Jul 17

Ethics at 3:AM

Ethics at 3:AM

QUESTIONS AND ANSWERS ON
HOW TO LIVE WELL

Edited by **RICHARD MARSHALL**

OXFORD
UNIVERSITY PRESS

OXFORD
UNIVERSITY PRESS

Oxford University Press is a department of the University of Oxford. It furthers
the University's objective of excellence in research, scholarship, and education
by publishing worldwide. Oxford is a registered trade mark of Oxford University
Press in the UK and certain other countries.

Published in the United States of America by Oxford University Press
198 Madison Avenue, New York, NY 10016, United States of America.

CIP data is on file at the Library of Congress
ISBN 978–0–19–063572–5

9 8 7 6 5 4 3 2 1

Printed by Sheridan Books, Inc., United States of America

CONTENTS

GLOSSARY OF ETHICAL TERMS

Cognitivism is the view that ethical sentences express propositions and can therefore be true or false (i.e., they are truth-apt). Thus, moral judgments are capable of being objectively true, because they describe some feature of the world.

Consequentialism is the doctrine that the morality of an action is to be judged solely by its consequences.

Contractualism is a distinctive account of moral reasoning "whereby an act is wrong if its performance under the circumstances would be disallowed by any set of principles for the general regulation of behaviour that no one could reasonably reject as a basis for informed, unforced, general agreement" (Scanlon, *What We Owe to Each Other* [Belknap Press of Harvard University Press, 1998] p. 153).

Deontological ethics or deontology (from Greek δέον, deon, "obligation, duty") is the normative ethical position that judges the morality of an action based on the action's adherence to a rule or rules. It is sometimes described as "duty-" or "obligation-" or "rule-" based ethics, because rules "bind you to your duty."

Expressivism is a form of moral antirealism or nonfactualism: the view that there are no moral facts that moral sentences describe or represent, and no moral properties or relations to which moral terms refer.

Moral realism (or moral objectivism) is the meta-ethical view that there exist such things as moral facts and moral values, and that these are objective and independent of our perception of them or our beliefs, feelings, or other attitudes toward them.

Noncognitivism is the meta-ethical view that ethical sentences do not express propositions (i.e., statements) and thus cannot be true or false (they are not truth-apt).

Rule utilitarianism is a form of utilitarianism that says an action is right as it conforms to a rule that leads to the greatest good, or that "the rightness or wrongness of a particular action is a function of the correctness of the rule of which it is an instance."

Utilitarianism is the doctrine that actions are right if they are useful or for the benefit of a majority.

Virtue ethics is currently one of three major approaches in normative ethics. It may, initially, be identified as the one that emphasizes the virtues, or moral character, in contrast to the approach that emphasizes duties or rules (deontology) or that which emphasizes the consequences of actions (consequentialism).

LIST OF CONTRIBUTORS

Nicolas Bommarito is currently a Bersoff Fellow in the Department of Philosophy at New York University and an Assistant Professor of Philosophy at the University at Buffalo.

Kimberlie Brownlee is an Associate Professor in Legal and Moral Philosophy at Warwick University.

Clare Chambers is University Senior Lecturer in Philosophy and Fellow of Jesus College, University of Cambridge.

Ruth Chang is a philosopher at Rutgers University, New Brunswick.

Jonathan Dancy is a philosopher at the University of Texas at Austin (half-time) and a leading proponent of moral particularism.

Stephen Darwall is the Andrew Downey Orrick Professor of Philosophy at Yale University and the John Dewey Distinguished University Professor Emeritus of Philosophy at the University of Michigan.

Kathinka Evers is a Professor of Philosophy at the University of Uppsala and a codirector of the EU Flagship Human Brain Project.

John Martin Fischer is the Distinguished Professor of Philosophy at the University of California, Riverside.

Luciano Floridi is Professor of Philosophy and Ethics of Information at the University of Oxford where he is also Director of Research and Senior Research Fellow of the Oxford Institute and Governing Body Fellow of St Cross College.

John Gardner is Professor of Jurisprudence at Oxford and a Senior Research Fellow at All Souls College in Oxford.

Allan Gibbard is the Richard B. Brandt Distinguished University Professor of Philosophy at the University of Michigan and is one of the leading figures working in contemporary meta-ethics.

Rebecca Gordon is a philosopher at the University of San Francisco. She is an applied ethicist.

Lori Gruen is the William Griffin Professor of Philosophy and Professor of Feminist, Gender, and Sexuality Studies, and Environmental Studies, at Wesleyan University, where she also coordinates the Wesleyan Animal Studies program.

Virginia Held is a philosopher at the Graduate Center of the City University of New York.

Philip Kitcher is the John Dewey Professor of Philosophy at Columbia University.

Matthew Kramer is Professor of Legal and Political Philosophy within Cambridge University and in his twenty-second year as a Fellow of Churchill College there. He was elected a Fellow of the British Academy in 2014.

Richard Kraut is the Charles and Emma Morrison Professor in the Humanities at Northwestern University.

Katarzyna de Lazari-Radek is a Polish utilitarian philosopher and a lecturer at the Institute of Philosophy at Lodz University in Poland and at the European Graduate School.

Christopher Lebron is Assistant Professor of African American Studies and Philosophy at Yale University.

Japa Pallikkathayil is an Assistant Professor in the Department of Philosophy at the University of Pittsburgh.

Joseph Raz is Professor at Columbia University Law School and Professor (part-time) at Kings College, London.

Thomas M. Scanlon is Alford Professor of Natural Religion, Moral Philosophy, and Civil Polity Emeritus.

Mark A. Schroeder is Professor of Philosophy at the University of Southern California.

Sibyl Schwarzenbach is Professor of Ethics, Political Philosophy and Feminist Philosophy at Baruch College and the Graduate Center at the City University of New York.

Torbjörn Tännsjö has been the Kristian Claëson Professor of Practical Philosophy at Stockholm University since 2002 and is the director at the Stockholm University Centre for Health Care Ethics, a collaboration among Stockholm University (SU), Karolinska Institute (KI), and the Royal Institute of Technology (KTH). Since 2007 he has also been an Affiliated Professor of Medical Ethics at Karolinska Institute.

Katja Maria Vogt is Professor of Philosophy at Columbia University and a recipient of the Distinguished Columbia Faculty Award.

Introduction

THIS BOOK IS MADE up of a selection of twenty-six interviews taken from a series of online interviews called "The End Times," published by the cultural magazine *3:AM Magazine* (3ammagazine.com) over a period of about five years. Putting them online each week means that the time lag between production and publication is minimalized, bringing a sense of freshness and urgency sometimes lost in slower production technologies. The interview format helps diminish the distance between the reader and the interlocutors: as outward-facing conversations they are able to cover subtle ground without becoming mired in insider terminology useful only for those already inhabiting the specialist tent. This combination of a weekly production schedule and an informal format is designed to publicize the work of some of the best contemporary philosophers working in the academy at the moment for a general readership.

The series started in December 2011. It doesn't focus on any single area of philosophy and has proceeded in its haphazard way ever since. Over two hundred interviews have been published at the time of writing. The series continues.

Limits of the Collection

These interviews give a snapshot of where philosophy of ethics stands at the moment. Although a wide range of views is presented, contemporary philosophy of ethics is a much broader landscape. The book includes some of the best thinkers in this area working at the moment, but inevitably there are missing voices who would have been here if I'd found them quickly enough, or had they not refused to do an interview when asked, or if I hadn't been ignorant about them and so never asked, or if there had been enough room to include everyone I did interview. But if the selection is partial and dependent on these contingencies, there is nevertheless more than just random whimsy at play in how this collection was constructed. I stand outside the academy and peer in.

I read as much as I can to try and sense what philosophers are finding interesting and important. That's how I manage to catch the ones I do catch, though of course it means I miss an awful lot. While there are limitations to what these interviews can deliver, nevertheless there's something worthwhile in doing this. Pulling the philosophers into a public, nonacademic domain of discourse is important if the broader public is to have access to their ideas. Since these interviews started, philosophers seem more visible than they were, and I hope that *3:AM Magazine* has been of some help in this positive trend, even though I still find them woefully underrepresented in the mainstream media.

The Selection

Turning to this particular selection, ethics, by its very nature, seems, arguably, to require this public exposure more than other areas of philosophy. Ethics is about what to do, how to live, what's valuable, what's right and wrong, who we are, and who we ought to be. These are things that most people struggle with at some time in their lives, and if there are thinkers who have ideas about these things then we should listen in and think about what they're saying, even if it's just to know what we're rejecting.

When invited by Oxford University Press's Peter Ohlin to collect interviews about ethics, I wondered whether I'd have enough material. But when I looked over the interviews published I found I had too much. There just wasn't enough room for all of them. Even without interviews with Christine Korsgaard, Cecile Fabre, and Elizabeth Anderson that had appeared in my first collection, *Philosophy at 3:AM*, there were still too many for a single collection. So unfortunately some great interviewees have not been included.

On top of having to select the interviews I also had to think about classifying them somehow. I fell back on doing it in a pretty conventional way. There are typically three types of ethical theories: meta-ethical theories, normative theories, and applied ethical theories. I took these as my organizing principles and went about slotting in the interviews where I thought they best fitted. As I did this, I realized that the categories were rather more porous than I had hoped. Many if not all of the interviews seemed to fit into more than one box. Some fitted into all of them. But I stuck to it because it gave some loose organizing structure to what I had even if it was all rather vague.

I took these three types of ethical theory to be trying to answer different questions. Meta-ethics looks at where ethics come from, what they mean, and so on. Theories answering these meta-ethical questions focus on the different kinds of accounts that might be given. They might answer the question of the source of ethics in terms of God's will, or human emotions, or psychological or social forces, or reason. They might argue that they are universal or relative to their social environment. They might examine what ethical language is like and how it works. Typical questions include whether ethics is objective or subjective, universal or relativist; whether it is grounded in egoism or altruism, emotion or reason; and whether gender is important to the kind of ethics one has.

Normative ethical theories, on the other hand, try and answer questions about how we ought to act, and so are more practical in their orientation. For example, an Aristotelian virtue theory argues that we need to develop good habits so we are able through this developed character to recognize the ethical thing to do in whatever circumstance develops; a Kantian deontologist might argue that we follow the edicts of universal Reason and do our duty; a consequentialist will focus on the consequences of an act, so for a Millian utilitarian a good act is one where consequences maximize happiness.

Finally, the applied ethical theorists turn to specific controversial moral issues of the day such as abortion, animal rights, torture, racism, and Internet privacy and try to work out how to understand and resolve the issue. In doing so they may mobilize insights from both the normative theorists and the meta-ethical theorists, but what they are interested in doing is showing what is peculiarly important to the specific case in hand.

As I said above, the lines between these are not sharp, nor are the divisions within each of the categories. So an applied ethicist will cross into the normativist realm and discuss different normative positions, and within a single realm, for example, a Kantian deontologist can be concerned with consequences.

So philosophical ethics is typically processed through these three lenses—meta-ethics, normative ethics, and applied ethics—sometimes separately, sometimes all together or in some combination—and the contemporary scene is one where there's a great deal happening. Virtue ethics seems to be thriving, as is a meta-ethics drawing on varieties of action theory where giving reasons is foregrounded. But so too are deontological theories where, again, giving reasons along lines analogous to legal juridical reasoning is shaping the discourse. And consequentialism is still alive and kicking: Derek Parfit's recent *On What Matters* argues for a kind of rule utilitarian position and although it hasn't convinced everyone, it has brought renewed life to various critiques of ethics generally. And areas of applied ethics being vigorously discussed, from sexism and racism to Internet privacy and torture, means that there is much that is directly and explicitly relevant to the contemporary world. Ethics today is an exciting domain.

One thing that is clear from the interviews is that most people want to use ethical discourse but don't want to be burdened with any esoteric metaphysics. In this sense naturalism—essentially a scientific, methodological view of ethics—is a default assumption of the contemporary theorist . But it's clear that there are non-naturalistic facts—numbers seem to be parade cases—so it's not clear what naturalism in ethics actually entails. Joseph Raz in his interview says that there are clear facts that natural science can't tell us about.

So, whatever one might think about this, it seems here is a consideration that remains a live debate. Meta-ethical commitments tend to be framed by those considerations, leading to the popularity of versions of expressivism—that our moral language does not imply the existence of objective moral values—and then defenses of or attacks on ethical realism.

In this volume's snapshot of current meta-ethics, the discussion is focused on expressivism. Gibbard, Dancy, Kitcher, Chang, Raz, Fischer, and Scanlon all present different versions of this. Schroeder presents a version of ethical realism. And other philosophers placed outside of the meta-ethical box in this volume defend one or the other side of this meta-ethical position. It might not be clear from this just what is at stake and why these positions oppose each other. Don't expressivists think their expressions are real? Well of course they do, but what they are doing is, in Schroeder's phrase, "metaphysically lightweight," while the realist is heavyweight. I think it's fair to say that here expressivism is in the ascendency but realism, which can involve a muted sort of Platonism about ethics, is still alive and kicking.

Turning to normative ethics, in this selection the leading discussions present the porousness of the three main categories (meta-ethics, normative ethics, applied ethics) but also provide evidence that all three areas are thriving. Deontological theories presented with a juridical flavor, as the two arising explicitly from considerations of the relationship between ethics and law are (Kramer and Gardner), can be understood as deontological but also, in a way, as versions of rule utilitarianism, and hence as a kind of consequentialism. Consequentialist theories are still actively developed and although Derek Parfit is not in the collection, his views developed in his two-volume *On What Matters*, which develops a rule utilitarian position, are discussed by several of the contributors. Kitcher's critique of the Parfit position is used to help him pivot to his version of expressivism in the meta-ethical discussion—arguing against the antinaturalism of Parfit—and to a version of ethics that accommodates virtue, deontic, and consequentialist theories without aiming to complete the project of ethical inquiry as he sees it, an inquiry "motivated by the aim of improving human conduct." Another deontologist included here is Stephen Darwall and his "from the second person" approach.

That the categories are porous is further illustrated by the case of Kramer, who could easily have been categorized as working in applied ethics as well as deontology, given his extensive work examining the ethics of capital punishment and torture. He could also be considered as a leading meta-ethicist, given his work on moral realism. Darwall's argument that a key feature of much contemporary ethical theory is its juridical nature means that both Gardner and Darwall could all have been put in the meta-ethicists box without any strain. Darwall himself is clearly doing meta-ethics as well, and he gives a good summary of the contemporary ethical scene within his discussion. As noted earlier, Parfit's

On What Matters has brought new energy to arguments regarding meta-ethics as well as normative ethics and ensured that the three normative positions I've used to organize the interviews are not so easily separable. Gardner defends ethical realism, which is a meta-ethical position. And, like Raz and Kramer, he discusses controversies surrounding the relationship between law and morality, such as rape, which would fit the applied ethics category as well.

Virtue ethics is also thriving, and here we have a range of approaches from Richard Kraut's Aristotelian, Katja Maria Vogt's Stoic, and Nicolas Bommarito's Buddhist approaches. Virginia Held's ethics of care is one that, although it isn't exhausted by understanding it as a version of virtue ethics, does have strong affinities with its general direction of travel. But she develops it into a feminist ethics of a distinctive flavor, and so I have put it into the applied ethics category even though it clearly has important things to say within the normative discussions as well. In fact it is clear that all the applied ethical positions develop, when relevant, positions that could be classified as normative and/or meta-ethics.

Consequentialist theories, as we have seen, are not always separate from deontological or virtue ethics, as several contributors notice, but there are still theorists who will approach ethics from a clear consequentialist vantage point. Torbjörn Tännsjö is a hedonistic utilitarian as he approaches the ethical issues of taking lives, and Katarzyna de Lazari-Radek defends the act utilitarianism of Henry Sidgwick.

Applied ethics is an approach to ethics that traditionally has not been as well regarded as meta-ethical and normative theorizing, but it seems to be gaining momentum. In this collection there are discussions of the ethics of sexism, racism, coercion, civil disobedience, care, civic friendship, torture, captivity, Internet privacy, and neuroethics. They may draw on perspectives from the normative and meta-ethical discussions, but all of them show how philosophers are engaging with some of the most pressing and controversial ethical issues of the day. They show that philosophy is offering interesting, important, and lucid insights into how we might wish to see human conduct improve in a wide range of domains.

Of course this is not an exhaustive range of interests, but it does give a clear indication of how the philosophical scene is producing relevant and theoretically sophisticated thinking that can help steer our thinking as the complexities of the world continue to pile up. It's not that philosophers expect to directly change the course of policies and behaviors. That's not what philosophy is for. Philosophers are here to raise important philosophical questions, set out how they might be answered and follow the arguments wherever they may take them. In this way we gain new knowledge and a more nuanced, more critical and deeper sense of what is at stake. Whatever practical benefits this brings, I think this greater awareness is in and of itself beneficial. It helps develop the inner self and opens us to a better understanding of what it is to be human and the choices we face. Some of the material here is challenging, and it can't all be right. There are real disagreements and genuine choices to be made. There is a sense of the urgency and importance of the questions that are being asked. And like lots of good philosophy, it's not clear what would make any of these perspectives wrong.

There is an additional context to contemporary ethical philosophy that should be noted, which is captured in an interview with Brian Leiter included in the last *3:AM* selection. There he identified a distinction that he thought tracked a genuine philosophical disagreement, a distinction,

> between those who think the aim of philosophy should be to get as clear as possible about the way things really are, that is, about the actual causal structure of the natural and human world, how societies and economies work, what motivates politicians and ordinary people to do what they do, and, on the other hand, those who think the aim of philosophy is to set up moral ideals, to give moralistic lectures about what society ought to do and how people ought to act. On the realist side, you find Thucydides, Marx, and Nietzsche, but also Max Weber, Michel Foucault, Richard Posner, and Raymond Geuss. On the moralist side, you find Plato and Kant, but also John Rawls, Ronald Dworkin and Martha Nussbaum, among many others. Many, but not all, naturalists are realists, since it's reasonable to think that if you want to understand the way things really are, you ought to rely on the methods of the sciences, which have been the most successful ones over the past several centuries.

Readers may find the ethical theorists in this book on the moralist side of the divide. But not all. And, as noted above, it would depend on the scope of naturalism as to whether the philosophers here count as naturalists or not. So maybe if there is a fruitful way of guiding readers approaching these interviews then it might be to suggest reading them in terms of this distinction and working out whether the distinction applies and if it does, which side of the line she is on. But that's no more than a suggestion: perhaps the best way is to read with openness and agnosticism and see what happens.

Finally, it is worth noting that of the twenty-six interviews overall, eleven are with women and three are with nonwhite philosophers. Both these groups are poorly represented in the profession and actually this book better represents those groups than does the profession overall. But it isn't good enough. There are signs that women are becoming better represented, but there is still much to be done to boost the representation of both groups. And as some of the contributors themselves have argued, this in itself is a pressing ethical issue.

1 | Meta-Ethics

1 | Philip Kitcher: "Life After Faith"

Philip Kitcher is the John Dewey Professor of Philosophy at Columbia University. Here he discusses his realist approach to ethics, Derek Parfit, the use of stripped-down thought experiments, intuitions, why we shouldn't try for ethical peaks, how he sees the ethical project, what life after faith means for religion and science, science and democracy, Dewey and pragmatism, science and values, science education, the point of philosophy, Joyce's *Finnegans Wake*, and why life without literature and the arts is a mistake.

3:AM: You've written books on *Science in a Democratic Society, Living with Darwin, The Ethical Project* and *Joyce's Kaleidoscope: An Invitation to Joyce's Finnegan's Wake.* This is a broad field of interests and captures the flavour of your philosophical position where you argue for the importance of both science and humanities. How did your philosophical career begin? Were you always asking questions, reading and thinking?

PHILIP KITCHER: I rather stumbled into philosophy. When I began my undergraduate career at Cambridge, I studied mathematics (pure and applied, with a dash of theoretical physics). Under the British system, I'd had to specialize at age 15, and I found it very hard to decide between mathematics and literature (English, French, and German). After two years of undergraduate study, it was clear that I was bored by the regime of problem-solving required by the Cambridge mathematical tripos. A very sensitive mathematics don recommended that I talk to the historian of astronomy, Michael Hoskin, and the conversation led me to enroll in the History and Philosophy of Science for my final undergraduate year. I'd originally intended to concentrate in history of science, but reading Thomas Kuhn's *The Structure of Scientific Revolutions* prompted me to switch to philosophy of science. Despite the fact that I hadn't done any serious philosophy as Princeton understood it, I was accepted as a graduate student in the philosophy side of Princeton's

HPS program (now defunct). I struggled at first, but eventually managed to correct some of my initial ignorance.

But I think that, all along, I was occupied by a range of questions, often different from those fashionable in the professional philosophy of the past half century, that have sometimes troubled philosophers in the past. It's taken me several decades to work out my own philosophical agenda, and it is, as your question suggests, wide. Some people would probably describe it as quite weird. Maybe this interview will dissolve some of that sense of weirdness.

3:AM: You wrote a review in The New Republic—"The Lure of the Peak"—of Derek Parfit's *On What Matters*, his massive two volume book that ambitiously tries to reconcile three approaches to ethics that are usually seen as irreconcilable: Consequentialists, Kantians and Contractualists. You ultimately judge this to be a grand and brave failure. The problem in the final analysis seems to boil down to views about naturalism. Can you say something about how the rejection of Parfit's vision of ethics sheds light on your own contrasting view?

PK: I have enormous respect for Derek Parfit, although he seems to me bound within an unfortunate philosophical tradition—rather like the extraordinarily brilliant exponents of Ptolemaic astronomy in the Middle Ages. Parfit believes that philosophers have a priori sources of knowledge that enable them to arrive at eternal truths. I don't think that anything of any consequence is known a priori: all our knowledge is built up by modifying the lore passed on to us by our ancestors in light of our experiences, and the best a philosopher can do is to learn as much about what has been discovered in various empirical fields, and use it to try to craft an improved synthesis. That seems to me what the great philosophers of the past did, even when (like Kant) they were declaring that their proposed principles were known independently of experience. That's part of my naturalism, which is more extreme than that of most philosophers (even Quine's): Dewey and Mill are the only two figures I know who have been uncompromising in their naturalism. Moreover, in the case of ethics, my naturalism follows Dewey in thinking of ethics as an unfinished human project. So Parfit's idea of a set of final principles from which all ethical truth flows strikes me as an illusion.

3:AM: Before moving on to look in detail at your own views, there are some things in the review that seem on the face of it rather strange. You don't approve of his use of thought experiments in the book. You say, "Sensible conclusions cannot be reached by pitting imprecise principles against fanciful cases." Isn't this a bit like criticizing philosophy itself? Aren't the thought experiments Parfit uses standard? They are even the basis of experimental philosophy investigations into what folk think, as in Joshua Greene's work.

So aren't you requiring standards that are themselves untypical and rigged to criticize Parfit's approach? So the criticism is that your criticism, if allowed to go through, would end much typical philosophical investigation.

PK: Thought experiments work when, and only when, they call into action cognitive capacities that might reliably deliver the conclusions drawn. When the question posed is imprecise, your thought experiment is typically useless. But even more crucial is the fact that the stripped-down scenarios many philosophers love simply don't mesh with our intellectual skills. The story rules out by fiat the kinds of reactions we naturally have in the situation described. Think of the trolley problem in which you are asked to decide whether to push the fat man off the bridge. If you imagine yourself—seriously imagine yourself—in this situation, you'd look around for alternatives, you'd consider talking to the fat man, volunteering to jump with him, etc. etc. None of that is allowed. So you're offered a forced choice about which most people I know are profoundly uneasy. The "data" delivered are just the poor quality evidence any reputable investigator would worry about using. (I like Joshua Greene's fundamental idea of investigating people's reactions; but I do wish he'd present them with better questions.)

Philosophers love to appeal to their "intuitions" about these puzzle cases. They seem to think they have access to little nuggets of wisdom. We'd all be much better off if the phrase "My intuition is . . ." were replaced by "Given my evolved psychological adaptations and my distinctive enculturation, when faced by this perplexing scenario, I find myself, more or less tentatively, inclined to say . . ." Maybe there are occasions in which the cases bring out some previously unnoticed facet of the meaning of a word. But, for a pragmatist like me, the important issues concern the words we might deploy to achieve our purposes, rather than the language we actually use.

If the intuition-mongering were abandoned, would that be the end of philosophy? It would be the end of a certain style of philosophy—a style that has cut philosophy off, not only from the humanities but from every other branch of inquiry and culture. (In my view, most of current Anglophone philosophy is quite reasonably seen as an ingrown conversation pursued by very intelligent people with very strange interests.) But it would hardly stop the kinds of investigation that the giants of the past engaged in. In my view, we ought to replace the notion of analytic philosophy by that of synthetic philosophy. Philosophers ought to aspire to know lots of different things and to forge useful synthetic perspectives.

3:AM: You also dislike the idea of there being a peak in the sense that Parfit uses it. For you this is an ideal that cuts away the point of the moral enterprise itself, and is something that I think Susan Wolf also wonders about in the book itself. Why do you object to there being a formula, or set of rules which, once known, we could thenceforth apply? Isn't this what ethics has always been about? In rejecting it, aren't you changing the subject?

PK: Ethical inquiry has always been motivated by the aim of improving human conduct. It doesn't follow from that that the goal is to produce a complete rule book that would be applicable to all cases. I'm very suspicious of the idea of a "final theory" in natural science, and the thought of a complete system of ethical rules seems even more dubious. You might even worry about whether, even if we could acquire the complete rule book, it would be ethically advantageous for people to defer to it.

A different vision of ethics is that of a collection of resources people can use to act better. The resources might be firm rules that could always be relied on. Or they might be ideals that could often be followed without thinking but that sometimes conflicted with one another. One goal of ethical inquiry might be to uncover strategies available for use when values conflict or when rules are incomplete. This different vision is Dewey's, and it's plainly visible in Aristotle; I'd argue that it's even present in Kant and Mill, in some of their writings.

3:AM: Ethical naturalism for you is facing the predicament of being alive and trying to work out, "by looking, as carefully and as comprehensively as we can, at the details of ethical practice and ethical change" what is to be done. From this you dispute the need for experts and suggest a much more democratic approach to ethical discourse? Again, haven't we always had ethical experts—the priests, the gurus, the philosophers and saints? Aren't you just tearing up the book and starting from some other place? To some, this might look like defeatism. The questions are too hard, so let's stop asking them and ask something else instead. And isn't then there a danger that the conjecture/refutation routine of scientific methodology that leads to discovery is lost. Is this where the influence of Kuhn is important in understanding your approach? Even Feyerabend? How do you respond to that sort of worry?

PK: My ethical naturalism sees us as facing the predicament of being social animals without evolved adaptations that make social life easy. The fundamental problem that sparks the ethical project lies in our limited responsiveness to one another. The only way we have to address that problem is through a representative, informed, and engaged conversation. Ethics, on this account, is a collective construction, constrained by the need to tackle the fundamental problem. We make ethical progress by obtaining—partial—solutions to that problem. Following Peirce and James, I take the ethical truths to be the stable elements that emerge out of ethical progress and that are retained under further ethical progress.

Although the conversation should represent all, and should thus be fully democratic, there's a role for experts. They should facilitate the conversation, helping people to see alternative points of view, and to understand the limitations and advantages of various proposals. The expert is a midwife. The expert is not someone who has the authority to pronounce the last word on the subject.

Feyerabend seems to have wanted to throw away objectivity altogether. Kuhn was different. He clearly accepted the progressiveness of natural science, but refused to adopt a teleological account in terms of the acquisition of some prior truth. I'm articulating a similar type of account. In ethics, we don't make progress by discovering pre-existent truths; we do so by solving problems. Truth is what we get by making progress. Because the problems are objective features of the human situation—social animals without the capacities for making social life come easily—ethics is objectively constrained. It's not the case that "anything goes." I suspect that this approach will still trouble many people. It's elaborated at much greater length in The Ethical Project, and in a more compressed (and, in some ways, improved) version in the second chapter of my most recent book, *Life After Faith*.

3:AM: One thing that surprised me in the article was that in your description of how ethical practices had developed you tell a kind of just-so story of the sort typically found in the cruder Darwinian-ethicist stories a la Pinker and Wilson. You have written against this sort of evolutionary psychology because it tends to be fanciful, dogmatic and over-elaborate in its purported explanations. Aren't you making the same kind of error?

PK: A reasonable challenge—especially since my *Vaulting Ambition* was very harsh on evolutionary story-telling. When I try to outline the history of ethical life, it's sometimes possible to find evidence for a hypothesis about how important transitions actually went. Often, however, that isn't so. There are many facts about human life in the Paleolithic we're never likely to know. But if I hypothesize that ethical life underwent a particular transition, I do owe the reader some account of how that transition could have occurred. So, in my historical narrative, I'm at some pains to distinguish "how-actually" explanations from "how-possibly" explanations. In this way, I avoid the questionable practice I have criticized elsewhere.

3:AM: Now you've taken an interesting position in the rather bad tempered discussions about the relationship between science and religion. You don't deny that religion's ontological claims (i.e. existence of Gods and spooks etc.) are bogus but you still think there is something valuable in religion. And you don't deny that scientific knowledge is genuine but you argue that bias in transmission, lack of transparency and undemocratic ownership of its knowledge makes science less than the highest good its apologists make for it. Is this right? Can you say something about this subtle and nuanced position that seems much more good natured than that of the belligerent Darwin wars backdrop?

PK: *Life After Faith* provides the best account of my views about religion. In that book, I argue against literal interpretation of religious doctrines. Religions make progress when they emancipate themselves from literalism, and take their doctrinal statements to be metaphors or allegories. Refined religion is aimed at realizing ethical values, including the fostering of human lives and human communities. At the present moment, many approximations to fully refined religion play a valuable role in sustaining the lives of disadvantaged people, in offering them genuine community, and in campaigning for social justice. Secular humanists should recognize those forms of religion as allies in the struggle for human advancement. They should also learn from them, as they try to build a fully secular world in which people can have the opportunity to live rich and fulfilling lives.

When we think about science, we tend to view its progress in terms of the accumulation of answers to questions. I've argued that we ought to go on to ask whether the questions are significant, to investigate what makes a question significant, and to consider whether the answers to significant questions are accessible to people who might benefit from them. My books *Science, Truth, and Democracy* and *Science in a Democratic Society* elaborate this socially-embedded approach to science and to scientific progress. As you point out, I don't deny that scientific investigation is capable of delivering important truths about nature, but that doesn't stop questions about whether, as it is practiced, science today lives up to its potential for benefiting humanity.

3:AM: Your intellectual hero is Dewey, and you go back to Milton and Mill to root your view that public democratic access to knowledge is a kind of ultimate requirement. You are arguing that science values and democratic values need to be put together. This strikes many as being wise and timely: many ask who gains from this great scientific knowledge being produced and there's a suspicion that any social benefits are merely lucky side-products of science. You have thought extensively about these symptoms of alienation from science. Can you say something about your Deweyian views on this and your perspective on the requirement of a better ordered science than we have now?

PK: I'm enormously grateful to the late Sidney Morgenbesser, who realized that many of the themes I was developing in the 1990s were akin to ideas in Dewey. Conversations with Sidney were immensely valuable (and delightful). Dewey is my ideal of the synthetic philosopher. He focuses very clearly on issues about values as they arise in his times. He develops philosophical tools to tackle them—his metaphysics and epistemology isn't an arid intellectual exercise but the prelude to investigation of concrete urgent problems.

In my work on science and democracy I'm both emulating Dewey's method and reaching conclusions similar to his. I also view The Ethical Project as elaborating further the kind of approach to ethics that is scattered throughout many of his writings. My current work, aimed at developing a Deweyan pragmatism for our times, attempts to synthesize ideas on a broader scale.

3:AM: Isn't there an inherent problem with a democratic science ideal in that science needs experts who do know better than the folk wisdom on matters of science? So how could there be democratic science in these circumstances? Isn't this an in built feature of scaled up social reality and its division of intellectual labour? The threat is that we can't all have expertise to understand what constraints we need to place on science?

PK: Of course expertise has a role. If there are to be appropriate judgments about what questions are significant, you need both the informed views of scientists who know what has been achieved and what future developments are promising and the reflective judgments of representatives of different groups who can identify what kinds of information are most urgently needed. My ideal of conversation that includes wide representation of perspectives, informed by the consensus view of current experts, pursued with an attempt to find a position with which all can live, brings the expert and the public dimensions together.

We can't realize that ideal. But we can certainly do better at approximating it. To cite just one possibility, we might consider how biomedical research would be different if the needs of people in the poorer parts of the world were fully taken into consideration. In trying to develop a more inclusive conversation, we might learn from the work of James Fishkin and Bruce Ackermann on democratic polling.

3:AM: Another challenge is the ownership of science. Much of it is privately owned. Copyright laws and so on mean that individuals (or corporations) own the products of science, not democratic communities. So like in science fiction stories like the tv series "Fringe" show a super smart scientific billionaire running amok in secret and there's a paranoia about that Frankenstein owns a plutocratic corporation. The issue of the plutocracy, and the secret state of a military industrial complex make science and technology out of democratic hands. So the argument that you put forward is really about politics, and this is a dimension that is left out of debates about science at our peril. Is this what you are arguing? Can you say something about this?

PK: I'm very concerned about the increasing distortion of research by the intrusion of the market. Universities, including my own, are beginning to see science as a means of attracting funds. Not only does that threaten types of investigation that might bring important future dividends, but it also intensifies the trend to orient research toward the felt needs of the wealthy. If the research agenda reflects "market forces," the problems of the poor are likely to be even more neglected than they already are.

3:AM: You link many of your views to an argument linking values and science. Science is supposed to be value free, and the suspicion is that it isn't. But doesn't placing democratic value on science distort science just as much as the anti-democratic values many suspect are driving it at the moment?

It's a very bad idea for scientific conclusions to be accepted because they fit with the political values of a group of researchers. It's not at all a bad idea for scientific questions to be chosen because a democratic deliberation would identify them as important for people's lives. Nor is it a bad idea for scientists who have partial evidence for a hypothesis to consider the value of the consequences that would ensue if that hypothesis were adopted and applied. There are many ways in which value judgments might enter into, or be absent from, decisions within the sciences. Some are problematic, others are welcome.

3:AM: Global warming, genetic engineering, bio-ethics are all issues that people are aware of and so what is at stake when you argue is pretty clear. But the impact of your ideas would bring about a pretty enormous social change wouldn't it? We need a new kind of politics, new ways of educating ourselves, a new kind of ethics? If religion survives, even that needs renewing? Is this right? What do you propose are the mechanisms for this? After all, I might be completely convinced by your arguments, but then wonder what I'm supposed to do about it?

PK: The point of philosophy, as I see it, is to change thinking, and thereby to change the conversation. In my current work on global warming, I argue that the only apparent solution to the deep problem of climate change would require very large transfers of wealth from rich nations to poor nations, so that the entire world can make the transition to renewable forms of energy as fast as possible. Of course, that is politically unacceptable, and to propose it initially seems absurd.

Yet an important part of my position is that this solution is not only just and feasible, but deeply in our interests. The supposed absurdity of proposing wealth transfers stems from blindness on the part of the citizens of the affluent world. Those citizens are distracted by the toys technology has supplied, and fail to recognize the ways in which what they most deeply want is made vulnerable by the coming disruptions of human relations on an over-heated planet. Making this clear is an urgent philosophical task. It requires going back, seriously and straightforwardly, to Socrates' old question: "How to live?"

As I work in this area, I'm often quite gloomy about the prospects for the human future. But, although I have no competence to intervene directly in a political movement, I hope that what I write may, in combination with the suggestions of others, cause a shift in perspective that will inspire a world-wide movement to accept the only solution to climate change. And before it's too late.

3:AM: A particularly interesting argument you have is about education. You talk about "scientific literacy." This has been dismissed in some circles as not real science but you are fierce in your defence of it, seeing it as the way of ensuring that there is science education for those who are not going to specialize. Can you say what science literacy is for you and why you think it is so very important?

PK: Current education in science treats all students as if they were going to have scientific careers. They are required to solve problems and memorize lists. For many of them, this kills interest very quickly. In my view, all students should be given an initial opportunity to pursue the science track as far as it goes. But for those who quickly decide that track isn't for them, a different style of teaching is in order. That should acquaint them with important concepts, give them a sense of the character of scientific work, present some of the wonderful surprises of scientific discovery, and, above all, show how important scientific research continues to be to human life. Science literacy consists in the ability and the desire to follow reports of new scientific advances, throughout your whole life.

3:AM: As someone engaged in the very frontline of science, philosophy and politics, are you optimistic or pessimistic about the situation at the moment. Are there examples that you can give to give us a sense of where you think we are heading?

PK: As I said in answering an earlier question, I'm quite pessimistic about climate change. This is an urgent problem, and much of the world is only now waking up to the easiest part of solving—the realization that anthropogenic global warming is real. Beyond that lie the problems of understanding how serious the issues are (how deep the waters are going to be, to make a bad pun), and of seeing that it requires concerted efforts by all nations. Finally, the hardest problem of all is to appreciate the facts that the poor nations are—quite reasonably—not going to forgo their development, and that they can only afford to develop by consuming fossil fuels.

3:AM: There's no doubt that this is philosophy very much engaged with the big issues of the day. So for the worried readers at 3:AM, are there five books you could recommend to help illuminate the deep issues at stake in this?

PK: Samuel Scheffler *Death and the Afterlife*
Helen Longino *Science as Social Knowledge*
Nancy Cartwright *The Dappled World*
Joshua Landy *How to do things with fictions*
John Dupre *The Disorder of Things*

3:AM: And finally, your interest in Joyce's *Finnegans Wake*, does this connect with your belief that to engage fully with the existential issues of the day we need to be able to work in diverse fields of intellectual enquiry and not think science is ultimate? Your approach is governed by the same question that governs all your philosophical enquiries it seems: "What makes a life worth living?" Can you say more about how you think reading FW can help us answer this fundamental question. And why this particular book is so life enhancing?

PK: I've already expressed my concerns about the stripped-down thought experiments many philosophers love. Those experiments should be contrasted with the detailed scenarios that literature often presents. I think we can learn an immense amount about how to live from reflectively engaging with literary works. (My book *Deaths in Venice* discusses this in some detail.) Like Joshua Landy (see recommendation above) I believe that the arts make indispensable contributions to our understanding.

Finnegans Wake is of philosophical importance because it deals so resolutely with the predicament of how to come to terms with the flaws and blotches on a human life at a stage when it's no longer possible to alter that life's fundamental pattern. In its probing of the retrospective view from old age, in which the same mistakes and failures are worked through, again and again, it invites readers to undergo an exercise of thorough self-examination.

I want to emphasize that this is only one way to read this remarkable book. It's a novel that prompts us to write the central narrative ourselves. People can do that in many moods and in many ways. My interpretation starts from a particular philosophical problem, one I think that jumps out from FW's most elegiac passages. But we should also remember that there's "lots of fun at Finnegan's wake."

3:AM: So finally, finally, other than Joyce, which other literature have you found enlightening as you wrestle with these big philosophical themes?

All Joyce's works are valuable in this regard. So are the major writings of other modernists—Proust, Thomas Mann, Musil. Above all, perhaps, are many of Shakespeare's plays—including some of the comedies and histories. But I'm not yet ready to write about them.

Philip Kitcher is the author of:

Abusing Science: The Case Against Creationism (MIT Press, 1982)

The Nature of Mathematical Knowledge (Oxford University Press, 1983)

Vaulting Ambition: Sociobiology and the Quest for Human Nature (MIT Press, 1985)

The Advancement of Science (Oxford University Press, 1993)

The Lives to Come: The Genetic Revolution and Human Possibilities (Simon and Schuster [US], Penguin [UK], 1996)

Science, Truth, and Democracy (Oxford University Press, 2001)

In Mendel's Mirror: Philosophical Reflections on Biology (Oxford University Press, 2003)

Joyce's Kaleidoscope: An Invitation to Joyce's Finnegan's Wake (Oxford University Press, 2007)

The Ethical Project (Harvard University Press, 2011)

Science in a Democratic Society (Prometheus Books, 2011)

Preludes to Pragmatism (Oxford University Press, 2012)

Deaths in Venice: The Cases of Gustav von Aschenbach (Columbia University Press, 2013)

Philosophy of Science: A New Introduction (with Gillian Barker) (Oxford University Press, 2013)

2 | Allan Gibbard: "Thinking How to Live"

Allan Gibbard is the Richard B. Brandt Distinguished University Professor
of Philosophy at the University of Michigan and is one of the leading figures
working in contemporary meta-ethics. He discusses what moral terms and
statements mean and what moral judgments are. He discusses the idea
that what something means is a normative claim and that this is about
the meaning not the nature of meaning. He talks about Kripke's book on
Wittgenstein, on what "ought" depends on, on expressivism, on ethics and
planning questions, on utilitarianism and contractarianism, and on the
current state of contemporary public ethical discourse.

3:AM: What made you become a philosopher?

ALLAN GIBBARD: I arrived at Swarthmore College as a freshman intend-
ing to major in math and physics. My impression of philosophy came from
reading Plato, whose arguments I had found lame and fallacious. I thought
that philosophy consisted chiefly in bad arguments for the existence of God.
But my parents had told me they thought I might be interested in philosophy,
and I registered for the introductory course just to find out what it involved.
My section was taught by Jerome Shaffer, who was a brilliant teacher able
to flummox us into avid disputes. It was a course on contemporary problems
with some historical background, and I was much more gripped by recent
philosophical writing than by older figures whom I really didn't know how
to interpret. Philosophy faculty at Swarthmore taught what we would now
think a heavy load, two introductory sections of 50 students each along with
a more advanced course. Some of the 50 students sat quietly in the back
and smoked, but about ten of us sat in the front engaged in arguing points.
Mr. Shaffer often had a bemused smile as he teased us with things that had
never occurred to us.

I came to think of philosophy as something any person should do seriously
whatever field one was in—but I didn't think I could make a living doing it.

I took the philosophy of science course of Stephen Barker, who was visiting from Johns Hopkins, which Mr. Barker taught as a relativity of the layman course. David Lewis, who I later learned had just returned from a year at Oxford with his family and had changed from chemistry to philosophy after engaging Oxford luminaries, sat in the back, a vocal auditor. Since we—and especially he had a better understanding of the issues than Mr. Barker had, we in effect taught the course from our seats. My big change at Swarthmore came my senior year, when I took Richard Brandt's moral philosophy seminar. Brandt was enthralling, and halfway through the seminar, I told him I had decided to go on in philosophy. A week or two later, I told him I had decided first to join the Peace Corps.

Brandt had built the Swarthmore department into one of the best in the world, with not only Shaffer but the two beginning Assistant Professors Larry Sklar and Jaegwon Kim. In a small department, he was convinced, the faculty needed above all to be able to talk with each other, even if that left gaps in coverage. He would sometimes interview a dozen candidates for a job and reject them all; "The only thing he could talk about was his thesis," Brandt complained of one candidate he had introduced me to. Harvard was of course wonderful in many ways, but it also felt like something of an anticlimax. The dean told us, "You may think you came here to get an education. We figure you already have an education."

3:AM: You're well known in philosophical circles for developing a theory of meaning. You claim that linguistic meaning is normative. Before discussing what this claim is, can you first say something about the competing theories that you found wanting?

AG: The view in my book isn't precisely that "linguistic meaning is normative." Rather, the thesis I explore is that claims as to what something means are normative claims. This is a view about the meaning of "meaning," about the concept of meaning rather than the nature of meaning. For the most part, so far as I can think, there aren't competitors around to my metatheory of meaning, because writers on meaning don't generally talk about what the things they say about meaning mean. The issue they address is what a word's meaning such-and-such consists in.

Metaethics, in contrast, in the wake of G. E. Moore, is a field that explicitly treats the meanings of terms. "Analytic" philosophy more generally for a long time followed Moore and centered on analyses of meanings. From standard taxonomies in metaethics, we can, if we like, devise corresponding views one might take on the meaning of meaning claims: theories that are versions of analytical naturalism, a non-naturalism that says that a term's meaning is a non-natural property of the term, and perhaps some form of non-cognitivism for meaning claims. The obvious approach to the meaning of meaning claims, though, is to try to define the concept of meaning in naturalistic terms, in terms that can fit into a purely empirical science. A central question for me, then, is why I reject treating meaning as a concept within a purely empirical science.

As early reviewers of the book point out, I'm rather perfunctory on this question. I don't come up with a knock-down argument that analyses in scientific terms won't capture the meaning of meaning claims. In a way I don't want to: as I say at one point in the book, I'm not convinced that treating the concept of meaning as a normative concept will be the most illuminating way to approach the theory of meaning. A search for a fruitful naturalistic reform definition might do better, in the spirit of Ruth Millikan. Another possibility, which I don't pursue, would be to attempt a treatment like that of Paul Horwich, seeking to give the meaning of "means" by identifying a "basic acceptance property" that characterizes the term's use. But Moore-like arguments, I suggest, will show that naturalistic analyses of the concept means go wrong, just as, as Moore argued, naturalistic analyses of the concept good go wrong. Perhaps we should go for a naturalistic reform of our concepts, but that will close some questions that might be worth asking. I try to identify what sorts of questions these might be.

Semanticists, so far as I am aware, don't have a standard gloss on what's at issue in questions of semantics. Perhaps they should say that semantic value is whatever fairly natural property—in David Lewis's sense of "natural"—best explains the phenomena their tests uncover. I argue, though, in a quick way, that semanticists can be interpreted as addressing questions of the normative kind that I try to elucidate in my book. A chief aim of the book is to try to show how fruitful a normative approach can be in identifying what might be at issue in questions of meaning.

3:AM: How important were arguments in Kripke's book on Wittgenstein to your approach?

AG: Very. I have to confess shamefacedly that I took a long time to get to Kripke's book. I am very bad at keeping up with philosophical literature. Many works don't engage me when I get to them, and when a work does engage me, it takes me a long time to try to think matters through. When I did read Kripke on Wittgenstein, I was thrilled. (I was sent there by a referee for my 1990 book *Wise Choices, Apt Feelings* who turned out to be John McDowell.) I had long struggled, off and on, to make something of Wittgenstein, and—whether or not Kripke got Wittgenstein right, and whether or not there is even such a thing as getting him right—here was a reading that made Wittgenstein intelligible as a philosopher. I was also perturbed, though. A lot in Kripke's Wittgenstein, it seemed to me, needed the sorts of distinctions that were standard in meta-ethics as I had learned it from Shaffer and Brandt. I had a sabbatical and had been invited to give the Hempel Lectures at Princeton in 1991. I also had the wonderful privilege of a discussion group, with Paul Boghossian, Peter Railton, David Velleman, and Steve Yablo. I was especially caught up by the famous line, "The point is not that, if I meant addition by '+', I will answer '125', but that ... I should answer '125'." I found this rich in possibilities, especially when joined to points in 20th century metaethics. (My quote here skips some words that I don't so much like.) The first of my three Hempel Lectures became the paper "Meaning and Normativity" published in 1994 and incorporated into my 2012 book of the same title. In the other lectures I tried to develop a positive view, but I got stuck, and it took me two decades to think I might be unstuck and could finish the book.

3:AM: Is the "ought" of your theory exceptionless or does it depend on the interests of the user, for example, or just for those interested in believing the truth?

AG: What I ought to believe depends on my evidence, in a way that doesn't depend on whether or not I care about the truth. What I ought to want to believe, in contrast, may perhaps depend on my interests. My interests might make it upsetting to believe what my evidence supports, and in that case, if I ought to want strongly enough not to be upset, it may be that I ought to want not to believe what my evidence supports. The question of what I ought to believe, on the other hand, is a substantive question in normative epistemology. As such, it isn't strictly a question for a meta-normative theory like mine. My meta-normative theory tries to identify what's at issue among theorists of statistical inference and the like, if they have competing substantive views on how one's degrees of credence ought to depend on one's evidence. My book is about meaning, and these questions are matters of substance, and so my book won't answer them.

Let me back up and approach your question in a more roundabout way. We must distinguish what it means to say that I ought to do a thing and what being what I ought to do consists in. Maybe, for example, being what I ought to do consists in something hedonic, such as being what will maximize my happiness. Even so, "ought" doesn't mean "would maximize one's happiness." If it did, as Moore argued, then "You ought to maximize your happiness" would just mean "Maximizing your happiness would maximize your happiness." It's a complex question whether Moore's arguments can be made to work, but in the book, I suppose at the outset that they do—and then at the end, I ask how you, a reader, could recognize whether they do for what you mean by "ought."

Back, then, to your question of whether or not what I ought to do depends on my interests. This, as I say, is a question of normative substance. A central, Moore-like point is that we can't define the concept ought in terms of interests, even if what we ought to do does depend on our interests. It is intelligible, for instance, to say that one ought not to inflict torment, even if it is in one's interest to do so—and I accept the Moore-like claim that the same would go for any naturalistic definition of ought. Of course I have some views about what we ought to do and why, but they aren't part of the metatheory the book develops. Here, for example, is a substantive normative view of mine: whether I ought to believe Darwin's theory of natural selection depends on my evidence, not on my interests. In addressing this substantive claim, we need to distinguish what I ought to believe from what I ought to want to believe. Whether I ought to want to believe Darwin might well depend on my interests, or on public benefits that my belief or disbelief might bring. Whether I ought to believe Darwin doesn't so depend, in my view. I draw a primitive sense of "ought" from A. C. Ewing, and talk couched with that primitive ought, I claim, is intertranslatable with Scanlon's and Parfit's talk of "reasons." Suppose I tell you I have reason to doubt natural selection as explaining our natures. If the reason I offer is that doubting it will promote my career, I'm changing the subject—unless I have very strange views about reasons to believe. Career success is at most a reason to want to doubt natural selection.

What, in this primitive sense, I ought to want does, it seems clear, depend on my interests among other things. (I say "among other things" in that, for example, if it is in my interest to torture you, that doesn't establish that I ought to torture you.) How what's the thing to do does depend on one's interests and how it doesn't is a central normative question that we face in various guises. It's a question that my book is devoted to understanding, but it's not an aim of the book to answer this question, even for cases where the answer is pretty obvious.

3:AM: Aren't there factual reasons for taking a particular expression to mean something rather than anything else, or are the arguments of Quine and Hartry Field decisive here?

AG: Of course there are factual reasons, if talk of meaning makes any sense. There are factual reasons to carry an umbrella when the sky looks threatening, and if the meaning of a word is a matter of when to accept sentences with that word, then in a like way, there will be factual reasons to accept some sentences with the word and to reject others. Those will be factual grounds for conclusions as to what the word means. Plausibly, they might be facts about one's proclivities to use the word in certain ways. (What these facts are is a substantive question in the theory of meaning, not a question of the kind my book addresses, not a question in the metatheory of meaning.) Quine was a skeptic about meaning: he thought that the only intelligible notions in the area—stimulus meaning, for example—were vastly different from the notions that had driven analytic philosophy. Traditional notions of meaning, his thinking suggested, aren't even meaningful. A central aim of my book is to find meaning in traditional notions of meaning. I draw substantially on Quine, but my aim is to find a way around some of Quine's main contentions. I don't claim to show that Quine was wrong and some or our claims are analytic, but I do claim to identify what it would mean to say that a sentence in one's language is analytic. Roughly, this amounts to saying to accept the sentence come what evidence may and on any intelligible supposition. Calling a sentence analytic is saying what to do with it.

3:AM: Do you say all statements about meaning imply an ought-statement? Can you say how this works?

AG: Not all statements about meaning entail non-trivial ought-statements. Some such statements are trivial, such as "A word means what it means." But in Chapter 6 of the book, I try to show how to translate sentences with "means" into sentences with "ought." With Quine and Horwich, I say the basic notion is one of synonymy. A Frenchman's sentence "La neige est blanche" is synonymous with my sentence "Snow is white," and this means that they are composed in corresponding ways of elements governed by the same oughts of acceptance. (The synonymy can only be rough, since, among other things, French has structural features like gender that English lacks, but I'll ignore such matters in what I say here.) We can build up synonymy with oughts from the ground up, recursively. So Pierre's word "blanc" is synonymous with my word "white," in that, among many other things, once we establish that his context "La neige est ..." is synonymous with my context "Snow is ..." then, for any evidence and under any supposition, Pierre ought to accept "La neige est blanche" if and only if I ought to accept "Snow is white."

3:AM: Quine argues that it is in principle possible for empirical evidence to allow [us??] to reject any sentence—even mathematical and logical ones— and so Quine is denying that we [don't??] have the normative obligations you claim we have. Is this a problem for you?

AG: Quine quines any distinction between changing beliefs couched with a term and changing what the term means. If quantum logic tells me to reject the sentence "The photon went through one slit or the other," Quine thought, we can't intelligibly ask whether the word "or" here means the same thing as it meant in the days before quantum theory. I agree that it might turn out we should stop thinking in terms of the classical inclusive "or," but it doesn't make sense to think in terms of it and deny the law of excluded middle. Quine, as I say, didn't think that the question of whether I'm thinking in those terms, with those meanings, makes sense. I try in the book to give sense to such questions.

3:AM: You're an expressivist about normative language aren't you? Can you sketch out what this commits us to?

AG: Huw Price has been arguing for expressivism for all language, even the most clearly naturalistic and factual—and I read Paul Horwich the same way, along with Robert Brandom. The issues involved are complex, and I have contributed to a volume on them. As I use the term "expressivism," I, like Price and Horwich, am a universal expressivist. Some writers build into the definition of "expressivism" that it denies that the claims it covers are true or false, and I myself made such denials in 1990 in *Wise Choices, Apt Feelings*, but I don't do so now. I now say that deflationary truth is the only kind I understand (though more needs to be said about it than is ordinarily said), and that "Torture for fun is wrong" is as true as anything could be. So what do I mean by "expressivism"? The basic pattern is that of Ayer's theory of what "wrong" means. Ayer holds, pretty much, that "X is wrong" means "Boo for X!" Booing a thing doesn't assert that one opposes it, but rather, expresses that opposition. My own view isn't Ayer's, but I adopt this pattern of explanation: explain the meanings of words, I propose, by explaining the states of mind they serve to express. That's expressivism as I mean the label. And in the explanation, this state of mind can't just be specified as believing that X is wrong. That would make the explanation uninformative.

3:AM: How do you put together your theory of meaning and your expressivist theory of normative language?

AG: In a nutshell: Claims about meaning are claims as to which sentences in one's language one ought to accept, in which circumstances, actual and hypothetical. Questions of which sentences one ought to accept are questions of which sentences to accept. And so questions of what a term means are questions of when—under what circumstances—to accept sentences that contain the term.

3:AM: Why don't you think linguistic meaning is causal-explanatory in nature when I can think of lots of examples where reading a sign, for example, explains what I do. "Turn left," it says, so I turn left. My knowledge of meaning helps to cause my behaviour. Why don't these count as empirically robust facts about language in the sense that you deny?

AG: As I am treating them, these are empirically robust facts in virtue of which we ought to accept various of our sentences in various circumstance. So they are facts in virtue of which our words mean what they do. That leads to your question, understood as a question about the meaning of meaning. When we say what a word means—that a Frenchman's word "chien" means dog, to take a stock instance—aren't we saying something analyzable as a purely empirical claim? Can't we put what we are saying purely in terms of the sorts of empirically robust facts you are speaking of? Well first, of course, once I answer no, I need an account of why what a person means by a word figures in explaining her behavioral proclivities. I offer such an explanation. The issue here is equivalent to that of how there can be "moral explanations," such as the purported explanation that slavery evoked such strong opposition because it was so bad. "Slavery was bad," plausibly, can't be analyzed in purely causal-explanatory terms, since believing that slavery was bad involves being against it.

How then could the badness of slavery explain why it aroused such opposition? My explanation is that, by its meaning, "Slavery was bad" agrees with various combinations of attitudes and causal beliefs. It agrees with the combination of opposing suffering and believing that slavery caused suffering, but it also agrees with opposing unprofitability and believing that slavery was unprofitable. Many of the relevant attitudes will go without saying, and so we adopt them implicitly in offering the explanations we give, but the pure logic of the claim "Slavery aroused such heated opposition because it was so bad" allows a wide range of combinations of attitudes with causal beliefs.

Still, why suffer these complications? You asked me earlier why I found alternative views of the meaning of "meaning" wanting, and I didn't give you much of an answer. But in the book, I look at some length at one debate about meaning, what classical physicists meant by "mass." I ask what's at issue in such a debate, and argue that the issue may not be settled unproblematically by classical physicists' proclivities of usage. We can give a normative account, though, of what might be at issue. What's at issue, I say, is, among other things, which sentences in one's language to accept if one is a 19th century physicist who ought, given his evidence, to accept the substance of Einstein's special theory of relativity.

3:AM: This takes us to your ethical theory. For you moral questions are not empirical questions about the natural world are they, but what you call planning questions. Can you explain what you mean by this and why it's crucially important if we're to understand the nature of morality?

AG: My term "planning" is misleading in a number of ways that I spell out in the book, but I still think it is illuminating. I talk about "planning" what to believe, what sentences in one's language to accept, and what degrees of credence to accord, even though one can't believe or accept sentences at will. Consider, though, planning in the most literal sense, contingency planning for what to do. Planning what to do issues in intentions—but just as one can't believe at will, one can't intend at will. One acts at will by forming an immediate intention and carrying it out. So what is the relation between "planning" what to believe, in my sense, and believing? It is the same as the relation between planning literally what to do and forming an immediate intention to do it. Plans are of course closely related to non-planning beliefs, but as Hume insisted, the relation isn't logical: it's not a conceptual contradiction to want to touch a hot stove tomorrow. Clearly, though, it's not the thing to do—and in saying that, I express having a clear plan not to do it, a plan with which you no doubt agree.

3:AM: You've written about your metaethical ideas under the title *"Thinking How To Live."* Your hypothesis in that book is that normative questions "are at base questions of what to do, what to believe, and how to feel about things." You don't ask whether it's true but rather, what difference would it make to us if it were. So can you sketch what conclusions you draw.

AG: I do claim that normative questions are questions of what to do and the like, but it doesn't follow that answers to them aren't true or false. Even Ayer, with his expressivistic version of emotivism, should have said that moral claims can be true or false. He was a deflationist about truth: according to him, saying "It's true that slavery is bad" is just saying that slavery is bad. So if "Slavery is bad" means "Boo for slavery!" then "It"s true that slavery is bad' must just mean "Boo for slavery!" Now I admit, of course, that we don't call "Boo for slavery!" true. Many philosophers think that this is a deep fact, but I can't find what's deep in it. Rules of usage, I agree, restrict "true" and "false" to declarative sentences, and so if you say "Boo for slavery!" I can't properly respond "How true!" whereas if you say "Slavery is terrible," I can. But to agree with the one is to agree with the other. By rules of usage, agreeing with a declarative sentence is regarding it as "true," whereas agreeing with an exclamation isn't. But reforming this rule away, I think, wouldn't make much difference.

3:AM: Are you a species of contractualist? Where would you part company with perhaps the two other major contractualist of recent times, TM Scanlon on the one hand and John Rawls on the other? Is one major difference that for you utilitarianism is still pretty compelling?

AG: At one time, it was widely thought that departing from utilitarianism would entangle one in contradictions. Hare thought indeed that conceptual logic and the nature of moral concepts pretty much forced one to be a utilitarian. That view is rare now, and we have to ask whether it has just gone out of fashion, or rather we have discovered something wrong with the arguments that used to convince people. The strongest arguments, to my mind, were the ones that John Harsanyi gave in the 1950's—although my impression is that these arguments still aren't widely known among philosophers. I myself think it is a disgrace to philosophical education that Harsanyi's arguments aren't standardly studied, even in graduate programs that pay some attention to ethics. Moral philosophers these days mostly think that utilitarianism goes against our moral intuitions and so fails, but we have to ask the further question of whether our moral intuitions can be made to fit in with each other coherently.

Can anti-utilitarian intuitions be fixed up so that they become consistent with each other but stay anti-utilitarian? Harsanyi's arguments seem to show that any non-utilitarian view has to be inconsistent. Rawls offers us many valuable ways of thinking, but his attempts to differentiate his system from Harsanyi's are strained. In fact he just sets aside rule-utilitarianism as not really utilitarianism, and then gives arguments which, if correct, would show that his system coincides with a rule-utilitarian version of Harsanyi. Tim Scanlon is the rare moral philosopher who has genuinely engaged Harsanyi, and he argues for a way around Harsanyi. My little book of Tanner Lectures *Reconciling Our Aims* accepts Scanlon's critique of Harsanyi, but then argues that the contractualist insights that ground Scanlon's system entail features that are close enough to utilitarianism that they will be counterintuitive in the same ways.

If these discredit utilitarianism, they discredit the bases of Scanlon's contractualism in the same way. As for these conflicts with intuition, I think that for the most part, something like rule-utilitarianism is the way to handle them. Disastrously, in my attempt to keep the the lectures at a proper length, I cut out saying this explicitly, and I was distressed that more than one commentator read me as rejecting rule-utilitaritarianism. I am glad to see that with Derek Parfit and Josh Greene, the right kinds of consequentialist views seem to be making a comeback.

3:AM: How do you respond to contemporary debates of morality, such as the new interest in the trolley arguments, Derek Parfit's *On What Matters* and Sam Harris's new and widely publicized book? I guess the broad question is whether you think the public discourse about ethics and morality is healthy or not?

AG: Your question is not, I take it, whether it is healthy to engage in public discourse about ethics and morality, but whether the public discourse that we are producing is in good shape. For the most part, philosophers aren't all that prominent in public discussions of morality, and I hope that more philosophical input into public discussion would make it better—though with some philosophers, I wonder. Some strands of philosophers' current discourse on morality, though, I find encouraging. My view on Derek Parfit's giant two volumes is divided: On the one hand, I disagreed with some of the metaethics in the volumes—though he and I have been pursuing the issues and our views turn out to be far more compatible than either of us had thought. With Parfit's exploration of what Kant could reasonably have maintained, I am much on board.

Much of my own interest in moral philosophy stems from hopes that getting clearer on what the issues are will help us to address them better. I think that public discourse on morality is a matter of thinking together what to favor and promote, and why—as well as how to feel about things that people do or might do. Once we join Socrates in rejecting the view that ethics starts with the supernatural, the real philosophical work begins. How, understanding ourselves as parts of the natural world, are we to get somewhere in addressing ethical questions that matter, and pursue the questions systematically? How are we to get started with the systematic pursuit of ethical questions. In most of my work in the past few decades, I have focused on questions of what we are doing when we address moral questions and, more broadly, questions of how to live. Some of my smaller pieces, however, have been on substantive issues in ethical theory, and this especially holds for my Tanner Lectures and replies in *Reconciling Our Aims*. My hopes are for more insightful thinking on public issues that is coherent and thus, I argue, broadly consequentialist.

3:AM: And for the readers here at 3:AM are there five books you could recommend that would take us further into your philosophical world?

AG: Much of my philosophical world most narrowly understood consists of subjects where I already have strong opinions, and so although I respect some recent books, I don't credit myself as learning central things I didn't realize before, apart from occasionally finding new arguments I must answer. Two philosophy books that have occupied me recently are:

Huw Price, *Naturalism without Mirrors*

Robert Brandom, *Between Saying and Doing: Towards an Analytic Pragmatism.*
Especially with Brandom, I'm still trying to master the framework, but his work is very rich. The books that most excite me in recent years are good presentations of scientific developments that bear on philosophical questions—especially on how to understand human thinking in a richly naturalistic way. I remember that when the psychologist David Premack looked around in a bookstore here at the University of Michigan, he commented that the textbooks assigned are pedestrian, whereas there are now a rich array of books for a popular audience that are first rate in their presentations of their subjects.

Three books that advanced my understanding of how evolution shapes our propensities are:

Sean B. Carroll, *Endless Forms Most Beautiful: The New Science of Evo Devo and the Making of the Animal Kingdom.*

Gary Marcus, *The Birth of the Mind: How a Tiny Number of Genes Creates the Complexities of Human Thought.*Jonathan Haidt, *The Righteous Mind: Why Good People Are Divided by Politics and Religion.*

Allan Gibbard is the author of:

Wise Choices, Apt Feelings: A Theory of Normative Judgment (Harvard University Press, Oxford University Press, 1990)

Thinking How to Live (Harvard University Press, 2003)

Reconciling Our Aims: In Search of Bases for Ethics (Oxford University Press, 2008)

Meaning and Normativity (Oxford University Press, 2012)

3 | Jonathan Dancy: "Ethics Without Principles"

Jonathan Dancy is a philosopher at the University of Texas at Austin (half-time) and a leading proponent of moral particularism. Here he discusses what reasons count in ethics and whether things like moral principles actually exist, and argues that no empirical inquiry is sufficient to establish relevance because the matter requires judgment in a way that lies beyond observation and inference.

3:AM: You've been a top philosopher for quite some time. What have been the satisfactions of being one so far, and what would you say to someone who questioned the relevance of philosophy?

JONATHAN DANCY: I don't feel like a top philosopher at all. If I am at the top, there must be a great many others up there with me. But I do think that my philosophical life has been far more successful than I ever expected, and the notion of success at issue here is grounded in what I take to be a common aim, or at least hope, of intellectuals, that their ideas will make a difference to the way in which others think, or change the intellectual agenda in some way. So the satisfaction for me comes when I see the ways in which my efforts have affected the contents of ethics courses, of readers, and of textbooks, and when I see that the possibility of particularism in ethics seems now to be taken seriously in a way that it never was before.

As for those who question the relevance of philosophy, they first have to say what it is not relevant to. There are normally two answers to this question, relevant to them and relevant to practical life. That it is not relevant to their concerns is something I find sad but inevitable; I don't see that everyone should be interested in what we do. The idea that it is not relevant to practical life seems, by contrast, to depend upon a rather limited conception of what practical life may be. Just to take an example close to home: surely the question whether there are any moral principles is pretty close to practice, since if we accept that there are none, this is likely to affect how we think and thereby what we go on to do.

3:AM: You make a striking point in an article responding to an idea by Christopher Hookway which gets at one area of your philosophical interests. That there are considerations implicated in believing something that are not in themselves reasons for believing something but are nevertheless "enabling conditions" giving us the right to believe something is something you have been arguing for the last twenty years. So what is the significance of this argument? What alternative view are you against here? Can you perhaps give us an example?

JD: The distinction between the things (or people) who do the work and those that don't themselves do the work but enable others to do it has widespread implications. A fairly trivial example is the distinction between the role of the actors in a theatre and the role of the backstage staff. The role of the latter is to enable the former to play their role. We just need a distinction between roles. More generally, though, there is a tendency in the theory of reasoning to see every relevant consideration as playing the same role, that of a premise.

But my view is that in order to understand reasoning, we need to distinguish between the different sorts of roles that considerations can play. In this, I find myself in agreement with Stephen Toulmin's suggestions in his *The Uses of Argument*. Just as a principle of inference should be distinguished from a premise, so should considerations that affect the ability of other such to stand as reasons for our conclusion.

Here is an example of the sort of thing I mean. That the gun was found in the butler's cupboard is, let us say, a reason to believe him to be the guilty party. That it did not appear that we were intended to find it plays, however, a different role. It is not a further reason to believe the butler to be guilty, but a consideration such that, had it not been the case, the location of the gun would have been a reason to believe the butler innocent. That is, if it looks like a plant, the fact that we found the gun in the butler's cupboard is now a reason on the other side.

In moral philosophy, I used the distinction between favourers and enablers to stop a certain form of anti-particularist argument. Suppose I offer a counterexample to a suggested moral principle of the form "All F actions are wrong," my example being an action that is F and G, and not wrong. A common response is to say that the relevant principle is really "All actions that are F and not G are wrong".

My response to this is, first, that this process might go on indefinitely, and second, that this supposes that being not-G has the same sort of relevance to the wrongness of the action as does being F; but it might be that being not-G is not itself a wrong-making feature, but simply a feature whose presence is required for the Fness of the action to make it wrong. If so, being not-G is an enabler, rather than a wrong-maker. It enables the Fness of the action to make it wrong, without itself counting against the action. So the supposed principle "All F actions are wrong," is false, and there is no true replacement "All actions that are F and G are wrong".

3:AM: In your book *Moral Reasons* you argue for a realist conception of ethics, which is the claim that there are facts of the matter in ethics. And then you attack consequentialism because you find consequentialists have far too narrow a view of reasons relevant for moral judgments. I guess these include your "enabling conditions" you just spoke about. But what would you say to the policy maker who says that the reasons for moral action on your account are too diffuse to be pinned down and measured and so lead to the consequence that public policy makers, condemned to work with mechanical algorithms are thus condemned to work outside of morality?

JD: I don't see that policy makers are condemned to work with mechanical algorithms. I do allow that the process of moral reasoning, whether in public affairs or in private life, is much more complex than traditional accounts have allowed. But that does not lead to pessimism, since I think that we also have the rational capacity to cope with the complexities that face us. But talk of pinning reasons down and measuring them makes me pretty uneasy.

I think that generally we all recognise the same reasons, and that disagreement arises when we assess their relative strength. Here talk of measuring may seem appropriate, but I would think that we estimate the strength of reasons rather than measure it. (There is, after all, no unit of measurement for reasons.) Such estimation is not easy, but politicians expect to differ from each other on such matters and do not expect (and never have expected) to be able somehow to prove that they are right.

3:AM: You used to argue that moral knowledge is of what in particular cases is a moral reason for what. There are no principles for moral reasons. (or any reasons actually). Basic moral knowledge is of contingent particular truths. But we know these a priori. Each new experience has to be worked out and judged but the judgment delivered is a priori. Is this right? Can you say something more about this and why you argued that this kind of judgment in the moral sphere is analogous to how we know what is relevant to what. Linked to what I asked in the previous question, but from a slightly different angle, does your view imply that we should be learning how to make judgments sensitive to these reasons rather than applying some cost accountancy model of measuring worth?

JD: Yes, in *Ethics without Principles* I did argue that our basic moral knowledge is of what is a reason for what in a particular case, and that such knowledge is a priori knowledge of contingent particular truths.

My reasoning was this. If we allow my starting point, that what is a reason in one case may not be a reason in another, the question whether it is a reason here seems to have to be a contingent one (since it might have been otherwise and would have been if the case had been relevantly different), and particular. But once all the empirical facts are in, we still have work to do to establish what features are reasons for what. So our decision on the latter front must be reached a priori, since it lies beyond anything that experience can inform us about.

The same argument applies to our decisions on another rational matter, what is relevant to what (in a particular case). No empirical enquiry is sufficient to establish relevance; the matter requires judgement in a way that lies beyond observation and inference. And if something can be deprived of its relevance by changes elsewhere, it must be a contingent matter whether it is here relevant or not. So yes, I do think that our sense of relevance can be trained, and that it should be, and I don't think that there is a possible unit of measurement for relevance (or worth) that would be capable of doing most of the work for us.

3:AM: Your view is a kind of moral particularism and if it is, how do you answer the argument that if we acquire all our moral concepts on a case by case consideration its difficult how we could ever learn anything like a generally realizable morality? You discuss this and other issues in your book that has the title that announces what for some sounds like a contradiction: *Ethics Without Principles*?

JD: I don't think I would say that we acquire all our moral concepts on a case by case basis. My view is rather that we acquire our moral knowledge on a case by case basis, starting, as I said above, from knowledge of particular reasons. It doesn't follow from this alone that we cannot build up a "generally realisable morality," even if what is meant by this that we cannot build up a principle-based ethic. Ross, after all, thought that we do start from particular cases, but that what we discern in such cases was capable of revealing to us the truth of certain prima facie principles, by a procedure called intuitive induction.

I don't say that this is impossible, but I do say that every suggested Rossian prima facie principle is subject to counter-example, and that I know of no real need for moral principles. Much of my time has been spent arguing that principles are at best redundant. In saying this I take myself to be, in a way, defending the possibility of moral distinctions. For if there are no available principles, or not enough to do all the work, some would say that this is the death of ethics. Not I, however. My view is that this wouldn't matter, since morality is in no need of principles.

3:AM: Did Christopher Peacocke change your mind? I was impressed by your remarks when writing about his book *The Realm of Reason* that twenty years of hard fought argumentation was severely challenged by his book. How hard is it to change your mind in philosophy, not on a minor detail but really on an argument which, as you wrote then, was something that a substantial amount of your philosophical career had been dedicated to developing and defending?

JD: Peacocke did not change my mind, but he did make it clear to me that I had more work to do. That is not much damage, for it is not as if I didn't really know this already. One can, however, conveniently forget such things and carry on regardless, and this was what I had been doing. And an occasional shock is nothing but salutary.

But your question does raise interesting issues about philosophical commitment. Many philosophers take up positions which they defend with vigor. I am one such. But when I ask myself whether I believe that my position is correct, I don't really know how to reply. I have committed myself to these things, but belief seems to require more than that sort of commitment. Still, whether I believe them or not, abandoning them would be a blow. Of course one can abandon an argument without abandoning its conclusion.

And indeed I did lose one of my favourite arguments when Michael Ridge and Sean McKeever persuaded me that holism in the theory of reasons does not actually entail particularism in ethics. To preserve my conclusion, I had to find another route from my premise to my conclusion. But all this is everyday stuff.

Suppose, by contrast, that I came to be persuaded that there was a need for principles of some type or other, in the sort of way that I have been officially denying for years. I would definitely have to try to find some way to come to terms with this, and I would probably console myself with the thought that at least I had forced people to do more than assume the necessity of principles, and actually to work out why they are so indispensable in ethics (when they seem not to be elsewhere, e.g. in aesthetics). I think I could come to think of this as an acceptable second best.

3:AM: You ask a pretty cool question which will help us understand some more about our views on the relation of reasons to acting. You ask in a recent paper; "Is it possible to run for the reason that the train is leaving when one doesn't know that the train is leaving?" So can we, and what does your argument show us?

JD: Can we run for the reason that p when we do not know that p? John Hyman and Jennifer Hornsby are convinced that we cannot, and I am convinced that we can. My view is that we cannot run for the reason that p if we do not believe that p, but that knowledge is not necessary. It is quite hard to work out how to argue about this. Take a case where I take myself to know what the bus time-table is, and in that light am running to the bus stop so as not to miss the bus. Actually I don't know this, because I have misremembered what is written in the timetable which I only consulted last week. Since then, however, the bus times have been changed, so that in fact I am right in thinking that the bus is about to leave. I would say, if asked what my reason for running is, that it is that the bus is about to leave. Hyman and Hornsby would say that this cannot be my reason, since I do not know it to be true; all I have is a luckily true belief. I think they owe us a reason for saying this, and I have not really seen one yet. But they certainly have some interesting things to say against my position, which may yet lead me to change some aspects of the position I defended in *Practical Reality*.

3:AM: What's the difference between the right and the good and why should it matter?

JD: There are various positions to be considered. Some people think that the best action is always the right one, and others don't. If the latter are in the right of it, there must be some difference between being right and being best. Even if the best action is always the right one, it might be that we are dealing here with two different concepts, and two different properties. G. E. Moore did say in *Principia Ethica* that it was there is only one concept here, but he later abandoned that view in favour of the view that there are two concepts and two properties, but that every action that has one property has the other, and so every instance of one concept is an instance of the other.

Those who think that the best action is always the right one can still allow that the action is right because it is best, and not best because it is right. Others think that though we do have a (prima facie) duty to make things go as well as possible, we have other duties which sometimes take precedence, so that we can be morally required to make things worse than we might have. On this view, the good and the right can conflict. This is significant because the basic intuition that underlies consequentialism is a sort of philosophical boggle, the thought that it cannot be one's duty to do anything other than the best one can. So the possibility of a non-consequentialist position is dependent, it seems, on supposing otherwise.

3:AM: An example of the great subtleness of your thought is the distinction you make between the prospective use of a moral principle to guide action, on the one hand, and its retrospective use to appraise the way an agent governed herself. You have a cool example to show why this is very important when you consider why we shouldn't kill a person so her organs can be used to save the lives of multiple other individuals. Can you say why this is important especially in the light of considerations about intentions and moral action.

JD: I am not quite sure what this question is aiming at. But one relevant fact is that assessing an action that has been done must be a very different activity from evaluating the merits of different alternative possibilities when deciding how to act. For when we are deciding how to act, there is as yet no actual action there to evaluate. All that deliberation can do is to tell us, not which action to do, but how to act—that is, it tells us that our action, when we do it, must have certain qualities, be of a certain sort.

Similarly, a reason to act is not a reason to do this or that particular action, but only a reason to act in a certain way, or to do an act of a certain sort. So the prospective question is quite different from the retrospective question. Intentions, too, can only be intentions to act in a certain way; one cannot intend a particular action. One can of course ask of an action, once it is done, whether it was intentional or not. But this last is not a question about the action, understood as a particular, but only about whether the agent's behaviour was intentional in some respects.

3:AM: You've a general worry that there's an orthodoxy current at the moment that doesn't make a distinction between reasons for action and reasons for why we ought to do something. Is that right? So how interested have you been in work of xphi and others who have looked at what the folk actually think about moral reasons and whether their intuitions square with those of philosophers?

JD: Yes, I think there is a distinction between two relations: the first is the favouring relation that relates considerations and actions (or beliefs, come to that, or emotions—any response, really) and the other is the making-right relation, which is a relation between consideration and rightness. To be a rightmaker is not the same as to be a favourer; being right is not favoured by anything.

Nonetheless a consideration that favours an action may succeed in making it right. It is all a bit complicated at this point and I am not at all sure that I have seen my way through it. I'm not sure, either, whether this issue is much connected to the results of experimental philosophy. I haven't been as interested in these results as I should have been, probably, but in the present case I don't see that one can learn much by asking the folk what they think or how they would respond to certain scenarios. The existence and nature of a subtle distinction like this one is not something about which I think the folk would have much to say, and if they did pronounce on the matter (which I would say is very improbable) I would not take their views to be of much significance. It is one thing to see how the folk operate a distinction that they understand, and another to see whether they can grasp a distinction in the first place.

3:AM: Isn't there a danger in your views defending judgment, thick concepts and the like that morals become fixed by the prejudices of an in-group. I recall Ernest Gellner worrying that consequentialism was thought of as being the ethics for the parvenu, the outsider who hadn't internalized the old-boy culture (I think his target was Michael Oakeshot). Given that so much of modern industrial society makes us all strangers don't your arguments make us all foreigners to morality because there is no single dominant culture in play?

JD: I do think that there are non-disentanglable thick concepts, but I don't think it impossible to abandon a thick concept for the reason that the distinctions that it draws are no longer ones that one feels comfortable with. Of course we are brought up with a way of looking at things, much of which is expressed using thick concepts, and it may be hard to escape from that viewpoint, but I would not say it is impossible. So we are not locked into the ethical perspective we have inherited from our parents, or that is common to our social group. And the (supposed) fact that there is no single dominant moral culture in contemporary (Western) society does not prevent people from having, and sharing with others, fairly ferocious moral opinions. So I don't see that danger either.

3:AM: In your introductory essay to Blackwell's *Companion to Epistemology* you make remarks that suggest that you feel that there are genuine distinctions to be made between analytic and continental philosophy. Is this right, and if so, what are they?

JD: Actually those remarks were a little tongue in cheek. Bernard Williams used to say that the distinction between analytic and continental philosophy is a cross-classification, like the distinction between Japanese cars and sports cars. I don't think that is quite the right way to look at it. Those who run this distinction tend to have certain writers in mind on both sides, say Quine at one end and Derrida at the other; and there are indeed huge differences in style between these two. But most philosophy is at neither extreme.

I remember a book by Julius Kovesi, *Moral Notions*, which argued that the supposed distinction between "good" and "yellow" was actually a matter of degree, and that many concepts lay between these two outliers. By choosing the two things at either end of the spectrum one gives the impression that there is a sort of chasm between them, and that everything must fall on one side or the other, when in fact there is no such chasm, and all we need to do is to plot the relevant differences carefully. The same applies to the differences between Quine and Derrida.

3:AM: I notice that you are partly responsible for Parfit writing his two volume *On What Matters*. He was supposed to write some comments to contributions to your book Reading Parfit but he went out of control and just wouldn't stop writing! So, given that you are (in a strange way) its midwife, what do you make of *On What Matters* and would you defend it against naturalist challenges such as Philip Kitchers's?

JD: I haven't read Parfit's *On What Matters* since it came out, though I have read many parts of it, or versions of many parts, many times over the years. I'll have to rectify this soon, because I will be teaching this book at UT Austin next Spring semester. Whatever one thinks of the book, I think it hardly deniable that Parfit is a genius, extraordinarily talented and inventive. One does not have to agree with him to say this.

But I do think that he is right about non-naturalism. It is one thing to show that non-naturalism is a live option, and another to show that it is the truth. The general question how there can be instantiations of non-natural properties and relations in a material world seems to me to be one without much of a bite. I am helped in thinking this by a sense that the favouring relation is unlikely to be naturalisable. Of course this does nothing to assuage those who feel that the very idea of a non-natural property or relation is a nonsense. But philosophers choose which attacks to respond to and which simply to leave aside.

3:AM: When not reading and writing philosophy, are there books that you have found inspirational or enlightening?

JD: The trouble with this question is that, though I know that it sounds a bit limited, the sort of inspiration and enlightenment I seek and recognise is going to be broadly philosophical. So anything I mention is going to be semi-philosophical in nature: Montaigne, for instance, or Sir Thomas Browne—two people whose minds seem so much better stocked than my own. But these are something of an acquired taste.

3:AM: And finally, are there five books you would recommend to the cool readers here at 3:AM wanting to learn more about all this stuff?

JD: In general it seems to me preferable to read the great classics of the subject, or shorter books that have stood the test of time pretty well, rather than the latest efforts of professional philosophers. Among the classics are Hume's *Enquiry Concerning the Principles of Morals*, Kant's *Groundwork of the Metaphysics of Morals* (but one really needs help with this), and Mill's *Utilitarianism*. More recent short books are G. E. Moore's *Ethics*, A. C. Ewing's *Teach Yourself Ethics*, and Bernard Williams' *Morality*. (I would love to write a book of this last sort myself, but it is not an easy task.)

Jonathan Dancy is the author of:

An Introduction to Contemporary Epistemology (Blackwell, 1985)
Berkeley: An Introduction (Blackwell, 1987)
Moral Reasons (Blackwell, 1993)
Practical Reality (Clarendon Press, 2000)
Ethics Without Principles (Clarendon Press, 2004; paperback edition, 2006)

4 | Ruth Chang: "The Existentialist of Hard Choices"

Ruth Chang is a philosopher at Rutgers University, New Brunswick. Here she confronts us with the philosophy of hard choices as she broods on the difference between incommensurate and incompatible and why the distinction counts, on how to handle hard choices, on different kinds, on why incomparability is rare but matters, on things being on a par, on causal determinism and agency, on being a closet existentialist, on the philosophical relevance of dirty socks to understanding love relationships, and on the recent spate of sexual harassment scandals in philosophy departments.

3:AM: What made you become a philosopher?

RC: I was working as a lawyer and I decided I wanted a 75% pay cut and to make my own copies.

3:AM: One of the things you've spent time thinking about is the difference between incommensurate and incomparable values. What's the difference between them?

RC: The terminology here is a bit of a mess, mostly because some philosophers like to use a fancier-sounding term—"incommensurability"—to mean incomparability, an idea for which we have a perfectly good ordinary term in English, namely "incomparability," while others—correctly—use the fancier philosopher's term of art to mean, well, an idea that we don't already have an ordinary English word, for, namely incommensurability. I really wish everyone would use "incomparability" when they meant incomparability and "incommensurability" for some other idea, preferably, the idea of incommensurability.

Here are the two ideas of interest. One of these is that of lacking a common unit of measure, or, equivalently, not being cardinally comparable. This idea traces back to Hippasus of Metapontum, a Pythagorean, who first noticed that the length of the diagonal of a unit square ($\sqrt{2}$) could not be measured by the same unit as any of its sides (1) since, as was thought at the time, rational numbers could not be put on the same scale as irrational numbers. The "discovery" that some lengths could lack a common unit of measure was a big deal because it threatened to throw into disarray the Pythagorean view that everything in the universe was measurable by ratios of integers. As the story goes, Pythagorean thugs took old Hippasus out to sea and drowned him in an attempt to keep his discovery secret. Of course, today we know about the real numbers, so the case of the length of diagonal and side of a unit square wasn't a good example of the idea of lacking a common cardinal measure. Still, the idea of incommensurability was born. Aristotle then used the idea—and, as Alan Code confirmed to me, employed the Greek equivalent of "incommensurable," asummetros—to refer to the idea that there is no common unit in terms of which the (true as opposed to expedient) value of beds and houses can be measured since a house isn't equivalent in value to any particular number of beds. So the etymology of "incommensurability" shows that we should use the term to refer to the idea of lacking a common unit of measure.

The other main idea is not being comparable. Given the ordinary language meaning of "incomparable," we should use that term to mean "cannot be compared," since that is in fact what the word means. There's no need to use a fancy-sounding philosopher's term of art to refer to the idea of not being able to be compared because we have an ordinary English word that will do the trick. So if things are incomparable, they can't be compared; if they are incommensurable, there is no common cardinal unit that measures them and by which they can be compared.

3:AM: So if two things are incommensurable, they aren't necessarily incomparable?

RC: Exactly. Being incommensurable is compatible with being comparable since you don't have to have a cardinal measure of two things in order for them to be comparable—they might be ordinally comparable. There may be no unit that measures the value of writing the Great American Novel and eating a slice of pizza, but the former could be better. So incommensurability does not entail incomparability. But incomparability entails incommensurability; if two items cannot be compared, they cannot be cardinally compared.

3:AM: Okay. Now that we've got the ideas straight, why does any of this matter? Why are incommensurability and incomparability important?

RC: Well, my own view is that incommensurability isn't all that important but incomparability is. To see why, we need to distinguish the relata, or the things that either incommensurable, on the one hand, or incomparable, on the other. The items that are typically said to be either incommensurable or incomparable are either abstract values, like justice and beauty and cruelty, or bearers of values such as policies, paintings, and actions. The main upshot of incommensurable values is that attempts to model values by standard utility functions, which presuppose cardinal measure of whatever the function is a function over, won't work. And if bearers of values—most significantly alternatives for choice—are incommensurable, then attempts to model the rationality of choice by such functions—for example by cost-benefit analysis—are similarly wrong-headed because the values of incommensurable alternatives do not admit of cardinal measure. There are other implications, but that's the main thing at stake if either values or their bearers are incommensurable. Since many people (but not economists and decision theorists!) already reject such modeling, incommensurability isn't really all that big a deal among most philosophers these days.

As for incomparability, if values are incomparable, again, not a whole lot follows. We have to reject standard decision-theoretic models of values, which, as I've said, a lot of people already do, and we have to accept that abstract values are incomparable. But this latter fact doesn't itself entail much—it doesn't entail that there are irreducibly plural values for instance since incomparable values—say, justice and beauty—may nevertheless be constituents of a single value—say, impartial goodness of outcomes. Nor does it entail that all bearers of those incomparable values are themselves incomparable since two abstract values can be incomparable without every instantiation of them (as manifested by bearers of value) being incomparable. That is, justice and beauty might be incomparable even though an insignificant beauty can be worse than a massive justice. So the incomparability of values, like the incommensurability of values or of their bearers, isn't such a big deal.

But if alternatives for choice are incomparable, then all hell breaks loose—at least if we accept certain natural assumptions. We naturally think that we're justified in choosing one alternative over the others so long there is some truth about their relative value, and being incomparable denies that there is any such truth. So if alternatives for choice are incomparable, practical reason breaks down; we haven't got any basis for being justified in choosing one alternative over the others. And if there's a lot of incomparability among our alternatives for choice, it looks like most of the choices we make aren't guided by practical reason.

Put dramatically, maybe the Enlightenment conception of ourselves as rational agents who go around discovering and responding to reasons is a sham—and maybe the existentialists were right after all. You think you're using reason when you decide to go vegetarian or start an exercise regime or buy this toaster rather than that one, but all you can do is existentially "plump" for this rather than that since incomparability is everywhere. What's a stake if alternatives for choice are incomparable is, then, our very understanding of ourselves as human agents.

3:AM: But you don't think there is a lot of incomparability—if any, right? Can you give us a sense of why, on the one hand, you think incomparability of alternatives is a big deal, and on the other, you think there isn't a lot of it?

RC: Fifteen years ago, when I was a grad student, I pored through the literature and collected what I thought were (and still think are) the seven main arguments for the existence of incomparability among goods or alternatives for choice. After raising objections against each argument and pronouncing each pretty much dead, I expected a rainshower of corrections, criticisms, and abuse from incomparabilists but surprisingly got very little pushback. I'm still waiting for incomparabilists to come up with a good argument for incomparability.

But of course this doesn't mean we shouldn't believe that there's no incomparability—I'm the first to believe that we should believe things for which there are no good arguments. Incomparability isn't one of those things, though, because I think there's a diagnosis for why we think we should believe it that has nothing to do with whether there is any.

The problem is that we need some way to understand "hard choices," roughly, choices between alternatives where one alternative is better in some of the relevant respects, the other is better in other relevant respects, and there seems to be no overall truth about whether one is better or whether they are equally good. Stock cases include whether to become a philosopher or a lawyer and whether to tell your friend that her husband is cheating on her or to stay silent because it's none of your business and they will work out their issues or not on their own. In many hard cases, you can be practically certain that neither alternative is better overall and nor are they equally good, so the hardness isn't simply a matter of uncertainty about the relevant facts. And since, so I've argued, the hardness doesn't seem to be in our language but rather in our values, we need to explain the hardness in terms of a normative fact about the alternatives. The fact that they cannot be compared seems pretty naturally to fit the bill. That's why the choice between them is hard. And since hard choices seem to be pretty common, we need a fair bit of incomparability to account for them.

If we inspect hard choices carefully, however, we'll see that there are two distinct sorts of hard case we need to separate: those that are hard because there is a complete breakdown of practical reason and so we must respond to them outside of the scope of our rational agency, and those that are hard simply as a substantive normative matter, perhaps in something like the way that some math problems are substantively—mathematically—hard. Maybe moral dilemmas, if they exist, are like the former. Maybe Sophie, in choosing between which of Jan and Eva to save from the Nazi gas chambers, was forced to do something that was not guided by reasons. When she chose to save Jan, she was not acting within the scope of her rational agency because practical reason had broken down—she had to existentially plump rather than rationally choose.

Hard choices of the second variety allow responses within the scope of rational agency—you remain a rational agent as you agonize over what to do just as you remain a mathematician as you painstakingly work out the next line of the proof. In these substantively hard cases, it makes sense to continue to deliberate, agonize, ask your mother for advice, and so on. When we choose in such cases, we are exercising our rational agency, not simply plumping like Sartrean existential agents.

When a hard choice falls outside the scope of practical reason, the right thing to say, I think, is that the alternatives are incomparable. When a hard choice is substantively hard, the right thing to say, I think, is that the alternatives are comparable, but related by some relation beyond "better than," "worse than," and "equally good"—I dub this relation "on a par."

Here's an example. Suppose you're choosing between spending Spring Break on a beach in Florida or camping with pals in Wyoming. You're practically certain that, with respect to whatever matters in the choice between them—say how costly, fun, and relaxing each holiday is –, neither is better than the other. If we improve one of the vacations—say, the price of the Florida vacation is reduced by $100—does it thereby follow that the Florida vacation is better? Probably not. If the alternatives are comparable—another argument suggests that they are—then they must be related by some fourth comparative relation beyond "better than," "worse than" or "equally good"—they are on a par. Roughly speaking, they are in the same league or neighborhood of value, even though their values are very different. I think a lot of hard choices are like this and that the cases that might be thought to be cases of incomparability are really cases of parity.

3:AM: Right. You're known for arguing that even if one thing isn't better or worse than another thing and they're not equally good, they can still be comparable—you say they are "on a par." Why should we think there is parity and what is it?

RC: Well, if someone asked me to say what it is for things to be better or equally good, I'd try to describe what those relations involve by describing features of the evaluative differences they denote. If A is better than B, then the evaluative difference between them favors A. If A and B are equally good, then there is a zero evaluative difference between them. If A and B are on a par, there is a non-zero evaluative difference between them, but that difference doesn't favor one over the other. One reason it's hard to wrap our minds around the idea of parity—or non-zero, non-favoring evaluative differences—is that we're so used to understanding value on the model of the reals. Once you assume that value behaves like mass or length, you're stuck with the view that one value has got to be more, less or equal to another since mass and length can be measured by real numbers, and real numbers must stand in one of those three relations. One of the upshots of entertaining the possibility of parity is that we begin to question at a really fundamental level understanding value in the same way we understand most nonevaluative properties in the world.

As for arguments for parity, that's too big a question to tackle here, but I can sketch a couple of big ideas that might help. We've already seen one argument: we need one concept—incomparability—to describe what's going on when practical reason breaks down and all we can do is existentially plump for an alternative, and another concept—parity—to describe what's going on when practical reason is humming along fine but there's a problem in the way the values or reasons relate that don't determine what we should do.

Here's a little exercise you can perform at home to help you get on the road to parity. Suppose you're contemplating a choice between two rather different things—maybe a career in law and one in sky diving—about which you're pretty sure that neither is better than the other. Now ask yourself whether a small improvement in one of them—say a $100 increase in salary—would necessarily make it better than the other. If not, then they aren't equally good. Now ask yourself whether they are comparable. One way to help yourself think about this is to consider successive detractions along a spectrum from one of the items and successive improvements along a spectrum in the other item until it's pretty clear that the detracted one is worse than the massively improved one. Now ask yourself whether it makes sense to think that somewhere along the spectrum we shift from comparability to incomparability. As we go down one spectrum and up another, we maintain comparability, but then somewhere in the middle we have incomparability and then moving in opposite directions along the spectra we again have comparability. The differences between each successive neighbor on the spectrum are by hypothesis small differences in whatever matters to the choice between them. I think it's pretty implausible to think that the items could be arrayed so that the items at the top of one spectrum are comparable with the items on the bottom of another, and yet the middle items of each spectrum are incomparable. There are complexities I'm ignoring over here, but the basic idea is that it's hard to believe that all such cases are ones where we've got incomparability instead of comparability. And if we've got comparability, we've got a comparative relation that isn't "better than," "worse than," or "equally good": we've got parity.

3AM: Can we go back to what you said about practical reason? Is this the right taxonomy of possibilities you have in mind? If incomparable, then we can't choose as rational agents because the choice involves a breakdown of practical reason; if equally good, then, I suppose, we flip a coin; if on a par, then … what? What are we supposed to do? Flip a coin? How does parity differ from equality?

RC: "On a par" and "equally good" are different relations because they have different formal properties. "Equally good" is reflexive—a is as equally good as a—and transitive—if a is as equally as good as b which is as equally as good as c, then a is as equally as good as c. "On a par" is irreflexive—a isn't on a par with itself—a is as equally as good as itself—and nontransitive—if a is on a par with b which is on a par with c, it doesn't follow that a is on a par with c. But they are both ways in which items can be compared.

You've put your finger on the other main importance of parity—besides its inviting us to give up our deeply held, implicit conception of value as akin to mass or length with respect to measurability. The most important difference between "on a par" and "equally good" shows up in what we should do, practically speaking, when faced with such alternatives. If alternatives are equally good with respect to what matters in the choice between them, it's always permissible to flip a coin between them. Not so when things are on a par.

The key thing about parity is that it opens up a new way of understanding rational agency that is a substitute for the usual Enlightenment conception according to which we are essentially creatures who discover and respond to reasons. On that view, our agency is essentially passive—our reasons are ones given to us and not made by us. Our freedom as rational agents consists in the discovery of and appropriate response to reasons given to us and not created by us. Parity allows us to see that our agency may have a role in determining what reasons we have in the first place. So we might be free in a deeper sense—we are free to create reasons for ourselves under certain conditions.

3:AM: Boo-rah! Say more! Is the thought that we aren't subject to causal determination but can break the causal chain with an act of agency that creates reasons?

RC: I don't think we can do anything to escape causal determinism—that is, if causal determinism is true.

The idea instead is that when our reasons are on a par, we have the normative power to create new, "will-based" reasons in favor of one alternative as opposed to another. Take a toy example. You can have the banana split or the chocolate mousse for dessert. They are on a par with respect to deliciousness, which is what matters in the choice between them. You have the normative power to put your agency behind—to "will"—the chocolateyness of the chocolate mousse to be a reason for you to have it, thereby, perhaps, giving yourself most all-things-considered reasons to choose the chocolate mousse. Your act of agency is what makes it the case that you now have most reason to choose the mousse. This is an active view of rational agency because instead of sitting back and discovering what reasons we have, we can create reasons—when our non-will-based reasons—what I call our "given" reasons—are on a par.

It's in this way, I suggest, that we forge our own identities as, say, chocoholics or people who love extreme sports or care about the environment or work to alleviate poverty or any number of things that help define each of us as distinctive rational agents with particular concerns and projects. This is, I think the most interesting way in which we are– as philosophers like to say—the "authors of our lives."

One way to get an intuitive handle on this alternative view of agency is by considering the way you spend your Saturday afternoons. Say you spend yours interviewing philosophers. Could it be true that you have most reason to spend your Saturdays this way, rather than, say, going for walks, learning the piano, or working in a soup kitchen? Probably not. Could it be true that you have sufficient reason to interview philosophers as well as many other things, and you just arbitrarily plump for interviewing philosophers, where this plumping isn't an exercise of rational agency but the agential equivalent of flipping a coin? Our choices of how to spend our free time don't always feel that deeply random. What we do instead, on the view I believe parity makes possible, is put ourselves behind one activity rather than another—we identify with it, we commit to it—for the time being perhaps—we take it on as something we'll do. When we put our agency behind something, it feels like we have most reason to do what we're doing. And that's because we have conferred normativity on that activity. Putting your agency behind spending your Saturdays interviewing philosophers is how you make yourself into the distinctive rational agent that you are—someone curious about things philosophical.

3:AM: Okay, so you're saying that when our "given" reasons are on a par—the reasons we discover and respond to—then I can create reasons for myself by putting my agency behind an activity, like interviewing philosophers. Presumably, my willing things to be reasons isn't itself something that is guided by reason but a pure act of agency. Doesn't this make you a closet existentialist?

RC: In a way, yes. I think that both Kant and the existentialists were right about some very deep matters. Kant—on some interpretations—was right in thinking that practical normativity could have its source in the will. Sartre was right in thinking that choices can be a matter of agential fiat. They both were too ambitious, however, and took their ideas to be the linchpin of human agency.

They were each partly right. Some reasons—the will-based ones—have their source in the will but others—the ones that are on a par when will-based reasons can kick in—are "given" to us just as the Enlightenment view says. And only some choices are a matter of agential fiat—for example, ones where we our "given" reasons are on a par. Crucially, the existentialists eschewed any possibility of normativity before the act of agential fiat. When we make ourselves into chocoholics or do-gooders or philosophical explorers, we do so in an already-existing normative landscape. Or so I think. So that's another way my view differs from existentialism.

3:AM: You also think that this agential fiat is what explains what's distinctive about love relationships, don't you? Can you explain what you have in mind here?

RC: Exactly what this agential fiat is is a big question but it shouldn't be thought of as something necessarily conscious or deliberate requiring effort and a furrowed brow. I've suggested that it's akin to stipulating the meaning of a word; you can just start using "gnarly" a certain way. That is indeed how slang gets going. Putting your agency behind something is something you do, but you might do it unconsciously and certainly not deliberately.

Here's a story that illustrates what I have in mind. Suppose you're invited to have dinner at the house of a casual acquaintance, and you see that she has left various pairs of her dirty socks lying on the living room floor. Your acquaintance might be a bit of a slob. Her socks don't strike you as providing you with a reason to pick them up. They're her socks, after all, and it's her home, which she can keep however she likes. Contrast this with the case in which you at home with your beloved. She has left her dirty socks strewn on the living room floor. When you see the socks, they might strike you as providing you with a reason to pick them up. You might desist (she's got to learn to pick up after herself) but the phenomenology of the socks is different in the two cases. What explains the difference in phenomenology? I suggest that the phenomenology is explained by something you do. By putting your agency behind her and her interests, you have given yourself special reasons of a committed relationship that you otherwise wouldn't have. Putting your agency behind things makes you see the world differently, including people. Your beloved, thought to be a cranky ass by everyone else, is your lovable honeycake.

3:AM: Now turning to something completely different. What is your take on the spate of sexual harassment scandals that have rocked the profession recently? What, in your opinion, can be done to help make the profession less susceptible to bad behavior by male senior philosophers pursing relationships with female philosophy students?

RC: Well, I can't believe that philosophers are worse than other academics, or people in general, although the distinctive, intense one-on-one discussions that mark training in philosophy probably makes our profession especially vulnerable to sexual harassment, inappropriate behavior, misread signals and the like.

The two most prevalent "unsympathetic" reactions to all the press about sexual harassment or sexually inappropriate behavior I've had—all from senior male philosophers, some of some fame—are both of apiece with what we do as philosophers and therefore not altogether surprising. But I find them pretty dispiriting.

The first is that we all have to remain neutral, that we can't express even conditional moral disapprobation or sympathy for a party until we ourselves have the proof in hand and we can make our own judgment about the matter. Allied with this reaction is the intellectual reflex to think of all the counter-arguments to any allegation or counter-interpretations to data with which we are presented. We are trained to be this way—to see the world in terms of arguments for and against a proposition, and to withhold judgment until all the arguments and data are in. This reaction is usually cloaked under cries of "due process!."

Now I'm a lawyer, and I love due process probably more than most philosophers, but I really think that these attitudes and reactions are misplaced. The real world is one in which none of us is ever going to get all the evidence and data needed to make the kind of well-informed, dispassionate judgment about a case, and—crucially—people who tend to be on the receiving end of harm require the profession's support rather than silence. So I think each of us has to make our own judgment, on the basis of whatever data we can be reasonably expected to get, including our understanding of how things typically roll in the world, and take a moral stand on cases of alleged sexual misconduct in the profession. It's not that we have to blog about it or call up the victim, whomever we might believe him/her to be, but even casual remarks to colleagues in a department go a long way toward establishing a departmental culture or professional community where, eventually, people in that community have the sense: "We are a place that cares about the harm sexual harassment does to junior people in the profession and will take that junior person seriously" or, to take just one possible alternative, "We are a place that cares more about the possible injustice done to an alleged perpetrator of sexual harassment and will stand behind such a person until he is proven guilty." Context really matters here. Given that sexual harassment is a very real and serious problem in the world, I would much rather be in the former culture than the latter. Of course, we can be wrong about any particular judgments we make. But that wouldn't be the end of the world since most of us aren't saddled with decision-making authority over the relevant parties. It's time to stop pretending that we are university disciplinary committees and quit creating a passive "due process" professional culture. Failure to build a welcoming, safe, and caring culture for the profession—one that reflects the realities of how the world usually rolls and thus errs on the side of supporting the alleged victim of sexual harassment—is, in my view, crucial to the health of the profession.

The second reaction I've had from senior male philosophers is that women undergraduates have all the power: with one little complaint they can ruin the career and reputation of a senior male philosopher who is guilty of nothing more than expressing romantic interest in her, and so the wisest thing a male philosopher can do is to steer clear of mentoring or working with any female student. The idea here is that if a senior male philosopher hasn't got the judgment to know when his behavior is inappropriate, unwelcome, and the like, he'll just punish all female students by taking his ball home and refusing to play with the girls. Louise Antony, in a NYT Opinionator piece, does a good job of skewering this view. I would add just one small point. At institutions where dating students is not prohibited, any senior person—graduate student or faculty member—obviously has the burden to make sure he's not unwittingly exploiting the power imbalance between himself and a female student when he begins to pursue a romantic relationship with her. One way to check whether he's doing that is for him to ask of every communication he has with the student, "Is this something I wouldn"t mind having videotaped/copied and shown to the university's committee on sexual harassment?' That might help pierce some self-deception.

I suppose that a silver lining in all the bad press philosophy has been receiving is that, like STEM researchers, philosophers might now be motivated to use the tools of their trade to figure out ways to make sexual harassment just unequivocally not okay within the profession. After the Larry Summers blowup, people in the STEM fields rolled up their sleeves and starting tackling the possibly related problem of the underrepresentation of women in those fields in the way they knew how—by collecting data, doing studies, and offering hypotheses based on rigorous analysis of that data. We philosophers are handicapped by not having the skills or resources—they have NSF funding—to collect data or to run proper studies about sexual harassment ourselves, but we can always try to do the same thing—to effect a shift in the culture of the profession—from our armchairs. I think that is already happening. But some people don't like it and are being dragged along, kicking and screaming. So it's a slow and painful process.

3:AM: Just so we don't end on the note of pain, for the readers here at 3:AM, are there five books that you could recommend that would take us further into your philosophical world?

RC: Aristotle, *Nichomachean Ethics*
Sartre, *Existentialism is a Humanism*
Kant, 1st two Critiques
Parfit, *On What Matters*
Korsgaard, *The Sources of Normativity*
Scheffler, *Boundaries and Allegiances*
I guess that's seven, but who's counting.

Ruth Chang is the author of:

Making Comparisons Count (Routledge, 2002)

5 | Joseph Raz: "From Normativity to Responsibility"

Joseph Raz is Professor at Columbia University Law School and Professor (part-time) at Kings College, London. He has spent a lifetime in the jurisprudential and ethical long grass. Here he engages with issues of the philosophy of law and wrestling with what it means to respect difference, the intelligibility of values, reasons and normativity generally and on their dependence on social practices. He discusses the connection between reasons and intentions, reasons and rationality, the nature of intentional actions, whether pragmatic factors can serve as reasons for belief, on law and morality, about legal institutions, about legal theory, about authority and interpretation and about the notion of "being in the world."

3:AM: What made you become a philosopher?

JOSEPH RAZ: I wish I knew, just as I wish I knew the answers to other questions about my childhood. For example, what made me at 14 enroll in and attend adult education courses in my hometown, lectures mostly populated by adults older than my parents, many of them retired, and why was I not intimidated by being the only child there? That may be even more puzzling than the fact that they were all philosophy courses. In other words I have been hooked for almost as long as I can remember. I think it was in my second year of this activity that I sought expert advice about what to read (I should mention that I was reading other adult books: history of economic ideas, military history, and more). Through various indirect connections I was invited to meet an elderly gentleman who asked me what I had read so far. Very proudly I told him that I was then reading Spinoza's Ethics. He was surprised and assured me that I might be reading it, but I did not understand what I read. I was somewhat shaken but did not desist. He was of course right, but knowledge of that fact did not dispel the charm.

I have to confess that my juvenile philosophical pursuits, even though they probably did not greatly advance my understanding of philosophy, did some good. I became familiar with philosophical books, (Plato, Descartes, Spinoza, and others) and that eases one's way to later more mature encounters with those same books and others. I did also benefit in a practical way. I probably was the only school child who subscribed to the Israeli philosophical quarterly, I doubt that I understood the articles I was so diligently reading. When in due course I applied to enroll as a law undergraduate at Hebrew University I approached the University's Academic Secretary (the head of the academic administration), with some requests. To my surprise he invited me to meet him. It was during my compulsory military service and I could only get weekend leave, so he invited me to his home. It turned out that he was a philosopher, teaching part time in the department, and also the executive editor of that philosophical quarterly. You can imagine my surprise that Mr. Pozñansky (that was his name) knew that while still at school I had subscribed to his quarterly for several years. Even though I was enrolling to read law, he encouraged me to pursue my studies in philosophy, saying that they needed someone in legal philosophy (not a branch of philosophy I had ever heard of). Some years later, when I graduated, he arranged for me to continue my studies in Oxford under the supervision of H.L.A. Hart. It was all his idea, and he secured both admission to Oxford and a scholarship to finance my studies there. I owe him more than I can say.

3:AM: One of the ideas you have argued for (in your 2000 Seeley Lectures) is that we ought to accept the legitimacy of difference. So you think someone can reasonably approve of normative practices that are positively hostile to each other, but that only commits one to respecting both positions and not engaging with them. Is that right, and if it is, doesn't non-engagement itself suggest a lack of respect?

JR: Accepting, or respecting difference is of course code. What we should respect are practices, styles of life, ideals and aspirations that are valuable, or that have some good, some value in them, and we should respect them for that reason (even when we have a very imperfect understanding of their value). I put it like that for pure gold is rarely found in human affairs. Our lives are wrought of alloys of mixed quality elements, some inferior or even seriously flawed. Human practices that have value often also enshrine prejudice or superstition, and perpetuate objectionable discriminations or exclusions. In saying, as it were, that that's life, I do not mean that we should be complacent about the unworthy aspects of our practices, or those of others. On the contrary, I suggest that we should not be complacent and should try to identify the less wholesome aspects of our own practices, as well as in those of others, distance ourselves from them and strive to rectify them.

So one reason why it is important to know about and to have a balanced view of practices we have no intention of sharing is that understanding them is close to being a precondition for understanding ourselves and our engagements with various practices. The recognition of the value in what is strange or alien to our ways anchors our humanity, protects us from smugness and intolerance. Our knowledge of and respect for other people's practices also creates for us the opportunity to change, to come to engage with people who might otherwise appear strange or worse, and possibly also to find that we can acquire a taste for the practices that initially were so alien to us—that is the second main reason for seeking to understand and for coming to respect the value of those practices. I am not suggesting that we should for ever be looking for new friends, or for a change in our activities and tastes, merely that it is good to have the option, and the option is made real in part through understanding what it is like to take it.

In the preceding comments I emphasized the barriers between people and the hostilities that sometimes accompany them that are bred by ignorance leading to narrow and misguided understanding of the range of activities and practices that can contribute to human fulfillment, to the quality of our lives. I also implied that being unaware of the shortcomings in our own practices may well contribute to such hostilities. Trivially, practices that are free from blemish will not be hostile to the good in other practices, even if they are incompatible, in the sense that one cannot fully participate in both. Such incompatibilities force choices on us, but these are no different from other choices forced on us by circumstances: my employer may require me to live within a certain distance from my place of work, and to refrain from working for competitors etc. When practices are literally hostile to other practices this is usually because they are committed (sharing them commits one) to inconsistent beliefs. Hence at least one of them is committed to false beliefs, which is one of its shortcomings.

A degree of hostility not literally between practices but between those who engage in them is common, and perhaps given our psychology inevitable, when the practices themselves prize highly qualities that may be detrimental to participation in the other practice. Some require quick decisive responses, others value measured slower responses, etc. It is "natural" that people in whose life certain qualities of mind, body or temperament are highly prized will tend to look down on those who lack them, and on activities that devalue them. My previous observations were meant to offer a corrective, a way of understanding that those others have their own way to a rewarding life. That may not be enough to rid us of the hostile opinions and attitudes that are bred by these incompatibilities, but they should enable us to contain them, and prevent them from leading to unjustified actions.

So far I have ignored your suggestion that non-engagement may itself indicate lack of respect. I tried to "blame" lack of respect (when respect is merited) on other factors. I do not see how lack of engagement can indicate or constitute lack of respect. Consider cases in which people make choices, of friends, occupations, pastimes, places of residence or whatever. It would be a mistake to think that in all such choices the rejected option is held to be impersonally inferior. Some of them may be. But others are no less worthwhile, but are not for me: I have stronger legs and weaker arms and that would make some sports more appealing to me than others. Must I think that the sports I do not respond to are inferior? Some occupations require one continually to make decisions, relatively important ones, on one's own. Others rely more on teamwork and collective decisions. I get anxious when burdened with responsibility without the chance to consult etc. Must I think that the job that requires solo decision-making is inferior rather than merely not suitable for me? Or must I think that those for whom it is the better choice are inferior to me, and that's why that job is best for them? Not all non- engagements are the same. But we are sufficiently aware of the difference between the value (impersonally speaking) of an option or a practice in which it is embodied, and our chances either of benefiting from engaging with it, or of responding to it emotionally, being drawn to it, or left cold by it in spite of its known virtues.

3:AM: Although you argue for the legitimacy of difference you argue that values are universal, and the notions of "partiality" and the social dependency of some values are resources you use to establish this. You argue that to be universal a norm has to be intelligible in terms of properties that can be specified without singular references and that they can be instantiated in any place and time. Can you sketch out your reasons for your conclusion that values are intelligible and universal?

JR: It is best to start with the intelligibility of values and of reasons, and of the normative generally, for it drives much of the rest. What is intelligible can be understood, and if it is intelligible to you then you understand it. But it is a special kind of understanding. Understanding generally involves knowing why what is understood is as it is, and an ability to use that knowledge to infer more truths about it and its context. The Intelligibility of the normative involves that, and more. It is difficult, probably impossible, to state literally and explicitly what it is in a way that would make it plain to someone who did not have the experience of understanding why some particular value is a value or some particular reason is a reason. It is like explaining what it is to see something—ultimately you have to rely on the people to whom you offer the explanation having eyesight and you just point to it—saying it is this experience I am talking about.

Therefore, we explain one normative idea, the virtue of integrity or of generosity, the value of good art, or of friendships, or of well-being, partly by relating them to other values, virtues, etc. and partly by relying on people who understand some of those values, virtues etc. to see the meaning, the good of the values and virtues that they are yet to understand, through imaginative thinking that enables them to see analogies between what they understand and what they are yet to understand.

If you agree that something like that is the way we gain understanding you will agree that it is gained through the grasp of concepts that can in principle be applied to a variety of instances, and whose application points to similarities, apprehension of which enables us to improve our understanding. The application of the concepts can be circumscribed by singular restrictions: they may apply only to instances occurring today, or to me, etc. But the restriction will defy understanding, and is not intelligible, unless it is itself an instantiation of a more general concept that lacks that singular restriction. That is why intelligibility requires universality, at least at the limit.

Why assume that values and normative reasons are intelligible? Perhaps it helps to put it slightly differently: why assume that only what is intelligible can be of value? Because, the brief version of the answer is, values are used, are invoked and referred to, to explain—to explain goals and aspirations, actions and intentions, and through them much more. Moreover the explanations we have in mind here are of a special kind. People's actions and aspirations etc. are motivated in many ways, often by factors of which the people concerned have little if any idea or understanding. Needless to say, their actions and aspirations can be explained by reference to such motives. But the explanations we have in mind are different. They explain actions or aspirations, by tracing the perspective of the agents who have them. How they saw matters in ways that made sense and, as they saw it, made the action worthwhile, or the pursuit of that aspiration worthwhile. They explain by factors that the people concerned regarded as intelligible, and which therefore enabled them to conclude that the action or aspiration is worthwhile. The claim is, and I am merely outlining a line of thought here—much more is needed to establish it -, the claim is that all values can feature in such explanations, and therefore they are intelligible. Whatever you think of the claim, the argument about it should not turn into a verbal dispute. It matters not whether the expressions "of value" or "has value" invariably refer to what can feature in explanations of that kind. What matters is that an important aspect of our life, the active aspect of our life, in which we have aspirations, pursue goals, form intentions and act to realize them, is governed by searching for and responding to factors that will make our involvement in the world, and our life, worthwhile. I, along with many others, use the terms "value" and "normative reason" to articulate the nature of that aspect of our life and the aspects of the world that enable us to have such life.

One familiar objection to claims about the universality of value is that it makes special attachments, to people, groups, institutions, objects, etc. unjustifiable, and indeed irrational. As you mention in your question I point to the ways in which the instantiation of value is, trivially, historical, thus acquiring features that, in the life of a group, an institution, or an individual, are unique even while they are an instantiation of a universal value, to explain why the universality of value is consistent with special relationships and attachments.

3:AM: Why do you think we can speak of evaluative knowledge? We can't speak of knowledge in a domain if we can't speak of error. Values are a problem for knowledge if belief in values depends on social practice and not the values themselves. So how do you answer this challenge, and is it a skeptical or irrealist one?

JR: I do not think that there is serious doubt that at least some values depend on social practices. The hard questions are whether there are any that do not depend on them. And what sort of dependences there are. Why does this dependence exist? And what does it tell us about the nature of value? I have tried to deal with these questions; here let me briefly and informally indicate some of the underlying ideas, and how they relate to the possibility of knowledge.

At the very least it seems that all cultural goods are socially dependent. I mean all valuable relationships, associations, attachments and forms of activities that are constituted by standards that can be sustained over time only by social practices. Commonly these are not stand-alone, single standards, or forms of activity, but whole webs of interconnected ones, as for example, all family relations and interactions, with their ceremonies, complex patterns of mutual expectations, normatively sanctioned demands, and duties, such as standards of privacy within families that allow greater interference with each other's affairs in some contexts, and a greater degree of distance in others, when compared to the norms and expectations governing such conduct among strangers.

Social goods, in other words, comprise much of what we and other humans care about. They include all artistic activities and products, all the activities, relationships and opportunities that are constituted in part by social, sometimes institutional, standards, such as dances, sporting activities, public organizations and involvement in them, including political structures of governance and participation in them, and much more besides. It is significant, but not relevant in replying to your question, that many if not all of those socially-dependent valuable forms of activity, of association, engagement, identification and more, come with their own distinctive forms of excellence. Nor is it relevant to your question whether these goods are created by social practices or merely made accessible to people through being sustained by social practices. What does matter is that the social dependence I am discussing is one of accessibility: That is because the ability to be in a relationship, any kind of relationship, or to participate, even if only as a spectator, in any sport, or to appreciate any work of art or artistic performance and so on, depends on understanding, broadly, their constitution, understanding what they are, an understanding that is required for engaging, and of course for enjoying or benefiting by one's engagement. And that understanding is inevitably acquired through familiarity with the practices that sustain the relevant cultural goods. Explicit explanation can help, but it cannot replace familiarity with the practices, since the cultural goods are too rich and complex to be learnt through explicit explanation only.

So the social dependence has nothing to do with what makes a relationship, pursuit or activity good or bad (for bad relationships etc. are also socially constituted). The dependence is of the ability to access those goods. It explains why different goods furnish the stuff of life in different societies, and in different eras. It explains, again, how misunderstanding and hostility can be bred through ignorance of the conditions of the availability of the good, and through ignorance of the possible diversity of forms of good. Understanding the social dependence of the availability of goods helps towards understanding the nature of value. But it does not determine it. This leaves of course the question of our ability to know about values untouched. But it means that there is no threat to the possibility of knowledge due to the social dependence of value.

3:AM: Throughout your work you've elaborated the importance of role of these normative reasons in our psychology—they are the kind of thing that can be explained by their subject's apprehension of something she thinks of as a reason for them. And when they are so explained, one has them for this reason. And actions, beliefs and intentions are then explained by these normative reasons. Have I got that right? Do you think that by starting with actions and beliefs and intentions your conclusions about normative reasons are different from what they would have been had you started elsewhere, such as with the role of emotions?

JR: I have already confessed, in some earlier replies, to pursuing some such approach. But obviously the direct answer to your question is that this approach should make no difference to the conclusions. The accounts I advanced apply to a number of issues: the explanation of value, the nature of normative reasons, the connection between reasons and intentions, and between reasons and rationality, and the nature of intentional actions. Each account is independently supported, though they are mutually reinforcing. These accounts should be improved, and the explanation of other issues should turn out to be consonant with those offered, before the latter can be deemed to be secure. Yet in principle, it does not matter where you start or the order in which you proceed. The conclusions should be the same.

However, there is, I hope, something suggestive in the approach that I have pursued. I hope that I have successfully pointed out that the central cases of intentional actions are actions undertaken for (what the agents believe are) normative reasons. If the value of those actions is the direct reason for them, and the value of other things bears on reasons to the extent that it affects the value of the actions, and if all this is in the very nature of value, then two broad conclusions become plausible: One is that some actions have value and others do not, and that some have more value than some others, for if none has value then all intentional actions and all plans to undertake them are based on a kind of error that it is really impossible to make. Second, that the explanation of normative reasons and of values does not seek for some mysterious existences. It is merely part of the explanation of intentional actions, though it is not only that. And we all believe that it is possible to explain intentional actions. These thoughts help, I think, calibrate our inquiries, deflating some aspirations, but also some alleged obstacles to their progress.

3:AM: Why don't you think pragmatic factors can serve as reasons for belief? Is it linked to your "no gap" thesis?

JR: This seems to me to be a confusing issue. On the one hand to believe that something is the case is to take the world to be so, and facts that point to it being so are reasons for that belief, they vindicate it. On the other hand, that believing something will assuage one's anxieties, while it does nothing to show that the belief is true, is a good thing. Other things being equal it is better to be free of anxieties. One may argue that it is good to be free of anxieties only if they are provoked by false beliefs, or at any rate by unwarranted beliefs. There will be cases regarding which such arguments are sound. But they will leave many cases in which it is genuinely good for a person to have a belief independently of whether it is true or not. Does that not mean that there are non-truth related reasons for belief? It does. The problem is that we cannot form a belief for such reasons. People who have beliefs have some, however incomplete and inarticulate, understanding of what beliefs are. They know that beliefs differ from fantasies, daydreams, suppositions, etc. and the difference is that beliefs, unlike other thoughts, are accountable to the standard of truth. That is, while there is nothing amiss in imagining oneself flying across the skies, and there is no reason to abandon the thought when confronted with evidence that one is not flying, one cannot believe that one flies given that one has evidence that that is not the case. One can daydream, fantasize etc. but not believe. So, that it would be, in some circumstances, good to believe that one is flying is a reason for having that belief, but it is a reason that cannot rationally sustain having the belief.

What to do when faced with this confusion? To start with we can try to distinguish two kinds of reasons. Practical reasons that show that it is good to have the belief, and epistemic reasons that support the truth of the belief. Given that distinction and the nature of belief we can observe that practical reasons cannot lead us to have the belief (though they can make us try to affect our circumstances so that we will come to have it), in the sense that we cannot reason from them to the belief (I'll be happy if I believe that I am clever therefore I am clever). Epistemic reasons (assuming that they are strong and adequate in the circumstances) once recognized do lead us to have the beliefs for which they are reasons (that is the no gap thesis that you refer to).

But didn't I admit that practical reasons can lead one to have a belief, however irrationally? If they are good practical reasons, why care whether one has the belief rationally or irrationally? True enough, practical reasons can cause one to have a belief, and that may be, if they are sound and adequate reasons, a good thing, even if one's believing or the process of acquiring the belief were irrational (which they will be sometimes, though not always). The difference is in the way the reason leads one to acquire or to have the belief. All reasons can figure in explanations of what they are reasons for. Epistemic reasons can figure in normative explanations of having the beliefs that they are reasons for, meaning that we can reason our way to a belief from premises that these reasons constitute. In a similar way practical reasons for having a belief can figure as normative reasons for action towards producing circumstances in which one would come to have or to maintain the belief. They may also, depending on the factual situation, figure in an explanation of why one has the belief, an explanation that is not normative, but an ordinary causal explanation. One may come to have a belief because the practical reason can induce self-deception, leading one into thinking that there are epistemic reasons for the belief, thus leading one to have it. In cases like that while the facts that explain the belief are practical reasons, the explanation is causal and not normative. There are more complications on the way to completing the account. But its nature is, I hope, clear.

What is common to all normative reasons is that they are facts recognition of which can lead people to respond in a certain way (form or sustain beliefs, act, or have emotions, etc.) because they (using their rational powers) recognize that the response is appropriate to the situation because those reasons are part of it. I illustrated this by referring to realizing through deliberation and reasoning that the response is appropriate. But sometimes no reasoning is involved when one grasps what response would be appropriate. Reasons being facts that make the response appropriate, practical reasons are facts that show the good that actions are likely to secure or protect, and epistemic reasons are facts that show that the belief is likely to be true. Note that epistemic reasons do not show that it is good to have that belief. That would require a practical reason. Hence, there may be nothing wrong in someone not bothering to form beliefs on certain issues even if epistemic reasons for the belief are readily available to him. There may be no practical reasons bearing on whether or not he should have a belief on the matter, or what it should be. However if one is aware of the facts that are epistemic reasons and aware that they are strong reasons, so long as one's rational capacities are not defective, one will form that belief. That is the no gap thesis.

What is common to all normative reasons is that they can figure in normative explanations of one's reactions (beliefs, actions, intentions, emotions) to one's situation. But they can fail to figure in normative explanations, and they can also figure in non- normative explanations, namely act as causal factors in the process that led one to react one way or another: a causal factor that does not influence one normatively, namely not through realizing, through the use of one's rational powers, that the reaction is appropriate, but through some other causal route.

3:AM: You have a distinct view of law: you say that it is essential that the law recognizes that its use of power is answerable to moral standards and claims to have reconciled power and morality, even if it may not live up to its aspirations. But you don't think that by its nature law reconciles the duality of morality and power: you think that its doing so is a contingent matter depending on the actual political reality of the society whose law is in question. Can you say something about this and why it's an important distinction?

JR: There is, of course, nothing special about the view that the law is answerable to morality. We, and our practices and institutions, all are. This is more an expression of what morality is, or of the meaning of "morality" that I use in my writings, than of what the law is (though—and I will return to the point—it is that too). Unlike some people who think of morality as a unified system of principles, I am with those who deny that there is a moral system, but believe that there are considerations that apply to us, and those of them that are basic, underived, cannot be further assessed (as good/bad, desirable/undesirable). Against that background I find little of theoretical interest in subdividing considerations of that kind into moral v. some other kinds. When writing about normativity, as you saw above, I do not mention morality, and write generally about values and normative reasons. When writing about the law I usually accede to the practice of discussing law and morality (using this term), but really having in mind the fact that the law, like all people, practices, institutions and more, can be normatively assessed. Needless to say, the hard questions are to determine which normative considerations are relevant to their assessment and which are not.

The thesis that you ask about is that the law, personalizing the institution here, recognizes that it is subject to moral standards and almost universally claims that it met them at least in one way. I make the claim on the basis of the language, normative, often moral, language legal institutions invariably use. This claim is not the minimal one implied when we act with an intention, namely that there is some good reason for the action (even when we act akratically we imply that, though we do not then believe that the reason for which we act is undefeated). Even gangsters who occupy and rule, let us say, a village by force and intimidation imply that they have good reasons for their actions. But they may well not think that those reasons have anything to do with the interests of the villagers, nor that they are reasons for the villagers to obey them. Legal institutions, and through them the law, act for reasons that they take to be good reasons for their subjects, and think that as a result their subjects should obey their laws and decisions. Institutions that do not make such claims are not legal institutions.

This is not primarily an observation about the meaning of the terms "legal institutions," "legal system" etc. It is about a type of social institutions of which law is one. It reflects the view that there is something important about institutions that make such claims (and there are of course many others that do make the claim). They can become a framework for co-operation, a focus of solidarity and an element in what constitutes a society or an organization to which its subjects feel allegiance, feel that they are members rather than mere subjects.

Two points to note here: First, the claim of legal institutions is not that their actions are based on the interests of the governed. It is that they are based on reasons that apply to their subjects. So, for example, governmental foreign aid need not be based on the claim that it serves the interests of the governed. It can be based on the moral duty of the governed to aid others. And of course it also means that the law can take account of the interests of all the governed, because each of them is subject to a moral reason to act in the interests of all. Second, the claim made by the law is not that it is perfect and cannot be improved. Rather, it is that everyone has reason to comply with the law because in doing so one would be complying with reasons that apply to one better than if one did not comply. My account of legitimate authority over people takes this to be the mark of authority. So it is my way of saying that the law claims to have moral authority over its subjects, so that they ought to comply with it even when it is imperfect.

But the law can fail to meet this standard, and thus it can fail to have legitimate authority. I take such failure to be a matter of degree. One can have a greater or a more limited authority, and when the law does not have the authority it claims it does not follow that it has none. Just that it has less than it claims. Some people think that a system that meets all the conditions that I have described, here and elsewhere, for qualifying as a legal system cannot fail to have legitimate authority over its subjects. I believe this to be a mistake about morality, and one that it is interesting to explore. What is not philosophically interesting is whether the word "law" or "legal system" is commonly used in a meaning that entails that there is an obligation to obey the law, whatever its content, or that there is a pro tanto obligation to obey, whatever its content. I think that we use "law" in legal contexts sometimes to imply such an obligation, and sometimes not. But this could become an uninteresting verbal dispute. What is important is that there are systems that are like legal systems that have legitimate authority but that do not have legitimate authority. This distinction is important because it helps us in forming moral attitudes towards political institutions, whether ours or not.

These matters are not more complex than those you touched on in your earlier questions. But I have spent more years thinking about them. Perhaps because of that I am more acutely aware of how crude and incomplete my answer here is. But it, like all the others, may serve as an introduction.

3:AM: What do you mean when you say that a theory of law is (in part) about the way legal actors understand themselves and their actions? What alternative approaches does your approach rule out?

JR: The point is important given that many people take the theories and explanations offered by the physical and the biological sciences as the paradigms of good explanations. The phenomena studied in those sciences, say fundamental particles, have no knowledge or understanding of the theories about and explanations of their conduct. Not so when you study human beings, or rather when we study the ways humans are and conduct themselves when they use capacities whose deployment involves people's rational powers. Needless to say, people can come to know and understand those explanations and theories, and adjust their behavior in reaction to the explanations. They can, for example, make false explanations true, by adjusting their conduct to make them true, as can happen under the influence of psychological suggestion, which as is well known can produce strong placebo effects. Economists tend not to notice that the fact that businesses in countries like the U.S. behave in the ways economic theories predict, whereas many businesses in developing countries do not, is due not to the rationality of the first and the imperfect rationality of the latter, but to the fact that many more business managers in the U.S. have been to business schools and follow the theories they were taught there, thus tending to verify them.

Taking a broader view: The task of explanation can be thought to be to account for what there is without changing it. When dealing with human conduct, aspirations, emotions and the like, the explanation involves getting the reader to understand how matters appear to the people whose conduct is explained. But these people are us, all of us. So the explanation, if successful, will improve our self-understanding. That in itself is a change with consequential changes in our hopes, aspirations, feelings and conduct. In fact, such changes are liable to be brought about by learning, perfectly or imperfectly, i.e. with mistakes and misunderstandings, explanations of the theorized-upon aspects of our life, whether these explanations are successful or not. For example, learning of the theories may make mistaken theories turn true by changing the explained reality to conform to them.

In sum the explanatory inquiry into aspects of human beings and their life is both a process of self understanding, and inevitably (and often unconsciously) a process of bringing about change, hopefully justified by the thought that at least up to a point the examined life is better than the unexamined one.

3:AM: You think that the content of the law can be devoid of moral considerations and so can be evil but that given that it imposes and enforces duties on people legal discourse is moral discourse. Why isn't this a problem?

JR: I am not sure that it is a problem. Though it seems to have encouraged some false views. It encouraged the view that there are different kinds of unrelated and non- comparable duties, rights etc.: legal rights are rights in a different sense of "rights" from moral rights, and so on. I tend to think that normative terminology is univocal in most of its uses, and that requires an explanation of why it can appear not to be. For example, how can one say correctly that one has a legal right even though one does not have a moral right, and even though it is immoral to have that legal right? If normative terms are used in the same way across the various normative domains then their use, and therefore the domains characterized by their use, must be inter-related. And they are inter-related even when they conflict. Much of what I wrote in reply to your earlier questions is meant, among other things, to contribute to such explanations.

3:AM: How do you explain the bootstrapping problem—how can duties and rights spring into existence on the say so of a person or an institution?

JR: If you mean "how can duties and rights spring into existence on the mere say so of a person"? The answer is that they cannot. When people or institutions can by their say so impose duties or confer rights on people that is because they are empowered to do so by normative considerations that exist independently of these actions. Most commonly that is because it is good for people if they or others can impose duties and confer rights. Earlier I alluded to an instance of such reasoning: when the conditions of legitimacy are met, legal institutions, which paradigmatically impose duties and confer rights, are part of the framework for the existence of politically organized societies that can foster solidarity and mutual respect and support. The existence of such societies is of great benefit to people, most directly to members of these societies, and therefore everyone has reason to support the generation and continued existence of these institutions. That is why they have the normative power to impose duties and confer rights by their say so. The accounts of the power to make promises, to enter into relationships such as marriage, and so on, would differ, but they are all unified by pointing to independently existing normative considerations that vindicate the power of people to change the normative situation by actions intended to do so.

3:AM: Some argue that in interpretive reasoning the distinction between law application and law creation is obscured and that this issue of interpretation is a pivotal issue dividing many philosophers of law. So the argument between Dworkin and Hart is about this isn't it? How do you respond to this debate?

JR: Let me say first that there are issues raised by Dworkin, and used by him in criticizing Hart's theory, that, as they are rather complex, I have avoided raising in my previous answers, and will not discuss here either. It is true that Dworkin associates them with his account of interpretation, but I think that they are best investigated independently of it. In other words I think that a proper inquiry into the nature of interpretation does not necessitate examining these views of Dworkin. I agree, however, that legal interpretation can obscure the distinction between law-application and law-creation.

However, to see that there is a problem with applying the distinction one need not think of interpretation. Anyone who has the slightest familiarity with the English Common Law, or with any of the common law legal systems or indeed with any legal system where some courts' decisions set precedents, is familiar with the fact that courts with the power to set precedents both apply and create law. To have the power to set precedents means (a) that one's decisions bind not only the litigants before the court, but also at least some future courts, and those who are subject to the laws that they adjudicate; and (b) that the decisions are so binding, at least in some cases, even if mistaken. So a court whose decision is a binding precedent may be creating a new legal rule even if it is duty bound, and even if it tries its hardest, not to do so. Because even if it is trying merely to apply the law as it is, should it make a mistake about that law, its decision will be binding even though the rule it enunciates was not binding until it was enunciated.

So, to determine whether a precedent-setting court's decision did or did not make new law one has to determine whether its statement of existing law is correct or not. That may not be an easy task. Moreover, the statement that was meant to be a mere restatement of existing law may be partly right and partly wrong, so that the precedent is partly reiterating and reinforcing existing law and partly creating new law—making the task of distinguishing what in the decision is application and what creation even more complex.

In actual legal practice the task is made complex by many additional factors, and we cannot discuss them here. I am focusing on the very elementary case of new law made, through the doctrine of precedent, when trying not to make new law, and when having a duty not to make new law, because it bears an important theoretical lesson: while sometimes even in this simple type of case disentangling what in the court's ruling is new and what a restatement can be fiendishly difficult, and perhaps even not a task that one can completely succeed in (i.e. it may be theoretically impossible to divide all strands in the ruling into application or creation), the difficulty casts no doubt about the very distinction between law creation and law application, and its inevitable application (in the case we consider) to the judicial process. It casts no doubt either on the distinction itself, nor on its applicability, for it is only with the use of the distinction that we can say (a) that the court has a duty merely to apply the law, (b) that the court has tried merely to apply the law, (c) that the doctrine of precedent means that its decision is binding even if it misapplied the law. And this last statement entails that since the decision is binding even though it does not apply the law, new law was made by it. That some material is made of two alloys woven together in an irreversible process, so that in the result one cannot say what is made of the one and what of the other, does not cast doubt on the fact that two distinct alloys are in the mix. Something similar is true of the law.

I offered this argument without referring once to the notion of interpretation in order to illustrate how the matter you raised does not depend on any deep, mysterious or controversial aspects of interpretation or of legal interpretation. But I do not wish to deny that the courts' reasoning about the law and about which legal conclusions to endorse, which ruling to make (as well as some other aspects of their reasoning) is interpretive. Why is it and what do we mean by saying that it is?

Interpretations are, generally speaking, explanations. At a stretch even interpretations offered by professional interpreters, i.e. live translation of speeches etc., can be said to explain what is translated in the minimal sense of explanation, namely by displaying or stating its meaning. In the same way interpretation through performance (of plays or music) contains an explanation in that it displays the meaning of what is interpreted. As you gather from this I take interpretation to be an explanation of the meaning of something: a text, an act, an intention, etc. "Meaning" is used here in its broad ordinary sense, not being confined to semantic meaning. We will not pursue the meaning of "meaning" here. It does not offer an easy clue to the nature of interpretation, as directly or indirectly we will need to refer to interpretation in explaining what has meaning and what that meaning is (whatever is explained in interpretations of it). For our purposes it is sufficient that the association of interpretation with the explanation of meaning locates interpretations primarily within the interpretations of human intentions, aspirations, emotions and action, and the products of human activities and practices. What makes interpretation a special kind of explanation is its connection to what people experience and do—and the problematic features of explanations of this kind that were discussed in my response to question 8 above—and the fact that many of the objects of interpretation are cultural goods, with their special features, some of which were discussed in my answer to question 4. Now, it is the mark of cultural goods that their meaning is detached from the intentions of their creators, even when they were deliberately created by someone, and this enables us to give Marxist explanations to works produced by authors who had no inkling of such explanations, and so on. It also explains why meanings change with history. It is not so much that meanings are lost (though they are often forgotten) as that new meanings are added since the work comes to mean new and different things to different people, often through familiarity with past interpretations of it. It is, as you can gather from these remarks, the existence of a plurality of acceptable, good, though incompatible interpretations that is one of the central, and essential, features of interpretative explanations. A common mistake is to think that the phenomena that establish interpretive pluralism show that there is no objective standard for correctness or acceptability of interpretations. They do not. They merely show that there is diversity as well as historical development not only in good interpretations but also in the standard for what makes interpretations good or acceptable. The standards may be historically, socially, dependent, but they are objective, independent of the interpreter's desires, and they guide both interpretations and their reception.

Needless to say, interpretive pluralism entails that preserving and reasserting known meanings of the interpreted objects is only one of the standards for correctness of interpretations. So we are back with the combination of applying, restating, reinforcing existing meaning and moving on towards new meaning. Interpretations can be conserving or creative and they are almost always a combination of the two, with all the impossibility, often the pointlessness of disentangling what is creative and what conserving in any given interpretation.

This combination of elements: continuity and change, plurality through reference to a common object of interest, sometimes of loyalty, points to the way interpretations function in our lives. They are crucial to the cementing elements of culture, of institutions and standards, as well as to the potential for creativity, development and improvement. We are united by our relations to a common history, a common heritage of cuisines, architecture, crafts, professional and leisure activities, arts and literature, and more which shape our imagination, providing us with the memory of smells and colours and patterns of response, and mutual expectations, which enable us to understand each other, and open avenues for individual development and creativity within the common bonds, individuality which makes itself understood to others, because its roots are in the common culture, and which can be freer and richer because of the richness from which it derives. Interpretations of cultural goods, of history and psychology, are crucial to these processes precisely because they combine preservation with change, plurality with relating to a common core, the common object of interpretation.

3:AM: Can you say something about how "Being in the World" is important to considerations of normativity and responsibility, and in using the term are you deliberately wanting us to connect your thoughts to other philosophers?

JR: It means more than I know, at least so far, how to say. I use the expression to indicate that what we, who we, are, and what life we have, depend on how we inhabit the world, and that that is not merely, not primarily, a matter of our internal or mental life, or attitudes. It goes further, it goes to the conditions that shape our mental life and attitudes. Perhaps some of what I have dimly in mind I can start to articulate (without I am afraid making things much clearer) in the following way. Many of the questions that occupied me over the years can be seen as various aspects of the explanation of normativity. I take its explanation to consist in explaining three aspects of reality and their interaction: How it is that we can pursue in our conduct a variety of ends (simple, like drinking water from the glass in front of me, or complex, like giving parties, or practising law, ends that are often nested in other ends, of our own or those we share with others). And how it is that in adopting ends we are guided by our own sense that those are ends to adopt, that their endorsement is not a whim or a product of some causal process that is opaque to us, but rather their adoption is intelligible to us as a reaction to how, as we see things, matters stand in the world in such a way that their adoption and pursuit is sensible, or even necessary, required. And of course the question of what it is about the world that can give point to or make necessary the adoption and pursuit of certain ends.

All these are ancient questions. But much discussion of normativity concerns the content of the normative phenomena: what should we pursue, and how powerful is the call on us to pursue ends of this kind or that, and what constitutes shared ends, and how are they related to individual psychology, and much much more besides. All these are important questions, but ultimately they can only be understood if we understand the way we inhabit the world, the relations between understanding how things are and the motivation to leave them alone, or even to preserve them or to change them etc. These more fundamental questions are also keenly debated. One of the more influential arenas for their debate concerns the truth and travails of expressivism. The very term intimates some of the limitations of that approach—it tells us that there is no special problem in knowing how things are in the world. What we need is an understanding of our attitudes that enable us to react to it as if it had features that it does not in fact have. This is obviously a tendentious characterization of the expressivist approach. But then there are no neutral ways of presenting the problems we deal with. My description of the approach here is not to be taken as more than an indication that mine is an alternative approach with a different focus, a difference that will disqualify it from belonging with the expressivist family. My approach suspects that the explanation of normativity, which is nothing less than the explanation of the possibility of normative action, must involve bringing into focus ways in which we inhabit the world and that they, in explaining our relations to the world, shed light both on it and on us.

3:AM: Have you changed your mind about anything fundamental to your philosophical position during your time as a philosopher or has it been more a process of deepening and further discovery within a rather settled framework of thought?

JR: For various reasons this is for me a difficult question. One is that I am not terribly interested in the question, and perhaps partly as a result, am often surprised when people point out, with actual quotations, what I wrote on some points in years past. One way in which I am sometimes surprised when confronted with previous writings is that I clearly remember that I felt tentative about this issue or that, and meant to express a partial or a tentative view only, and lo and behold: that is not how I wrote. I sound very definite. Have I changed my mind, or am I one of those people who tend to sound confident when they are not? But there are other difficulties with the question.

Sometimes a deepening of a view may go so deep as to change its character without actually changing its letter. Ever since my student days I was interested in the social character of the law. More recently I have written on the social character of value in general, and on the ways in which the characterization of these two forms of social dependence differ, and the ways in which they are nevertheless interdependent. The result is that once embedded in the wider context my old views on the social character of the law while unchanged may have acquired, in my mind, a different meaning. There is more to say, but it is probably of no interest to anyone but myself. Similar changes probably affected other of my views.

Joseph Raz is the author of:

The Authority of Law (Oxford University Press, 1979. Second edition, 2009)
The Concept of a Legal System (Oxford University Press, 2nd ed., 1980)
The Morality of Freedom (Oxford University Press, 1986)
Ethics in the Public Domain (Oxford University Press, 1994)
Practical Reason and Norms (Oxford University Press, 1999)
Engaging Reason: On the Theory of Value and Action (Oxford University Press, 2000)
Value, Respect, and Attachment (Cambridge University Press, 2001)
The Practice of Value (Oxford University Press, 2003)
Between Authority and Interpretation (Oxford University Press, 2009)
From Normativity to Responsibility (Oxford University Press, 2011)

6 | John Martin Fischer: "Deep Control, Death and Co."

John Martin Fischer is the Distinguished Professor of Philosophy at the University of California, Riverside. Here he discusses semicompatibilism, freedom, determinism, moral responsibility, responsibility practices, different kinds of control, death, anti-Epicureanism, and issues relating to the meaning of life.

3:AM: What made you become a philosopher?

JOHN MARTIN FISCHER: I'm not sure, but I suspect that various factors played roles in this disaster! From early on, I liked the idea of going into teaching as a profession. Both of my father's brothers were university professors, and I admired them greatly, and I especially admired their opportunities to travel all over the world as part of their profession and to be mentors to young people (and to keep in touch with their students, who sometimes became their friends). As an undergraduate at Stanford, I really enjoyed my philosophy classes, and slowly I became hooked. Michael Bratman was a huge influence on me—he was a great teacher, and he introduced me to Harry Frankfurt's work in an upper division "action theory" class. In that class we read Frankfurt's 1969 article in which he presented his famous (putative) counterexamples to the Principle of Alternative Possibilities (according to which moral responsibility requires access to alternative possibilities). I was definitely addicted to philosophy at that point—and how could I have done otherwise?

I had a wonderful experience in graduate school at Cornell University, where I was especially helped by Carl Ginet, Terry Irwin, and Sydney Shoemaker. I've always thought that I became a Semicompatibilist because Carl Ginet was an incompatibilist, while Terry Irwin and Sydney Shoemaker were compatibilists. One wants to please one's parents, as it were! (Semicompatibilism is the doctrine that causal determinism is compatible with moral responsibility, even if casual determinism rules out freedom to do otherwise.)

3:AM: Most people hold themselves and others morally responsible. And you think we need a philosophical foundation for this. Others might say that it's just biology, or culture, or education or psychological biases or a supernatural element underwritten by a deity that makes us do this and that there's not space for a philosophical foundation. How do you think we should answer this mix of challenges?

JMF: In some ways it can be helpful to have an explanation of our responsibility practices. Perhaps in the end they are just "brute" or unexplained by deeper philosophical ideas, but I think it can be fruitful at least to explore ways in which our responsibility practices can be explained by simpler, more basic ideas (where these are distinctively philosophical ideas). If we have such an explanation, we can (perhaps, at least) answer certain moral responsibility skeptics, and we might be able to provide answers to questions about moral responsibility in "hard cases," such as psychopathy and other disordered agents. After all, our actual responsibility practices can (and should) be called into question, and they don't in themselves answer questions about certain contentious or difficult cases. Can a severely depressed individual be deemed morally responsible? An individual suffering from Alzheimer's Disease? How about an individual with unusual or atypical brain structures (suggestive of a higher probability of violent behaviour)?

Similarly, I think it is desirable to have a way of engaging more productively with the moral responsibility skeptics. That is, we want to take their worries very seriously, and seek to address them as much as possible on their own terms. This is perhaps a way in which I differ from the approach taken by Peter Strawson (although we both think that moral responsibility should be sequestered from certain metaphysical issues). I believe in a moderate sequestration of metaphysics, whereas Peter Strawson argues for a more extreme sequestration of metaphysics. Here (as elsewhere) I prefer the path of moderation.

3:AM: You take this to mean that we are committed to a framework involving freewill and moral responsibility and you argue that "control" is a key to working out this framework. So can you first tell us about the two kinds of control you identify—"regulative control" and "guidance control."

JMF: Yes, regulative control involves a "dual" or "two-way" agential power. If an agent with regulative control does X, he or she could have refrained from doing X (and done some Y instead). I assume further that the agent would have been acting freely along either path, that is, along the X path and along the Y path. Alternatively, one might say that an agent with regulative control exhibits guidance control along both paths—the actual path leading to X, and the alternative path leading to Y.

3:AM: It's guidance control that you think is significant for morally free agency don't you?

JMF: Yes. I claim that guidance control is all the freedom required for moral responsibility. An agent need not have regulative control over her behavior in order to be morally responsible for it; all that is necessary is for the agent to have guidance control of it. I have argued that the Frankfurt cases are situations in which agents have guidance control without also possessing regulative control.

3:AM: There are concerns about the impact of causal determinism on our ability to be free moral agents. On the face of it, it seems to deprive us of the control needed but you argue that the beauty of guidance control is that it is compatible with causal determinism don't you?

JMF: Yes. And I do think it is a beautiful and elegant theory. On my view, guidance control is the freedom-relevant condition necessary and sufficient for moral responsibility. To exercise guidance control of behavior, the behavior must issue from an agent's own, appropriately reasons-responsive mechanism. It is not simply required that the agent in question have the capacity for reasons-responsiveness; in addition, the behavior much issue from this general capacity. I further contend that "ownership" of the mechanism that issues in the behavior, and the "reasons-responsiveness" of the mechanism in question, are entirely consistent with causal determinism. So even if causal determinism would rule out regulative control, it would not thereby (or for any other compelling reason) threaten guidance control (and robust moral responsibility)

3:AM: You argue that moral responsibility is connected with artistic self-expression, in fact you argue that being morally responsible is a species of artistic self-expression. This is derived from your idea that the value of moral responsibility is connected to the value of exhibiting freedom. Is that right?

JMF: Yes. In my view, and based on Aristotle's approach, there are two conditions for moral responsibility: an epistemic condition and a freedom-relevant condition. I contend that guidance-control is the freedom-relevant condition. But these are "first-order" conditions on moral responsibility. One can step back and ask the question, "Why do we value acting in such a way as to be fairly (or legitimately) held morally responsible?" Here we are asking a second-order question, "What is the value of acting from one's own, reasons-responsive mechanism"? Here I suggest that this value is the same as the value we place on artistic self-expression. In acting freely, we are (in a sense) writing a sentence in the narrative of our lives. Our free will transforms us into authors of the stories of our lives, and endows us with an irreducible "narrative" dimension of value.

3:AM: From this foundation you argue that death can be a bad thing for a person—even though of course that person can't experience harm. Epicureans disagree. So how do you argue that they're wrong?

JMF: I follow an anti-Epicurean tradition (at least if one interprets Epicurus in a certain way) in arguing that death can be bad for an individual insofar as it is a deprivation of what would be on-balance good (including some positive experiences). (It is anti-Epicurean in the sense that it holds that something can be bad for an individual without the individual's experiencing anything unpleasant as a result of the thing in question.) I have sought to build on examples and arguments suggested by such contemporary anti-Epicureans as Thomas Nagel, Joel Feinberg, Jeffrey McMahan, and Robert Nozick. They have offered compelling (in my view) examples in which it seems that an individual can be the subject of a misfortune without experiencing it as unpleasant or bad in any way, and without being able so to experience it. I have offered a defence of the notion that we can extrapolate from these (and related examples) to the badness of death, where (I stipulate) there is not even an individual left to be the subject of the purported harm or misfortune.

3:AM: We've all been dead before and don't worry so much about that; and we're going to be dead again one day and it strikes me as a damn scary thing coming. Some people say there's no reason justifying this asymmetry of attitudes towards death but you say there are good reasons for it. So why is my attitude rational and defensible?

JMF: Anthony Brueckner and I have argued that it is rational to have asymmetric attitudes toward prenatal and posthumous non-existence as a special case of a more general rational asymmetry toward past and future pleasurable experiences. We here employ certain Parfit-style thought-experiments to motivate the idea that it is rational to care especially about future pleasures. Given that death deprives us of future pleasures, and the fact that we are born "late" deprives us of past pleasures, our commonsense attitudes toward prenatal and posthumous non-existence turn out to be a rationally defensible particular instance of a more general asymmetry.

The Brueckner/Fischer line has it that our asymmetric attitudes toward late birth and early death are a special case of a more general asymmetry. I have offered a sketch of an argument for the rationality of this more general asymmetry; in future work I hope to fill in this sketch a bit.

3:AM: Heidegger and Bernard Williams thought immortality would be a bore or worse but you think it could be good. How do you argue for living forever?

JMF: I think that there are two kinds of projects that could give us reason to live forever (assuming relatively favorable physical, economic and environmental circumstances). The first kind of project would be "other-directed"—scientific, artistic, social, and so forth. I don't see any reason to suppose that we would necessarily run out of such projects, even in an infinitely long life. It seems to me that to suppose otherwise might be to buy into a misleading metaphor—the metaphor of the library of books with a large but finite collection. The idea is that our projects are the books in this library; with an infinite amount of time, one could read all the books, and one would be left then with nothing but oneself, as it were. But this is problematic for various reasons. I think the most obvious reason is that there we should not suppose that life's projects are accurately represented by a finite set of books. After all, to stick to the metaphor, people are writing new books all the time. So by the time we would have read all the books in the original collection, there will be new books to read. Also, even if there were merely a finite set of books, why can't we appreciate a book we have read before when we come to it after having had a new set of experiences?

So I don't think we would necessarily run out of other-directed projects, such as finding the cures to diseases and maladies, economic and environmental challenges, writing compelling novels and poetry and philosophy, and so forth. But there are also "self-directed" projects, such as enjoying music, art, food, and sex, or meditating or praying. Suitably distributed over time, and given variety in the content of the experiences, I don't see why these kinds of projects could not also give one reason to live indefinitely. I certainly would not reduce all value or meaningfulness to such projects; but they do seem sufficient to give one reason to prefer continued life to death.

3:AM: Is it your view that by reflecting on death we get a grip on what is of value in life? Is this what you're getting at by saying that in acting freely our stories matter?

JMF: I do think that reflection on the badness of death can help us to illuminate questions about what makes life meaningful. Also, I think that reflection on immortality and whether immortal life could be choiceworthy and meaningful can help us to understand in a deeper way why our finite lives are meaningful (if they indeed are).

But my views about the relationship between acting freely and our stories are a bit different. I hold that in acting freely we transform the chronicles of our lives into genuine narratives. Our stories are not just descriptions—they are narratives. And in evaluating our lives, there is an irreducibly narrative dimension. That is, the value of our lives is determined by a function that takes into account more than just the total welfare or happiness as aggregated over our lifetimes. This value also depends crucially on relationships between parts of our lives that have important structural similarities to the parts of narratives. In particular, the meanings or values of certain parts depend crucially on relationships with other parts. Here I rely on important ideas of David Velleman. I add the contention that our acting freely—exhibiting guidance control—is the crucial ingredient that transforms the chronicles of our lives into narratives and thus makes us artists (authors of the stories of our lives).

3:AM: "Deep control" is the moderate position between the extremes of "superficial control" and "total control." Why is it "deep control" we need for the distinctive sort of self-expression you contend we need to be morally responsible?

JMF: We need more than "superficial control" because of obvious inadequacies in various "superficial" analyses of control, such as the conditional analysis of freedom (and so forth). One clear set of problems pertains to the possibility of manipulation. On the other hand, "total control" is too much to ask—it is manifestly impossible and intuitively just too much to ask for. (Well, at least in my opinion, and not Galen Strawson's!) I think that a certain kind of reflective maturity will naturally issue in a middle-ground here: we need more resources than mere invocation of certain "springs of action," such as choices, but we do not need to travel back to the very beginning of the sequences that issue in our behavior. This then gets us to the Middle Way represented by guidance control.

3:AM: You dismiss total control as a kind of "metaphysical megalomania"—what's the error here?

JMF: The error here is kind of like the error of the kid who keeps asking "why?" and never stops. But admittedly it is an error which is such that it is hard to explain exactly why it is an error! (And I grant that there are those who do not find it an error at all!) Well, in most contexts it just is inappropriate to keep asking "why" and not to recognize that certain answers are perfectly reasonable or fitting in the context of what is being asked. Since we can't be the cause of ourselves, some (following Galen Strawson) conclude that we can't be morally responsible for our behavior (I've oversimplified unconscionably here). I'd rather turn this point on its head and conclude that the requirement that leads to the need for self-causation is over-rigorous, since it apparently leads to absurdity. We do need to own the mechanisms that issue in our behavior, but it does not follow that we must be the first causes of that behavior. I think it is a kind of intellectual maturity to realize that, if one's perhaps initial thought that we need to be originators of our behavior leads us to a manifest absurdity (that we are causes of ourselves, as it were), it should be reconceptualized so that it is not extreme.

3:AM: "Judgment sensitivity" and "conditional freedom" get it wrong not by wanting to go all the way back but by not going back far enough. You think they're too shallow to contribute to moral responsibility don't you?

JMF: In my opinion these ideas might "contribute" to an understanding of moral responsibility, and they—or something like them—might be elements of a more comprehensive account of moral responsibility. But they don't get it right, in my view, just as they are (or without further supplementation). For instance, it is well-known that the conditional, "If I were to choose to X, I would X" is insufficient for "I can X," since it might be the case that I am unable to choose to X. Similarly, I do not think that judgment sensitivity is necessary for moral responsibility, since a Frankfurt-style counterfactual intervener could render an agent judgment-insensitive without interfering in the actual sequence leading to the behavior (and thus not etiolating the agent's moral responsibility.) So a more nuanced, refined set of conditions must be developed. I would suggest that such an account must make use of devices similar to the two key elements in my account of guidance control: ownership and reasons-responsiveness. The mix will involve holding some factors fixed, while allowing others to vary. At a deep level my approach arguably shares these abstract elements with the approach of the so-called "New Dispositionalists," who contend that even in Frankfurt cases the agent has a certain sort of ability to do otherwise. Note that I need not disagree with these theorists about the presence of alternative possibilities interpreted in their more abstract way in the Frankfurt cases.

3:AM: You've argued that your position is compatible with causal determination but it is also compatible with causal indeterminacy as well isn't it?

JMF: Yes, my account of guidance control has the virtue (in my opinion) of being compatible with causal determination and also with the lack of causal determination. This helps to achieve a goal I think is worthwhile: rendering our responsibility practices resilient with respect to certain scientific discoveries. Our moral responsibility should not "hang on a thread."

I do believe that our moral responsibility practices presuppose certain contingent, empirical features of the world. I think they presuppose that we are "in the space of reasons," just for one example. By this metaphor I mean at least that we are reasonably good at identifying reasons for action and responding to them. (This is, of course, a somewhat contentious view these days.) But I just don't think that these deep and important features of our lives presuppose either the truth or falsity of causal determinism. We wouldn't, and shouldn't, give up our view of ourselves as morally responsible if we were to wake up to the New York Times headline, "Causal Determinism is True!" Nor would we be obliged to give up our basic view of ourselves as morally responsible if we were to wake up to the headline, "Causal Determinism is False"! It is an advantage of an account of moral responsibility that it does not conceptualize responsibility as dependent on these sorts of empirical theories.

3:AM: And for the readers here at 3:AM are there five books other than your own (which we'll all be running out to read straight after this) that would help us get to grips with this philosophical world of yours?

JMF: Michael Bratman, *Intention, Plans, and Practical Reason.*
Peter van Inwagen, *An Essay on Free Will .*
Harry Frankfurt, *The Importance of What We Care About .*
Gary Watson, *Agency and Answerability .*
Robert Kane, ed. *The Oxford Handbook on Free Will* Second Edition.

John Martin Fischer is the author of:

Moral Responsibility (ed.) (Cornell University Press, 1986)
God, Foreknowledge and Freedom (ed.) (Stanford University Press, 1989)
Ethics: Problems and Principles (coed., with M. Ravizza) (Harcourt Brace Jovanovich, 1991)
The Metaphysics of Death (ed.) (Stanford University Press, 1993)
Perspectives on Moral Responsibility (coed., with M. Ravizza) (Cornell University Press, 1993)
The Metaphysics of Free Will: An Essay on Control (Blackwell, 1994)
Responsibility and Control: A Theory of Moral Responsibility (with M. Ravizza) (Cambridge University Press, 1998)
My Way: Essays on Moral Responsibility (Oxford University Press, 2006)
Introduction to Philosophy: Classic and Contemporary Readings (with John Perry and Michael Bratman) (Oxford University Press, 2009)
Our Stories: Essays on Life, Death, and Free Will (Oxford University Press, 2009)

7 | Mark A. Schroeder: "Being For"

Mark A. Schroeder is Professor of Philosophy at the University of Southern California. Here he discusses meta-ethical thinking: why it ensnares all of us, meta-ethical expressivism and noncognitivism, its relationship to semantics, its relationship to natural languages, the importance of "not," technicality and depth, slaves of the passions, moral realism, Bernard Williams, hypotheticalism, and the Humean theory of reasons.

3:AM: What made you become a philosopher?

MARK ANDREW SCHROEDER: I was raised in a home where critical thinking—especially of received cultural ideas—was emphasized by my father and highly valued, by parents who are both two of the most compassionate, and two of the most principled, people I know. So when one of my first college courses—taught by Jennifer Manion at Carleton College—sought to apply critical thinking to the subject matter of moral philosophy, it was love at first sight. After that I was lucky to be in a supportive undergraduate environment with lots of good role models of other students who went on to do PhDs, and I always, at least early on in my career, believed that I could work harder than anyone else, so that gave me the confidence to see it through, even when the path looked dim.

3:AM: You work in meta-ethics—what are we to understand by that term and why do you find metaethics something we're all likely to get snared up in at some point?

MS: The simplest definition is probably that metaethics is concerned with questions about ethics—paradigmatically, with questions in the philosophy of language, philosophy of mind, epistemology, and metaphysics, about moral or ethical language, thought, knowledge and reality. We're lucky to be in a period, however, in which metaethics is often construed much more broadly—many questions start off as of interest in arguments about traditional metaethical questions, but end up having great interest in their own right, and are not obviously classifiable as just questions about moral language, thought, knowledge, or reality. If you attend the annual Wisconsin Metaethics Workshop, for example, which I think is a showcase for the range of issues that are of interest under the heading of "metaethics" today, you'll see that the range of issues covered is incredibly diverse—which I think is absolutely wonderful, and why I'm lucky to be working in this field today.

The easiest way of seeing why metaethics is something that can easily ensnare all of us is just to focus on simple cases in which real-world people disagree about important moral issues. In my introduction to *Noncognitivism in Ethics*, I focused on the case of a procedure called infibulation with excision, which is a particularly problematic variety of female genital mutilation. Most readers will find it obvious that it would be wrong to have this procedure—which comes with many well-documented drastic medical risks—performed on one's daughter, but not only is there a large population that continues to perform this procedure, it is actually often seen as a duty, a matter of giving one's daughter the best chances in life. These are very different perspectives. Because these issues are so important to us, it's hard to avoid getting caught up in reflection over how such deep disagreements are possible, and to even begin that reflection is to get caught up in metaethics.

3:AM: Metaethical expressivism is what you call the heir to noncognitivist views in ethics. So what do you take noncognitivism to be in ethics, and briefly, what went before metaethical expressivism?

MS: "Noncognitivism" is a term of art that has been used differently by different people. When I was an undergraduate, a visiting speaker once chastised me for misusing this term when I followed Michael Smith's use, from whom I had learned it. I guess that what I take to be interesting, here, is a tradition that starts with Axel Hagerstrom and Ogden and Richards, is popularized in the 1930's, particularly by Ayer and Stevenson, and continues through Hare, Blackburn, Gibbard, and others today. There are many threads to this tradition, so we can define "noncognitivism" in many plausible ways. But I think all of these theorists share the idea, at a minimum, that words like "good" and "ought" have a fundamentally different job description from words like "square," "tall," and "green," in a way that plausibly makes them in some sense metaphysically lightweight, and also tells us something about what Stevenson called the "magnetic" uses of moral language—ways in which moral language seems to exert a kind of pull or sway, or to be inherently practical in some way.

3:AM: Metaethical expressivism asks us to revise important issues in semantics. Can you say what's at stake then in this theory?

MS: The basic turn, for the expressivist, is from characterizing the meanings of predicates in terms of what it takes for them to apply—their extensions—to instead characterizing them in terms of what it takes to think they apply. What is particularly fruitful about this turn is that in some sense everyone can make it, because if you can characterize meanings in the former way, you can characterize them in the latter way. But the advantage of this turn is that it allows for the possibility that for some predicates—perhaps moral terms among them—there is a fact of the matter about what it takes to think it applies, but no perspective-independent fact of the matter about what it takes for it to apply. Put differently, the expressivist framework is one that gives a particularly natural way of making sense of how moral predicates could have a kind of meaningfulness without determining any extensions solely in virtue of that meaning. Described in this way, it is an alternative to relativism and some kind of dynamic theories of meaning, as well as to some kinds of inferentialism.

One way of thinking about this, from a metaethical point of view, is as making room for the idea that in some sense there are no moral facts—since "wrong," for example, does not determine any extension in virtue of its meaning, there is no property in the ordinary sense that we are responsible to, when we use the word "wrong," because it is ordinarily assumed that properties determine extensions. But the big idea of expressivism is important far outside of metaethics. It may even be that it gives us a much more fruitful perspective on semantic theorizing in general that is less prone to paradox.

The expressivist turn offers something more promising—a way in which we might actually be able to describe the meanings of the words in the language that we are actually speaking, without courting paradox. So I think its interest extends far beyond metaethics.

3:AM: You argue that you can't understand natural languages if this type of expressivism is true—and the word "not" seems to have a big role in your thinking here. What's the problem and is this a knock down reason for saying metaethical expressivism cannot be true?

MS: That's a great question—I have written a great deal about a problem sometimes called the "negation problem" for expressivism. But this is a little bit misleading. In fact, there isn't anything special about the negation problem; it's just the simplest case of a much more general problem about structure that any adequate expressivist theory needs to respect. To get a sense for the problem about structure, note that on a naïve gloss, an expressivist might tell us that to think that stealing is wrong is just to disapprove of stealing. So now compare the following three sentences:

N1) Caroline does not think that stealing is wrong.
N2) Caroline thinks that stealing is not wrong.
N3) Caroline thinks that not stealing is wrong.

According to the expressivist, to know the meaning of "stealing is not wrong," we have to know what it takes for N2 to be true. But unfortunately, our naïve expressivist view doesn't allow for enough distinctions. We can distinguish:

1*) Caroline does not disapprove of stealing.
3*) Caroline disapproves of not stealing.

And some simple reasoning shows that 1* has to correspond to N1, and 3* has to correspond to N3. But there is nothing left to correspond to N2, which is what we really want to understand. So there is a problem understanding the meaning of the logically complex sentence, "stealing is not wrong." The problem gets some more constraints when we observe that it's not enough just for the expressivist to tell us some story about what it is to think that stealing is not wrong; she also needs to tell a story that explains why "stealing is not wrong" has all of the right logical and semantic properties. Note that none of this is a special problem about negation; we could easily have started by distinguishing sentences like the following:

v1) Caroline thinks that stealing is wrong or Caroline thinks that killing is wrong.
v2) Caroline thinks that stealing is wrong or killing is wrong.
v3) Caroline thinks that stealing or killing is wrong.

Again, there is an important distinction between the first and second sentence, and another important distinction between the second and third. And again, to understand the complex sentence, "stealing is wrong or killing is wrong," according to the expressivist, we need to know what makes v2 true. But again, there are not enough distinctions in "Caroline disapproves of stealing" to go around.

To solve this problem, the expressivist needs a robust notion of content. As I would put it now, they need a surprising theory of the nature of propositions. There are different ways of going about constructing such a notion, and the one I developed and then criticized in Being For is just one of them. I don't know of one that I find wholly satisfactory; the one I developed in Being For runs into troubles with certain natural language expressions, and I worry about others for different reasons. I don't know that this is a knock-down argument against expressivism, but I think it tells us a great deal about what a successful expressivist view would have to look like, and I think that the vast majority of people who continue to write and publish about this and related problems are still focused only on special cases of the problems, without thinking about them in full generality.

3:AM: Why get so technical—why not just say it fails for "deep" reasons like many metaethicists do?

MS: I'm extremely skeptical of high-level attempts to say why a view like expressivism must fail, without getting our hands dirt with the details. The basic reason is that expressivism constitutes such a different perspective from that occupied by many of its high-level critics, that it's very easy to take for granted things that look very different from an expressivist perspective, or to misunderstand how an expressivist could actually treat some phenomenon. More generally, the fact of the matter is that we don't have a birds-eye perspective on our own language and minds—we understand them from the perspective of our language and minds, using our own minds to formulate ideas in our own language. That gives the expressivist—in principle—enormous resources for making sense of things that puzzle people about naïve statements of expressivism, because how our minds and language work are themselves some of the free variables, for the expressivist. It's an ongoing question, I think, the extent to which those resources can be utilized.

3:AM: You're a moral realist aren't you and take a naturalist reductionism position don't you? What's this and why is supervenience important?

MS: I would characterize myself as a reductive realist, yes. I don't get too worried about the title of "naturalism," because that's not something I ever set out to defend, although I think that by most ways of counting, the view I defended in Slaves of the Passions would qualify. I don't have a lot to say about why to be a realist in the first place outside of what I think goes wrong with particular irrealist views, metaethical expressivism among them. But I'm attracted to reduction in metaethics, largely because I think it promises to explain what to me is the most puzzling feature of moral facts: their necessary relationship with the non-moral facts, as exhibited by the fact, generally referred to as the supervenience of the moral on the non-moral, that there can't be any moral difference, without some underlying difference in the non-moral facts. Necessary connections between distinct existences strike me the kind of fact that can't be just a brute, unexplained fact about the world—I see them as in need of some kind of explanation, and a reduction would provide that explanation.

3:AM: Why is it better than other kinds of realism for you, such as Moorean non-naturalism defended by David Enoch, for instance?

MS: I think that David and I part ways over the importance we attach to explanatory power in theory selection. I start doing philosophy with things that puzzle me, and looking for ways to explain them. David, I think, sees things he finds deeply right or deeply wrong. He and I share a holistic perspective in the assessment of philosophical theories, which he often characterizes by considering how many "plausibility points" a view receives for this or that feature. But in addition to disagreeing with him, in some cases, about the measuring of these "plausibility points," I guess that I don't think the relevant points are all exhausted by plausibility considerations. The reason is that it's merely a conceit to think that the philosophical theories that we are comparing are full-formed theories. In many cases, they are more like research programs.

As an investigator who is making decisions not about which research program to bet on before some divine oracle reveals the answer tomorrow, but about which research program to invest my own time and efforts in over the long haul, the upside potential of a view is of much more significance to me than the work required to realize that potential. I'm not sure if this answers the question, exactly.

3:AM: If realism wasn't true—and many philosophers don't think it is—then what would you believe instead?

MS: The short answer is that I would still believe it but be wrong! But if you talked me out of realism, it would probably be into some form of expressivism. I don't know what that form would be, but over the last 5-6 years I've become increasingly sympathetic to the idea that we need expressivism for more pressing applications outside of metaethics—particularly, as an account of truth. And I don't really see how to give an expressivist account of truth that won't make room for metaethical expressivism. So that has warmed me up to that idea a little bit.

Depending on how we define "realism," a contextualist theory like that of my colleague Steve Finlay might also qualify as a retreat from realism, and in that case I would be cautiously sympathetic to some variant of a view like his End-Relational Theory, which I am most impressed about for his treatment of deontic modals. And if you talked me out of reductionism but not out of realism, I think I'd be split between adopting the views of my colleague Ralph Wedgwood whole cloth, on the one hand, and trying to develop some of what I think are the most interesting threads in Ralph Cudworth, Richard Price, and H.A. Prichard, on the other. I'd probably fight a valiant fight on Cudworth and Price's behalf before conceding that Ralph is right.

3:AM: The Humean theory that reasons for action are instrumental, "slaves of the passions," is an unpopular theory these days but you're drawn to it and defend it don't you. What's at stake with this theory?

MS: The biggest thing at stake over this theory is the universality and prescriptivity of morality. On a standard interpretation, Mackie assumed that nothing could be wrong, unless it was based on rules that apply to absolutely everyone, no matter what they are like, and are genuinely normative, in the sense of giving them reasons to act. But since he assumed that whether a person has a reason depends on her aims, it depends on what she is like. So, he inferred, there can't be rules that both apply to absolutely everyone and give them reasons, and hence nothing is wrong.

Gilbert Harman argued, around the same time, that morality doesn't really require such universal rules, on the grounds that moral judgments of the right kind do require reasons, but for Humean reasons, no reasons can be universal in this way. And Philippa Foot famously argued, again around the same time, that morality can maintain a kind of absoluteness by not providing reasons—again for the same Humean reasons. To me, these three authors in the mid to late 1970's, and Bernard Williams, in "Internal and External Reasons," which followed just a few years later, set the agenda for much of the most interesting work about morality and reasons over the next twenty or more years, by people like Christine Korsgaard, David Velleman, Michael Smith, Jean Hampton, Warren Quinn, and many others—particularly including Foot herself. The theory is unpopular today because these three authors made vivid its natural consequences.

3:AM: Bernard Williams has been an important philosopher in how the theory has been formulated for contemporaries—is it your view that he and others haven't been careful enough in formulating it?

MS: I don't think Williams lacked care in formulating his version of the theory—though there are many difficult features of the article, "Internal and External Reasons," which began this literature. I think, rather, that by taking care over different things than Williams did, it's possible to formulate a general view that has much weaker commitments, and that by standing on his shoulders, we can worry about different things, now, than he had to be worried about when he originally wrote. Sometimes we can recognize the achievements of an article that set an agenda without constraining ourselves to think within the space of possibilities set out by that article.

3:AM: You're interested in background assumptions that moral philosophers import into their arguments—why are these so important to your approach?

MS: I don't think they're important only to my approach—I think we should all care about when it is that we find our arguments persuasive only because we are working with some implicit picture. Interesting philosophical arguments are complex and often resistant to straightforward formalization, and philosophical prose that insists on formalizing every important argument is not only stilted, but sparse on important arguments and ineffective at communicating its most important points.

So some of the key pieces are in place for there to be gaps in our arguments that we don't, ourselves, recognize. We know these gaps are real, and coming to grips with them is at least one important first step toward trying to imaginatively inhabit the views to which we are unsympathetic. If good philosophy ultimately involves the holistic comparison of packages of ideas, as I think it does, you can't do it well while importing assumptions that are tacitly rejected by proponents of the package of views that you are considering.

3:AM: You defend a version of the theory called Hypotheticalism don't you? So how do you formulate the Humean theory of reasons and why do you call it a "parity" thesis?

MS: My formulation of the Humean Theory of Reasons starts with what I take to be a paradigmatic example of a desire-based reason. The Humean Theory of Reasons is the theory, essentially, that all reasons are relevantly like the reason given in the example. This is why I call it a "parity" thesis, because at bottom it says that two things are the same, without building in a lot of theory about what makes them the same—though you can arrive at more specific versions of the Humean Theory by adding more about what makes the reasons the same, or, put differently, by adopting more specific views about what is going on in the paradigmatic example.

3:AM: So how does your approach handle those arguments against the Humean thesis?

MS: There are a lot of different arguments against the Humean thesis, but the argumentative task of *Slaves of the Passions*, my first book, is to show that each of them is really only an argument against some versions of the Humean Theory, because each turns on assumptions about what is going on in the paradigmatic example. I also argue, for each of these assumptions, that the best version of the Humean Theory of Reasons has independent grounds to reject the assumption, and hence has independent grounds to take a form that is immune to the objection. That, at any rate, is the organizational conceit of the book.

3:AM: And finally, are there five books you could recommend to readers here at 3:AM to help us explore further your philosophical world?

MS: Aside from some of the historical canon, my own engagement with many of the issues I think of as broadly metaethical derives from two books published in the mid-'90s that I think have been formative for everyone of my generation: Christine Korsgaard's *The Sources of Normativity* and Michael Smith's *The Moral Problem*. I was lucky enough to have teachers who steered me toward both of these as an undergraduate, I spent a lot of time with each early in my philosophical development, and both have deeply informed my work, in different ways. The best source, I think, for insight into what metaethical expressivism might be and what you might do with it is Allan Gibbard's *Thinking How to Live*, which I was lucky enough to have a chance to start thinking about while in graduate school, while it was still in manuscript. The hardest material in the book is quite difficult, but Gibbard writes with a lucid and charming style that makes it a great pleasure to read, and its scope is stunning. David Lewis has always been a role model for me, and his *On the Plurality of Worlds* is, in addition to being justly one of the most widely cited works of contemporary philosophy, a model of constructive theorizing. Finally, my "philosophical world" is grounded in the history of philosophy, and particularly in the history of moral philosophy. I'm not sure if it's the right thing to mention, here, but I'm currently working through Terry Irwin's *The Development of Ethics*, which is a massive but wonderful take on one perspective on the history of ethics from Socrates through Rawls, and has the virtue of including a lot of discussion of figures from the tradition who are slighted by sparse conceptions of the canon. There are many other books worthy of mention, here, but those are five that illustrate different things of importance to me.

Mark Andre Schroeder is the author of:

Slaves of the Passions (Oxford University Press, 2007)
Being For: Evaluating the Semantic Program of Expressivism (Oxford University Press, 2008)
Noncognitivism in Ethics (Routledge, 2010)

8 | Thomas M. Scanlon: "The Contractualist"

Thomas M. Scanlon is Alford Professor of Natural Religion, Moral Philosophy, and Civil Polity Emeritus. Here he discusses what he takes meta-ethics to be and its developments since the 1970s, his realism and cognitivism, why and how he takes reasons to be fundamental, why he disagrees with Mark Schroeder's desire theory, why irreducible normative truths pose no problem, reason's guiding practical force, contractualism, rights, the doctrine of the double effect, and Kantianism and consequentialism in relation to his response to Parfit.

3:AM: What made you become a philosopher?

Thomas Scanlon: In my junior year at Princeton I took a seminar on the philosophy of mathematics with Paul Benacerraf. It was a terrific course, based on Paul's dissertation on logicism, which he had recently finished. This led to my writing a senior thesis under Paul's direction on mathematical Platonism, the question of whether sets and numbers exist. I was vehemently of the opinion that they do exist. (Isn't it surprising that questions of ontology seem to give rise to so much passion?) During that year I found that I loved thinking about philosophical questions so much that I did not want to give it up. Chapter 2 of my 2014 book on reasons was in part a working out (a generalization and refinement) of ideas from that senior thesis, fifty years later.

3:AM: You've been a leading figure in metaethics. Before examining your ideas, could you sketch out what metaethics is and what has happened to this area of investigation since Mackie's book on ethics back in the 1970s.

TMS: The metaethics I was first introduced to, in the early 1960s, was mainly concerned with the question of motivation: of how it could be that accepting the judgment that an action would be morally wrong involved being motivated no to do it. Given the spirit of the time, this was mainly addressed as a question about the meaning of moral terms, such as "ought" and "good." The dominant views were forms of non-cognitivism, which held that moral judgments do not make factual claims but express feelings of a certain sort (Stevenson) or the acceptance of imperatives (Hare.) Mackie's book added, to the charge that an interpretation of moral judgments as stating facts could not explain moral motivation, the ontological charge that facts about objective rightness and wrongness would be "queer" entities, "unlike anything else in the universe," and the epistemological charge that we would have no way of coming to know such facts. He objected to moral facts because of their claim to objectivity. He seems to have had no problem with facts about reasons for action that depend on the agent's desires.

In this period, the main alternatives to non-cognitivism were forms of moral realism that took moral truths to state facts about the natural world, such as the views developed by Richard Boyd and Nicholas Sturgeon at Cornell and by Peter Railton. Sophisticated versions of non-cognitivism, such as Simon Blackburn's quasi-realism and Allan Gibbard's related views, came a bit later. These views incorporated a shift in the discussion from the earlier focus simply on moral judgments to the broader question reasons for action more generally. This shift was evident in the title of Christine Korsgaard's influential book, *The Sources of Normativity*.

3:AM: You are a realist and a cognitivist about ethics aren't you? In saying this, what and who are you setting yourself up against?

TMS: I am a cognitivist about normative judgments in general, not just moral judgments, in that I take these judgments to be capable of truth or falsity in a straightforward sense. This sets me against many forms of non-cognitivism, and also against Kantian views that take normative judgments to be grounded in the will.

3:AM: You argue that truths about reasons are fundamental. What do you mean by this claim and why doesn't this commit you to some sort of normative metaphysical fact that would escape our best scientist and therefore be at best dubious?

TMS: "I take facts about reasons to be fundamental in two ways. First, I believe that facts about reasons are not reducible to or analyzable in terms of facts of other kind, such as facts about the natural world. Second, I believe that reasons are the fundamental elements of the normative domain, and other normative notions, such as goodness and moral right and wrong can be explained in terms of reasons. I am less firmly committed to the latter view, which is a purely normative thesis, than to the former. The former view is controversial for the reason you cite, but I believe that reasons for thinking it to be in conflict with science rest on a mistake. I agree that science is the best way of understanding the natural world, and therefore that we have reason to believe what the best science tells us about the objects in that world and the relations between them. But this does not mean that the natural world is the only thing we can have true beliefs about. The status of material objects such as the desk I am writing on as things that are "real" is a matter of their having physical properties, such as weight, solidity, and spatio-temporal location. In order to be real, such things need not have, in addition to these properties, some further kind of metaphysical existence."

In order to be real, such things need not have, in addition to these properties, some further kind of metaphysical existence. Numbers and sets are not parts of the natural world, and facts about them are not facts about that world. They are mathematical facts, about, say the mathematical relations that hold between numbers and between sets. What these facts are is a purely mathematical matter, not dependent on the existence of numbers, sets and facts about them in some metaphysical sense that goes beyond the literal mathematical claims involved. If physical objects do not require a further kind of metaphysical existence beyond the physical, why should mathematical objects and facts require some further kind of existence beyond their obvious mathematical properties? In the same vein, whether certain natural facts would, if they were to hold, be a reason for me to behave in a certain way, is a purely normative matter. No further "dubious" claim about metaphysical existence is involved.

Argument about the ontological status of mathematical and normative truths seems often to take the following form. Critics insist that in order for perfectly ordinary claims about numbers or reasons to be true they must be claims about facts that have some special metaphysical status. They then, quite reasonably, to say that these claims, so interpreted, involve a lot of hot air, and should be rejected. But they then go on, unfairly, to say that those who object to the hot air having been put in in the first place are "deflationists."

3:AM: Why don't you think a desire theory of reasons can explain everything that needs to be explained? Is Bernard Williams wrong in this?

TMS: Desire theories come in two forms. Reductive desire theories, such as Mark Schroeder's view, take facts about reasons for action simply to be facts about what would satisfy agents' desires. What I call normative desire theories are based on very general normative claims that agents have reason to do what will satisfy their desires (or at least certain desires.) Reductive desire theories deprive judgments about reasons of their normative force. Normative desire theories preserve the normativity of judgments about reasons, since they are based on a general normative claim. For that reason, they do not escape the ontological and epistemological objections that normative facts are supposed to be subject to. I would of course not reject them for that reason, since I do not think that those objections are substantial. But normative desire theories entail conclusions about what reasons we have reasons that seem to me false. I find myself in the course of a day having desires for many things that I in fact have no reason to seek or bring about. Attempts to avoid such implications by trimming back the class of desires that generate reasons seem to me to rely covertly on judgments about what I have reason to want that are independent of desires. There is also the problem that desire theories do not describe accurately the relation between reasons and desires from an agent's own point of view. (This is my main reason for rejecting desire theories.) To desire something is to see some fact about it as a reason to seek it. The fact that I desire something thus always presents, but leaves open, the question for me of whether this purported reason to seek it is actually a good reason.

For many years, before I had thought very carefully about the question, I assumed that many, perhaps even most, reasons for action depend on an agent's desires, even though there are some reasons, such as moral reasons and perhaps some prudential reasons, that do not depend on desires. But when I thought more seriously about the question, I was surprised to be led to the conclusion that desires never provide reasons for action, except perhaps is certain trivial "tie-breaking" cases. When I considered carefully cases in which it seemed that a person had a reason because he or she had a certain desire it always turned out that the reason was being provided by some underlying fact about the object of that desire, such as that it would be pleasant. I argued for this view in Chapter 1 of my book, *What We Owe to Each Other*. I was rather shocked when I first realized that this was what I believed, but in the twenty years since then I have become more and more convinced that it is correct.

The idea that reasons for action depend on desires is more plausible, and even correct, when taken as an answer to the explanatory question about what an agent's reason was for acting a certain way. This is a psychological question, about what an agent saw as a reason, not a normative question about what reason he or she actually had. Bernard Williams' view is complex and not easy to interpret, but I believe that one element of it was an attempt to forge a tighter link than I would between these explanatory and normative questions. He was also, I believe, drawn toward the idea that in order for it to be true that some consideration is a reason for a person it has to be also true that it would be irrational for the person to refuse to recognize this. The idea of such a link between reasons and rationality is widely shared—common to desire theories and some Kantian views, I believe—but it seems to me to be mistaken.

3:AM: How can we know irreducible normative truths?

TMS: What is the problem supposed to be? It seems to me as clear as anything that I know some such truths, such as that the fact that I would die if

I jumped out the window next to me is a reason for me not to do that. (Even if a normative desire theory is correct, this is, at base, a normative truth.) If normative truths, in order to state facts, would have to be about some kind of metaphysical objects, there might be a question of how we could "be in touch" with these things. But, as I said in response to your earlier question, this is a false and misleading picture. We can have knowledge of mathematical facts because we can engage in the right kind of reasoning about mathematical questions. Similarly, we can arrive at valid conclusions about reasons by thinking carefully about them. Relevant doubts about the conclusions we reach are first-order doubts about whether we are, normatively, correct. Normative judgments are much more open to such doubts than mathematical judgments. We have well-worked out accounts of various parts of mathematics, which give us justified confidence in our particular beliefs about those subjects and, more generally, confidence that there is a fact of the matter about at least many questions that are as yet undecided. The problem with normative judgments is that we lack such an overall account of the subject matter of reasons for action. This is a first-order, normative problem, not a metaphysical or epistemological one.

3:AM: Another challenge a realist theory like yours faces is to show how it can maintain reasons' "action guiding," practical force. Can you sketch out the problem here for us and say how do you fix the problem?

TMS: The problem was this. It seems that the fact that a person accepted a moral judgment, say that a certain action was morally required, can explain the fact that the person acted in that way. But, following Hume it was assumed that the acceptance of a "factual" or "descriptive" judgment could not explain action in this way. The "explanation" in question had two dimensions. First, accepting a judgment was assumed to make it rational for a person to act a certain way (and perhaps even irrational not to do so.) Second, the acceptance of such a judgment was thought to be connected with the person's being caused to act in this way. Non-cognitivist views were supposed to avoid this problem. Hare, for example, held that the acceptance of an imperative is the only kind of judgment that is "logically" linked with action. I suppose he also assumed that we are physically constituted in a way that explains our normally, if not invariably, behaving rationally. My view is an exact parallel with this. Rational agents are creatures that are capable of making judgments about what they have reason to do. And insofar as they are not irrational, they act in accord with the judgments about reasons that they accept. So even if judgments about reasons are the kind of things that can be true or false, the acceptance of such judgments has "practical force" in just the way that hare thought the acceptance of imperatives did.

3:AM: You are a contracturalist as well as a realist aren't you? Was it through finding that you believed that morality depends on reasons that require no further moral facts, reasons that no reasonable people could reject that led you to this position, or were you a realist first and that led to you discovering that for it to work a realist position followed?

TMS: I was a realist (that is to say a cognitivist) about normative judgments before I became a contractualist about morality. I was, as I have said, unsure about the degree to which reasons depend on desires, but as I have also said even a normative desire theory would be a form of normative realism. Thinking about contractualism, however, forced me to formulate a general view about reasons, which turned out, as I said, to involve rejection of the idea that desires generate reasons.

3:AM: In thinking about freedom of expression and toleration you had to think about the notion of rights. Have you a settled view of what rights are now, and what are the main features of such a view. Are you still a consequentialist?

And why don't you call yourself an instrumentalist anymore with respect to rights?

TMS: The view of rights that I formulated back in 1975 held that rights are constraints on the discretion of agents to act (or not act) that are justified by the fact that they are needed in order to protect certain important interests and that they do this at a tolerable cost in terms of other interests.

I thought of this as at least akin to a kind of consequentialism since I thought of the interests in question in terms of states of affairs that it is good to have obtain. I thus described my view of rights as "instrumentalist" because I saw rights as justified by the fact that their being observed promotes these states of affairs.

I put things this way because I saw some version of consequentialism as the only alternative to direct intuitionism about rights, which seemed to me unacceptable, because we need some way of justifying rights and of thinking systematically about what they require. But contractualism provides such an alternative, and once I started seeing things this way the original formulation of my view of rights came to look like a special case of the contractualist account of right and wrong: To say that a right is a limit on discretion to act that is necessary to protect a certain interest is just to say that there would be a reason to reject a principle permitting people to act in the way the right forbids (namely a reason that a person has who has the "important interest" in question. And to say that the right protects this interest in a way that is feasible is just to say that no one has good reason to object to being constrained in the way the right involves, so the rejection just mentioned is reasonable.

So my current view is that rights are no more "instrumental" than any other facts about right and wrong. The question remaining is whether there is anything distinctive about rights, as contrasted with other facts about right and wrong. This is connected with the current discussion about "directed duties." I am inclined to think that there is nothing distinctive about rights (i.e., that there is no important class of directed duties that is narrower than the realm of "what we owe to each other" which contractualist moral theory describes.) But I am not sure about this at the moment.

3:AM: You've rejected the doctrine of double effect, which is a doctrine which seems to be something in the news at the moment via discussions of various trolley thought-experiments which is often invoked to explain the permissibility of an action that causes a serious harm, such as the death of a human being, as a side effect of promoting some good end. Can you say why you reject the doctrine?

TMS: For many years, roughly from 1969 until 1999, I was a semi-unwilling believer in the doctrine of double effect. On the one hand, I felt pulled to accept it because I did not see any other way to explain what seemed to be obvious facts about right and wrong in various cases. But I could not see any general explanation of why an agent's intentions should have this kind of right-making and wrong-making significance. I also felt challenged by objections to the doctrine of double effect raised by Judith Thomson and Jonathan Bennett, among others. So I was greatly relieved in 1999 when I came to the conclusion that the cases I had been concerned about could all be explained in other ways, which did not depend on the intentions of the agents. The appeal of the doctrine of double effect, I concluded, arises from a failure to distinguish between two kinds of judgments, judgments about what makes an action wrong, and judgments about what is faulty in the thinking that leads an agent to think that an action is justified. Judgments of the latter kind must make reference to what the agent intended (what he or she took to be good reasons for acting in a certain way) whereas judgments of the former kind need not do so.

I did not conclude that facts about agents' intentions (about what they see as reasons for acting as they do) are never relevant to the rightness or wrongness of what they do, although I have sometimes been interpreted as holding this. My main conclusion was just that an agent's intentions are not relevant to the permissibility of actions in the particular way that the doctrine of double effect maintains. I think there are also other cases in which an agent's intention may appear to be relevant but is not. For example, people sometimes say, "Doing X in order to bring about Y would be wrong," which appears to be about the agent's intentions in doing X, when the relevant truth about permissibility is really, "The fact that doing X would bring about Y does not justify doing X," which is not about intentions at all. (This is just the distinction I mentioned in the previous paragraph.) There are, however, cases in which the wrongness of an action does depend on the agent's intentions. For example, intentions are relevant to understanding the wrongfulness of coercive threats

3:AM: Does your understanding of moral permissibility end up making you a Kantian alongside a contractualist and a consequentialist (of some stripe), and does that mean you are sympathetic to Parfit's arguments about metaethics in *On What Matters*?

TMS: As I explain in my contribution to volume two of Parfit's *On What Matters*, I am not a Kantian either about moral permissibility or about practical reasoning more generally. I do not believe that Kant's Categorical Imperative is a requirement that any rational agent must recognize. Nor do I think that the authority of practical reasons flows from what we will, or can will. The various forms of the Categorical Imperative are naturally read as stating some very appealing moral ideas. But these ideas are distorted when they are embedded within Kant's metaphysics of the person and of action, including his distinction between autonomy and heteronomy. I am in more agreement with the position that Parfit calls Kantian, although for reasons given in my contribution to that volume I do not think it is very Kantian. I am not a consequentialist although, like any sensible person, I think that the consequences of actions do matter to their permissibility. In my view they matter because permissibility depends on the reasons individuals have to object to principles permitting certain actions and those reasons depend on how they would be affected by the consequences of these actions. As far as metaethics is concerned, Parfit and I are in quite full agreement.

3:AM: Is the "naturalism" that Parfit discusses in the second volume a threat to your position? Is there anything that this "naturalist" argues that gives you pause?

TMS: I do not see any reason to accept what Parfit calls "metaphysical naturalism" or what he calls "normative naturalism."

3:AM: And finally, are there five books you would recommend to the readers here at 3:AM wishing to go further into your philosophical world?

TMS: Thomas Nagel, *Mortal Questions*
John Rawls, *A Theory of Justice*
Joseph Raz, *The Morality of Freedom*
Derek Parfit, *On What Matters*
Joseph Fishkin, *Bottlenecks*

Thomas Scanlon is the author of:

What We Owe to Each Other (Belknap Press of Harvard University Press, 1998)

The Difficulty of Tolerance: Essays in Political Philosophy (Cambridge University Press, 2003)

Moral Dimensions: Permissibility, Meaning, Blame (Belknap Press of Harvard University Press, 2008)

Being Realistic About Reasons (Oxford: Oxford University Press, 2014)

2 | Normative Ethics

1 | Virtue Ethics

9 | Richard Kraut: "Against Absolute Goodness"

Richard Kraut is the Charles and Emma Morrison Professor in the Humanities at Northwestern University. Here he discusses ancient philosophy and ethics; why utilitarianism and Kantian and neo-Kantian Rawlsianism are hedonistic and faulty, why Aristotle is very relevant, and how goodness figures large in our everyday thinking.

3:AM: What made you become a philosopher? You've been one for some time now. In that time, what have been the biggest changes you've witnessed to the way philosophy is done and its status? Has it been as satisfying as you hoped?

Richard Kraut: I started developing an interest in philosophy when I was in high school (Erasmus Hall, in the Flatbush section of Brooklyn). My older sister had completed college, and had been a philosophy major, so there were some philosophy books lying around the house. I can't recall reading any of them, but their titles intrigued me. And somehow or other I fell in with a group of brainy kids who were reading Bertrand Russell—*Unpopular Essays* and *Marriage and Morals*, not his "technical philosophy," but, even so, enough to make me want to take a philosophy course as soon as I went away to college (University of Michigan).

THE SUBJECT TOOK HOLD: I enrolled in philosophy courses every term, enjoyed them all, became a philosophy major, and had no doubts about going to graduate school (I wound up at Princeton). It was a smooth, easy process. I've never had any regrets, and have never felt conflicted about the value of philosophy or whether it was something I should be pursuing. Yes, it's been as satisfying as I hoped it would be—perhaps more so. I was extremely lucky, because there is no way of knowing in advance whether one's interest in a subject is going to continue to develop or fade. Or whether new ideas will keep coming.

You ask about changes in the way philosophy is done and its status. I was an undergraduate and a graduate student in the 60s, and when I look back at the 40 years of philosophical work that has been done since then, my sense is that it has been a period of tremendous growth and accomplishment. The subject of moral philosophy has been enriched by many great figures like Rawls, Nagel, Scanlon, Williams, and Parfit. In the study of ancient philosophy, there have been many advances in our understanding of the three main Hellenistic schools (stoicism, epicureanism, skepticism), while the study of Plato and Aristotle has also flourished. My sense is that as an intellectual practice academic philosophy is in a healthy condition. The importance of such major thinkers as Hegel and Heidegger is more widely acknowledged than it was when I was a student, and there is a broad consensus among academic philosophers that the subject should never lose touch with the canon of great historical works of earlier centuries.

Since philosophy is inherently an adversarial activity (one is always arguing against someone), it is in a way remarkable that we agree as much as we do about which problems ought to be taken seriously and which authors should be read. One unhealthy change should be mentioned, however: it has become necessary for academic philosophers to do quite a bit of publishing in order to remain in the profession. Graduate students are encouraged to have one or two publications in professional journals. At research universities (and even at some teaching-oriented liberal arts colleges), junior faculty members must have five or six publications or a book, if they want to become tenured. There is nothing unfair about any of this; these or comparable quantitative standards apply to every academic field. But I think philosophy is a field in which it often takes decades to reach a point at which one has something very important and worthwhile to say. One result is that some talented philosophers who might have done valuable work leave the field because they are developing too slowly. I suspect that many other academic fields do not suffer in the same way from the pressure, which arose in the 1970s, to publish and establish one's reputation at an early stage of one's career. Is economics, for example, losing talented economists because of the need to publish? I doubt it. But I'm pretty sure that philosophy is.

I'm not sure what is meant by the "status" of philosophy, but here are some thoughts that might be relevant. In my experience, philosophy is a subject that has a deep hold on a significant number of intellectually curious young people. They naturally love the questions it asks, and they appreciate the rigor and depth of the great historical figures. Some people will be bitten by the philosophy bug; they need only be exposed to it. But there are other people who are annoyed when they encounter philosophy, because they expect it to be at the same time profound and easy to understand. If they have to work hard at it, they think that somehow or other this is the fault of the writer—that it should be as easy to read philosophy as it is to read a work of popular history or a magazine article. They don't think that mathematics or physics or ancient Greek should be easy, but for some reason they do have that expectation of philosophy. This attitude exists, I think, even within academia. There too, philosophy is regarded as insular and needlessly obscure. In that respect, I think the "status" of my discipline is not what it should be. I don't think this is a problem that has become worse over the years. But it has not become better.

It's not as though I think that philosophers should be entirely let off the hook. I often come across philosophical writing that could have been made more reader-friendly, had the author been aiming to write for an audience of people who are interested in philosophy but are not yet specialists. Often, just a bit more effort would have allowed the author's thoughts to reach a wider audience. So, my view is that the "status" of philosophy suffers for several reasons, and that philosophers are partly, but only partly, responsible for this.

3:AM: You're an expert in ancient philosophy, but you use this expertise to engage with vital contemporary moral and political issues. Is this something that drew you to this domain, or was it something that grew out of realising that the Ancients had something to say to us?

RK: I fell in love with Plato's writings as soon as I started reading him, and this made me want to learn Greek (which I began studying intensively between my sophomore and junior years). Plato's ethical and political works are accessible to beginners and have a powerful protreptic quality—they are emotionally powerful and make philosophy seem more important than any other human pursuit. (I am thinking particularly of his Gorgias.) It took me more time to appreciate Aristotle. As a separate interest, I also started reading widely in contemporary moral and political philosophy.

It may sound strange to say that this was a "separate interest" but what I mean is that I didn't, at first, think that Plato or Aristotle had to be compared with philosophers of the twentieth century. I found their ideas intriguing and worth exploring for their own sake, and I wasn't committed to any notion that modern or contemporary philosophy was inferior, or that philosophy had better turn back to its roots in antiquity. But over the years, I started developing an interest, which grew stronger, in the question of which ideas (if any) in Plato or Aristotle (or later ancient Western philosophers) could still be defended— and of providing a defense for them. So I turned increasingly from primarily historical and interpretive questions to the project of assessing the strengths or weaknesses of what these historical figures were saying. When I had a year's leave of absence in 2004, I wrote the first draft of *What is Good and Why*, which defends some very Aristotelian ideas about human well-being.

3:AM: In that book you challenge two mainstream strands of contemporary ethical theories with ideas developed from the Ancient Greeks don't you? You argue that neither utilitarianism nor neo-Kantian Rawlsian contracturalism are adequate. Before you say what you propose in their stead, what are the main difficulties that you identify with these two approaches to ethics?

RK: Utilitarianism in its classical formulation (the utilitarianism of Bentham, Mill, and Sidgwick) says that there is one supreme principle of morality: maximise the good. Much of the opposition to it in the twentieth century has recoiled from it because of the way in which this seems at odds with our ordinary thinking. As W. D. Ross pointed out in *The Right and the Good*, it is an awful reason to break a promise that, after giving one's word, one discovers a better use of one's time (better in utilitarian terms). No promisee would accept that as a legitimate justification for failing to honor a commitment—and who could blame him?

Rawls also used a powerful example, in *A Theory of Justice*: it would not be a justification of slavery if it turned out that it produced the most good—if the suffering of the slaves was sufficiently outweighed by the well-being of the masters. It's not an adequate reason to enslave people that other people would benefit a great deal from being slave-masters.

There is another problem with classical utilitarianism: it was committed to the thesis that the good that is to be maximised is one thing only—pleasure (and similarly the only bad thing to be avoided is pain). Early twentieth century philosophers who wanted to remain utilitarians—I am thinking of G. E. Moore and Hastings Rashdall—were attracted, for good reasons, to a more pluralistic conception of what is good. They held that such things as knowledge, virtue, beauty, and friendship are good in themselves, and are not merely to be valued as sources of pleasure.

But the more fundamental problem is the one that Ross and Rawls identified. Even if utilitarianism embraces a pluralistic conception of the good, their objections will remain powerful against that new version.

As to your question about "neo-Kantian Rawlsianism": there are several things to say here. Kant himself has a hedonistic conception of the human good, and so his theory has that weakness in common with classical utilitarianism. Rawls did well to reject hedonism in *A Theory of Justice*, but what he replaced it with is not very satisfactory. His idea (and here he borrows from Sidgwick) is that what is good for a human being is the fulfillment of the plan that he would rationally choose were he to deliberate fully and clearly about his options.

Basically, the thought is that you construct what is good for you by following a certain procedure: whatever the outcome of that procedure is, that's where your good lies. He acknowledged that according to this view if someone rationally chooses to devote his life to counting blades of grass, then that really is best for him. Obviously, the notion of rationality is doing a lot of work in this theory, but Rawls, like most philosophers, makes the standards of rationality rather low—it requires little more than thinking coolly and consistently. So, he is saying: if someone coolly and consistently decides to spend his life doing something that strikes other people as boring and trivial, he is nonetheless doing what is most of all in his interest to do, because what is best for someone is defined as whatever arises from a rational procedure. My reaction to this example, like most people's, is that it would have been better for the grass-counter to devote himself to other activities. We can recognise that such a life has less of what is good for the person living it than do other human lives. There's a standard we use to evaluate how good his life is for him, and judged by that standard, the grass-counter could have done better—even if he made his decision without violating the very weak norms of rationality that Rawls has in mind.

In his second great work, *Political Liberalism*, Rawls portrays his theory of goodness (which he calls "goodness as rationality") as one that is to be used solely for purposes of constitutional design and basic justice. It is not meant to be in competition with hedonism or any of the historically important theories of goodness: all such theories (which he calls "comprehensive") are inherently divisive and controversial, and so they should be used primarily in the private sphere. That form of liberalism, which adopts a stance of neutrality between competing conceptions of the good, has many defenders and opponents. It is currently one of the great divisions in contemporary political philosophy.

A point that is often overlooked is that Rawls remains committed, even in *Political Liberalism*, to the thesis that some conception of the good must be used in the political realm. He never suggests that political theory can get by simply with a theory of justice or moral rightness—or that these notions can be understood independently of a conception of what is good for citizens. Rather, his idea is that the theory of goodness that he proposes in *A Theory of Justice* – what he calls "goodness as rationality"—is the theory that ought to be used by citizens when they reflect on matters of basic justice and constitutional design.

It's therefore a fair question to pose about Rawls: what is it about this theory of goodness (goodness as rationality) that makes it the best theory of goodness for a political community? I don't think his work directly addressed that question, but presumably the answer he would give is that justice requires one to use goodness as rationality in one's dealings with fellow citizens. In other words, goodness as rationality does not (for Rawls) need to be the correct or best answer to the question, "what is good for human beings?" It only needs to be the theory of goodness that justice requires us to use.

I find that an implausible view because it amounts to saying that in the political realm we ought to treat others as though goodness consists in one thing, even if we think and publicly announce that it consists in another. It's much more attractive to look for a theory of what is good for human beings that can be defended on philosophical grounds and that can at the same time serve as a publicly recognised standard of well-being. Rawls thought that this has become an impossibility in the modern world, but I am not that pessimistic.

3:AM: Your approach is largely a mix of Platonism and Aristotelianism, isn't it? I think you call it a developmental theory of well-being that places the idea of "flourishing" at its heart, don't you? But you're not using that term to mean "human flourishing" are you? You say at one point: "Good poetry, good wolves, goof thieves, and good people are all good in the same way: in all cases, some contribution is made to what is good for someone, and that is what supports the judgment that S is a good K." Can you say something about this crucial idea and then how your ethical system works?

RK: My approach does have both Platonic and Aristotelian elements, but probably the Aristotelian aspect of it is more pronounced. There is a kind of realism that both Plato and Aristotle share, and I'm very attracted to it. They both rejected the view that goodness, beauty, justice and other such properties are human constructions—that there is no other standard of correctness than an individual's preferences or whatever norms happen to prevail in this or that society.

Against this, they think that what is good for someone is rather like what is healthy for someone: it's not the creation of our thinking but a real property that is "there" whether we realise it or not. You can have a disease that will make you die at an early age, and neither you nor anyone else might realize that you are unhealthy in this way. That disease is bad for you, even though no one knows of it. Similarly, a society can be unjust even if no one thinks of it as unjust.

The way in which Aristotle has had a greater influence on my thinking is this: Plato tends to think of goodness as a property that mathematics can help us understand. The idea is that what makes things good (a good poem, a good person, a good building) is a certain proportion, balance, structure, or harmony. It's not a silly idea. So, he concluded that if we study the geometry of planes and solids, or the harmonies of music, that will help make us better decision-makers (provided we have been well educated in other ways). That strikes me as an intriguing idea that has not been very fruitful.

Aristotle shows no interest in it, and I think his instincts were right. So he pares away the parts of Plato that rely on this mathematical conception of goodness, and what remains is a conception of the well-lived human life as something that arises out of the good dispositions that children normally have and the good habits they acquire when they are well brought up. It's a process in which certain potentialities of human nature are actualised through a long and gradual process—a process in which we become more skilled at recognizing what we have reason to do and why, and in which our emotions become more responsive to those reasons.

People sometimes say that in Aristotle's writings the Greek word that is often translated "happiness" (eudaimonia) really would be better translated "flourishing." That's not quite right. It would be better to say that eudaimon means something like "living well," and that Aristotle's distinctive conception of what it is for a human being to live well calls for that individual's rational and emotional powers to unfold properly over a long period of time. "Flourishing" and "thriving" are good ways of capturing this idea.

As you point out, it's part of my view that the concept of flourishing has very broad application. It applies not just to human beings but to many other living things. We can say that certain kinds of animals do not flourish in captivity. Or that your hibiscus is not flourishing in that windowsill. That leads me to the thought that what it is for any living thing to have a life that is good for it is for that organism's potential to grow and develop and be exercised in a mature form. What makes a good human life good for the one who is living it is, in this respect, similar to what makes any living thing fare well.

Of course, this idea is too abstract to provide any answers to the concrete questions we face about how to manage our lives. But it fits with the realism that I find in Plato and Aristotle. Just as a plant's flourishing is not a matter of it's living according to a standard that it devises (plants can't do that sort of thing), so too with us.

I want (finally) to respond to your question about good poetry, good wolves, good people, good thieves, and so on. One of the hypotheses I endorse in *What is Good and Why* is that when we evaluate things in relation to the kind to which they belong (a poem is not just plain good—it's good as a poem), we should consider whom they are good for. Here's an obvious example: a college or a university can't be a good college or university unless it is good for someone. Even All Souls (in Oxford), which admits no students, has to be good for the scholars who have positions there—if it is to be a good college. More typically, good schools have to be good for students. Good people are also good for someone—they ought to be able to help at least some others.

These are very plausible and unambitious claims. But I admit that there are cases in which my hypothesis could be challenged. Must a good poem, for example, be good for someone? That's a difficult issue in the philosophy of art, but I'm inclined to think what makes poetry good is the way in which it exercises and expands our imagination and our emotional life. A mind exposed to good poetry grows, and that's good for the mind. But there are other hard cases. What about a good thief—is someone's being a good thief good for anyone? Most people would say that being a good thief is simply a matter of skill at thievery, and that whether such a skill does anyone any good is irrelevant. But why do we assume that one skill a thief ought to have is the ability to avoid detection? Obviously because we take it to be bad for the thief (or for his employers, or the government he is working for) to be detected. The skills a thief ought to have are simply the ones it would be good for him (or those on whose behalf he is working) to have.

3:AM: You argue that most parents would agree with your ideas. Why do you find that this is a far better system for understanding ethics than the alternatives?

RK: What you have in mind here is my point that when parents reflect on the well-being of their young children, they often think in terms of the unfolding and training of natural capacities. This indicates that the conception of well-being that I favour is not a philosophical invention alien to common ways of thought—something that a philosopher dreamt up out of the blue. It is part of our conceptual framework that infants and children are beings that need to grow, and that this process is good for them. There are wonderful things that we experience in childhood, but Peter Pan to the contrary, refusing to grow up is not healthy.

Other theories of well-being simply overlook this aspect of our common normative framework. Rawls, for example, as I've noted, focuses on rational planning: what is good for us is to achieve the plan that we would adopt with full deliberative rationality. But infants and small children are not yet able to engage in the sophisticated intellectual activity we call planning. They can't look for reasons to pursue this end rather than that. Yet it is undeniable that much that they do is good for them, much that they do is bad for them, and much that willy-nilly happens to them is good or bad for them. It can't be the case that we have two different concepts of what is good for a human being—one of which is applicable to infants and small children, and the other of which is applicable to later stages of life.

Of course, the things that are good for small children are different from the things that are good for adults. But there is only one relation here: the relation of being good for someone. I think that one point in favor of the developmental conception of well-being that I derive from Aristotle is that it recognises this unity.

3:AM: Your approach endorses the idea that there is a single best way of arriving at the good. This is a key distinction isn't it between contemporary ideas and the Ancients. Bernard Williams criticised the arrogance of moderns who sneer at the Ancients for holding such an unsophisticated view, but isn't there a little bit of truth in the claim that its unlikely that there is just a single best way to decide on the good?

RK: Bernard Williams was a formidable philosopher. The questions he raised about the over-ridingness of morality and about what he called "internal" and "external" reasons were extremely fruitful. I also admire him for the breadth of his learning and interests. His familiarity with Greek antiquity—he especially loved Sophocles and Thucydides—allowed him to make important contributions to the study of both Plato and Aristotle. But I also think he underestimated them.

In *Ethics and the Limits of Philosophy*, he gives them credit because they, unlike many modern philosophers, ask the very broad question, "how should one live?" rather than the narrow question, "what does morality demand of us?" But he didn't think their answers to that broad question were very plausible, and he also thought that "how should one live?" is actually too broad and abstract a question.

You are right that he criticised the arrogance of the "moderns who sneer at the ancients"—that is one of the main themes of *Shame and Necessity*. But although I don't think he sneered at the ancients, I think he was not a great fan of the philosophers of Greek and Roman antiquity. A large part of the reason for that is that Williams was not sympathetic to their realism. This emerges in his denial that there are such things as what he called "external" reasons. When he says that all reasons are "internal," he means that whatever you have reason to do must be based ultimately on preferences, desires, dispositions that you already have.

On this basis, I think he would agree with what you are suggesting: there isn't, as you put it, "just a single best way to decide on the good." That's because there are lots of differences between people, and what is good for someone must arise out of what is peculiar to that person.

A theory of well-being can easily say "here is the one best way for a human being to live" and then add "but there are as many different ways of instantiating that general formula as there are human beings." For example, Rawls's theory of well-being says that the best way to live is to achieve the ends that you would adopt with full deliberative rationality. But that allows for the possibility that no two people will achieve a good life in exactly the same way, because no two people will have exactly the same ends. In the same way, the approach I favour holds that there is something that all good lives have in common: in each case, certain natural powers have been developed and are being exercised.

But that leaves the door open to the possibility that no two individuals are exactly alike in the way they should develop. People differ in their talents, temperaments, and tastes. A child who has one kind of personality and set of skills should develop in way that brings out the best in these; another child's developmental path will be at least somewhat different, perhaps radically different. So, I want to say that there is a great variety in the species of human well-being, but that all of these species belong to a single genus.

3:AM: Implicit in all ethical enquiry is the question of method. You argue that Aristotle's ethical method was "endoxic" which I think means something roughly like dialectic, doesn't it? And I think you endorse the idea that this approach is something that Aristotle proposed as a general method and not just for ethics. Is that right and, if so, does this mean that Aristotle put the philosopher in a neutral stance—someone presenting the position that reconciles a dispute rather than being an active player? And I guess one has to wonder if this is the right way to find out the truth?

RK: Aristotle had a crucial insight about philosophical methodology: it thrives on disagreement. Typically, when he wants to work out a theory about something—about the soul, or the nature of change, or the good—he starts by taking a look at what other people have said about that subject, and he acknowledges that although they contradict each other, much of what they say has some initial appeal. That's still a common way to teach philosophy. It's not the way science is taught, and some people regard this as an indication that philosophy is intellectually inferior to science. But the fact that they have different methods doesn't show that there is something suspect about philosophy.

One of the most attractive features of Aristotle's way of proceeding is that it forces each of us to look beyond ourselves and to see what can be learned from others. (It is part of the method to look not only at other philosophers, but to look at what non-philosophers think—as Aristotle would put it, what "the many" think. Sometimes philosophers go off the rails and the views of "the many" are superior.)

It's quite different from the methodology that Descartes made famous in the *Meditations*. Of course, Descartes proposes that methodology because he thinks it serves his agenda: he wants to propose a way of thinking about matter and mind that will replace the grip of the Scholastic framework. As a general strategy for arriving at philosophical understanding, it is not a good idea to doubt everything you think you know, in an effort to find a starting point that cannot be put beyond doubt.

I agree with you that Aristotle's methodology would have a serious defect if it required anyone who is engaged in a philosophical inquiry to look only at what others have said about the matter. In fact, you have put your finger on something that Aristotle failed to make explicit in his various remarks about methodology. He ought to have emphasized that a philosophical inquirer is "an active player," as you put it—someone who is not merely adjudicating the disagreements of others, but is also creatively proposing new possibilities that others have overlooked. I don't think he says anything to rule out that creative factor as one component of a good philosophical method. So, I'm inclined to say that he provides an excellent starting point for finding a good method, but that his views need supplementation.

3:AM: You say: "Although ethics must be judged by the same endoxic method used to prove truths in every other field, we should recognise that it is a field in which some of what is shown to be true holds only for the most part." So you argue that ethics always has to be open to exceptions and that this is what Aristotle thought too. But was this supposed to distinguish ethics from, say natural science and if so, do you think it did, given that many argue that natural sciences are also open to exceptions? Perhaps there's a difference between how Aristotle conceived of the natural sciences and how contemporary philosophers do so that explains this?

RK: Aristotle thinks that in both the study of nature and the study of ethics we encounter many truths that hold only for the most part. But it's important to be careful here: he doesn't mean that we encounter only truths of this sort. He gives a few examples of universally true statements in ethics, though they are not accepted by everyone. He says that adultery, theft, and murder are always wrong; to call an act adulterous, for example, is already to say that there is no occasion in which it is right.

Obviously, not everyone agrees. But most people would accept his point, using different examples. A common example used by philosophers these days is that torturing people just for the fun of it is always wrong. This is hard to reject because the description of the act builds in a reference to the motive, and obviously if that goal is the only proposed grounds for an act of torture, it fails to justify it.

How common is it for the sciences to affirm generalisations that are recognised as holding only for the most part? That is a very complicated question, and I don't know the answer. On my understanding of thermodynamics, when you put a cold object into a warm glass of water, there is some possibility that the cold object will get colder and the water will get warmer. If it happens, that calls for no revision in our understanding of the laws of physics. So, in a certain sense, you might say that it is only for the most part true that the cold object will warm up the water to some extent. I think of the social sciences, the life sciences, and our common sense framework as resting much more heavily than do physics and chemistry on generalisations that are true only for the most part. Smoking cigarettes tends to lower longevity and health, but there are exceptions.

But in any case Aristotle deserves a lot of credit for his attempt to show that the natural world is something about which we can, with the right methods and the right experiences, have a systematic understanding. I don't think it can be shown, as he believed, that the very best human activity is one in which we contemplate the orderly nature of the universe. In that respect, his theory of well-being fails to accept, as it should have, the variety of human flourishing. It is too ambitious in its attempt to single out one kind of human career as best.

3:AM: Although you doubt if there's anything positive in Plato about ideas of human equality, freedom of conscience, rights to political participation, limited government, constitutional rule, democracy, you think there are valuable lessons that can be drawn from Plato for political theory even in our contemporary modern nation state context. Popper infamously called Plato a totalitarian, but Alan Gilbert reads him as arguing against tyranny. How do you assess his political theory? Is the *Republic* its centre, or did he develop between the *Republic* and his *Statesman* and *Laws*?

RK: I think that it's pretty clear in the *Republic* that Plato thinks that the kind of democracy that Athens had was an extremely bad regime. It's not the worst kind—it is not as bad as a tyranny; but it gets very bad marks. His way of criticising Athenian democracy is to imagine a city that takes its guiding principles—equality and freedom—to an extreme. There is so much equality in his imagined democracy that children and adults are on an equal footing (so that children have no respect for adults, and adults act like children). There is so much freedom that whether or not you have to submit to the laws is up to you.

A natural reaction to his critique is to say that this is unfair—it is just a caricature of a democracy. But even so I think Plato has a point: if freedom and equality have to interpreted in a way that allows for other sorts of principles and values, then they cannot be the only considerations that are relevant to the assessment of a constitutional design. To put the point differently: it is not every kind of equality that we should have and not every kind of freedom that we should enjoy. If democracy rests on a refusal to make distinctions of this sort, and if these are the only two values it recognises, then it is in trouble.

Aristotle is also a critic of democracy, but his way of criticising it takes a different form. He is not against the rule of the many—which is one way of thinking about what a democracy is. What he opposes is the use of power to secure the interests of one's own economic class—whether rich or poor. He is just as opposed to rule by the few who are rich as he is to rule by the many who are poor. Today we tend to be suspicious of the idea that those who have fewer economic resources will use the power of their great number to mistreat the wealthy.

In our society, the political power that comes with great wealth can be enormous, and wealthy elites have devised very successful methods of insuring that their wealth will remain available to them even in democratic constitutions. But the power of wealth was far smaller in fifth and fourth century Athens, and Aristotle may have been right that the poor were just as prone to mistreat the rich as the other way around.

To get back to Plato: It's clearly his view that if a community could find an small group of human beings (men and women) whose ethical and intellectual skills were of the highest order, then there would be no point in giving them decision-making authority for only a limited period of time. Making political decisions is not something that everyone does well—so why not leave it to people who are moral exemplars and have a deep understanding of justice and human well-being? That's one of the basic ideas of the *Republic*.

It's not a silly idea. (He is not saying that we should give absolute power to anyone who has a Ph.D. in philosophy.) I think it has important implications for the way we think about voting. To vote is to undertake a serious responsibility, and it should be discharged only if one measures up to certain standards of fairness, objectivity, and understanding. Many voters are pretty bad voters, in that they don't make enough of an effort to vote well. It's hard to be in love with a democracy in which that is the case.

After Plato wrote the *Republic*, or perhaps even while he was writing it, he must have realised that it does not serve as a guideline or blueprint for how actual regimes should be governed. He thinks it is important to see what the best realisable regime would look like, but that is compatible with acknowledging that it would be a disaster for a political community to turn absolute power over to just any group of elite politicians. So, that leaves a huge gap in his political thinking: how should existing political communities be reformed? What model should they look to, if not the model provided by the Republic?

The answer to that question is the (very long-winded) one he gives in the *Laws*. And one of the fascinating things about this dialogue is that Plato relies to some extent on some of the mechanisms of democracies. The most important offices are filled by means of a complicated series of elections. Safeguards are put into place to insure that magistrates do not misuse their power. There are fixed terms to most positions of power. There is an assembly in which all citizens meet. Women are to be educated in many of the same ways as men.

Of course, this is not a regime that would we or Plato's contemporaries would classify as a democracy. Citizenship is restricted to those who have at least a modest amount of land. Even so, it has some democratic features. And I don't think there is anything in the *Laws* that requires him to retract his picture of an ideal society in the *Republic*.

3:AM: You think that valuable intellectual activity need not take the form of knowing that something is so, don't you? So, devoting your life to something even when nothing known is gained is a desirable form of cognitive growth even when it falls short of a goal of knowing. This is something that seems hard to land with people greedy only for results and certainty. Do you think that deeper consideration of this point would help contemporary debates about the purpose of universities, education, philosophy and life, especially in the context of a culture that seems rather anti-intellectual and somewhat philistine?

RK: I like the words you use in framing your question—"greedy only for results and certainty"—because of the analogy they draw between an obsession with money and acquisitions and an obsession with the accumulation of known facts. Of course, in certain contexts, knowledge is exactly what we are and should be looking for. We don't want to punish someone who is accused of a crime unless we know that he has committed it. In the sciences, we want knowledge not only of what is the case, but also of why it is so; the most valuable scientific theories are the ones that do the most work in answering these why-questions. But it is form of intellectual narrowness to think that the best or only worthwhile use of the mind is to acquire knowledge.

Listening carefully to a complex piece of music, studying a poem, being aware of the complex relations between the characters in a novel or play—all of these are forms of intellectual exercise, but it would be a distortion of why they are valuable to view them as ways of acquiring knowledge. Someone can be quite knowledgeable in a certain area without having much in the way of understanding or insight. (Think of someone who has memorised a lot of historical facts, but does not have a larger picture in which they take on deeper meaning.) Works of art need to be understood in order to be appreciated—but here too understanding is not the same thing as knowledge. And it would be silly to set oneself the goal of understanding as many works of art as possible.

As Socrates saw, it is already a worthwhile accomplishment to rid oneself of the assumption that one knows something, if in fact one only thinks one knows. One is in a better condition, intellectually, if one is aware of one's cognitive limitation than if one is not. That is partly because one will never improve if one does not recognise any need for improvement. But someone who has become aware of how much more difficult a problem is than he had realised has already done something worthwhile and admirable—even if he does not solve the problem.

That's one of the reasons why philosophy is such a valuable activity. There are deep, difficult problems in our intellectual framework, and they should not be evaded; it is already an accomplishment to become aware of them, even if we cannot settle on one right solution to them. One of the dangers of seeing scientific theories as a model of intellectual accomplishment is that one loses sight of these other forms of mental growth.

3:AM: You ask the deep question in your book *Against Absolute Goodness* which is this: "Are there things we should value because they are, quite simply, good?" What seems an easy question gets trickier once we start to consider that often we relativise the term good to "good for such and such a purpose" or person. But that's not what you are after is it? G.E. Moore in his *Principia Ethica* wrote, "The only possible reason that can justify any action is that by it the greatest possible amount of what is good absolutely should be realised." Moore seems to be answering your question with a "yes." You think he is wrong because absolute goodness isn't a reason-giving property? Is that right?

RK: I'm fascinated by the large role that goodness plays in our everyday thinking, and the philosophical tradition that goes back to Plato has also placed "the good" at the centre of moral philosophy. My project in *Against Absolute Goodness* was to show that a certain way of thinking about goodness—the way that G. E. Moore advocated (and perhaps Plato as well)—is a mistake. Moore thought that he was simply making explicit and clarifying something that common sense already presupposes. He called the property that is taken for granted in our common ways of talking "absolute goodness"—meaning that it is not what is good for someone or good for some purpose, but simply good.

"Because it is a good thing" seems, at first sight, to be a way of answering the question, "why should I value that?" Similarly for badness: it seems obvious, for example, that if you should take aspirin to avoid a headache, that is partly because pain is not in itself neutral in value; it is by itself a bad thing. I wrote *Against Absolute Goodness* because I think that these seemingly obvious points are not at all obvious, on second thought. There is, in fact, nothing to be said in favour of the idea that goodness is a property that some things have, and others lack; and that it's because certain things have the property of being good that we should value them.

I think that pain is not bad absolutely. It's not something whose presence in the world makes the world a worse place, as Moore supposed. Rather, the sensible thing to say about pain is that (in many circumstances) it is in itself bad for the person who feels it. Even if the pain you feel does not interfere with your ability to accomplish your goals, it is often a bad experience. (There may be exceptions: there are pains so mild we don't mind them; and sometimes even severe pain forms a part of a larger whole that needs the pain in order to be good on balance). But a bad experience is not bad full stop; it is bad for the one who has that experience.

This may sound like an issue so abstract that it could have no practical implications, but it does. Some people say that knowledge should be advanced because knowledge is by itself a good thing. According to this view, knowledge need not be good for anyone to have—its pursuit is justified whether or not it benefits anyone. I have no objection to the thesis that knowledge need not be useful—a means to a further end—in order to be worth pursuing. Philosophy, for example, is often valuable without being instrumentally valuable.

But I would never say that philosophy's value consists in its being good full stop. The more plausible thing to say about philosophy is that it is a mind-expanding subject: your mind is deeper, broader, enriched, through its exposure to philosophical questions. If you are interested in philosophy and study it in the right way, you are better off than you were before, simply because your mind has been transformed for the better. That is to say: it is good for you. We don't have to say "it's a good thing (period)" because it is more plausible to say that the reason why you should learn this subject it is good for you.

It's sometimes said that people should be kept alive, however much they are suffering, because human life is in itself a good thing—even when it is not good for someone to be alive (or good for other people that he is alive). But this view can't be right, if being good (period) is not a reason-giving property. So, this issue, seemingly so abstract and inconsequential, has an important political dimension.

3:AM: How does this approach square with the idea that there is one way of achieving goodness? As we noted earlier, you have written that "there is just one legitimate route—the route of goodness—for arriving at practical conclusions," so why doesn't that thought endorse a kind of absolute goodness, understood in terms of this one legitimate route?

RK: The word "absolute" is used in many ways, and this can easily create confusion and misunderstanding. Sometimes it is used interchangeably with "objective." To be committed to the existence of "absolute values" is to be committed to "objective values," that is, values that are "out there" in the world, values that exist whether we recognise their existence or not. Hamlet is denying that there are "absolute" or "objective" values when he says: "there is nothing either good or bad but thinking makes it so."

I think he is wrong about that. None of us really believes that we can make something valuable or good or worthwhile just by thinking that it is. My thinking that I am a good tennis player does not make me a good tennis player. My thinking that I am a good person does not make me a good person. I may be wrong in thinking that I have chosen the option that is best for me. And so on. When we struggle to make good decisions, we assume that it is all too easy to decide badly; we presuppose that there are objectively better and worse ways of handling our practical problems. In that sense, we all believe that there are objective values, and since "absolute" is sometimes used to mean "objective," we all believe that there are absolute values.

The word "absolute" is used differently when Moore and other philosophers talk about something being good absolutely—good full stop, or good simpliciter, or quite simply good (period). These philosophers are not saying, with Hamlet, that nothing is good but thinking makes it so. Rather, they are saying that some things are good without being good for anyone. That is what I am skeptical about. In *Against Absolute Goodness*, I express my doubts about whether something's being good (period) is a reason for valuing it.

But I don't have any doubt at all about the importance of the concept of what is in a person's interest—what is advantageous, or beneficial, or good for someone. It would be crazy to deny that sometimes (in fact quite often), the fact that an action would be good for someone is a good reason to undertake it. Doctors ought to devote themselves to what is good for their patients. Teachers ought to devote themselves to what is good for their students. It's part of normal social life that we pay attention to what is good for the people we encounter and the people with whom we are affiliated.

One of the most controversial claims I make in *What is Good and Why* is the one you cite in your question. My thesis is that whenever we have reason to do something, one part of the reason is that the action chosen will be good for someone (or not as bad for someone as the alternatives). For example, if you have reason to do something that you have promised to do, then keeping your promise will be good for someone (yourself, or the promisee, or some third party). A promise that will do no good for anyone is a promise that one has no reason to keep.

Putting these reflections together, I can now answer your question: my thesis that what is good for someone is a ubiquitous component of good practical reasoning allows me to accept "absolute" goodness in one sense, but it does not commit me to "absolute" goodness in another sense. It allows me to reject Hamlet's thesis. That is, it allows me to say that what is good for me is something that I could be wrong about. But it does not commit me to saying that something's being good absolutely—good (period)—is a reason for valuing it.

3:AM: We've already talked about Plato's politics. But superficially at least, Aristotle's politics seems pretty repulsive. You say that Aristotle's politics were full of doctrines that are not now and probably never were credible. He thought slavery was justified, that women should stay at home and that manual labour is degrading and those engaged in it should be barred from full citizenship. He thinks democracy corrupt, and so on. And its linked to an ethical theory that is embedded in a metaphysical theory that probably can't accommodate modern science. But despite all this, you think there are riches that have been either missed or undervalued don't you? So why should we take Aristotle's politics seriously and what are these riches?

RK: Aristotle takes over from Plato the extremely plausible thesis that the design of all political and social institutions should be governed by a conception of the good. It is with these two figures that the notion of a "common good" enters political thought. By calling it a "common good," they mean to convey the idea that the good of each member and segment of the political community is equally important. If any portion of the political community lacks the resources to live a good life, then political institutions are failing to achieve their proper function.

A contrasting idea, which guides utilitarianism, is that although everyone's good counts for something, institutions should aim at the greatest total good, even if that requires sacrificing the good of some for the sake of the larger good. But Plato and Aristotle hold that something is deeply wrong with a political regime if it allows some citizens to achieve their good at the cost of the good of others. No just society would tolerate that. (Even in Aristotle's defence of slavery, the idea is not that the institution is justified because the good of the master outweighs the good of the slave. He thinks that the slave is better off being guided by the rational foresight of the master.)

Many contemporary liberal theorists find it very attractive to say, with John Rawls, that political institutions must be designed so that no conception of what is good for people is favoured over any other. The state must be neutral between competing conceptions of the good—that is their way of explaining why the state must be secular. This means that for Rawls and other like-minded liberals, a state cannot support cultural institutions. It cannot, for example, give tax exemptions to museums on the grounds that enjoying great works of art is part of a good life. I think it would be hard for Rawls to justify the teaching of music, arts, and literature in public schools. That would be akin to teaching Catholic dogma: it would presuppose a conception of what is good that cooperative citizens need not share.

I find Aristotle's approach to the design of public institutions far more plausible. It is very hard for a society to be a good society—one that is not only just but is good for people to live in—unless the resources needed for human flourishing are transmitted from one generation to another through education and cultural institutions. Aristotle's political philosophy rests on a conception of human flourishing that is extremely attractive, and it can be employed by modern democracies. We can say that he was badly mistaken in his assumption that certain people are naturally inferior in their cognitive skills; we have thousands of years of historical experience that he lacked, and we can more easily see that assumptions about the natural inferiority of whole peoples or groups lack empirical support. When we throw out that part of Aristotle, much is left standing.

I even think we can learn something from Aristotle's antipathy towards democracy (which he shares with Plato). Neither of them was opposed to giving significant political responsibilities and powers to the general citizenry—provided that the citizens are fair-minded, impartial, and have some understanding of what is worthwhile. For Aristotle, the Greek word, demokratia, means rule by a large group of people whose outlook on politics is biased by the fact that they have less wealth than those few who are able to avoid the necessity of working for a living.

He uses a different word—politeia, which can be translated "republic"—to name the kind of political system in which power is widely distributed among citizens and these citizens are not biased in their own favor or in favor of their own economic class. His view is that this is one of the good ways of organizing politics, and that democracy (in his sense) is not.

Aristotle is as deeply opposed to oligarchy (the rule of the rich) as he is to democracy (in his sense of that word). When he studies a political society, he looks not only at the legal system, but at the norms and practices that hold sway, and this leads him to recognise that the rich can dominate the poor even when the laws formally grant equal power to both classes. He would have no trouble, then, with the idea that many of the states that we call "democracies" are really oligarchies.

3:AM: Do you think understanding the context of his work and life mitigates his class and gender biases or is he just an apologist for inegalitarian views we find morally repulsive these days?

RK: Aristotle's attempt to justify slavery is a great moral defect. So too is his failure to follow Plato's lead in challenging contemporary attitudes towards women. Plato is completely serious about giving women a much larger role to play in political life. In the Laws, he does not give them complete equality, but even so, his proposals that they should receive an equal education, serve in the military, and hold some political offices are obviously meant to be taken at face value. But Aristotle simply follows traditional Greek biases and allows women no important roles outside the household. The one thing we might give Aristotle some credit for, in this area, is that he (unlike Plato) saw the importance of addressing the question whether slavery can be justified.

I don't think we can let either Plato or Aristotle off the hook by saying that their biases regarding slavery or women or both were quite common in fourth century Greece. They themselves realised that philosophy must look beyond social conventions and must ask whether prevailing norms have a deeper justification. So, they were not living up to their own intellectual standards.

But it would be a failure of our own if we refused to take Aristotle seriously as a political thinker because he tried to justify slavery. Here was a blind spot in his thinking. That does not show that he had no insights, or that we have nothing to learn from him.

3:AM: Are there political theorists that you find have been able to develop ideas from Plato or Aristotle into the modern setting. Rawls, for example, is the most profound political philosopher of the modern era, but he springs from Kant rather than the Ancient sources doesn't he? So is there anyone, or any current political tradition, that is rooted in either of these two giants?

RK: Amartya Sen and Martha Nussbaum deserve a lot of credit for making use of certain concepts that play a large role in Aristotle's political philosophy. Rawls himself borrows little from Aristotle, even though he makes some very perceptive remarks about him. (He takes nothing from Plato, so far as I can see.) But I entirely agree with you about the profundity of Rawls, and his place in the Kantian tradition. There is something profoundly wrong in both Kant and Rawls—they underestimate or ignore the strength of an Aristotelian approach to well-being, and the role it can play in political philosophy. But philosophy makes progress when it throws up competing theories for our consideration. It would be a mistake for someone with Aristotelian sympathies not to take Kant or Rawls seriously.

3:AM: Scott Berman has recently argued that Platonist metaphysics is consistent with modern epistemology and science. He calls himself a Platonist! Do you agree with his assessment of Platonic metaphysics and are you a Platonist too? Or an Aristotelian?

RK: I think that the most important part of Plato's metaphysics is still extremely attractive and plausible. What I have in mind is his notion of "carving nature at the joints" and his insistence that what we call "the world" does not merely contain physical objects. What he saw was that human conventions (linguistic, social, etc.) cannot be the sole basis for our classificatory schemes. The distinction between oxygen and hydrogen is not just a human construction—there really are different sorts of things out there, and we had better pay attention to them. And we should agree with Plato that things made of physical parts are not the only real things. Justice, for example, is a property that some social institutions or people or laws have and others lack; but justice is not made out of stuff in the way trees are.

All of this is completely acceptable to Aristotle. I think of him as enhancing the Platonic tradition rather than rebelling against it, by showing the importance of concepts that Plato had neglected—notions like potentiality and actuality, capacity and realisation, matter and form. So, I think of myself as both a Platonist and an Aristotelian, and I think large portions of their metaphysics are still viable.

3:AM: And finally, for the readers here at 3:AM wanting to delve further into the world of Plato and Aristotle are there five books (other than your own, which we'll be dashing away to read straight after this) that you could recommend for us?

RK: Some of my recommendations (those of Cooper, Hadot, and Frede) are works that move beyond Plato and Aristotle, so I hope you don't mind my including them.

JOHN M. Cooper: *Pursuits of Wisdom: Six Ways of Life in Ancient Philosophy from Socrates to Plotinus*

PIERRE HADOT: *Philosophy as a Way of Life: Spiritual Exercises from Socrates to Foucault*

MELISSA LANE: *Plato's Progeny: How Socrates and Plato Still Captivate the Modern Mind*

DANIELLE ALLEN: *Why Plato Wrote*

MICHAEL FREDE: *A Free Will: Origins of the Notion in Ancient Thought.*

Richard Kraut is the author of:

Socrates and the State (Princeton University Press, 1984)
Aristotle on the Human Good (Princeton University Press, 1989)
Aristotle: Politics Books VII and VIII (translation with commentary) (Clarendon, 1997)
Aristotle: Political Philosophy (Oxford University Press, 2002)
What Is Good and Why: The Ethics of Well-Being (Harvard University Press, 2007)
How to Read Plato (Granta Books: 2008)
Against Absolute Goodness (Oxford University Press, 2011)

10 | Katja Maria Vogt: "The Pyrrhonian Sceptic"

Katja Maria Vogt is Professor of Philosophy at Columbia University and a recipient of the Distinguished Columbia Faculty Award. Here she talks about ancient inspired alternatives to doing ethics, Pyrrhonian skepticism, what abstention from dogmata might mean, how Pyrrhonians can act, the defects of belief, not solving Moore's paradox, why the Stoic political theory isn't crazy, why Stoics aren't scary, on changing the conversation in ethics by following the lead of Elizabeth Anscombe, and her own theory of agential action and ethics.

3:AM: What made you become a philosopher?

KATJA MARIA VOGT: The same thing that sometimes makes me reconsider my choice: people who are too sure of themselves.

3:AM: You're an expert in aspects of Ancient Greek philosophy but what's interesting is how the issues they grapple with are still alive today. Is your work proof that philosophy doesn't make progress, or is it evidence that what progress looks like isn't what some critics of philosophy think it looks like?

KMV: I think of philosophy as a long-term, large-scale conversation. The ancients ask questions that one can phrase without first buying into a conceptual framework, in other words questions anyone can ask. Once you think through these questions, things can get very technical. But you start with things that can puzzle you simply as you go through life. This is a common denominator between ancient philosophy and contemporary philosophy, and to me anyway it makes for a strong connection.

So, progress? Of course the ancients don't have everything figured out. I once had a student in an Aristotle class who asked me whether I think

Aristotle is right that women can't think, as the student put it. Well, there's a nice paradox. At a minimum, or so I'd argue, ancient philosophers develop methods of inquiry that help one become a better thinker. I give them more credit, though. There are questions about the nature of value, knowledge and ignorance, epistemic norms, norms of assertion, and so on, where in my view it makes a lot of sense to engage with their views.

Along these lines, I'm wrapping up right now a book project entitled *Desiring the Good: Ancient Proposals and Contemporary Theory*. It is laying out an ancient-inspired alternative to the way G.E. Moore conceives of the question "what is the good? ." The *Principia Ethica* begins in this seemingly odd way, as if it was obvious that the main and first task of ethics was to ask what the good is. Surely, there are lots of ethicists who don't think so. While I agree with Moore, I think one needs to spell out why this is the starting-point. And one needs to offer explicit reasons for the way in which one construes the question "what is the good?" Here I depart from Moore, in ways that are ancient-inspired. Plato and Aristotle both think that the version of "what is the good?" that gets ethics started is "what is the good for human beings?" They have lots to say about the difference between good and good-for; the relationship between the good for human beings and the good for, say, fish; and the good as the object of desire. These are the sorts of things where, to me, ancient philosophy is immediately alive. It takes a lot of work to make it, fully, a live contender. But the effort seems very much worthwhile to me.

The conversation I am interested in is also facilitated by the fact that most Greek philosophy pre-dates monotheistic premises. This doesn't mean that for Plato, Aristotle, Chrysippus, Epicurus, and so on, there is no such thing as divinity. But for them it is a question, and not one to which the answer is simply available, how one should think of a god. And for all the ancients know, the soul may well be physical. The main interlocutors of ancient skeptics, Stoics and Epicureans, think so. This is one reason why ancient skeptics would not come up with external world skepticism. To them, it is an alien idea that "the mind" is different in the relevant, radical way, from "the world." Instead it is a highly complex part of the world. I think this is along the right lines, and a good reason to study these theories.

3:AM: The Pyrrhonian skeptic is a crucial figure in your work isn't she. Can you sketch for us what makes this species of skepticism so interesting?

KMV: For better or worse, I think my deepest motivation remains a dislike of unqualified assertion. I share the skeptical idea that embracing falsehoods has significant practical impact. This idea is behind all ancient skepticism, Pyrrhonian and Academic, and very different from external world skepticism. Declarative statements that may be false are risky. We act based on what we take to be information, and run into trouble. It seems natural to me that, for pretty much everything, less than full credence—and less then full assertion—is warranted. And I think that ordinary language is on my side. We routinely use qualifiers such as "for all I know" and the likes. Or we do this implicitly, using sentences that, on the surface, have the form of assertions, but we say "hmm ..." or signal to our interlocutors in some other way that we're not fully sure: we're telling them what seems to us, and we flag that this may not be what really is the case. I recently turned to spelling these things out independent of ancient sources, in papers co-authored with Jens Haas, on ignorance and action.

In general, I want to pursue these ideas with respect to challenges today. Here is one such paradox: assume the norms of assertion say we all should use a lot more qualifiers, refraining from full assertion; and assume the gender dynamics and workings of bias in professional philosophy are such that we should encourage female students to drop qualifiers because if they do not, their modes of speech are perceived as self-deprecating. Where does this leave us? Do women not have the luxury to rationally respond to the difficulty of the questions we all tackle?

3:AM: How do you understand their idea of abstaining from dogmata?

KMV: As a philosopher, you are likely to find certain ideas compelling. And you are also likely to be aware of relevant objections. Even if you aim to reformulate your ideas in the light of these objections, you may feel the pull of considerations that your approach cannot accommodate. This is precisely what abstaining from dogmata means: you are still thinking it through, and you are not pretending that the matter is settled.

3:AM: Can the Pyrrhonian state her position? Wouldn't any statement be self contradictory, along the lines of "I believe nothing." Isn't any assertion a problem? Are the Pyrrhonians condemned to silence?

KMV: Metrodorus, a pre-Socratic atomist, puts things nicely: None of us knows anything, not even this, whether we know or do not know; nor do we know what "to not know" or "to know" are ... So the ancient skeptics were duly warned. They did not walk into the trap of saying "I believe nothing" or "I know nothing." Instead they say that they continue to investigate. And yes, I think they can say this–that they continue to investigate–without getting in trouble. Pyrrhonian skeptics say that they "lay open" what is going on in their minds. On my analysis, this manner of speaking has the form "X appears F to me now." It is called a report, as opposed to an assertion. It is intentionally elliptical, i.e., it is supposed to be different from "X appears to be F for me now." The idea is that, by dropping "to be" one doesn't refer to reality. This is where things become troublesome. Elliptical utterances only work because others understand them as equivalent to their non-elliptical versions. Others will think that "X appears F to me now" just means "X appears to be F." Skeptics, or so I have argued, can communicate, but only by relying on non-skeptical speaking conventions as default interpretations of their talk.

3:AM: You argue that Michael Frede is wrong to think the skeptic has an alternative kind of belief to the usual one and say that they have no beliefs. What kind of mental life do they have if they have no beliefs? Is theirs a life of continuous inquiry? Is this where Socrates is coming from?

KMV: Skepticism is formulated in controversy with its opponents. It proceeds by "borrowing" their terms. For purposes of addressing the question "do the skeptics have beliefs?", the only plausible notion of belief is the notion that Stoics and Epicureans employ. And they employ an on/off notion of belief where beliefs are actively formed judgments. This is why I disagree, in a sense, with Frede. He ascribes beliefs of a sort to the skeptics that, in the debates that skeptics are immersed in, just do not count as beliefs. In another sense I agree with Frede. There are doxastic attitudes that today we characterize as beliefs and that are not actively formed judgments. Skeptics can hold those attitudes. As I see it, skeptics cultivate ways of thinking that typically leave one with less-than-full belief, hypotheses, interrogative attitudes, and so on. I'm invested in spelling out a larger picture, also in ethics, on which this is an ordinary way, and a good way, to think and live.

And yes, it is Socratic. Like Socrates, I think that important questions tend to be pretty hard. It is not to be expected that, without a commitment to long-term investigation, one gets things right. In Plato's dialogues, the question that gets ordinary people into ethics is how to raise their kids, which teachers to send them to, and so on. Plato thinks this is one of the hardest questions, for it is the question of what is good for human beings. This seems right to me. And it seems to me that parents typically never conclude their thinking about this, even though they do one thing or another all the time to help their kids grow up well. Indeed, I think kids greatly prefer parents and teachers who have not made up their minds once and for all, about, say, gender norms or whatever it may be. Work-in-progress-thinking is not a failure, precisely where things matter; it is a rational response to the fact that things matter.

3:AM: If I don't have beliefs I might think that I can't act—and if they can't act they can't inquire. The Pyrrhonian has no beliefs according to you—so how do they act?

KMV: Pyrrhonian skeptics have been under attack for this since antiquity. I have distinguished a couple of versions of the problem. The Animal Charge says that, without beliefs to the effect that x is good and y to be done, the skeptic does not act rationally, but instead merely like an animal. The Paralysis Charge says that, in following appearances (which the skeptics say they do) one may often have too many and conflicting things to do. Like in Buridan's example, if "walk to the right" seems to you and "walk to the left" seems to you, and that's all you have—no further criterion that prompts movement one way or another—you may not walk at all. The Inconsistency Charge says that the skeptic, by leaving a room through the door rather than walking into the wall, is shown to be inconsistent. Contrary to her claims, the skeptic believes that "this is the door" just like the rest of us. And so on. I'm interested in these questions for two sets of reasons. First, I think they zoom in on core problems in the philosophy of action. Second, I am invested in developing an account of rational action without full belief or knowledge.

3:AM: Is it your claim that not just the Pyrrhonians but also Plato, skeptical Academics and the Stoics thought of Beliefs as defective, "shameful" cognitive attitudes. Does this mean that they all thought that no belief can be true or false?

KMV: Yes, though for a variety of reasons. The most technical reason is formulated by the Stoics: they think that strictly speaking propositions are true/false. Basically, I think the Stoics are right about this. Chrysippus, the leading Stoic logician, said that he's not interested in policing the language. In that sense, it's alright with me if people say that beliefs are true/false. But I think it is more precise to assess the contents of beliefs, i.e., propositions, as true/false.

You quote from Plato's *Republic*. "Shameful" refers to the idea that one shouldn't assert what one doesn't know. When Socrates is asked "What is the good?" he refuses to put forward a mere belief (doxa) and says that doing so would be shameful. What does he do instead? He offers comparisons, models, and hypotheses in order to think them through. This seems like the right way to go. That is, not knowing the answer to "what is the good?" is not a reason to stop talking and thinking about it. Far from it! This is the spirit in which I'm doing ethics even though I'm an ancient skeptic at heart. Not endorsing an account of the good is one thing. Wanting to figure out what is good is another, and entirely compatible with it.

3:AM: The position seems to make knowledge a rare thing for these philosophers. Does it make knowledge something very different from belief, and rules out ideas of knowledge as a species of belief (e.g. justified and true belief)? Tim Williamson has argued for not seeing knowledge as being grounded on belief, so should contemporary epistemology take these Ancient guys seriously?

KMV: Yes, knowledge is a rare thing! Still, I don't think that we should just give up on knowledge and talk entirely in terms of lesser doxastic states. In the end, I guess the fact that we want knowledge and find it valuable doesn't go away, even if knowledge is elusive. And yes, to know something is not to hold a true/justified/etc. belief. The word that is translated as "justification" when people say that Plato anticipates the JTB account of knowledge—that knowledge is true justified belief—is "logos." Logos, however, is better translated as "account." Plato thinks that, when one works one's way toward an account, one is getting rid of one's earlier doxastic attitudes. The account is going to replace them.

That seems pretty plausible to me: the doxastic attitudes you may have had during the first weeks of Chemistry 101 don't survive when you become a scientist. That doesn't mean that the things you learnt in the first few classes were false. It means that once you get a grip on the relevant concepts, become familiar with larger-scale theories in chemistry, and acquire the ability to develop these theories further, you'll think different thoughts.

And: "yes" on your question whether contemporary philosophers should take ancient epistemology seriously. Williamson also seems aware that his epistemic view on vagueness is pretty much the Stoic view. I say pretty much because there's a difference: the Stoics never do just epistemology, they do normative epistemology. Their interest in vagueness is related to their interest in training oneself to be able to pause, not say "yes" or "no," in cases that seem borderline. They play sorites games in logic class in order to cultivate the ability not to assent rashly.

3:AM: Is "I believe it is raining outside but I know it isn't" no longer a self – contradiction on this position? Does your position solve Moore's paradox?

KMV: Well, that would be nice! But I guess one can only solve Moore's paradox if one shares its premises. And those include the very premise that I reject, namely that to know that it's raining entails that one (also) believes that it's raining.

Suppose someone talks herself into thinking that mist in the air is evidence that it's raining. She's very much hoping for rain—she's a farmer and fears that her crop otherwise goes bad. Or consider an alternative background story— she promised herself that she'll go running if it's not raining, but she hates running; and now the mist really looks rather rain-like to her. The farmer and the would-be runner may in the back of their minds know quite well that it is not raining. But they get themselves to believe that it is raining. This is belief/doxa of the sort I've been writing about: a changeable attitude, badly integrated with one's firmer epistemic attitudes, subject to wishful thinking, and so on.

How does this bear on Moore's paradox? The upshot is, I guess, that there's not so much a paradox, but a lack of integration of the person's mental states. And this is what interests me. There may be failures to integrate that are rather charming. Say, your sciency lover and life companion doxa-thinks it was fate that you two met, a belief that is entirely at odds with everything a scientist may take herself to know about the world. But on the whole, integration seems better. Wishful thinking, not wanting to believe what the evidence suggests, wanting the evidence to suggest something we are antecedently invested in, and so on, are pervasive phenomena. On the larger picture I defend, these are topics that ethics and normative epistemology, in conversation with philosophy of mind and cognitive science, must explore. And the case of the moonstruck scientist suggests that we may even want to keep an open mind on whether integration is always better than not-integration.

3:AM: You've looked at Stoic political theory. Did they place perfect rationality as the constitution of their "Cosmic City" and virtue? What did they mean when they call the cosmos a city? Can you sketch for us what the Stoic political philosophy was and why you don't think it's as crazy as some have thought.

KMV: You're right, I don't think it is crazy. Indeed, I don't think it is crazy at all. The main upshot of Stoic political theory is that all human beings are fellow-parts of the world and have to find a way of living together in the world. I think this is right. I think traditional political philosophy is wrong to assume that we "only" have to figure out how to live together in a given state, though that of course is already a tall order. But it's just one component of the larger task each of us has, namely, to be a good part of the world. The Stoics mean this quite literally. They are physicalists who think of the world as a complex whole with parts. We are some of these parts. Tigers, palm-trees, glaciers, grains of sand, and so on and so forth, are other parts of the world. We are fellow-parts also of them, though not in the same way in which we are fellow-parts of the world with other human beings. This latter relationship is "political" in the sense that we have to figure out how to live together in the world.

The contentious idea here is whether there can be a normatively relevant relationship between "everyone." Sam Scheffler, for example, thinks that only special relationships (say, between friends or family members or fellow New Yorkers) can be normatively relevant. A relationship between everyone, the thought goes, just isn't a relationship. This is where the Stoics, and I, disagree.

It's been a while that I've written on this, but I recently had a chance to lay out this kind of cosmopolitanism at the book launch for Cruft/Liao/Renzo's Philosophical Foundations of Human Rights. I am quite committed to a cosmopolitan approach to human rights, starting from the idea of human beings as fellow inhabitants of the world. And I'll continue to spell this out in contemporary terms.

3:AM: Perfect deliberation seems worrying—so many sc-fi programmes have shown how the perfect reasoning of the machines and computers threatens rather than enriches. Isn't this why the Stoics and their sages are dangerous? Isn't it the Weberian bureaucratic mind gone wild?

KMV: Luckily, my Stoics are not that scary. One of Frede's proposals is to take seriously that ancient skeptics and Stoics come in tandem. They are like two camps in one of today's debates. They keep talking to each other and they share the terms of the debate. And they share premises. First and foremost, that it is hard and important to figure out what to do. Second, that, given the way the human mind works, we easily jump to conclusions. We do that all the time and for all sorts of reasons. For example, we jump to the conclusion that someone was offending us, and get angry. Or we jump to the conclusion that "7 is many" because the logic teacher, who plays a sorites game with the class, manipulates us into being too hasty. And so on.

So the claim is that we need, more than anything else, the ability not to accept impressions in rash ways. The skeptics develop forms of argument that reliably keep us away from rash assent. The Stoics put forward a set of epistemic norms that have the same objective. And they construct a model of a perfect reasoner. This helps them spell out what reasoning would look like in a person who forms no beliefs and who has attained knowledge—and, importantly, the affective attitudes that reflect this knowledge are affective attitudes of wanting things to go well for others. But none of the Stoics think that they are this perfect reasoner. Instead, the aim of the perfect reasoner-model is to find some strategies for the likes of us, flawed and imperfect, to do better. This is what interests me.

Here is a disclaimer. I said "my Stoics" because the Stoics I'm talking about are people like Zeno and Chrysippus, interlocutors of the skeptics. This constellation stays in place for a while. For example, Cicero, whose treatises contain lots of skeptic-Stoic debates, self-identifies as an Academic skeptic. But there are also Stoics who aren't my Stoics. They populate much of the pre-Barnes/Cooper/Frede/etc. secondary literature. They are too preachy and admonitory for me. They lack the edge and the epistemic modesty that comes from talking to skeptics.

3:AM: How has the Aristotelian idea that agents want their lives to go well fused with proposals coming from Elizabeth Anscombe in your recent work on ethics? Are your arguments and the position you establish aimed at changing the way contemporary ethics is done, or at least an attempt to put back key elements from Ancient sources that you think are currently missing?

KMV: It's interesting that you ask this. The answer is yes—the new book you are referring to, *Desiring the Good*, is an effort to change the conversation in ethics. In "Modern Moral Philosophy," Anscombe says that before doing normative ethics we should do philosophy of psychology. People often take this to mean "moral psychology"; but that doesn't seem quite right. At the time when Anscombe wrote, people in Oxford used "philosophy of psychology" pretty much as we today use "philosophy of mind." And this is the path Anscombe herself took. She started philosophical debates about intention and about pleasure, ever since major topics in the philosophy of mind.

I want to pursue this path, and I think that Plato's *Philebus* as well as Aristotle's *Nicomachean Ethics* lay out the kind of approach in ethics that Anscombe was gesturing at. Here ethics starts out with normative questions, but quickly hits the breaks: it becomes apparent that, if we want to get clear about what is good and bad for human beings, we need a better grip on what is going on in our minds. How does motivation work? What kinds of cognitive activities make up our mental lives, and how do they mix with affective attitudes? And larger questions follow suit: if we examine human decision-making, we will need to better understand the metaphysics of the domain of action. We need to understand contingency and what Aristotle calls for-the-most-part regularities. Say, when you explain to a kid why she shouldn't hit her sibling, you'll say "it hurts!" and "she'll be upset." Now, of course one can think of instances of one person hitting another person that don't hurt and there are people who don't get upset when hit. But we say "it hurts" and "she'll be upset" anyway, and we believe that this rightly orients action. These are for-the-most-part regularities. Part of the upshot is that McDowell's insight in the metaphysics of the sphere of action is seriously incomplete. He argued, and lots of people accepted, that situations in which we act are particulars. That seems right. But it is equally important that the sphere of action displays for-the-most-part regularities. Otherwise there would be no rational planning and ethical thinking.

When thinking about what to do, we need to assume that patterns and non-necessary regularities are in place, in people and in the sphere in which we act. Aristotle likes comparisons with medicine and navigation. Consider a boat trip. There'll be particular moments where the sailor's reactions have to be spot-on, acting quickly in the light of given features of this particular situation. But there's also planning and that takes non-strict regularities into account. Making up her mind when to sail and whom to take along, she'll think thoughts like: there's more/less wind in the morning; there are more/fewer storms in August than July; fellow-sailor Queequeg is the best harpooneer; for the kind of trip we have in mind, we need a boat like Quint's; and so on. But none of these regularities are strict. This year's July may be atypical; Queequeg may miss; something may come up and a bigger boat is needed; and so on. The challenge of practical thinking is to take non-strict regularities into account, not mistaking them for the absence of regularities and not mistaking them for strict regularities either.

How does this relate to my work on skepticism and normative epistemology? As a student, I found convincing Plato's and Aristotle's claim that ethics is not for the young. It's too hard, in part because, if understood along the lines I sketched, it involves forays into philosophy of mind and psychology and epistemology and metaphysics. So I thought it worthwhile to spend a couple of decades to collect at least some of the pieces of the puzzle. And more recently I have started to put these pieces together.

3:AM: Can you sketch your theory of agential action and ethics?

KMV: Standard versions of the Guise of the Good say that in any action, the agent is motivated by seeing the action or its outcome as good—and these standard versions take themselves to be Aristotelian. I argue that they miss Aristotle's core idea, namely that agents aim to have their lives go well. That is, the Guise of the Good in Aristotle is not exclusively and not primarily a theory about small-scale actions. I introduce a three-fold distinction between small-scale particular actions, mid-scale actions (pursuits), and the largest-scale motivation to have one's life go well. Based on this distinction, I defend what I take to be a genuinely Aristotelian version of the Guise of the Good. Though I'm pretty much done with this book manuscript, I have a few related things that I want to work more on, including the Aristotelian dictum that deliberation is about the possible and the role of epistemic norms in ethics. The latter is, of course, the common denominator of everything I've done so far.

3:AM: And for the readers here at 3:AM, can you recommend five books (other than your own) that will take us further into your philosophical world?

KMV: Well, I'm sure you heard that ancient philosophers, as in philosophers working in ancient today, are a prickly bunch! For any of us to recommend five books, i.e., not to recommend hundreds of other books, could only amount to instant professional suicide. With that in mind, here are five books that, at least in spirit, deeply shaped my views. For anyone who has a couple of decades to spare, Plato's *Philebus* is it; for anyone interested in ancient skepticism: *The Original Skeptics: A Controversy*; Thomas Nagel's *The View from Nowhere*, squarely within the monotheistic paradigm or rather, within the set of premises that are its philosophical counterpart, but a creative masterpiece; Aristotle's *Metaphysics*, like the *Philebus* for those who want to keep busy for

the rest of their lives; and for more lighthearted moments, Bernard Williams'
Moral Luck.

Katja Maria Vogt is the author of:

Law, Reason, and the Cosmic City (Oxford University Press, 2008)
Belief and Truth: A Skeptic Reading of Plato (Oxford University Press, 2012)
Skepsis und Lebenspraxis: Das pyrrhonische Leben ohne Meinungen (Taschenbuch, 2015)

11 | Nicolas Bommarito: "Buddhist Ethics"

Nicolas Bommarito is currently a Bersoff Fellow in the Department of
Philosophy at New York University and an Assistant Professor of Philosophy
at the University at Buffalo. Here he discusses Owen Flanagan's three
styles of working with Buddhist philosophy, whether Buddhism has
religious content, its relationship with applied ethics, the metaphysics and
epistemology of Buddhism, comparative links with Western philosophy,
whether the Bodhisattva is a virtue ethics, Logong, patience as a moral virtue,
why anger toward those who hurt us is never justified, modesty as a virtue of
attention, private solidarity, and his status as an anti-expert.

3:AM: What made you become a philosopher?

NICOLAS BOMMARITO: It's hard to say because it wasn't until I was
nearly 20 that I learned philosophy was something you could study. I was
raised Catholic and around 13 or 14 I decided that it wasn't for me. At that
time I was sort of operating on the assumption that there was some religion for
me, so I started reading around about other religions. As a result I read, among
other things, Śāntideva's *Way of the Bodhisattva* and *The Questions of King
Millinda*. This was the first I thought critically about how to live or what reality was like, but that was long before I ever even heard of Plato or Aristotle.

When I started at the University of Michigan I was a computer science
major, but after a few long nights searching hundreds of lines of code for a
misplaced semicolon I gave up on that. I was able to take Tibetan language
courses and was taking a lot of courses on Buddhism; Andy Quintman and
Ben Bogin ran a study aboard program in Tibet and that really got me hooked
on studying Tibetan language. Off we go again . . .

I got into philosophy after I took a few classes by Louis Loeb, Rachana
Kamtekar, and Stephen Darwall (The first book on virtue that I ever read was a
wonderful anthology he edited; I alluded in a conversation that couldn't afford

to buy it and he immediately offered to loan me a copy!). I think part of what pulled me into philosophy was that you could read a text and say something like, "That seems wrong because . . .," which seemed to be a taboo in my Asian Studies courses.

I was also really lucky to land a job as a student librarian in the Tanner Philosopher Library—that was wonderful because I got to have a key to the library so I could stay there reading very late. I got in the habit of skimming the books as I reshelved them, so I got a good sense of what people were reading. Plus I got to talk to lots of really smart graduate students all the time!

3:AM: You're interested in Buddhist philosophy. Owen Flanagan has three different styles working across the border of western and Buddhist philosophy: a comparative approach; a fusion approach (where we try a unify them) and a cosmopolitan one (where we are ironically poised to accept whichever comes through as best). Do any of these help capture your own perspective on what you're about?

NB: Of the options, I suppose I'm closest to the cosmopolitan approach (though I'm not sure I'd describe myself as "ironically" positioned). I see my interaction with Buddhist philosophy in the same way I think of my interaction with people I know. When I meet a philosopher that I respect, I'm not interested in just comparing our ideas and I'm not really out to develop some fusion of our views. I'm going to listen to them and think about what they say. I won't accept everything they argue, but they'll likely show me things I've not really worked out or things I didn't see before. I relate to Buddhist philosophy in the same way.

3:AM: You've written about Tibetan philosophy. Although Plato has Apollo and Descartes God its kind of easy to be philosophically interested in their work without any theological or mythical commitments. Is it the same with the religious content of Buddhism? It seems to be more tightly wrapped to religion.

NB: One wrinkle here is that it's often hard to tell what counts as "religious content"—You suggested Apollo for Plato, but does his belief in The Forms count as religious? How about his belief in reincarnation or the immortality of the soul? Lots of Buddhists so dislike the idea of theological or mythical commitments that they don't even like to call Buddhism a religion at all.

As with Plato, whether or not the interesting stuff is separable from the religious content depends a lot on what gets included in the religious content and what you find interesting. Some people think the Myth of Er is just a silly story tacked on the end of the Republic, but other people think it's really important. This is particularly pressing when it comes to Buddhism since it has been received in a lot of different cultures; people in Tibet, Japan, Korea, China, Europe, America all had to import it and all face this challenge of figuring out what the important parts are. One of the main tasks people interpreting Buddhism face is determining what's the product and what's the wrapping. So for example, some people will think the practice of reciting mantras is critical to Buddhism, while other people will think it's not.

I'm not in the business of arbitrating what "real" Buddhism is, but as someone who isn't particularly fond of theological or mythical commitments, I can say I've had a much easier time with many Buddhist texts than I have with people like Plato or Descartes.

3:AM: Is it fair to say that the philosopher of Buddhism is working in the field of applied ethics rather than metaphysics or epistemology or are there metaphysical and epistemological commitments that you have to have to get to the ethics?

NB: One of the reasons that Buddhist philosophy is interesting is there is so much to work on—so you can find things relevant for ethics (not just applied, but normative theory and metaethics too), metaphysics, and epistemology.

There's a boring way in which everybody relies, at least implicitly, on metaphysical and epistemological views. Saying, "Don't shop there because they mistreat their workers" makes assumptions about actions, persons, causation, and how you might know about those things.

Less boring is when there are interesting connections between theory of what there is and how we know and how we should live. In general, for Buddhists there is a strong connection. This is partly because many Buddhist thinkers share the assumption that living well involves seeing things as they really are and that the way to reduce suffering is to get rid of mistaken ways of experiencing the world.

When you get down to particulars, however, I think the answer is the same as in Western philosophy: It ends up being different for different thinkers and different texts. So there definitely are metaphysical and epistemic commitments, but how much of the ethics one can accept without relying on varies a lot. For example, many people read Śāntideva (a famous 8th century Indian Buddhist) as arguing that a kind of altruistism follows from metaphysical truths about emptiness. But other figures like Dōgen (a famous 13th century Japanese Buddhist) seem to see emptiness as superseding ethics.

3:AM: What are the salient features of this metaphysics and epistemology?

NB: Well one is the idea of karma. This literally means action, but generally refers to the idea that our actions produce effects. So saying that something is your karma is really saying, "It's your doing!" Of course, there's debate about how to interpret the idea—whether we should think of it naturalistically, as the same cause and effect of science, or as being supernatural aspects like past and future rebirths.

Another important one is the idea of emptiness. To say that something is empty is to say it is empty of a particular kind of essence. To say that all things are empty is to say that nothing has a static and persisting essence. The classic example is that of a chariot—when we examine a chariot we find various parts, wheels, axel, reins, etc. To say that a chariot is empty is to say there's nothing to it beyond those parts, there's no extra chariot-ness to be found. A common metaphysical claim in Buddhism is that all phenomena are like this. When applied to people this is called non-self. When Buddhist say that there is no self what they mean is that, like the chariot, there is no you-ness beyond the parts that make you up.

On the epistemology side, there's discussion about what the sources of knowledge are. These are categories like: perception, inference, analogy, and testimony (among others). There's debate about which ones are reliable and when, which ones reduce to other types and why. Of course, these issues are not unique to Buddhism; there's lots of discussion of these concepts by non-Buddhist philosophers in India too.

3:AM: Are there comparative links with anything in western philosophy?

NB: In terms of taking metaphysics and epistemology to be important for ethics there are a lot. So Spinoza's *Ethics*, for example, spends a lot of time on metaphysical issues before getting to the ethics. Or think of all the ethical conclusions that Kant derives from metaphysical ideas about our freedom. Or think of the all the people Aristotle inspired to base ethical conclusions on ideas about a thing's natural function. The general aim of trying to get ethical stuff out of metaphysical theory seems to happen in both places.

I suppose consequentialists in general share a view of the importance of the effects of our actions. People have found Derek Parfit's view in *Reasons and Persons* similar to Buddhist ideas of non-self.

3:AM: What is the Bodhisattva? Is it a kind of virtue ethics?

NB: A Bodhisattva is a kind of ideal being in Buddhism. It initially referred to the historical Buddha in his previous lives. There is a collection of stories called the Jātaka Tales that describes these lives. They commonly involve the Buddha as a king or some kind of animal and he makes these huge sacrifices to help others. Later, the term comes to refer to someone who purposely forgoes their own enlightenment in order to help others. So rather than escape from suffering, the Bodhisattva chooses to remain in the world in order to help others.

So it is a kind of ideal being, but that doesn't mean it must be a kind of virtue ethics. Lots of theories can describe ideal beings and are not thereby a type of virtue ethics—So Utilitarians can describe an ideal utility maximizer or Kantians can describe an ideal person who never takes inclination as a reason for action.

It's an extra interpretive step to claim that all other ethical notions are derived from the concept of the Bodhisattva. In a lot of cases, that's going to be tough work—one would have to argue that suffering is bad because the Bodhisattva wants to eliminate it. That seems rough going to me.

I'm with Jay Garfield in that I don't find the project of trying to fit so-called "Buddhist ethics" into one of our theoretical categories to be very interesting. Partly because I'm skeptical that there is one theoretical view that is Buddhist ethics; it seems implausible that a tradition spanning thousands of years and multiple cultures will have a single ethical theory. It's also partly because I'm not sure what they payoff of such a project is; I'm less interested in making a case that a particular philosopher or tradition is virtue ethical or consequentist than I am in what new ideas I can learn from them.

So for me, the more exciting projects in Buddhist ethics are those that take Buddhist thinkers on their own terms and try to build on what's useful in them. Some that come to mind are Jay's work on the role of experience in ethics, work by Bronwyn Finnigan on the role of fear and how we should think of spontaneous action, and work by Emily McRae on the place of emotions like anger in ethics.

3:AM: And what is Lojong and what is of philosophical interest in it?

NB: Lojong literally means "mind training" and it's a collection of techniques to cultivate mental, emotional, and behavioral changes. Here's a version of one such technique called Exchanging Self and Other: First you imagine yourself from the point of view of someone beneath you in some respect (could be wealth, professional respect, or even moral development) and let feelings of jealousy and envy towards yourself arise. You think to yourself, "Ugh! They are doing so well and I really suck!" You examine those feelings and observe what they're like. Next you do the same with a rival who is equal to yourself in this respect. You imagine yourself from their point of view and observe your feelings of competitiveness and insecurity. Finally, you take up the point of view of someone above you and let yourself see your accomplishments, skills, and successes as small and trivial.

Of course, this is just one example and this particular practice won't be what everyone needs. This one is supposed to be an antidote to a variety of negative mental habits. So it's supposed to combat things like the tendency to see our own position and qualities as absolute and fixed. It's aimed at breaking the habit of thinking of our own success and skills as fixed and intrinsic qualities of who we are. By getting used to the fluid and perspectival nature of these feelings, this technique can help rob pride, jealousy, and resentment of their power and make us more sympathetic to others.

I think the philosophical interest in Lojong is in ideas about how moral development works. A lot of philosophers in the West take after Aristotle and think of moral development on the model of developing a skill. It's almost taken to be a truism that the way to develop a virtue is by doing the actions associated with the virtue. You get to be a generous person by doing generous actions, a just person by doing just actions, and so on. I think Lojong puts pressure on this; it is a collection of techniques for developing morally important traits like compassion, selflessness, and kindness that doesn't involve doing any of those actions. I think it offers a well-developed picture of how we can also cultivate virtue via imaginative practices that should be more central in how philosophers think about moral development in general.

3:AM: You've offered a Buddhist-inspired account of patience as a moral virtue. What's the argument and what does it add or change to non-Buddhist approaches?

NB: In Buddhist thought, patience is essentially about not getting shaken up by various things in life. This is a bit broader than non-Buddhist notions in that it's not essentially temporal, it's not only about waiting. This, to me at least, is a more natural way to think about things. There is something similar in managing to keep from getting agitated when stuck in a traffic jam and keeping your cool when a co-worker insults you. When you're insulted you're not waiting for anything, but there's a kind of basic relation to the world that you have in both cases.

I start with that notion and give my own explanation of how having that relation to the world can make you a morally better person. In a nutshell, my answer is that if patience is a moral virtue it is about what we value and how we experience that value. At the time, I expressed the idea in terms of perspective; someone who "has perspective" has a sense of scale in that they see the place of particular desires or values in their desires and values as a whole. They also have a sense of themselves in a larger context—their family, the human race, the environment, or whatever.

I think this best captures why not all failures to get angry count as patience. It doesn't make you patient if you don't get angry at the jerk in the meeting because you drained half a bottle of NyQuil right beforehand or because you're distracted thinking about a paper you're revising. I think it also best captures when getting angry doesn't make you impatient. So someone who is angry when stuck in traffic on an ordinary day seems impatient, but someone who is angry when stuck in traffic when driving his pregnant wife to the hospital doesn't. The former lacks perspective in a way that the latter doesn't.

So I think impatience is essentially a way of being out of tune with what is really important. This isn't to say the impatient person doesn't know what's really important, but their emotional experience, particular with regard to anger and annoyance, doesn't bear that out.

3:AM: Why don't you think that anger towards those who hurt us is never justified?

NB: I think it's important to have some way to distinguish anger towards someone who intentionally hurt you and anger towards someone who did you no wrong. There's a difference between an awful parent who is angry at his child, not because of anything the child did, but because he's stressed at work and someone who is angry with a person who has been constantly bullying them. Call that difference one of "justification."

So I'm not willing to say that people who are angry about being racially profiled, harassed, or abused are making a mistake, that their anger doesn't make sense. It's a further question whether or not anger is desirable or useful. So if I'm upset about a past failure, a friend might tell me that being upset isn't desirable or useful; it's making me miserable and I'd be better off not feeling that way. She can tell me this without having to say that my feelings are unjustified, that I didn't really fail or that failures never warrant getting upset. I think something similar is going on with anger. You don't need to think that anger is always unjustified to say that it is often better to avoid it.

3:AM: Is your view that modesty is a virtue of attention rooted in Buddhism? What's the case?

NB: It's not really rooted in anything Buddhist. The idea is that to be modest (in the sense that a morally good person is, not in the sense of dressing a certain way or being a Victorian prude) isn't really about whether you know how good you are. Instead, it's about how you direct your conscious attention and why. Modest people don't pay much attention to their own goodness because they don't care about puffing up their own egos. They experience the world in a certain way that reflects a concern for others. At the heart of immodesty is a kind of self-centeredness; immodest people are self-involved in a way that leads them to over-attend to their own goodness. I think this best explains a variety of features of modesty.

There are some strands in Buddhist thought that might be working in the background. One might be the idea of avidyā. This is often translated into English as "ignorance" and in Buddhist thought is one of the root causes of suffering. But in addition to not knowing something about the world, it can also mean not seeing something about it. So for Buddhists, the kind of ignorance that causes suffering isn't limited to simply having false propositional beliefs, but also includes experiencing the world in a way that misrepresents it or leaves something out. I think having this notion floating around my brain might have helped me to think of modesty in terms of experience rather than just belief.

3:AM: You've also argued in favour of what sounds rather paradoxical: "private solidarity." How is it possible for anyone to support others and show solidarity in private and without producing change? It sounds like a cop-out! But you argue that it is ethically virtuous?

NB: I think the only reason it might seem paradoxical is if you think that solidarity must be shown. I started thinking about solidarity that isn't displayed or performed for others when reading a biography of Simone Weil. When she was only 5 or 6, she learned that French soldiers fighting in WWI didn't have access to sugar and so gave up eating sugar in solidarity with them. The description of the case is kind of bare, but I thought it had some striking features. It's naturally described as solidarity (a few biographers explicitly describe it as such), but one gets the feeling that she didn't have the aim of starting a political movement or raising awareness. I was puzzled by this because I thought it reflected well on her moral character even if she didn't tell anyone and just thought to herself, "Well, if they can't have any sugar, I won't either."

It's important to note that I don't think private solidarity is the only kind of solidarity or that it's necessarily better than public solidarity. In fact, I think cases of purely private solidarity are pretty rare and are often in cases where actually doing something to bring about change isn't an option. It's plausible that as a five year-old child, Simone just wasn't in a position to be able to do much about the situation (and, as her life bears out, once she did have the chance, she did try to bring about change). What makes it virtuous, I think, is that it connects us with others even if they never learn about it and is a way in which our concern for others can manifest.

3:AM: Another rather paradoxical sounding claim you argue for is that it is sometimes rational to self-describe as an anti-expert. How do you argue for your position?

NB: I think that someone can be more rational for taking their own beliefs to be false, particularly in cases where you have good evidence that they are false but can't change them. Consider two people who just can't shake their belief that aliens abduct people and experiment on them. They have the same irrational belief, but they have different beliefs about the truth of this belief. One thinks it's false, he sees it as a sticky bit of wishful thinking from his childhood spent reading too much sci-fi. The other thinks it's true, when he reflects on his belief he takes it to be true. I think the former is more rational than the latter, because at least he responds appropriately to the evidence about the status of his first-order belief in aliens.

The beliefs don't have to be anything wild about aliens either, could be something common like, "If I don't watch the Red Wings play, they'll lose!" Lots of superstitions like this can be hard to shake: I need to use my lucky pen on the exam or I need to wear my lucky t-shirt or I won't do as well in the race tomorrow. I think the rational way to respond to these beliefs is to think that they're false even if you can help but have them.

I think this is true even in cases where you can change your first-order beliefs, but it takes time. So if a geologist suddenly gets some strong evidence that many of her geological beliefs are false, it may take her a while to get rid of her false beliefs. After all, she built a career on them and is very attached to them. But I think what will motivate her to do the doxastic housecleaning is the thought, "but those beliefs are false!"

3:AM: Do you think that Buddhism brings new philosophical ideas to the table that need to be a part of all philosophers' repertoire, or is it always going to be a rather marginal influence in the academy?

NB: I do think Buddhism offers analytic philosophers interesting concepts and new ideas. I wouldn't say that they need to be part of all philosophers' repertoire though. I've found it useful and interesting, but other people will find other things useful and interesting. I really do hope that Analytic philosophy will broaden its horizons and include a broader range of topics, figures, and ideas. Buddhism is one direction to expand, but it's certainly not the only one. I'm also happy to meet people expanding in other directions: I learn a lot by talking to people thinking about Feminist philosophy or African philosophy. I think it's a bit like foreign language study: I think it's good for people to learn a foreign language, but I don't think they have to learn the same one that I did.

Of course, I would like Buddhist ideas to become more mainstream and more accessible to non-specialists. I would absolutely love it if in 50 years from now, Analytic philosophers could make references to the ideas of Śāntideva or Buddhaghosa as casually as they can for Plato and Aristotle now.

3:AM: And for the readers here at 3AM, are there five books you could recommend that will take us further into your philosophical world?

NB: *Unprincipled Virtue*—Nomy Arpaly
This is the book that made me want to become a philosopher. It definitely hit me like an atom bomb. I loved how it discussed interesting theoretical issues in a way that was grounded in realistic examples. It's also written in this way that makes hard issues feel easy and clear. It set the ideal for philosophical writing that I've been chasing ever since.

Way of the Bodhisattva—Śāntideva

If I've at all managed to stop being the know-it-all, condescending, asshole that I was in my late teens and early 20s, it's largely because I was fortunate enough to have read this book. Plus, it's one of those texts with so many interesting little bits that you keep coming back to it.

Uneasy Virtue—Julia Driver

When I started thinking about virtue more I was discouraged because I started getting the feeling like you had to build on Aristotle or get out. This book helped me see that there are other options that are really attractive views. And it has these amazing examples that would really throw me—I'd have to keep thinking about them for weeks and weeks.

Discourses—Epictetus

This is the first historical work in Western philosophy I read that seemed relevant to my life. Very few works of philosophy can make me feel better when I'm feeling down, but this one can.

Land of No Buddha—Richard Hayes

I love how Hayes writes about Buddhist philosophy. You can see he's really invested in it, but also not afraid to be critical. It helped me to see that you could write about Buddhist thought in a way that didn't boil down to total and blind acceptance.

II | *Deontological Ethics*

12 | Matthew Kramer: "Law and Ethics"

Matthew Kramer is Professor of Legal and Political Philosophy within
Cambridge University and in his twenty-second year as a Fellow of Churchill
College there. He was elected a Fellow of the British Academy in 2014. Here
he talks about where law and morality meet, about the different varieties of
legal positivism, about rights, about objectivity and the law, about H.L.A.
Hart, about the ethics of capital punishment, about Achan and the purgative
rationale, about why "evil" still has traction, about torture and moral integrity,
about moral realism as a moral doctrine, about freedom, and about moral
responsibility.

3:AM: What made you become a philosopher?

MATTHEW KRAMER: I've been fascinated by philosophical issues since
my early boyhood. I remember that, at the age of 7, I initiated a conversation with my mother about the nature of time. She had studied Philosophy
as an undergraduate, and she supplied me with a few of the books that she
had retained (anthologies of extracts from philosophers over the centuries).
I first became familiar with legal philosophy at the age of 11, when I read
some excerpts from H.L.A. Hart in an anthology lent to me by my oldest
brother. Around that same time, I also became familiar with moral philosophy
through some of Bernard Williams' writings. Not too long thereafter, I became
interested in Stoicism; I've retained that interest, which has indeed shaped my
highly regimented lifestyle as well as my intellectual orientation. I continued
to read philosophical works intermittently during the years leading up to my
undergraduate studies. Hence, the decision to major in Philosophy was pretty
straightforward — though I did also major in Government (Political Theory)
and History (Intellectual History), and I naturally took courses in quite a few
other subjects as well. Similarly straightforward was my resolve to carry
on with philosophical work at the postgraduate and professional levels. I've

always felt most comfortable in thinking at high levels of abstraction, and I'm grateful to be able to engage in such thinking as my livelihood!

3:AM: You're interested in both law and ethics, in fact you write that they do meet. However, your overall position is as a legal positivist isn't it? I always thought that that was a position that kept the two apart and this was the main difference between positivists and natural law thinkers. And within the positivist camp don't Raz and Shapiro disagree with your position? So perhaps you could begin by outlining what your position is?

MK: Legal positivists are often said to insist on the separability of law and morality (or to deny necessary connections between law and morality). Although that common characterization is not incorrect, it is seriously misleading in more than one way. First, any legal positivist would accept that there are numerous necessary connections between law and morality; most of those connections are trivial, but some are of more significance. They are all consistent with the proposition that law is not an inherently moral phenomenon. Second, the proposition just stated is itself not indicative of a single point of contention between legal positivists and their natural-law opponents. Natural-law philosophers have affirmed a multiplicity of necessary connections that are supposed to establish the inherently moral character of law, and legal positivists have sought to controvert those connections; the ensuing debates are largely distinct from one another. Third, not everybody who is predominantly a legal positivist is invariably on the positivist side in those debates, and not everybody who is predominantly a natural-law theorist is invariably on the natural-law side. (I myself am on the legal-positivist side in every one, or virtually every one, of those debates.)

Legal positivism is a species with many varieties. I can't discuss most of them here, but the division to which you have adverted is between Inclusive Legal Positivism and Exclusive Legal Positivism. Along with quite a few other positivists (such as Wil Waluchow and Jules Coleman and Ken Himma), I belong to the former camp; Joseph Raz and Scott Shapiro are among the positivists in the latter camp. Debates between Inclusivists and Exclusivists are themselves multifarious, but they usually center on either or both of the following propositions: (1) It can be the case, though it need not be the case, that a norm's consistency with some or all of the requirements of morality is a necessary condition for the norm's status as a law in any particular jurisdiction. (2) It can be the case, though it need not be the case, that a norm's correctness as a moral principle is a sufficient condition for its status as a legal norm in any particular jurisdiction. Most Inclusivists affirm both of these propositions, and most Exclusivists deny both of them — though, again, I'm here glossing over a lot of complexities and cross-cutting allegiances.

3:AM: So what are the affinities between morality and law even though they are strictly separable?

MK: As I've remarked, there are many such affinities. Perhaps the most obvious, and also one of the most important, is the shared deontic vocabulary. Both in regard to law and in regard to morality, we speak of duties and rights and obligations and liberties and authority and so forth. Another obvious necessary connection is that individual laws and whole legal systems are always properly susceptible to moral assessment. There are also subtler affinities, however. For example, in my writings on the nature of legal rights, I've argued that the delimitation of the class of potential right-holders — that is, the delimitation of the class of beings who can hold legal rights at all — is partly and inherently an ethical matter. Given as much, we can't provide a full account of the deontic relations in any system of legal governance without drawing on substantive ethical considerations.

Of course, if the scope of your question here is broadened to encompass contingent connections as well as necessary connections, every legal positivist would accept that the links between law and morality are — and should be — multitudinous. Hart emphasized this point in his famous discussion of legal positivism in the ninth chapter of *The Concept of Law*.

3:AM: Do you think of your position as an extension of legal positivism and what if any are important new implications of your position?

MK: On matters relating to the general connections and disconnections between law and morality, my position is pretty close to Hart's. One respect in which I go beyond Hart (especially in my 2007 book *Objectivity and the Rule of Law* but also to some degree in my 2004 book *Where Law and Morality Meet*) is that I conjoin legal positivism with a wide-ranging account of the nature of legal objectivity. Another respect in which I go beyond him is that I more carefully differentiate among aspects or dimensions of morality that are at issue when philosophers debate the separability of law and morality. Similarly, in the final chapter of my 1999 book *In Defense of Legal Positivism* I ponder at length the implications of legal positivism for the matter of political obligation (i.e., the matter of the moral obligation to obey the law), whereas Hart's own reflections on that issue are far sketchier. Moreover, although Hart was an Inclusive Legal Positivist avant la lettre, he largely finished his career before the Inclusivism/Exclusivism controversies gained momentum; consequently, he never ruminated sustainedly on the points of contention that have divided Inclusivists and Exclusivists. In *In Defense of Legal Positivism* and in some of my other books I have also criticized Hart on a number of additional points, but overall I immensely admire his contribution to the philosophy of law, and I regard my work on legal positivism as an extension of his work.

On other philosophical questions, I'm more often in disagreement with Hart than in agreement with him. For example, his account of the conditions necessary and sufficient for the holding of legal rights is directly opposed to my account. Likewise, I am a moral realist — and I take moral realism to be a moral doctrine — whereas Hart's own position on the nature of morality was rather nebulous. Similarly, although I warmly applaud Hart for his continuation of the liberal tradition of John Stuart Mill, his allegiance to utilitarianism (albeit an allegiance tempered with some substantial doses of Kantianism) is something that I decidedly do not share. And so on. Greatly though I esteem Hart, my alignment with him on philosophical issues is largely limited to the merits and implications of legal positivism.

3:AM: Capital punishment is a live debate at the moment throughout the UK and USA. You've examined the arguments for and against it and conclude that most arguments justifying it fail. However there is a position that you think justifies a tiny range of cases being punished by capital punishment. Before getting to that can you sketch for us what a good argument for capital punishment has to do to succeed? Is William Edmundson right to say that it has to deal with both justification of punishment in general and the place of death in any such theory?

MK: In my 2011 book *The Ethics of Capital Punishment*, I do indeed argue that all the standard rationales for capital punishment — deterrence-oriented, retributivist, incapacitative, and denunciatory — fail to establish that such punishment is morally legitimate. Each of those standard rationales is the application of a general theory of punishment to the death penalty. To succeed as a justification of that penalty, a rationale has to establish that the execution of a convict is both morally obligatory and morally permissible. Since none of the standard rationales does establish the moral obligatoriness and moral permissibility of the death penalty (either when each of those rationales is considered discretely or when they are considered in combination), none of them can properly serve as a basis for the imposition of that penalty.

My own rationale for capital punishment in a very limited range of cases, the purgative rationale, is not an offshoot of a general theory of punishment. Hence, I reject William Edmundson's claim. Like quite a few other philosophers of punishment, I'm a pluralist. In my 2011 book I've argued that there is no single theory that will justify all the sanctions which a system of criminal justice is morally obligated and morally permitted to impose. In particular, there is no general theory of punishment that will also justify the use of the death penalty. The purgative rationale is a free-standing justification derivable not from any general theory of punishment but from an account — broadly Stoical in its inspiration — of the conditions for warranted self-respect.

3:AM: And do you think that the most common arguments for capital punishment fail because they're associated with a wide-ranging theory addressing all types of crimes rather than a particular and limited range of wrongdoing?

MK: Yes, as a pluralist about punishment, I've contended that the considerations sufficient to justify the imposition of most other criminal sanctions are insufficient to justify the use of capital punishment. I've never committed myself to any wide-ranging theory of punishment, but my discussions of such theories make clear that I am far more sympathetic toward retributivism than toward any of its consequentialist rivals. Nonetheless, retributivism fails to vindicate any use of the death penalty. Of course, many contemporary retributivists view that apparent failure as a strength of their doctrine, because they are opposed in principle to capital punishment. However, if one believes (as I do) that capital punishment is in principle morally legitimate in certain cases of extreme evil, one will conclude that retributivism falls short of being a comprehensive justification of punishment.

3:AM: What is the purgative rationale for capital punishment? Why is the execution of Achan a good illustration of what you are driving at?

MK: The purgative rationale is a complex deontological justification that is applicable only in cases of extravagant evil. It maintains that, in some such cases, the sustainment of an evildoer's life (even through lifelong imprisonment) is at odds with the conditions for the warrantedness of a sense of self-respect on the part of every member of humankind. My 2011 book begins its discussion of the purgative rationale with the story of Achan that is recounted in chapter 7 of the Book of Joshua. Achan appropriated for himself some of the booty that had been seized by the Israelites at Jericho. When his misappropriation became evident, God enjoined the Israelites to purge their community of the taint with which they had been defiled through the presence of the wrongdoer. God instructed them to execute Achan, and they complied. Now, although this story is grotesque (like so many of the other narratives in the Book of Joshua), it is serviceable for my purposes in one key respect. That is, it presents vividly the idea that the continued presence of an evildoer within a community can defile the community even if there was no collective responsibility for the original crimes. That idea is not unique to the Bible, of course. It is also present in Greek mythology — prominently so in the story of Oedipus, for example. Nonetheless, various books in the Hebrew Scriptures chiefly helped to give form to my inchoate sense of the purgative rationale for capital punishment. (As I say in the preface to my 2011 book, that inchoate sense arose when I was 8 years old. At that age, I learned about the Holocaust and about the judgments at Nuremberg that followed the Second World War.)

Now, my invocation of the Bible (and perhaps also my invocation of Greek mythology) will immediately set off alarms in the minds of some philosophers. I should therefore remark that I have been robustly atheistic since the age of 8. On the one hand, I read the Bible every day for 60-90 minutes, and I have been working on a Biblical commentary as my principal avocation for nearly 32 years. On the other hand, my preoccupation with the Bible is purely intellectual and philosophical and literary rather than devotional. I became interested and remain interested in the Bible primarily because of its vast influence on Western culture, but over the years it has also been quite stimulating as a source of philosophical ideas (albeit no more so than Shakespeare's plays, every one of which I read annually). Because I am unremittingly atheistic, I thoroughly secularize any ideas that I draw from the Bible — as I have secularized the purgative rationale.

3:AM: Why do you think the purgative rationale "does not succumb to the moral vices or the empirical snarls that undermine the standard justifications for the death penalty"?

MK: Because the purgative rationale for the death penalty is strictly deontological (though non-Kantian), it is not dependent on empirical contingencies like those on which the deterrence-oriented and denunciatory rationales are dependent. It therefore does not become bogged down in the futility of the myriads of conflicting empirical studies through which social scientists have sought to ascertain the presence or absence of those contingencies. The wording which you've quoted from my book is slightly too strong, however. Although the in-principle pertinence of the purgative rationale is not dependent on empirical contingencies, its legitimacy in practice — that is, the morality of its implementation — is subject to such contingencies. In the lengthy final chapter of my 2011 book, I discuss the problems that afflict the implementation of the death penalty, and I leave open the possibility that the imposition of such a penalty will never be permissible in practice notwithstanding its legitimacy in principle. (Indeed, that book closes with a call for a moratorium on capital punishment.)

The phrase "moral vices" in the quoted wording refers to several things. First, in some circumstances, most of the standard rationales for capital punishment call also for the infliction of supplementary sanctions such as prolonged torture. Second, some of the standard rationales deem the execution of innocent people to be morally permissible and morally obligatory in certain credibly possible contexts. Third, most of the standard rationales contravene the principle that a necessary condition for the permissibility of any governmental measure M is that M be the least invasive feasible means of attaining the legitimate end in pursuit of which M is undertaken. Fourth, some of the standard rationales favor the organizing of executions as public spectacles with especially brutal methods of putting capital prisoners to death. Those and several other moral failings in the standard rationales are all avoided by the purgative rationale.

3:AM: Does this position depend on the idea of "evil" having traction? I'm thinking that in modern times it is a concept that doesn't command universal acceptance is it?

MK: The notion of evil is indeed discountenanced by a number of contemporary philosophers, and even more widely discountenanced is the notion of defilement. Given that I marshal both of those concepts in my elaboration of the purgative rationale, I've had to do a lot of work to explicate them in philosophically respectable ways. Having said as much, I should immediately add that I benefited from many illuminating accounts of evil that have been propounded by philosophers over the past few decades. My own account is quite different from any of those, but I've profited considerably from engaging with them. (By contrast, I discovered very little good philosophical work on defilement in recent decades. I do mention a few writings in my discussion of the matter, but for the most part I had to find my own way.)

Clearly, the main challenge has been to secularize ideas that were originally developed in religious contexts. I think that I have succeeded in doing as much. There is certainly nothing mysterious or eerie or numinous in the concept of evil as I expound it. My account of evil in a nutshell is as follows: Evil conduct is underlain by sadistic malice or heartlessness or extreme recklessness that is connected to severe harm in the absence of any significant extenuating circumstances. Of course, I've had to flesh out that bare-bones statement greatly in my 2011 book, but my point here is simply to indicate that the property of evil as I expound it is a secular moral property rather than anything that smacks of the supernatural.

As for the notion of defilement, the key to it in the Hebrew Scriptures and in Greek mythology is that a community transgresses against God or the gods by harboring (perhaps unwittingly) an evildoer in its midst. To secularize that notion, I have refocused it on the relationship between any community and humankind, specifically in connection with the sustainment of the conditions necessary for the warrantedness of everyone's sense of self-respect. The idea in a nutshell is that some crimes are of such extreme turpitude that the continuation of the life of the perpetrator of those crimes — a life whose ethical tenor is thoroughly dominated by the iniquity of those crimes — is inconsistent with the aforementioned conditions. I've devoted many pages to expanding on that skeletal idea, but its independence from any religious doctrines should be apparent even from this one-sentence encapsulation.

3:AM: If capital punishment is a central contemporary issue so is the use of torture. Why do you argue that torture is always wrong?

MK: There is no single answer to that question, because there are many different types of torture, and the explanation of the wrongness of torture is not uniform across those types. (When I refer to the sundry types of torture, I am not differentiating among them on the basis of the techniques employed; rather, I am differentiating among them with regard to the chief purposes for which torture is undertaken.) Let me say a bit here about the most frequently discussed type, interrogational torture. My 2014 book *Torture and Moral Integrity* maintains that such torture is always and everywhere morally wrong. The gravity of the wrong varies, but the wrongness itself does not. Hence, it should be apparent that that book is as robustly deontological as any of my previous volumes. ("Robustly deontological" is definitely not equivalent to "robustly Kantian." My book on torture contains numerous objections to Kantianism as well as to consequentialism.)

Interrogational torture involves the deliberate infliction of severe pain for the purpose of extracting information from someone (either from the person on whom the pain is directly inflicted or from someone who is likely to care deeply about that person). The deliberate infliction of severe pain for that purpose is always morally wrong because of the overweeningness of the control exerted both through the infliction itself and through the aim which it is undertaken to achieve. The overweeningness of the control exerted by the infliction itself has been brought out especially incisively in recent years by David Sussman, and the overweeningness of the aim pursued has been brought out especially incisively in recent years by David Luban. Hence, I draw upon their writings as well as those of many other philosophers in my ruminations on torture.

3:AM: Given that you think capital punishment is justified in rare cases why doesn't an analogy to the purgative rationale justify torture in rare cases? If a consequence of torture is to prevent an act of mass killing of innocents that would trigger your purgative rationale for a death sentence then wouldn't that situation elude moral vice?

MK: At some length in my book on capital punishment and at considerably greater length in my book on torture, I highlight the main differences between various types of torture (including punitive torture) and deliberate killing — in order to explain why each of those types of torture is always morally wrong whereas deliberate killing is sometimes morally permissible. Punitive torture is always morally wrong because, in light of the availability of alternative sanctions (including the death penalty), its infliction of severe pain serves as a means of attaining vengeance. By contrast, the purgative rationale is wholly dissociated from any quest for vengeance. The only rationale for capital punishment that presents it as a means of vengeance is the denunciatory rationale. (Some retributivists over the centuries have associated their doctrine with a quest for revenge, but most contemporary retributivists differentiate sharply between retribution and revenge.)

If the contrast is instead between capital punishment and interrogational torture (or several other types of torture that are relevantly similar), the key differences bear on the overweeningness which I mentioned above. Because the infliction of pain is strictly incidental if it occurs at all in a purgative execution, capital punishment is not overweeningly controlling in the first respect identified above. Similarly, because capital punishment is not aimed at gaining fine-grained control over someone's behavior, it is not overweening in the second respect identified above. Its effects are more wide-ranging than the effects of most non-lethal techniques of torture, but the agony-exploiting and minutely controlling properties of interrogational torture are absent from a purgative execution.

Why is the overweening controllingness of interrogational torture so important? The answer to that question is signaled in the title of my 2014 book, for I understand moral integrity as conformity to a deontological ethic of self-restraint. Although my elaboration of that ethic has been inspired partly by Stoicism, it is not tied to any Stoical doctrines. Some of Rawls's remarks on self-respect are also a source of inspiration for my pondering on the matter — since the notion of self-restraint is integrally connected to that of warranted self-respect. I expound that connection in my books on capital punishment and torture, but I develop it in much more detail in the book on which I'm currently working, *Liberalism with Excellence*.

Your second sentence here also asks why torture would be wrong if it serves to avert a calamity. I naturally discuss calamity-averting torture, especially calamity-averting interrogational torture, at many junctures in my 2014 book. On the one hand, the ticking-bomb scenarios peddled by proponents of interrogational torture — scenarios in which hundreds or thousands or millions of deaths are averted through the use of such torture — are generally fanciful. On the other hand, far more realistic is a situation in which the use of torture can avert a single death or some other small-scale calamity. Such situations are very rare, but they are not fanciful. Why would interrogational torture be morally wrong even in such a situation? The short answer to this question is that all the wrong-making properties of interrogational torture are present when it averts a calamity as well as in any other context. Its calamity-averting role affects the gravity of its wrongness but not the wrongness itself. Hence, although the recourse of somebody to interrogational torture in one of these extremely rare situations might conceivably be the less grave of two very serious wrongs between which he or she has to decide, it is still a wrong. At the end of my answer to your next question below, I briefly touch upon one of the implications of this point.

3:AM: Your approach across these issues is to mix abstract with concrete argumentation. Can you say something about this and why you think this the best way to approach these philosophical issues?

MK: Yes, this pattern was especially evident in my book on torture. Chapters 1 and 4 deal with very abstract and somewhat technical issues relating to moral conflicts and the nature and sustainability of deontology, whereas the other chapters deal with more concrete matters pertaining to the specificities of torture. Although positions on the abstract issues do not logically entail positions on the more concrete questions, the links between them are quite strong. I expand on this point by contrasting my account of torture with the account propounded by Michael Moore, who was generally supportive of the Bush Administration's interrogational practices. My marked differences with Moore over that matter are closely related to the differences between us concerning the importance of moral conflicts and the rationality of deontological absolutism. Connections between the highly abstract levels and the more concrete levels ramify all the way down into the details of the appropriate legal responses to the perpetration of torture. Whereas Moore's doubts about the frequency of moral conflicts and about the rationality of deontological absolutism lead very smoothly to his opposing the imposition of legal sanctions for instances of interrogational torture that avert calamities, my affirmation of the frequency of moral conflicts and my defense of the rationality of deontological absolutism lead very smoothly to my insistence on the moral obligatoriness of legal sanctions for all instances of interrogational torture perpetrated by public officials.

3:AM: You defend a moral realist position that claims that ethics is both objective and that that objectivity is itself an ethical matter don't you? Can you sketch out this idea and also say whether your approach to law and morality depends on whether you are or are not taking this view that objectivity is itself ethical?

MK: Yes, my 2009 book *Moral Realism as a Moral Doctrine* argues that morality is strongly objective in several different ways, and that the objectivity of morality in each of those dimensions is a moral matter. More specifically, the book underscores the mind-independence of all basic moral principles and of many derivative moral principles; it contends that there are determinately correct answers to a vast array of moral questions; it affirms the categorical prescriptiveness of moral principles and the other ways in which such principles are uniformly applicable; it highlights the invariance of morality in major respects, while also readily acknowledging the variability of morality in other respects; it accounts for the knowability of moral principles and for the transindividuality of our epistemic access to them; it expounds the ways in which moral deliberations can be impartial and thus truth-conducive; and it maintains that any number of moral assertions are truth-apt and that some of them are true. In so arguing, the book addresses the semantics and metaphysics and epistemology of morality, but it comes to grips with all such issues as substantive moral matters.

The closing portion of your question here is not easily answerable. On the one hand, I'm inclined to say that my espousal of moral realism as a moral doctrine is independent of my espousal of legal positivism, because the former position aligns me quite closely with Dworkin whereas the latter position aligns me quite closely with Hart. On the other hand, there are certain points in my defenses of Inclusive Legal Positivism against Exclusivism where I rely on claims about the observational mind-independence of morality. Moreover, I'm doubtful that a thoroughgoing moral nihilist could meaningfully come to grips with most of the questions addressed by legal positivists and their natural-law opponents (save through radically revisionary understandings of those questions). Thus, although one's stance on questions about the objectivity of morality severely underdetermines one's stance on questions about the relationship between law and morality, there are some connections.

3:AM: There's been quite a lot of discussion about whether people have freewill and whether responsibility is conditional on us having it. Pat Churchland and others have pointed out that long before freewill and autonomy were an issue responsibility (and punishment) were well established. So do you think freewill is important for your theories about punishment, responsibility and morality to work or could you retain your views without any freewill foundations? And does this connect with more general considerations of freedom?

MK: Although my longest book (*The Quality of Freedom*) is on political and social freedom, I explicitly prescind there from questions about metaphysical freedom. I say more about those latter questions in *Moral Realism as a Moral Doctrine* and in *The Ethics of Capital Punishment*. I'm a compatibilist, and — naturally — I'm a compatibilist for moral reasons. On the one hand, like most compatibilists, I readily accept that an individual's freedom of will can be vitiated by factors such as coercion, fraud, severe inebriation, and hallucinations or mental illness. On the other hand, the sheer fact that a person's willing is itself causally determined does not deprive the person of responsibility for her decisions and actions, whether they be creditable or discreditable. Thus, insofar as the property of freedom of the will is understood to consist in the will's not being causally determined, that chimerical property is not a necessary condition for moral responsibility. If freedom of the will is instead understood (as I understand it) to consist in the absence of the vitiating factors mentioned here and any other vitiating factors, then it is indeed a necessary condition for full moral responsibility. (Of course, the presence of some vitiating factor does not necessarily negate moral responsibility altogether. In many contexts, various factors attenuate — rather than eliminate — moral responsibility.)

The connection between moral responsibility and freedom of the will in the latter sense just outlined is presupposed by most social practices of blaming and praising and by most legal practices of punishment. However, it should not be regarded as merely a presupposition of those practices. Rather, it is also an objective moral fact by reference to which the appropriateness of those practices in their broad contours is to be gauged. (As the phrase "in their broad contours" suggests, I am obviously not suggesting that any actual practices in all their details are derivable from the abstract concepts of moral responsibility and freedom of the will. Those concepts are vague in the technical sense as well as in an ordinary sense, and many of the details of their cashing out can legitimately vary across societies. Moreover, as is apparent, many actual practices of blaming and praising and punishing are morally dubious to greater or lesser degrees. Even if they conform to the general connection between moral responsibility and freedom of the will, they can of course go badly astray in their specifics.)

3:AM: And finally, for the readers here at 3:AM, are there five books you could recommend that will take us further into your philosophical world?

MK: As I've already suggested, two of the books that would take people further into my philosophical outlook are the Bible — Hebrew Scriptures, *New Testament*, and *Apocrypha* — and the *Complete Works of Shakespeare*. (Let me emphasize again that my study of the Bible has nothing to do with any sentiments of religiosity.) However, I shan't include those volumes here. Nor will I include anything by anyone who is currently alive. Here, then, are five books that have heavily influenced my thinking:

> H.L.A. Hart, *The Concept of Law*
> Wesley Hohfeld, *Fundamental Legal Conceptions*
> John Rawls, *A Theory of Justice*
> John Stuart Mill, *On Liberty*
> Gregory Kavka, *Hobbesian Moral and Political Theory*

Compiling a list of this sort is extremely difficult. On a different day, I might have included Locke's *Second Treatise of Government* or Hobbes's *Leviathan* or Berlin's *Four Essays on Liberty* or Foot's *Virtues and Vices* or Spinoza's *Ethics* or. . . . Still, each of the five listed books has profoundly shaped my outlook — by provoking me to disagree as well as by eliciting agreement in me, of course!

Matthew Kramer is the author of:

Legal Theory, Political Theory, and Deconstruction (Indiana University Press, 1991)
Critical Legal Theory and the Challenge of Feminism (Rowman & Littlefield, 1995)

Hobbes and the Paradoxes of Political Origins (Macmillan Press, 1997)

John Locke and the Origins of Private Property (Cambridge University Press, 1997)

A Debate over Rights (with N. E. Simmonds and Hillel Steiner) (Oxford University Press, 1998)

In Defense of Legal Positivism (Oxford University Press, 1999)

In the Realm of Legal and Moral Philosophy (Macmillan Press, 1999)

Rights, Wrongs, and Responsibilities (editor and principal contributor) (Macmillan Press, 2001)

The Quality of Freedom (Oxford University Press, 2003)

Where Law and Morality Meet (Oxford University Press, 2004)

Freedom: A Philosophical Anthology (coed., with Ian Carter and Hillel Steiner) (Blackwell, 2007)

Objectivity and the Rule of Law (Cambridge University Press, 2007)

The Legacy of H.L.A. Hart: Legal, Political, and Moral Philosophy (coed., with Claire Grant, Ben Colburn, and Antony Hatzistavrou) (Oxford University Press, 2008)

Hillel Steiner and the Anatomy of Justice (coed., with Stephen de Wijze and Ian Carter) (Routledge, 2009)

Moral Realism as a Moral Doctrine (Blackwell [Wiley-Blackwell], 2009)

Crime, Punishment, and Responsibility (coed., with Rowan Cruft and Mark Reiff) (Oxford University Press, 2011)

The Ethics of Capital Punishment: A Philosophical Investigation of Evil and Its Consequences (Oxford University Press, 2011)

Torture and Moral Integrity: A Philosophical Enquiry (Oxford University Press, 2014)

13 | John Gardner: "Law as a Leap of Faith"

John Gardner is Professor of Jurisprudence at Oxford and a Senior Research Fellow at All Souls College in Oxford. Here he takes the label "legal positivism" mainly to problematize it, thinks deeply about the "chicken and egg" puzzle, finds Dworkin's idea of constructive interpretation bewitching but mistaken, thinks it's misconceived to think judges can only be constrained by rules in their decisions if the rules preexist the decisions, has much to say about the role of customary rules, asks whether there can be a written constitution, defends the Razian thesis that the law makes moral claims and reconciles it with the possibility of immoral laws, writes about law as a leap of faith and connects Kelsen with Kierkegaard, and says rape is wrong as sheer use of person.

3:AM: What made you become a philosopher? And why legal philosophy?

JOHN GARDNER: I started by studying law, which is an undergraduate subject in the UK. I was lucky enough to study law in the intellectually liberal environment of Oxford, where my tutors encouraged wide-ranging critical reflection and took a dim view of rote learning (except as a necessary evil come exam time). I think Nicola Lacey was the person who gave me the initial support I needed to develop serious philosophical interests. As well as teaching me philosophy of law in the most inspiring way, she sent me to Jonathan Glover for moral philosophy tutorials. Jonathan in turn knew just how to deal with the knee-jerk value-scepticism of a 19-year-old know-it-all law student. He tormented me with the nihilistic implications of my views until I couldn't take it any longer. I have been an in-your-face moral realist ever since. One more success for aversion therapy.

At that point I was still pretty sure that I was going to end up practising law. So I took the view that I should study as much philosophy as possible while I still had the time and the access. As a masters' student in the Oxford Law Faculty of the mid-1980s, studying for a degree so highly prized in the English legal profession that nobody would care what I actually learnt, I was lucky enough to be able to develop my philosophical interests and skills in some more advanced philosophy-of-law courses laid on by Joseph Raz, John Finnis, and Ronald Dworkin. I also attended in a more recreational way (I was such a geek) the seminars of Amartya Sen, Jerry Cohen, Derek Parfit, Steven Lukes, David Miller, and many other local philosophical luminaries. The seminars jointly held by Sen, Cohen, Dworkin, and Parfit were known among the students as "Star Wars"—that name helps to capture both the mood of the meetings and the spirit of the age in which they took place.

I was irreversibly contaminated by all of this and when I headed off to London to qualify as a barrister the following year, my heart wasn't in it. I soon contrived to get back to Oxford for a doctoral degree. I was helped in doing this by the fact that I had meanwhile won, as it seemed to me by lottery, a "Prize Fellowship" at All Souls College. This gave me decent funding and fascinating colleagues. The indefatigable Tony Honoré, with whom I still teach to this day, was my college mentor and my thesis supervisor. Later, on Honoré's retirement from official duties, Parfit took over the former role and Raz the latter. My thesis was about moral and legal responsibility. It was all over the place. Bad for my progress with the degree, but good for my philosophical education. My examiners (Bernard Williams and Antony Duff) smiled on the resulting artefact and let me out into the world as a moral and legal philosopher.

It's just occurred to me that maybe you didn't want the story of who I worked with, how I was funded, what I was occupied with before I became a philosopher, and all that David Copperfield kind of crap. Maybe you wanted to hear about the philosophical puzzles that kept me awake at night and the ideas that inspired me. Alas, I forget. I only know that there were a lot of them, and that I had a massively exaggerated sense of how many of them I could tackle and how quickly.

3:AM: You're a legal positivist aren't you? You wrote a famous paper about it—5 1/2 Myths. What's at stake?

JG: For people who like that kind of label, that is the kind of label they like. I help myself to it mainly to problematize it, and to some extent to poke fun at it. "5½ Myths" was a pedagogical exercise. I noticed that my students associated "legal positivism" with all sorts of only very loosely connected propositions. I also saw that articles in the law journals often treated "legal positivism" as an all-purpose bogeyman. I didn't care and still don't care who is a legal positivist and what assortments of things people who are called by that name happen to believe. But I did care, and still care, about the sloppy herding together of a number of only very loosely connected propositions to create an all-purpose bogeyman. So in "5½ Myths" I set about what I later came to call the "unbundling" of the propositions in question. Along the way I endorsed what I identified as the core teaching of the legal positivist tradition and hence what I called, for the purposes of the paper, the "legal positivist thesis" or "LP". This is the thesis that law is made by people. In any legal system, the law of the system is what the relevant people made, never mind whether that is the law they ought to have made.

What is at stake? A lot. "5½ Myths" sets out to show that there are many implications that LP does not have, and many puzzles, therefore, that it does not throw up. But there are of course many other puzzles that it does indeed throw up. Here is one. Once we endorse LP we will need an account of what makes an person a "relevant" one, or, in the terminology favoured by H.L.A. Hart, an account of how one might qualify as a "legal official". One of the great puzzles of legal philosophy, which LP foregrounds, is what Scott Shapiro calls the "chicken and egg" puzzle. Legal officials make law, says LP. But law also makes legal officials. How is it possible for law to make its own makers? Hart had an answer, which I think is broadly right. (Shapiro has a rival one, which I think is broadly wrong.) Hart's key move, in my view, is to recognise that not all law is made by the relevant people's attempts to make it. Often law is made by accident, including by people who are trying only to follow or apply law that they take to exist already. If they are the relevant people they can sometimes change the law by misunderstanding it. From this one can build a picture of how they come to be the relevant people. They become the relevant people by treating each other, mistakenly, as already being the relevant people. It is a collective and accidental form of self-appointment. Hart called the gradually mutating customary norm by which officials recognise each other as officials (and hence become the officials of a system of norms in which they are so recognised) the 'ultimate rule of recognition' of a legal system and he claimed, I think rightly, that every legal system necessarily has at least one of them. (He sometimes said "one and only one", but that was in my view a slip.)

The chicken-and-egg puzzle is just one of many puzzles that are thrown up by LP. Many people interested in the law think such puzzles are mere diversions, like Sudoku. After a recent lecture she gave at Boston College, my former tutor Nicola Lacey nicely raised some very wide-ranging doubts about LP and propositions like it (namely, those which are supposed to be necessarily true of all legal systems). She wondered out loud : "Is it just philosophy? In which case, how do I explain to my students that they should be interested in it, except as a very fascinating intellectual game?" My experience is that if people don't have philosophical interests, there isn't much to be gained by trying to sell philosophy to them as "relevant" to something else that they are interested in. The same is true of history, maths, astronomy, and other intellectual pursuits. Either they grip you or they don't. Nevertheless, as someone who does have philosophical interests, I find that my views about the nature of law have many repercussions in other parts of my work.

To give just two examples. The view that I defend in chapter 5 of my book *Law as a Leap of Faith,* according to which law makes moral claims, is the key to understanding why and how the problem of moral luck comes up in the law. I showed the connection in a paper called "Obligations and Outcomes in the Law of Torts" (2001), And the view I align myself with in "5½ Myths" (chapter 2 of the same book), according to which the legal invocation of moral standards does not turn those standards into legal standards, turns out to be central to understanding the workings of many criminal law defences. I explained how the two are connected in a paper called "Justification under Authority" (2010). People who are not interested in philosophical inquiry into the nature of law may not be very interested in philosophical inquiry into these specific areas of legal doctrine either. But there is no doubt that the general and the specific are closely connected at many points. As I put the point in *Law as a Leap of Faith*, chapter 11: If there is no general jurisprudence, then there is also no special jurisprudence (e.g. philosophy of criminal law or philosophy of private law).

3:AM: Given that you oppose "package deal approaches" to legal philosophy that get to grips with issues by setting up positions in adversarial terms—such as "Hart vs Dworkin" or "Legal positivism vs Natural Law", what alternatives are you ruling out with Legal Positivism?

JG: The main rival view I am ruling out is that, in at least some legal systems, the law is not straightforwardly made by people. On this view, what counts as law can depend, at least in part, on its merits—moral or otherwise.

This rival view has enduring appeal and various aspects of legal life combine to lend credibility to it. The one I will mention here is the prevalence of judicial interpretation, which is often conducted, at least nowadays, on the footing that judges should read a legal text as succeeding in doing the valuable things that it was designed to do (sometimes known as "purposive" interpretation). In Law's Empire, Dworkin brilliantly recasts purposive interpretation as a species of a larger genus that he calls "constructive" interpretation. If a legal text sometimes means what it would be better for it to mean by some standard, argues Dworkin, then it cannot be the case that the content of the law is whatever content the authors of the text gave it. They did not have the power to make law, the content of which is worse than it would be better for it to be by the relevant standard. This is a bewitching idea. But it trades on the mistaken view that interpreting a legal text is finding meaning that it already has at the point at which it is presented for interpretation. In fact, judicial interpretation may give new meaning to a legal text—hence new content to the law—and may do so on moral grounds. When that happens the legal text has whatever new meaning the judges now give it thanks to their new interpretation of it. That they give it that new meaning on moral grounds does not alter the fact that its meaning is the meaning that they now give it, never mind whether that is the meaning they ought to have given it. Which is what LP says.

No package deals in sight here! Plenty of other things that Dworkin says are right. He is absolutely right to commend constructive interpretation if by that he simply means that judges should interpret legal texts with an eye to making the law that they contain morally better than it would be on other interpretations.

3:AM: Is it because Ronald Dworkin doesn't acknowledge that customary laws and case laws are man-made that you disagree with him?

JG: I can't recall what might at first have motivated my disagreements with Dworkin. It is true, however, that part of the original impetus for Dworkin to introduce principles (which he claims to be LP-inconsistent legal norms) into his analysis of the nature of law was to explain features of legal reasoning that I prefer to explain in LP-consistent ways. I have already mentioned customary law so let me say a word about case law. And I have already mentioned Dworkin's 1986 work on interpretation, so let me reach back to his earlier conceptualisation of his position in terms of "legal principles".

Dworkin's original argument has something like the following shape. (1) Judges who are faced with what he called "hard cases" have to find a moral justification for what they already regard as law, and they apply that moral justification to resolve the "hard case". (2) When they do so, they do not reach outside the law. So (3) some law is supplied (its content determined) by the moral justification for it. There are three claims here. I have some quarrels with the first and the third. But the relevant quarrel here is with the second claim.

Why should we think that judges who identify these principles are not reaching outside the law? Dworkin gives several reasons. Some are wildly question-begging (e.g. that if judges were reaching outside the law, that would be bad.) But a reason that law students often find attractive is that judges who reach for these principles almost always talk as if they are only applying the law and not changing it. Judges often say that the "hard case" before them is already covered by the law and calls for no legal innovation. One possible response to that fact: Well, judges would say that, wouldn't they? They have every reason to fib about what they are doing, given that there are so many people like Dworkin who wrongly think that judges' reaching outside the law would be bad. But one need not accuse judges of fibbing in order to understand what is going on in an LP-consistent way. One can point out that legal changes can be made accidentally by judges who reasonably but mistakenly imagine that they are only applying and not changing the law by their decisions. That is why they say they are only applying and not changing the law by their decisions.

3:AM: Do judges rely on rules, or do they just make a decision that is much looser than rule following. Didn't Richard Posner suggest something like this, that the law is more untethered than is supposed? Isn't this how opponents to positivism criticize the position, that if law is just man-made it is arbitrary?

JG: A common view is that judges can only be constrained by rules in their decisions if the rules pre-exist the decisions. This is a misconception. There are (at least) two different ways in which decision-makers can be constrained by rules. First, they can be bound to apply an existing rule in making a given decision. Second, they can be bound to explain or show what the reasons for their decision are in such a way that those reasons are capable of being understood and used as a rule from then on. The first constraint, when it applies, distinguishes judges from legislators. But it often does not apply, either because there is no existing rule or because the judge is not bound by the existing rule. That is when the second constraint comes into its own. It is what distinguishes judges from arbitrators. Arbitrators need not bring their decisions under rules, even under new rules. Judges, however, are bound to do so.

"Arbitrary" is sometimes used as a pejorative term meaning something like "capricious" or "on a whim". But arbitrators are paid to arbitrate, and in that sense to be arbitrary. This does not mean they act on a whim, still less that it is alright for them to do so. Like judges, legislators, and other makers of morally significant decisions, they should make their decision on the strength of adequate reasons. What "arbitrary" means (applied to arbitrators) is simply that the adequate reasons need not be organised into a rule that is capable of being used by future arbitrators to decide further cases. Each case can be arbitrated, as it is sometimes said, "on the facts". Not so in a court of law. A judge in a court of law, to repeat, is bound to organise her reasons for decision into a legal rule. That is what tethers her even when it is up to her to determine what the legal rule in question is going to be.

Dworkin made much of the fact that judges use principles as well as rules. The remarks I just made assume that principles are also rules, albeit possibly more abstract ones or less fully-formed ones or less decisive ones. Actually, I don't really mind whether we speak of principles or rules here. So in a more Dworkinian idiom I would be happy to say: Judges, unlike arbitrators, are constrained by the fact that they must explain or show what legal principle (either existing or created for the purpose by them) underpins their decision.

Do opponents of LP really say that "if law is just man-made it is arbitrary"? I have not encountered that particular criticism. It is clearly fallacious. It confuses the question of what qualifies as law (LP says: only man-made norms) with the question of whether the makers of a particular law or body of law had enough reason to make it. As I have just explained, LP allows one to insist on the highest rational standards for intentional law-makers to follow. All it adds is that, if the law-makers fail to live up to those standards, unfortunately one still ends up with law (to be precise, yet more crappy law).

I have a feeling that I may have been repeating myself a bit, making the same point in several ways. The point is that many people are rightly interested in how judges set about making law, which is often by argument about the merits of the law they are making. But it is also possible to be interested in why what judges make counts as law. The LP-compliant answer is that it counts as law in virtue of its having been made by the right kind of person, and irrespective not only of its merits as law but also of the merits of any argument that went into making it.

Have I made that point that in enough different ways now?

3:AM: So let's go back to Hart's "rule of recognition". The notion makes a lot of the idea of "social rules" and "customary rules". Given the fluid nature of modern social reality, how are we to make sense of these? Who is in charge of saying what these are given that our big cities are now full of so many different communities all with a host of different social rules and customs? How does the law know which ones to use? Given that most judges tend to be disconnected from the ordinary folk, how do they know anything about these social rules and customary rules?

JG: As you say, different populations may have different customs, even in the same place. Some are customs of wider populations and other are customs of narrower populations. Hart's explanation of the nature of law emphasises this very point. He argues that the ultimate rule of recognition of a legal system is supplied by a narrowly elite custom, the custom of a population of officials. It is a custom of mutual recognition whereby they all treat each other as officials. Each official purports to follow what he or she takes to be the existing official custom. Over time officials make errors in what they take the official custom already to be. Occasionally they wilfully misrepresent the custom. Either way, if their error or misrepresentation takes hold in the official population, the custom is changed.

One implication of this is that an ultimate rule of recognition of a legal system is typically indeterminate, at any given time, in respect of at least some of its applications. Of course all rules are indeterminate in respect of at least some of their applications; I don't mean to deny that. What I mean is that there is a special indeterminacy that comes of the fact that an ultimate rule of recognition is a customary rule. It is in a perpetual state of flux as parts of the official population fall behind with changes in the purported rule-following behaviour of others. Some people think that this is somehow a problem with or objection to Hart's explanation of the nature of law.

Some were drawn to "legal positivism" by the belief that it would cleanly answer, if not every question of law, then at least the legal question of where to look for an answer to any question of law. But let me disabuse you of that expectation right away. It is absolutely no part of the sales pitch of legal positivism as I understand it, or as Hart understands it, that it offers a clean answer, in every case, to the question: Is that the law? It is not even part of legal positivism's sale pitch that it offers a cleaner answer to that question than do anti-positivist alternatives that make the identification of law depend on moral considerations. If the limits of law are indeterminate—if there are at any moment rules of which it is neither true nor false that they are rules of law—then an explanation of law's nature needs to capture that fact. I regard it as a positive virtue of Hart's explanation of the nature of law that it shows one very important source of such indeterminacy in the very foundations of every legal system. It is the fact that every legal system has customary rules as its ultimate rules of recognition.

A more radical objection has it that the perpetual state of flux in these ultimate rules of recognition is also a perpetual state of fragmentation, inconsistent with their existence as rules. When half of the officials treat the rule as covering cases ABCD and the other half as covering cases BCDE (it is said) then it is not one customary rule with indeterminacies but two rules, neither of which is found in the custom of officials generally, so neither of which is capable of being the ultimate rule of recognition of a legal system. So (it is said) legal systems cannot have ultimate rules of recognition. A particularly sophisticated version of this objection is found at the start of Dworkin's *Law's Empire*. The objection, however, is misconceived. It rests on the thought that the identity-conditions for a customary rule are extensional. Hart goes to great lengths (which I have already summarised) to show that, in identifying a customary rule, the intensional has primacy. That is one thing he is trying to get at with his famous "internal aspect of rules" move (not that he executes the move very well). Dworkin tries to outflank him here by suggesting that an intensionally-structured identity thesis could only succeed by relying on agreement among rule-users about the rationale for the rule, i.e. the reasons for having it and following it. That would be inconsistent with the prevalence among judges of what Dworkin calls "theoretical disagreement". But this represents a misunderstanding of the nature of rules. They are capable of being regarded and used as reasons quite apart from the reasons for having them and using them. Hart is right to think that one and the same rule may be treated as a reason for action by two or more agents even though (a) one of them treats the rule as applying to cases to which, for the other or others, it does not apply and (b) they do not agree at all about the further reasons for having and using the rule.

It doesn't make sense to ask "who is in charge of saying what the customary rules are". Once someone gets to rule authoritatively on what a rule says, it is no longer a customary rule. Now it is an authoritatively created rule that is merely based on a customary rule. The ultimate rule of recognition of a legal system is not authoritatively created and cannot be authoritatively created. Attempts may be made to formulate it (e.g. in legislation or in a judgment of a court) but the formulations of it cannot be more than mere commentary or gloss. An ultimate rule of recognition exists in the actions of members of the relevant population, whatever they may say about it. If what they do and what they say differ, it is what they do that counts.

3:AM: You make much of this in what you say about Constitutions. So what's the link between these rules of recognition and Constitutions?

JG: In a paper called "Can There be a Written Constitution", which is chapter 4 of *Law as a Leap of Faith*, I have some fun with the possibility that "written constitution" is an oxymoron. You can probably imagine how I set this up from what I just said. Many think that, where there is a written constitution, the rules in the written constitution comprise or include the ultimate rules by which legal officials are identified. If Hart is right then an ultimate rule of recognition of a legal system cannot be authoritatively stated. It must be an unwritten rule. We can draw any of the following three conclusions: (1) Hart is wrong about the ultimate rules of recognition of a legal system; (2) there cannot be a written constitution; or (3) the rule of recognition is not, at least in the case of written constitutions, a rule of the constitution. Many writers have opted for (1), accusing Hart of being excessively influenced by the British situation, where the constitution is unwritten (or uncodified, at any rate). Hardly anyone has considered (2) so that is where I start. But of course I end up, after quite a lot of hard labour, at (3). I argue that where there is a written constitution, there is an ultimate customary rule of recognition, not in the written constitution, that says: "Follow the constitution!" or "Bow to the framers of the constitution!" Some people think that these two possible rules come to the same thing, that (for an LP-endorser) "Follow the constitution!" must mean "Bow to the framers of the constitution!" I devote some energy in the paper to showing that this is a mistake, that even for a written constitution following the constitution is not exactly the same as bowing to those who enacted it.

This reminds me to say that one problem on which my work hardly touches is the problem of identifying the correct mode of or technique for interpretation to be used by courts. I do not believe that this is a philosophical problem. It is an ordinary problem of politics. How "originalist" or "textualist" judicial interpretation should be depends on how reactionary judges should be. Many talk as if it is the other way round. Thus reactionary judges, and their reactionary supporters, like to roll out "theories of interpretation" on which their reactionary positions are supposedly premised. To which I reply: that "theory of interpretation" you are offering is really the conclusion, not the premise; conversely 'let's be reactionary' is the premise, not the conclusion.

A further step to go with this line of thought: If we value the checks and balances of political pluralism (government and opposition and independents, upper and lower houses, legislature and executive, etc.) we should value, on the same basis, pluralism of judicial approach. The common law doctrine is that the three main canons of statutory interpretation (the literal rule, the mischief rule, the golden rule) are permissive. Judges get a free choice about how to interpret, within these three rival approaches, subject to binding interpretative precedents. This seems eminently sensible to me. All three canons have their rival advantages. So why not take the same view with constitutional interpretation, e.g. in Canada or the United States? In one way the resulting legal indeterminacy is healthy. It makes it harder for those who lay down written laws to predict what exactly their laws will achieve, and that tends to instill a measure of caution or humility in law-makers who may otherwise be too keen to leave their indelible stamp on the world. It is part of the ideal of the rule of law that politicians and their apparatchiks must be kept under control by the law, even by the law that they themselves made. (Former British Home Secretary David Blunkett is once reputed to have said (to his paramour) "I know the law. I made the law." That remark, if correctly attributed, shows a politician drunk on power and in need of a harsh lesson in humility at the hands of the courts. Alas his repeated encounters with the British and European courts showed him to be, in this respect, incapable of learning. Like a recalcitrant teenager, his arrogance only grew.)

3:AM: Joseph Raz argues that "the law" is moral. You defend this view don't you? Can you say what the argument is and how it handles the idea of, say, laws that are blatantly immoral, such as those of a monstrous regime? Does the position require a particular view of morality to work, such as anti-realism?

JG: I would hesitate to summarise Raz's views as you do. The thesis that "the law is moral" is so vague that, on one reading or another, it could be attributed to almost any philosopher of law known to me. I think the thesis of Raz's that you may have in mind is the thesis that the law makes moral claims, i.e. that legal statements are purported moral statements. I do indeed defend this thesis, in chapter 5 of *Law as a Leap of Faith*. I expend quite a lot of energy there reconciling the thesis with the possibility of immoral laws. My main point is that claims can be false, and can also be believed to be false by those who make them. Often the law makes false moral claims. Sometimes it makes insincere ones. Many people (most recently Scott Shapiro) argue that the law can be morally misguided, but they doubt whether it can be insincere. Theirs is known as the "moral aims" thesis, and it makes room for accidental immorality on the part of the law. The "moral claims" thesis makes room in legal life for an additional form of immorality in the form of intentionally immoral laws that are made or applied under the pretence of moral justification. Such laws may be associated in people's minds with the Nazis and other depraved regimes. I am not so sure that the Nazis were just pretending. But laws made on moral pretences are shamefully common in contemporary democracies, where vote-seeking politicians pander to what they know to be the obnoxious views of their electorate, e.g by demonising asylum-seekers or welfare benefit claimants. In the UK right now there is a lot of this going on under the fake-moral guise of "fairness". There are vulnerable people being legislated into destitution by ruthless liars.

Not all of this lying is lying by the law, however. We should contrast moral claims made in the making of law with moral claims made in the applying of it. I argue that the law makes its distinctive moral claim at the point of application. Moral claims made by legislators about the law they are making—e.g. spurious Tory claims to fairness—are not (yet) the claims of the law.

In these remarks the law is personified, and many people wonder whether that personification is in order. This has been the most challenging critique of both the "moral aims" and the "moral claims" thesis. Most of my chapter 5 is devoted to deflecting it. I argue that the law makes claims in a non-metaphorical way. It literally makes claims through the officials who represent it at the point of its application. I argue that making the law's moral claim is part of what makes a law-applying official such that she speaks on behalf of the law. I illustrate the point copiously, most extensively from the judgments of Justice Holmes (a.k.a. Oliver Wendell Holmes) who is said by Dworkin to constitute a counterexample to the moral claims thesis. I show that Holmes is no counterexample.

As I said at the start, I am an in-your-face moral realist. So I hope that my views about law don't presuppose or support any kind of moral anti-realism. Whether they are compatible with any kinds of moral anti-realism I don't know. I am not the sort of philosopher who tries to make his positions as uncontroversial as possible by showing that they are compatible with falsehoods. I don't think avoiding or minimising philosophical controversy is a valid reason for any philosophical move (unless one is playing some kind of philosophical Russian roulette and one's life, or some other morally important matter, depends on one's avoiding or minimising philosophical controversy).

3:AM: How do you counter claims that you and Raz conflate "what is important for a person" with "is morally important for a person" and that it makes sense to say that a judge is compelled by the law but not morally compelled by the law?

JG: I can't say I have seen that criticism aimed at Raz. But some people have criticised me for making the following argument: (1) law claims to give reasons; (2) law regulates morally important matters; therefore (3) law claims to give moral reasons. That is clearly not a valid argument as it stands. Fortunately, it is also not an argument I made. My argument in the same neighbourhood was: (1) law claims to create obligations (a.k.a. duties); (2) not all obligations are moral ones; but (3) all obligations relating to morally important matters are moral obligations; (4) all the obligations that the law claims to create relate to morally important matters (if only because of the moral importance of the way law regulates them); therefore (5) law claims to create moral obligations. That argument is valid. The most vulnerable premise might seem to be (3). But I have yet to see a good counterexample. Prudential requirements cannot be a counterexample because they are not obligations. Requirements of etiquette or of games cannot be a counterexample because they do not relate to morally important matters. Or rather: when they do relate to morally important matters they also become moral obligations.

Am I not missing the most important and obvious counterexamples, namely legal obligations themselves? No. A legal obligation is, more fully spelt out, just what the law claims to be an obligation. It is no obligation except according to the claims of the law. It does not follow that we should think of such an obligation, as Holmes and Llewellyn thought, as merely an "obligation" in scare-quote marks. Nor should we think that it is an obligation only in some specialised legal sense, as Hart and Kelsen sometimes suggested. It is, according to law, an obligation. Hence: a legal obligation. No scare quote marks required.

3:AM: Are you saying that rationality requires moral requirements? And isn't this close to what the "Natural Law" people say? It sounds like something John Finnis would agree with doesn't it?

JG: I say that moral reasons are reasons. One does not need some further reason to treat them as reasons. If rationality requires us to act for an undefeated reason (as I think it does) then rationality requires us to attend to applicable moral reasons like any other applicable reasons. We are irrational if we attend to non-moral reasons and refuse to attend to moral ones on the same footing. Some people say: Why be moral? But one might as well ask: What reason does one have to care about reasons? The question answers itself as soon as one understands the categories that it invokes.

Is this the same as John Finnis's thesis that basic goods are self-evident? Certainly not. I am not sure that any goods are self-evident and I am not sure that any are basic in the sense that Finnis has in mind. I do think some things are good independently of whether anyone judges them good. This may make me more of an in-your-face moral realist than Finnis is. Unlike him, I don't feel the need to appeal to either basicness or self-evidence as part of my case for moral reality. In that way I am not as meta-ethically defensive as he is.

What does any of this have to do with Natural Law? Mill, to take an example at random, is never called a Natural Lawyer by anyone. But he is clearly in-your-face moral realist who agrees with me that it is rational to be moral.

I take it that Natural Lawyers are not distinguished by their meta-ethical views. They are distinguished by their views on how morality and law are related. In an article called Nearly Natural Law (which appears as chapter 6 of Law as a Leap of Faith) I express a great deal of sympathy for most (though not all) of Finnis's views on this front. I merely add that, whenever they are right, they are consistent with LP.

3:AM: You don't think justice is the first amongst the virtues of the law or legal systems do you? Why do you limit the scope of Justice as you do?

JG: Justice is but one moral virtue among many. I am interested, among other things, in which moral virtue it is. For many years I was equally interested in charity, which is another moral virtue. Few disagree that justice can be contrasted with charity, and hence that the just person and the charitable person are contrasting types. But attempts to analyse the contrast between them have mostly been hopeless. I began my work on this topic many years ago by thinking about the differences of opinion between just people and charitable people, noting that the just person is interested, as the charitable person is not, in whether people get all and only what is due to them. A lot of modern writers in political philosophy have assumed (though rarely argued) that all questions of public morality boil down to questions of what is due to people and how to get it to them, or (as I have also expressed it) questions of propriety in allocation. Many others have said: questions of propriety in allocation, although not the only questions of public morality, do take priority in public morality. I have set myself against both these views (the exclusivity view and the primacy view). I know of no reason to think that public officials are primarily let alone exclusively in the business of allocation, and I very much regret the contemporary tendency to convert every question in public affairs into an allocative question, a question of justice.

However judges are primarily in the business of allocation. This is something they have in common with arbitrators, as indeed with sporting umpires and referees. Adjudication, in all but the rarest of cases, is a matter of deciding who wins and who loses. Since there is no legal system without adjudication, this shows an intimate connection between law and justice. Judges should be just above all. What this does not entail is that the law should be just above all. Indeed it shows one of the risks of excessive juridification, namely that the law and the rest of public policy will become excessively preoccupied with justice because everything in law and public policy will be seen from the start as a potential site for litigation and hence adjudication. That is regrettable. I am all for access to the courts, and generous legal aid to make it possible. But I am quite unhappy about the rest of public affairs being conducted on the model of litigation. In my view, the Rawlsian tradition in political philosophy has given succour to this way of modelling public affairs, even if Rawls himself saw a much more limited role for the primacy of justice. (Or did he? It isn't at all clear.)

3:AM: Your last book is called *"Law as a Leap of Faith'*, and is the title of one of the essays inside. You're working there with ideas of Hans Kelsen and the title refers to a Kierkegaardian idea too doesn't it? So could you say what you mean when you argue that law is a leap of faith? Doesn't it take law outside of the space of reasons, which sounds like an invitation for arbitrary law? And do you endorse this conception, or just saying that's what it turns out to be?

JG: Yes, I do connect Kelsen with Kierkegaard, mostly in respect of their understanding of normative "points of view", of which the point of view of the law is one. Kelsen and Kierkegaard, however, tended towards an ultimate normative irrationalism. They thought that normative questions were always questions from within a point of view, and could not be point-of-view transcending questions about which point of view to adopt. Here I part company with them, and in the process bring faith in God, as well as faith in law, back into contact with rationality. However I give Kelsen and Kierkegaard full credit for noticing what might be called the rationality gap, viz. that one's reasons for adopting a certain point of view (sufficient to warrant doing what from that point of view one should do) need not be reasons for doing those very things had one not adopted the point of view in question. The adoption itself makes a difference. This is very important to my entire way of thinking about law, and about many other topics in practical life. We often align ourselves with particular people or institutions or systems of thought to guide us through life. Doing so may be rationally eligible without being rationally required. But by aligning ourselves with these systematic guides, we may make certain actions rationally required that would otherwise have been merely eligible. Perhaps, like Abraham, we may occasionally even make certain actions rationally required that would otherwise have been ineligible.

You may call this "arbitrary". If so it is arbitrary in the sense in which arbitration is arbitrary (see above), namely in a non-pejorative sense. We need to arbitrate in the relevant sense because rationality is pervasive and inescapable, but radically indeterminate. It tells us what counts towards what we should do and how to count it, and it often rules out doing certain things. But it only rarely tells us what, in the round, to do. That is the rationality gap. We usually fill the gap for ourselves by rationally acceptable but not rationally determined commitment: by decision, promise, self-identification, and other determinacy-adding measures. Timothy Macklem and I have written together about this feature of the human predicament. He and I are old pals and we see these things in pretty similar ways.

3:AM: Your essay "The Wrongness of Rape" is a great example of your philosophy of criminal law in action. So what exactly is wrong with rape—and what is wrong with some alternative claims about the wrongness of rape?

JG: When Stephen Shute and I wrote that essay we were drawn to a rather Kantian answer. Rape is wrong as sheer use of a person. It is not the only sheer use of a person (of course) but like slavery it is one, the social meaning of which lends a special moral significance to it. At this stage in the story, you will notice, consent is not of the essence. People may freely put themselves forward for sheer use (think of prostitution or pornographic performance) and that sheer use is in the same branch of immorality as rape. Nevertheless consent comes in with great importance at the next stage. People have an autonomy-based right, or sometimes they do, to put themselves forward for sheer use. We thought that sexual autonomy had particular importance, enough importance to protect consensual sexual activities even of a mutually sheer-using variety. So—we concluded—while (consenting) prostitute-use is in the same branch of immorality as rape, the law should not prohibit it (or for that matter consensual prostitution itself).

I still think that this answer is in the right neighbourhood. I am not as confident about the details as once I was. However I do stand by an important critical position that Steve and I took. We criticised those who regard the wrongness of rape as stemming primarily from the negative experiences of those who are raped, from how bad rape seems to them. We thought, and I still think, that before we give credence to how bad rape seems to those who are raped we had better be sure that there is something wrong with rape independently of how it seems to those who are victims of it, such that the way it seems to them is rationally defensible. I had a terrific exchange with Danny Statman about some aspects of this critique in a recent symposium about my 2007 book Offences and Defences. Danny took me to task for demanding too much in the way of rational explanation for our feeling humiliated. I took him to task for failing to notice that our actually being humiliated is exactly the rational explanation we need for our feeling humiliated.

3:AM: And finally, are there five books you could recommend to our readers which would take us further into your philosophical world?

JG: Aristotle, *Nicomachean Ethics*. H.L.A. Hart, *The Concept of Law*, Joseph Raz, *Practical Reasons and Norms* , Bernard Williams, *Moral Luck* and Martha Nussbaum, *The Fragility of Goodness*.

John Gardner is the author of:

Law as a Leap of Faith: Essays on Law in General (Oxford University Press, 2012)

14 | Stephen Darwall: "From the Second Person"

Stephen Darwall is the Andrew Downey Orrick Professor of Philosophy at Yale University and the John Dewey Distinguished University Professor Emeritus of Philosophy at the University of Michigan. Here he discusses what happens if the second-person stance is adopted in ethics; why contractualism is the most naturally grounded position for it; its juridical character; its implications for autonomy; Joseph Raz's challenge; nuancing Jonathan Dancy's position; on morality, authority, and the law; honour, history, relationship, and Adam Smith; vengeance and John Stuart Mill; Nietzschean *ressentiment* and dark worship; Kant; what is to learn from psychology and x-phi; and the relative status of P. F. Strawson to Quine.

3:AM: What made you become a philosopher?

STEPHEN DARWALL: In a way, I want to answer that philosophy did: philosophy's power to compel philosophy. It is pretty much impossible to engage appreciatively with philosophy without beginning to do it. I don't think I was clear when I was growing up that there was such a subject that one could actually study. For various reasons, I wasn't a voracious reader, and my (K-12) education (much of it in the time just after Sputnik went up in 1957) was focused more on math and science. (For younger readers, this was a time of massive public investment in math and science, with tremendous spillover benefits for fields like philosophy as well as general support that helped to create a system of excellent public universities that were the envy of the world. Of course, all this is pretty much unimaginable now.)

But more to your question, when I went to Yale as an undergraduate in 1964, I was a prospective math major. In my sophomore year though, I had the good fortune take some really difficult math courses (in real analysis with Shizuo

Kakutani, who proved the Kakutani fixed point theorem) at the same time that I was taking my first philosophy courses. These showed me two things: first, I didn't have the talent or even really the interest to do serious mathematics, and second, that the rigorous thinking that had attracted me to mathematics could be put in service of things I was actually interested in thinking about. Growing up with an Episcopalian clergyman father (check out the hymn tune "Darwall's 148th" in many Protestant hymn books—by John Darwall, my great great great great grandfather) I was drawn to thinking about questions about the relation between religion and morality and the foundations of ethics. But I had no idea that this was a subject of academic study. Lucky me.

3:AM: You're a top moral philosopher, and connected with the notion of "the second-person standpoint." So what is this?

SD: Well, suppose, I answer by saying that it is the standpoint you and I are in right now, though the people who are "overhearing" our conversation may not be. I am writing these very sentences in an attempt to answer the questions you addressed to me, and you addressed them to me in the expectation that I would take the fact that you asked them as at least some reason to answer them. This fact is an example of what I call a "second-personal reason." In asking the question you were presupposing some standing or authority to ask them of me, that I would (do) recognize this authority, and take myself to have some reason thereby to answer them. Of course, this is a pretty lengthy list of questions (constituting, after all, a kind of interview), so you couldn't just send me these questions out of the blue. But you could presuppose the standing to invite me to participate in an interview, which you did, and I agreed, thereby giving you the standing to send me with these questions with the expectation (not just the prediction) that I would answer them.

In relating to one another in these ways, we presuppose, I argue, that we each share a common basic second-personal authority to make claims and demands of one another and hold each other mutually accountable. We each presume this authority when we exercise our respective (second-personal) normative powers to make agreements and hold one another to them.

3:AM: What difference does it make to the kind of reasons one can use to justify moral beliefs? Is consequentialism, for instance, in difficulties if second personhood is adopted?

SD: My claims are, in the first instance, about the second-personal nature of certain moral concepts—more specifically, the deontic concepts of moral right and wrong, duty, obligation, requirement, demand, and related ideas of moral rights and so-called "directed" or bipolar duties that we owe to others. For example, I argue that it is a conceptual truth that if I am morally obligated to do something (if it would be wrong for me not to do it), then my action is of a kind that it would be blameworthy of me to fail to perform were I to do so without adequate excuse, and that would therefore warrant my feeling guilt. As I understand them, moral blame and guilt are Strawsonian reactive attitudes through which a holder of the attitude implicitly addresses demands to its object and assumes the authority to hold him or her accountable.

It follows that any theory of right, that is, as Ross put it, of "what makes right acts right," must be an account of what can make an act something we are accountable in this sense to do or not to do. This certainly doesn't rule out even act consequentialism on conceptual grounds. It just means that if act consequentialism is advanced as a deontic moral theory, as a theory of moral right and wrong, then it must say that it is blameworthy for moral agents to fail to perform optimific acts, so long as their failures are not excused by mitigating circumstances. Most consequentialists have reluctant to say that. Mill, for example, when he says in Chapter V of Utilitarianism that we don't call actions wrong unless we think they are fittingly responded to by guilt or sanctions (a version of the conceptual thesis mentioned in the last paragraph), ends up making remarks that are much more rule utilitarian than act utilitarian. In my review of Derek Parfit's *On What Matters*, which will be coming out soon in The Philosophical Review, I argue that something similar is going on in Parfit's move from defending act consequentialism in Reasons and Persons to defending rule consequentialism as part of the "Triple Theory" in *OWM*.

In The Second-Person Standpoint, I argue that the normative ethical theory that is most naturally grounded in the second-person standpoint is contractualism. But one could accept my conceptual arguments and advance other theories on their basis. For example, one might argue for a version of rule utilitarianism as grounded in the idea of equal second-personal authority.

3:AM: What is distinctive about morality as an ethical concept from this perspective?

SD: Given what I have said above, I can be relatively brief. In "The Distinctiveness of Morality" I agree with Sidgwick, Anscombe, and others that what distinguishes the "modern" concept of morality is its juridical character: its consisting of duties or obligations that are incumbent on any moral agent (and its deep connection to rights that any moral agent has). It just follows from what I have said about deontic moral concepts above that morality distinctively implicates accountability and (reactive) attitudes through which we hold ourselves and one another answerable. Similarly, the idea moral rights just is the idea of what moral agents have the authority to claim or demand from one another.

3:AM: And does this approach lead to a particular view of autonomy? Is self respect a key attitude of someone taking a second personal attitude toward herself?

SD: I believe that it does. First, autonomy of some form is built into the idea of what I call "individual" second-personal authority as it is implicated in a moral claim right or an obligation owed to someone. These entail the notion that the right holder has the authority to claim or demand something at her own discretion. And autonomy has been central to conceptions of human (claim) rights from at least the time of Grotius. Grotius calls it "power over ourselves" and argues that it is a fundamental "perfect right" that individuals have the authority or "faculty" to demand. I argue that this second-personal aspect is central also to what Hegel calls the "modern" idea of a "right of subjective freedom," that is, that everyone has a right to lead his or her own life, and consequently has the authority to demand that others let him or her do that.

3:AM: Joseph Raz's "normal justification thesis" poses a challenge to your second personhood thesis doesn't it? Can you first say what Raz's positions is and why it creates difficulties? And how do you propose to meet the challenge?

SD: Raz's normal justification thesis says that the normal way of justifying a claim of authority that some person or institution makes over someone to direct that person's conduct is that the latter would do better in complying with reasons for acting that apply to her independently were the latter to treat the former as having this authority and comply with them for that reason. I argue that this fails to distinguish between whether it would be desirable for the latter to treat the former as having authority and whether the former actually has the authority to make legitimate demands of the latter, which can only be justified by reasons of the right kind that would simultaneously justify the legitimacy of the former's demands and the latter's holding herself accountable to the authority.

As I see it, these reasons are second personal; it follows that all claims to authority must be justified within a second-personal framework. The challenge posed by the normative justification thesis is that if it were true, this would not be so. Seeing, however, why justifying the desirability of treating someone as an authority is different from establishing that person's authority itself helps one to see why a second-person framework is indispensable.

3:AM: You argue against Jonathan Dancy's moral particularism. What's the problem with particularism?

SD: I don't argue against particularism as Dancy actually advances it, at the level of reasons. I argue that that position is inaptly named "moral particularism," because, when it comes to morality, there actually are features of deontic moral concepts that push in the direction of formulability in general principles. If what is morally wrong is what we are justifiably held accountable for not doing, then there just has to be some presumption that some common and public way of determining what is wrong is possible. In this way, morality is more like the law than, say, art. The point is not one about objectivity, but about a public standard of accountability. It is hard to see how we could intelligibly hold people accountable for complying with standards that are not publicly formulable in some way or other, even if only with pro tanto principles that it takes some judgment to apply, that admit of exceptions, and so on.

3:AM: You also argue that the second person framework can shed light on the nature of law. So what distinctive things does it illuminate?

SD: As I see it, the concept of law is second personal in its nature. It is essential to law that it is promulgated or addressed to those whom it purports to bind and make accountable for complying with it. Whether one is a legal positivist or not, it is hard to deny that law purports to have de jure authority (that doesn't mean that it has it), so if I am right in my claims about the conceptual connections between authority, obligation, and accountability, law's second-personal character derives from that. A second-person framework can also illuminate the difference between criminal and civil or private law, e.g., torts and the law of contracts. I make a distinction within morality between moral duties or obligations period and bipolar obligations that are owed to others. The latter entail correlative claim rights that the obligor has to the obligee.

I analyze the difference in terms of who has authority or standing to demand compliance. In principle, we can, as representative persons, demand compliance with moral obligations pure and simple, for example, through what Strawson calls "impersonal" reactive attitudes like moral blame. These therefore implicate a representative authority any person has. Someone with a claim right to whom someone else owes an obligation has a distinctive authority to demand compliance and hold the obligor personally accountable, for example, through the "personal" reactive attitude of resentment. An obligor with individual authority also has a standing to forgive a violating obligor at her discretion that others do not have. The difference between these two authorities, representative and individual authority, respectively, illuminate the difference between complementary legal authorities that are implicated, respectively, in criminal and private law.

For example, only a victim can bring a tort action to gain compensation for violation of his legal rights, whereas it is up to the people and their representatives, through, say, the district attorney, to bring criminal cases. This difference is reflected in the way cases are referred to. When O. J. Simpson (first Google example) was accused of murder, the case was named The People of the State of California vs. O. J. Simpson, whereas the civil case against

Simpson was brought by Nicole Brown Simpson's estate and the parents of Ronald Goldman.

3:AM: How does respect and honor fit into this approach, and why do you find Adam Smith interesting here with regard to honor?

SD: In "Respect as Honor and as Accountability," I argue that honor cultures are mediated by forms of recognition respect and contempt that I had heretofore failed to distinguish from the recognition respect for persons that is the hallmark of morality. Honor respect and contempt socially construct status and rank in a kind of social drama in which participants enact what Goffman called the "presentation of the self in everyday life," with a persona or face. When others recognize this presentation, "support" and "countenance" her countenance and her occupying the social roles she aspires to, then that person is able to maintain the social face she presents. If, however, others regard this with contempt or "look her out of countenance," she loses face, which contempt can be internalized felt emotionally as shame. Honor respect is thus a kind of recognition respect for persons, only "person" understood not as an accountable moral agent, but as having a distinctive place in a social hierarchy that honor respect and contempt construct. This sense of "person" is precisely the sense in which the law is said to be "no respecter of persons," (a phrase that can sound odd until you see what it means); it treats everyone equally as equally accountable citizens. Of course, this is the sense of "person" as equally accountable moral agent of morality's signature idea is equal respect for persons.

Adam Smith is interesting here because of his ambivalence about honor. On the one hand, some of Smith's normative views about the importance of responding to insults reflect the ethos of honor culture. But, more importantly to my mind, Smith also holds that what "our resentment is chiefly intent upon" is not that the insult be avenged, but that the other be "sensible" that "the person whom he injured did not deserve to be treated in that manner."

3:AM: That's relevant to my next question I think. John Stuart Mill thinks vengeance lies at the heart of justice, and is just nothing to do with morality. You argue that a second personhood perspective on reactive attitudes changes this, and does turn them moral . Is that right? How does that happen?

SD: The form of "animal resentment" that Mill takes to be central to the sense of justice is a desire for revenge that makes sense in hierarchies of dominance and submission and in honor hierarchies. Revenge is a form of getting even in which a dishonoring agent who has raised his relative status in lowering yours is humiliated by dishonor in return, which "turns tables" and reverses the relative hierarchy established by the initial insult. I agree with Mill that vengeance has nothing to do with morality. The difference between the kind of "justice" vengeance involves and justice as an important moral idea is that the latter involves holding someone who has acted unjustly accountable, whether by representative persons, or personally by the victim, or by the unjust agent himself (for example, through guilt, apology, compensation to the victim, and so on).

The crucial difference is that holding someone accountable is not returning evil for evil or getting back or getting even. Holding someone accountable in the sense I am elaborating is itself a form of recognition respect for someone as an equal moral person—holding him to demands that we and he have the authority make of him as an equal person. Although vengeance is taken against another person, it is not second personal in the sense of holding another accountable through a respectful demand for respect. Unlike second-personal reactive attitudes it involves no implicit demand that the other hold himself accountable.

3:AM: You similarly approach Nietzschean ressentiment—you have a great sentence—'Repressed, ressentiment bores into the unconscious, a "dark worship" in which morality's distinctive ideas of guilt, moral responsibility, and moral evil are fashioned.' How does second personhood help nuance your approach to ressentiment?

SD: The point is quite similar here. Ressentiment as Nietzsche understands it is a repressed expression of self-hatred that attempts to get back at an envied superior in a way that will lower him to one's level. It seeks a kind of revenge, not openly or honestly, but mendaciously from a position that cannot admit its own weakness and so is secretive and self-deceptive. Nietzsche's view is that psychological mechanisms like these are the source of the distinctive moral ideas of moral accountability. Naturally, I disagree. I think Nietzsche has a quite brilliant and insightful analysis of a recognizable psychological syndrome that is responsible for much mischief, but he fails to appreciate the ways in which, properly conceived, morality involves a form of mutual respect that is quite positive and life affirming and that develops naturally out of our capacity for mutual response.

3:AM: Kant thinks dignity is a value that we all can achieve but only when we properly exercise our capacity for moral choice rather than a standing a person has regardless of merit. Do you agree?

SD: It is widely believed that this is not so, that Kant thinks that dignity of persons is rooted in the capacity itself, but I argue in "Kant on Respect, Dignity, and the Duty of Respect" that what Kant actually says at least sometimes admits of the interpretation you mention. (Richard Dean argued for this point earlier in his The Value of Humanity in Kant's Moral Theory.) There are other places where Kant gets much closer to a view I think he should hold, namely, that dignity consists in a standing any moral agent has to claim or "exact respect" (Kant's phrase), what I would call, equal second-personal authority. But even here there are probably ways of interpreting Kant in terms of merit and what I call "appraisal respect," as when we say someone's character "commands" respect.

3:AM: What is the relationship between your moral philosophy and cognitive science and xphi investigations into behaviours and attitudes and beliefs? Can you learn from biologists, for example?

SD: I have a chapter in SPS titled "The Psychology of the Second Person" in which I lay out some of the experimental evidence for second-personal psychological phenomena, for example, in producing cooperation in prisoners' dilemma situations. People are prepared to expend resources to hold others accountable. But what is especially interesting is that this tends to elicit the others' cooperation only when the latter view their doing so as legitimate. More recently, a former student of mine, Brendan Dill, and I have been writing a paper, "Moral Psychology as Accountability," which reviews the experimental literature on moral motivation and emotions in psychology and argues that it can be best explained and unified if morality is conceived in the fundamentally second-personal terms of accountability. So I think there is a lot of benefit from mutual exchange there.

I am sure there is much to learn from xphi also. For example, I can't really lay out the case properly here, but I think that the original Knobe effect cases can be explained in second-personal terms. Roughly, when an action (as I would put it) involves a violation of a moral norm that we are accountable for complying with, it is sufficient to for us to consider that intentional that it was done knowingly. When however, no such norm is in question and the (implicit) issue is whether someone is to be (positively) credited with something, we assess intentionality, not just by whether the agent knew what she was doing, but by her end or purpose. What the second-personal framework offers here is the idea that the attitudes of blame and praise (esteem) are not really contraries. Blame is a second-personal, holding-responsible reactive attitude that implicitly involves address, whereas esteem (crediting) is third personal; it does not implicitly involve address.

I haven't thought as much about the interactions with biology, so I'm not sure what to say there.

3:AM: PF Strawson seems an important figure in your work. He's someone who isn't discussed as much today as say, Quine is , even though thirty years ago he was considered a contemporary giant. Is he underrated at the moment and due for a reassessment? And is it because a certain self image of scientific naturalism is rather predominant in the USA at the moment, overshadowing Kantian preoccupations?

SD: Strawson is certainly discussed a lot in the literature on responsibility, freedom of the will, and so on. Evidence is pretty equivocal on the relative prominence of Strawson and Quine, however. When I do a Google Book Ngram Viewer search of relative cites of Strawson and Quine, Strawson systematically dominates Quine (and a search of Strawson alone going up to 2008 shows the great interest Strawson has received relatively recently that I just mentioned). On the other hand, Word and Object has many more Google Scholar cites than any of Strawson's works. Just from my own sense of things, though, I would say that Quine's influence in philosophy these days is decidedly less than it was thirty years ago. So I'm not sure I'd endorse your diagnosis in terms of American scientific naturalism (though there is no doubt that that has been a strong current from the early twentieth century on).

3:AM: And finally, are there five books (other than your own) which you could recommend to the readers here at 3:AM that would help them go further into your philosophical world?

SD: Let's see, how about, in no particular order:

> Adam Smith, *The Theory of Moral Sentimen*
> Samuel Pufendorf, *The Law of Nature and Nations*
> Laura Blumenfeld, *Revenge: A Story of Hope*
> Immanuel Kant, *Groundwork of the Metaphysics of Morals*
> P. F. Strawson, *Freedom and Resentment and Other Essays.*

Stephen Darwall is the author of:

Impartial Reason (Cornell University Press, 1985)

The British Moralists and the Internal "Ought": 1640–1750 (Cambridge University Press, 1995)

Moral Discourse and Practice: Some Philosophical Approaches (Oxford University Press, 1997)

Welfare and Rational Care (Princeton University Press, 2004)

The Second-Person Standpoint (Harvard University Press, 2006)

Honor, History, and Relationship (Oxford University Press, 2013)

Morality, Authority, and Law (Oxford University Press, 2013)

III | *Consequentialist Ethics*

15 | Torbjörn Tännsjö: "The Hedonistic Utilitarian"

Torbjörn Tännsjö has been the Kristian Claëson Professor of Practical Philosophy at Stockholm University since 2002 and is the director at the Stockholm University Centre for Health Care Ethics, a collaboration among Stockholm University (SU), Karolinska Institute (KI), and the Royal Institute of Technology (KTH). Since 2007 he has also been an Affiliated Professor of Medical Ethics at Karolinska Institute. Here he discusses the ethics of acts of killing, moral realism, repugnant conclusions, reasons and norms, utilitarianism, hedonism, human enhancement, genetic technologies in sport, global democracy, populist democracy, and conservativism.

3:AM: What made you become a philosopher?

TORBJÖRN TÄNNSJÖ : When I was in my late teens I was already interested in philosophy. In high school I read Bertrand Russell's The Problems of Philosophy and his My Philosophical Development. I don't know what brought me to the subject in the first place. And my interest was theoretical. I wanted to know what it means to know something, whether we can know at all, and, if so, how. These were typically the questions raised by Russell. However, two simultaneous personal experiences drew me to moral philosophy. I describe this in the preface to Taking Life. This is how it happened. I was conscripted to military service, and my gut feeling was to refuse to serve. I did not want to kill other people. This seemed to me wrong, if not in principle, so at least in practice. There were no serious military threats facing Sweden, and if the situation would change there was no guarantee that I would turn out to be a just rather than an unjust combatant. Moreover, the kind of values for which I was supposed to kill, such as democracy and national independence, were better served, I thought, through non-violent action. This was during the heydays of the civil rights movement in the American South. Again Russell, not the philosopher, this time, but the political activist, inspired me. My arguments were met with no sympathy from the military authorities. They threatened me with jail, if I was not prepared to serve.

At the same time my father got ill. It soon turned out to be serious. He suffered from cancer in his liver with metastases in many places of his body. The prediction was that he should be dead within a few months. This prophecy was born out by realities. My father reacted with good sense and courage to the prophecy. He was sad to leave in such an untimely manner, he told my mother and me, but he had had more than fifty rich years, so he wasn't resentful. And he swiftly took care of all sorts of practical matters relating to his death. However, something he had not expected happened. His sufferings turned out to be unbearable. The medical doctor who treated my father was his personal friend, and my father was given morphine and all sorts of palliation. However, his pain could not be controlled. His last weeks were terrible. He sometimes fell asleep. When he woke up he was still in a delirious state caused by the morphine, and he asked me, his only child, and my mother, whether he was dead or alive. We had to inform him that he was not yet dead; he had to struggle on for yet another while. He asked his doctor to assist him in his dying. He begged for euthanasia. His doctor turned down his request with the words that euthanasia was not only illegal, but it was "at variance with the principles of medical ethics." My father's agony increased and culminated in a state of terminal agitation and ended only with his very last choking breath.

I was much concerned with what had happened. It did not only affect me emotionally. I was intellectually in a state of deep confusion. How could it be that I had a legal obligation to kill people I did not know, and who did certainly not consent to it, while my father's doctor could not help my father to die when my father asked for it? My consternation brought me to moral philosophy and a life-long search for an answer to the question when and why we should, and when we shouldn't, kill. To kill or not to kill, that was the question that haunted me. I began to study practical philosophy at Stockholm University in 1966, with a particular interest in the ethics of killing.

3:AM: So this issue, the act of killing, is one of your central concerns as a philosopher. This is a sensitive issue—in fact one that has proved very sensitive in both Sweden and elsewhere hasn't it. Can you say something about the reactions you've faced when you've asked for surveys to be completed, and when you've tried to discuss the issue in publications for the general public such as the "repugnant conclusion" debacle last year.

TT: My interest in bioethics started some 25 years ago. The first topic I addressed was prenatal diagnosis and abortion. I published an article in Dagens Nyheter, the leadings Swedish newspaper, where I argued that the pregnant woman should be free to seek whatever prenatal diagnosis she wanted, and then do as she saw fit with regard to abortion. The argument was simple. If society regulates this kind of abortion and decides, for example, that it is permitted to have an abortion if the child has a chromosomal defect (Down), but not if it has the "wrong" sex, then society sends a nasty message: a child is welcome regardless of its sex, but not if it is mentally retarded. The reaction to this article, with its simple and straightforward message, was very strong. A media Hype was created, and the leader of the Christian Democratic Party in Sweden, Alf Svensson, demanded publicly that I should be removed immediately from my position as Associate Professor of Practical Philosophy at Stockholm University.

I also met with resistance when much later I took up my systematic studies on the ethics of killing. I wanted to make a survey of the reactions among Swedes to the kinds of killing I was going to discuss: murder, suicide, euthanasia, capital punishment, killing in war, and so forth. I had obtained funding from the Swedish Research Council for the survey and I approached the Swedish state authority for official statistics and asked it to perform my survey, only to receive the following letter from the Chief Executive Officer of the authority, called SCB (Statistics Sweden):

After careful discussions within the authority SCB has decided not to undertake the proposed survey you describe in your letter of 4 February 1999. The reason is that SCB, like other institutes in the world, has very little experience of the gathering of this kind of highly sensitive data. We do not want to risk that a survey like the proposed one should initiate psychological reactions among the respondents that are difficult to handle. We think here of respondents who have suffered in war, who are suicidal, or who have experienced difficult decisions in relation to abortion ... The final decision was taken by the Chief Executive Officer of SCB after a discussion within the board of the office. (My translation)

I succeeded to have my survey made, however, by approaching another firm. And eventually, and quite recently, when I was preparing my Taking Life, I got my data not only from Swedes about this, but from Americans, Russians, and the Chinese. This time, the Chinese turned out to be a problem. At first I could not have my survey made in China, for roughly the reason it had been a problem in Sweden. Eventually, the resistance withered, however, and in my book I can report the answers from random samples of 1000 Americans, Russians, and Chinese about the all the kinds of killing I investigate

A recent American experience was when Vox last year commissioned a piece from me on the "repugnant conclusion." I delivered it on time, Vox carefully edited it in cooperation with me, to my satisfaction and theirs, but then, at the very last moment, they refused to run it. It was supposed to be too sensitive in an American liberal context, according to the editor in chief. My defence of the repugnant conclusion, saying that an extensive population of people living lives just worth living, if they are many enough, is to be preferred to a population of ten billion extremely happy people, could be seen, the editor in chief thought, as an attack on the right to free abortion. Hence he stopped the publication. Actually, I defend the right to free abortion, but this was of no avail. My argument could still be seen as supporting moral conservatives, it was maintained. I was surprised. You don't expect such a narrow minded response from liberals! The result was that I had my paper published elsewhere instead (by the Gauker:), and indeed, there was much discussion about it. Vox had created a Streisand effect!

I have always enjoyed the media Hypes I have created and I enjoyed this one, for the same reason that I liked the others: it meant that many people (now Americans), who would not have thought of the problem I discussed, now had to do so. Many even took up a their own stance to the problem, some in defence of my position, others in opposition to it, and they tried to give their own arguments. I wouldn't be surprised if some of them have turned to a serious study of philosophy.

3:AM: Why are you a moral realist and what difference does this make to how you go about investigating morals from, for example, a non-realist?

TT: I am indeed a moral realist. In particular, I believe that one basic question, what we ought to do, period (the moral question), is a genuine one. There exists a true answer to it, which is independent of our thought and conceptualisation. My main argument in defence of the position is this. It is true (independently of our conceptualisation) that it is wrong to inflict pain on a sentient creature for no reason (she doesn't deserve it, I haven't promised to do it, it is not helpful to this creature or to anyone else if I do it, and so forth). But if this is a truth, existing independently of our conceptualisation, then at least one moral fact (this one) exists and moral realism is true. We have to accept this, I submit, unless we can find strong reasons to think otherwise. Moral nihilism comes with a price we can now see. It implies that it is not wrong (independently of our conceptualisation) to do what I describe above; this does not mean that it is all right to do it either, of course, but yet, for all this, I find this implication from nihilism hard to digest. It is not difficult to accept for moral reasons. If it is false both that it is wrong to perform this action and that it is right to perform it, then we need to engage in difficult issues in deontic logic as well. So we should not accept moral nihilism unless we find strong arguments to do so. So are there any good arguments in defence of moral nihilism? I think not and I try to defend this claim in my From Reasons to Norms. On the Basic Question in Ethics . It is of note that for a long time moral nihilism was a kind of unquestioned default position in analytic moral philosophy. What initiated the interest in moral realism was the fact that, in 1977, two authors, John Mackie and Gilbert Harman, independently of one another, put forward arguments in defence of the nihilist position. This triggered an interest in what had up to then been a non-issue. When thinking carefully about their arguments for nihilism I didn't find them convincing. I was not alone. At first there was a trend towards moral realism in its "Cornell," i.e naturalist, style. In my book Moral Realism I didn't take a stand on the naturalist/non-naturalist issue. I am now a decided non-naturalist realist. And today we may even speak of a trend towards non-naturalist moral realism (for example Derek Parfit, David Enoch, apart from myself).

Being a moral realist I see normative ethics as a search of the truth about our obligations and a search of explanation; the idea is that moral principles can help us to a moral explanation of our particular obligations. The method I employ is simple and straightforward. One could speak of it as hypothetically deductive. I look at the most promising putative moral theories. I construct crucial thought experiments in areas where they give conflicting advice. I confront their conflicting advice with my own moral sensitivity, my moral intuition. I take the theory that can best explain the content of my intuitions as gaining inductive support through an inference to the best explanation. One possible such area is the ethics of killing. Here we can construct our moral laboratory and arrange with our thought experiments.

3:AM: You think there are three basic moral theories that someone might apply to killing don't you? Can you sketch them for us?

TT: Different areas present us with possibilities to test different theories. My main interest is in utilitarianism. One may think that the ethics of killing should be a serious obstacle to it. If anything is wrong in principle, one may think, it should be the intentional killing of an innocent human being. Deontological thinking in both a Kantian and a Thomistic version prohibits this. According to deontology it is wrong to kill an innocent human being, period. Or, one may think that, if there is anything we should be allowed to do as we see fit with, it is ourselves. We own ourselves. This is the core of a libertarian theory of rights. But on this theory, while we are at liberty to kill ourselves (regardless of the consequences of others), we are not allowed to kill others, not even if this means that there we be fewer murders in the future, totally speaking. Now, utilitarianism condones killing of innocent human beings, even murder, if it makes the world a better place. This is at variance with both deontology and the moral rights theory, then. We can see that this is a fruitful field if we want to assess these three theories and employ the method I recommend.

3:AM: Is it possible to hold all three at the same time?

TT: These theories, deontology, the moral rights theory, and utilitarianism, contradict one another. Moreover, they give conflicting (inconsistent) recommendations. It is hence not possible to hold them together, in a pursuit of moral truth. If two norms conflict, if they are mutually inconsistent, then at least one of them must be false. It is possible to hold on to a revised version of the three theories, however. You may think of them as not providing you with absolute true answers to moral questions, but with merely prima facie obligations or pro tanto reasons to act. But this is a fourth normative theory, in competition with all the three I discuss in my book. And I try to show that it is not superior to any one of them. Moreover, it has its own severe problems with practicality. It is difficult to apply it to concrete cases, and it is outright impossible to apply it in abstract thought experiments. We should only resort to this kind of intellectual compromise as a last resort, then, when we have failed to find a "deterministic" principle giving an answer to what we ought to do, both in real cases and in abstract thought experiments. And utilitarianism is such a plausible and deterministic moral principle, I argue.

3:AM: Why do you find utilitarianism the best of the approaches?

TT: There is no way to answer this question briefly. You have to work through all the examples I present, tease out the implications of the theories, and confront them with the content of your intuitions. You should not take your intuitions at face value, moreover. This is an important addition to the method I sketched above. You should not take the content of your intuitive response as evidence until you have submitted your psychological reaction to what I call cognitive psychotherapy. You should do what you can to learn as much as possible about the origin of your reaction. You are only allowed to treat the content of your intuition as evidence if the intuition stays after you have exposed it to cognitive psychotherapy; in some cases you have to reject it even if it does indeed stay. An example of this if you have learnt that your intuitive reaction is an example of "quick" thinking, an heuristic device, which works in most cases, but which may have failed in the present one. In discussion of the trolley cases we can see examples of this. Our reluctance to push a big man onto the tracks in order to save five lives is an example of such quick thinking, I argue. Hence, even if we intuitively feel that it is wrong to perform this action we should not take the content of our intuition as evidence. This does not mean that we have evidence in support of pushing the big man either, however. Some people claim that this is their intuition in relation to the case. I suspect, however, that, to the extent that they believe that it is all right to push the big man, this is the result of an application of utilitarianism (or some similar theory) to the case. But then the content of the intuition gives no independent support of the theory. So the upshot is, in this case, that we lack evidence for and against pushing the man.

When I examine all the thought experiments I conduct in the book utilitarianism seems to deliver the right answer, where we meet with conflicting advice from the theories. Moreover, it strikes me that much of the opposition to utilitarianism stems from a difficulty people have with keeping two questions apart: what is the right thing to do in a particular case, and what sort of person one should attempt to become. Once we realise that utilitarianism comes with the idea of blameworthy rightdoing (such as when you push a big man onto the tracks in order to save five lives) and blameless wrongdoing (such as when you don't push a big man onto the tracks in order to save five lives), then utilitarianism all of a sudden appears to give the right answers. It is indeed right to push the big man, but we should attempt not to become people who are prepared to do this, since this would, even if it helps us to the right decision in this abstract thought experiment, make us dangerous, nasty, and ones no one should want to socialise with. Hence, if you do push the big man you are blameworthy, not for doing this in the situation, but for being a person capable of doing this. It is right, according to utilitarianism, to become a person who doesn't push, but yet, for all that, it is all right (if you can) to push. And this also explains why you are blameless when you don't push. Your reluctance to push is a sign of the fact that you have succeeded in becoming a good person. No blame on you for this, not even if it were possible for you to push! This is subtle but it seems to me, at any rate, to be the correct verdict of the case.

It is of note that even if utilitarianism has proved to be superior to deontology and the libertarian moral rights theory in the area of killing, we are not allowed to say that it has been finally vindicated; it has to face other challenges in other areas, in particular in situations of distributive justice. If we construct crucial thought experiments where utalitarianism has to compete with egalitarian and prioritarian thoughts, how does it succeed? This is something I am working on right now.

3:AM: Do Chinese and Westerners respond differently to the trolley problem, and if they do, doesn't that make problems for your moral realist stance? And to generalize a point made recently by Alex Rosenberg, isn't the systematic inability to find deep universal moral agreement proof that even if morals are objectively real, there's no way we know them—and we'd be better off accepting that they're not objectively real?

TT: We cannot take the result of surveys such as the one I have made as evidence for or against moral theories. At most they can help us to a better understanding of our own intuitive responses. They can form part of our cognitive psychotherapy. We can be certain that, if there are conflicting views in different cultures, some of these views must be false. This may help us to transcend our own narrow cultural horizon. Of course, even where people in different cultures agree they may all have gone wrong. However, now it is at least possible that the best explanation why people agree is that they have converged on true answers. It has been thought that some thought experiments are better than others, in that they do not trigger special cultural cues. Abortion, for example, is extremely problematic exactly in this regard. People in different cultures think very differently about abortion. Abortion is not seen as a moral problem for example in Sweden or Russia, but it is seen as a difficult moral problem in China and in the USA. It has been thought that the so-called trolley cases can present us with thought experiments where no cultural cues are struck. It is not that everyone agrees about the answers, but it has been thought that roughly the same pattern emerges in all cultures: a majority is for example prepared to flip a switch, killing one in order to save five, while a majority finds it wrong to push a person onto the tracks in order to obtain the same result. My results from China indicate that there may exist a cultural difference also in this case. The Chinese are generally speaking much more reluctant than Westerners to killing as a means to the rescue of lives. If this is correct, then this means that we cannot take for granted that our reactions in relation to the trolley cases are not determined also by cultural idiosyncrasies. This renders them less helpful, then, to the kind of search of the moral truth that I am interested in.

Does all this show that even if moral realism is true moral knowledge is not possible? I think not. There are some particular moral truths that I believe we have access to (such as the one not to inflict pain on a sentient being for no reason). Moreover, I am quite optimistic that the method I recommend will yield also more principled moral understanding. This might be the place to repeat what Derek Parfit has said. Normative ethics, pursued as a free, systematic, and critical attempt to find moral truth, regardless of religious and other authorities, is a rather new adventure. Let's wait and see what will happen!

3:AM: Are you a hedonist then?

TT: I am indeed a hedonistic utilitarian. I have defended hedonistic utilitarianism for quite a while. When I wrote my book Hedonistic Utilitarianism. A Defence (1998) this was a very controversial position. Now many people seem to be drawn to it. There are both moral and methodological problems with hedonism. I have tried to rebut the moral criticism of the sort raised by, say, Robert Nozick, with his "experience machine." And I have tried to deal with the methodological problems. If you take happiness to be a kind of mood, then it is reasonable to assume that at each moment we are at a certain level of happiness (mood). If this is so, then we can answer what has been called the heterogeneity objection to hedonism. It is true that it feels very differently to enjoy a good meal, taking part in an interesting conversation, or to think of how successful your children are. Suppose we do all these things at a particular time. How happy are we at the time? We do not need to calculate the value of each such feelings on any singular scale to answer this question. We need not see our happiness at the time as a mathematical function of these items. It is rather that all these experiences, together with many other factors, causally puts us at the time at a certain level of happiness, i.e. in a certain mood. And we have access to this mood. We can compare it to the mood just before the present one, and so forth. And this prepares the way to meet a second methodological challenge to hedonism, to do with measurement. Given this idea we may speak with good meaning of comparisons of happiness, both intra- and interpersonally (in a manner suggested by the economist Francis Ysidro Edeworth, putting a stress on the least noticeable difference of happiness). I put forward these ideas in the old book and I have kept developing them since then.

3:AM: Can you say something about how using your applied ethical approach you approach the issue of controversial issues such as abortion or IVF or mercy killing?

TT: My standard approach to problems in applied ethics has been roughly this. It is of interest to try to find out the implications of different basic moral approaches to problems such as these ones. It is of interest to find out to what extent an overlapping consensus is possible (where different basic theories point in the same practical direction). It is also of interest to find where this is not possible. I have been able to find much room for overlapping consensus in my discussions about the role of coercion in health care (my book Coercive Care bears witness to this) while I have been utterly pessimistic with regard to topics such as euthanasia and abortion (where I have published articles such "Why No Compromise Is Possible").

3:AM: You are a philosopher who is a member of the ethics board of Karolinska Institutes. How does your approach help clarify existing discussions?

TT: In such boards (I have served in several) what is needed from a philosopher is indeed applied ethics of the kind I just described.

3:AM: Is capital punishment ever morally permissible?

TT: One way of submitting your moral intuitions in relation to some issue to cognitive therapy is to learn more about how people in other cultures think about it. I have been brought up in a culture where capital punishment is indeed anathema. I have always thought of myself as a principled opponent to capital punishment. However, when thinking about how the topic is handled in other cultures, in particular the American, Russian and Chinese ones, I have realised that my own tack on the issue was utterly superficial. I have now come to the conclusion (roughly) that capital punishment is defensible, if it can be shown to have a deterrent effect on murder. In that case, a few executions save not only some people from being murdered but also some people from becoming murders. It is hard to tell, however, if capital punishment has such an effect. And even if, in some contexts it has (such as in the American South with a very high incidence of murder), this effect may very well go away if a decent welfare state was replaced for the existing social order. I want to think that there are better ways of obviating murder than to resort to capital punishment, but I realise that this may be wishful thinking on my part.

3:AM: With science and technology developing as it is, what are the ethical concerns regarding human enhancement, such as the use of genetic technologies in sports?

TT: There comes a time where next to everyone will resort to techniques that enhance cognitive, mental including emotive, physical, and other capacities. When this has happened, if not before, the ban on doping in sport will have been lifted. There are good reasons to lift it anyway (I wrote about this recently in an article in The Boston Globe), so I do not see this as a problem. Actually, I see mainly one huge problem with human enhancement and it has to do with the possibility of life extension. The possibility to go on indefinitely with our lives may become a reality and it will present us with a temptation. Why not hang around for yet some time? My conjecture is that most people will refuse to let go, even when their lives have become boring (at least in comparisons with possible lives lived by new generations). If this happens, there will eventually be no room for new generations. A kind of collective irrationality will lead to a bleak life for the last generation that decides to stay around. Unless we put and end to the human race (through global warming, for example), before this happens, individual egoism will block the path to a better world.

3:AM: The world looks a mess at the moment—wars, global warming, poverty, inequality etc. Could a global government be a good step forward to dealing with all this. You argued the case in 2008, are you still in favour?

TT: The book Global Democracy is out in a new printing with a new preface where I still defend my view. It is obvious, I think, that national democracy withers. This has to do with globalisation. It is also obvious that humanity faces existential threats of a global nature. They are global in the sense that is not possible to deal with them unless we resort to global governance. Take global warming as the most obvious example. When the leaders of different nations negotiate about the problem, each leader is supposed to make as small concessions as possible on behalf of her own nation, while urging others to do more. We face a giant tragedy of the commons. What we need is legislation, not negotiation, for the entire globe. Only a global government of some kind can provide the needed solutions. Global governance need not take a democratic form, however. Just think of organisations such as the World Bank. It is quite possible that we will soon come to live under some sort of global despotism, enlightened or not. This is not a nice prospect. And there is only one way of avoiding that this happens: to establish a global democracy. And it is not too late to strive for such a democracy, of a straightforward populist nature, where people on the globe elect a world parliament, which in turn elects a world government. It is natural to build on the United Nations in this endeavour. A modest first step in the right direction is to introduce a parliamentary assembly in the UN framework. There exists such an initiative and I strongly support it.

3:AM: With Donald Trump making the populist case for democracy, are you still in favour of populist democracy? And he's a right winger too, so do you still defend a political conservativism?

TT: My take on conservatism (as opposed to radicalism) cannot be explained in this short space. I am a left winger, thought. And I do believe that what I have called populist democracy is to be preferred to what I have called elitist democracy. In many European countries we have populist indirect democratic systems. The people elect, in a proportionate manner, a parliament. The parliament with all its parties is representative of the political opinions among the citizens. It is reasonable to claim that the people rule itself through the political institutions. The US two party system is very different, of course. Here the people decides about who should rule them, but it is not reasonable to claim that the people rules itself through the political institutions. In comparison, I find that the standard European system is better, also as a model for global democracy. Again, to defend such a position would take more space than is available right now.

3:AM: And finally, for the readers ere at 3:AM, are there five books you could recommend, other than your own, that would help take us further into your philosophical world?

TT: Sure:

> Robert Nozick, *Anarchy, State, and Utopia* is (still) the best introduction to, and defence of, the libertarian theory of rights, which I discuss and reject in my *Taking Life*.
> Jonathan Glover, *Causing Death and Saving Lives* is a minor classic on the ethics of killing.
> Jeff McMahan, *The Ethics of Killing* is a highly instructive and more up to date book on the subject, which is written from a point of view very different from mine. One could perhaps speak of his method of "inductive" where mine is "hypothetically deductive" (to use terminology from the theory of science).

The kind of moral realism I defend is best compared to the moral nihilism defended by John Mackie. However, the best book on Mackie and his argument from queerness in particular and the "error theory" in general to this date is not his own *Ethics* but Jonas Olsson, *Moral Error Theory*.

In my *Global Democracy* I argue that global democracy is not only necessary if we want to solve pressing global problems, but also of value in its own right. For a defence of the opposite position one should turn to John Rawls, *The Law of Peoples* with its Kantian insistence that a global state is bound to deteriorate into global tyranny.

Torbjörn Tännsjö is the author of:

Moral Realism (Rowman & Littlefield, 1990)

Conservatism for Our Time (Routledge, 1990)

Populist Democracy: A Defence (Routledge, 1993)

Hedonistic Utilitarianism (Edinburgh University Press, 1998)

Coercive Care: The Ethics of Choice in Health and Medicine (Routledge, 1999)

Understanding Ethics: An Introduction to Moral Theory (Edinburgh University Press/ Columbia University Press, 2002. Second, revised edition, 2008)

Global Democracy: The Case for a World Government (Edinburgh University Press, 2008)

From Reasons to Norms: On the Basic Question in Ethics (Springer, 2011)

Taking Life: Three Theories on the Ethics of Killing (Oxford University Press, 2015)

16 | Katarzyna de Lazari-Radek: "From the Point of View of the Universe"

Katarzyna de Lazari-Radek is a Polish utilitarian philosopher and a lecturer at the Institute of Philosophy at Lodz University in Poland and at the European Graduate School. She is the philosopher who is always pondering contemporary ethics from the point of view of the universe, with Peter Singer. Here she discusses Sidgwick and why he's not widely read, his approach to ethics and why he's significant, what we mean by "the point of view of the universe," Sidgwickean rationality and Kant, reflective equilibrium, self-evident axioms, Parfit's "future Tuesday indifference" and his *On What Matters*, hedonism, esoteric morality, the repugnant conclusion, and why Philip Kitcher is wrong to think naturalism in ethics is defensible.

3:AM: What made you a philosopher?

KATARZYNA DE LAZARI-RADEK: This may sound a bit naïve but I did always want to make the world a better place. And though you can do it without studying philosophy, it is easier to have influence on people when you understand the world better and you have certain abilities to formulate arguments, analyse problems, seek a fault in your own as well as someone else's thinking. I wanted to know what would be the thing that makes the world a better place, what is the good, what should I do, what are our obligations and who are these that I should take care of. These are all ethical questions that you need to think over. There is no better place to find answers than philosophy. It gives you enormous possibilities to think. Hannah Arendt once said that evil comes from the lack of reflection. I think I agree.

3:AM: You have joined forces with Peter Singer to defend act utilitarianism. Most people will have an inkling about Mill and Bentham but not perhaps the philosopher you want to return to—Henry Sidgwick. He's the guy who might be the very first of the analytic philosophers isn't he—messing up the usual time line that tends to see the analytics kick starting with Frege, Russell and Moore. Why isn't he so well known as the rest of the utilitarian band? Is it that he tends to be quite boring to read compared to the others?

KLR: I think that the main reason for Sidgwick not to be widely read is simple—his prose is really difficult. It is very complex and you often lose the line of an argument as it is so complicated. Sidgwick sometimes writes a few pages, you think he presents his own ideas but at the end of the section he rejects all of what he has argued so far. You need to get back, look at the argument again and find a mistake in it together with Sidgwick. I think English speaking people are used to simpler English texts. You know, Kant or Hegel are very difficult, but an English philosopher is usually much more straightforward. As for Sidgwick being the first of analytical philosophers I agree that he gave a good start to Moore. Many people forget that without Sidgwick's The Methods of Ethics there would be no Principia Ethica. The naturalistic fallacy was not Moore's invention—it is already in Sidgwick.

3:AM: You've two aims in the book—one to make Sidgwick accessible, and to defend utilitarianism. On the first aim first—do you think there's a problem with contemporary philosophy requiring that we always read the original text rather than a "made easy" text book. Wouldn't we get more progress if philosophers were a little less precious about the originals and got on with making things more accessible? Is that a reason why you treat him as if he were a serious contemporary rather than someone from the history of ideas?

KLR: As for your first question, I believe a lot depends who is supposed to read philosophical texts and for what purpose. You cannot really study philosophy seriously on the basis of what you called "a made easy text book." Also why not exercise your brain a bit? We would definitely hope that our book is not treated as a substitute for The Methods, but rather as an introduction to The Methods. On the other hand, if you study something else, political thought, let's say, you read Rawls and you want to know who that guy Rawls often refers to was and what he said, our book will be a good summary, I would think.

3:AM: So for Sidgwick, what is ethics, its methods and what is a philosopher up to when she's investigating them? And what does it mean to say there is a "point of view of the universe"?

KLR: Sidgwick defines ethics as a study of what we ought to do as opposed to other studies such as psychology or biology that tell you what is the case. The methods of ethics are rational procedures which we, individual beings, use to determine what we ought to do. In everyday life we are often not very consistent: we use many different methods, and we mix them as well. But Sidgwick is a scholar and he wants to make them scientific. Therefore he will separate them carefully and underline differences between them. He will talk of egoism, intuitionism and utilitarianism.

As for the most important expression: "the point of view of the universe" that is to symbolize an impartial concern for everyone. Sidgwick calls for impartiality in ethics and thinks that when deciding what we ought to do, we should try to take an impartial perspective—not mine, not yours, not my children's but "the point of view of the universe." Rawls, Nagel and Parfit will all refer to that perspective in their works later on.

3:AM: What does rationality add up to in Sidgwick? Is this a return to Kantianism and a kick back against Hume and Hare and is it part of the reason why Sidgwick rejects common sense ethics?

KLR: I do think Sidgwick was influenced by Kant in this respect, but also by such English intuitionists as Thomas Reid or William Whewell as well as Coleridge. He did believe in reason and rationality. But he also saw a great crack in it. Claiming that both maximizing my own good and maximizing impartial good is rational, he could not reach a final answer to the most important question of his inquiry: what ought I to do? When in a tragic situation, should I save my own child or rather a few children of complete strangers? Sidgwick regretted to say that but he confesses at the end of The Methods that reason may not give us a final answer. That would be tragic indeed as it would open the door to subjectivism again. Peter Singer and I tried to help Sidgwick to overcome that chaos. We claim that only impartial action is fully rational.

As for his rejection of common sense. He is not satisfied with rules given by common sense as he finds them unclear, vague, not self-evident.

3:AM: And does this mean that he is out of line with someone like Rawls who'd argue that we need to find a "reflective equilibrium between theory and considered moral judgments? Where do you stand on this?

KLR: This is an interesting question but I treat it more as a problem of justification. First, unlike Rawls, both Sidgwick and we are interested in truth and finding true moral principles. Now the question is do we use coherentism or foundationalism to find out the truth. Reflective equilibrium seems a useful tool but as Hare, in his review of The Theory of Justice, recalled Plato saying: "If a man starts from something he knows not, and the end and middle of his argument are tangled together out of what he knows not, how can such a mere consensus ever turn into knowledge?" (Rep. 533 c). On the other hand, foundationalism can lead easily to dogmatism. We tried our best to stand somewhere in between those two.

3:AM: Are you sympathetic to the foundational self-evident axioms Sidgwick uses? Is this where the idea of 'rational intuition" comes in—and your use of Parfit's "Future Tuesday Indifference"? Can you explain the argument here? And why wouldn't this be congenial to contemporary economists who might have expected to find a defence of their models of rationality in this approach?

KLR: Yes, we are sympathetic to Sidgwick's appeal to self-evident axioms, especially his axiom of rational benevolence, which is linked to taking "the point of view of the universe." We argue that this is a rational axiom, because, in contrast to many other moral intuitions, our acceptance of it cannot be debunked by an evolutionary explanation.

Parfit's uses the idea of "Future Tuesday Indifference" in a slightly different context, to argue against the subjectivist view that what is rational is always dependent on a person's ultimate desires, or ends. A person who is indifferent to what happens to him on any future Tuesday (and therefore, when offered a choice between being pinched today and hours of torture next Tuesday, chooses the torture) may be acting in accordance with his bizarre set of desires, but he is still irrational. Contemporary economists assume that a view of rationality that is subjectivist, or as they would call it, instrumentalist, so they won't find this argument congenial. It will force them to reexamine their fundamental assumptions about rationality.

3:AM: Unlike Parfit's *On What Matters* you defend act utilitarianism don't you? Can you explain what this is and why you don't go all the way with the Parfit approach?

KLR: Yes, together with Sidgwick, we are act-utilitarians. When you think of how to maximize the good, there are two main types of utilitarian theory: act utilitarianism and rule utilitarianism. The former tells you that you should decide what to do, to maximize the good, each time you need to take an action. But rule utilitarianism tells you first to decide on certain rules that, generally, will lead to maximizing the good. For example, it is generally better for us that we do not deceive each other and can trust each other. Therefore it is desirable to have a rule forbidding lying. When in a situation where you have to choose whether to lie or not, a rule utilitarian will apply a rule, no matter what are the further consequences; an act utilitarian has to think whether in this very situation a lie will bring about better overall consequences, if so—then it is better to deceive at that moment.

In *On What Matters*, Parfit works on putting together three seemingly very different moral theories: contractualism, utilitarianism and Kantianism. I think that rule utilitarianism goes better with his idea of reaching the same summit even if taking different routes. But next year, we should be lucky to have a third volume of *On What Matters* where Parfit will spend much more time discussing act-utilitarianism.

3:AM: This is a form of hedonism isn't it? How does Sidgwick understand hedonism—and are you sympathetic?

KLR: Well, you can be a hedonist no matter whether you are a rule or an act utilitarian. A hedonist defines the good which you should maximize in terms of happiness or pleasure. For Sidgwick the two were the same thing and he defines pleasure as desirable consciousness, that is a state of mind which you desire at the time of feeling it. We do argue for hedonism and for the idea that we ought to maximize certain states of minds. I think it is interesting to see how Peter Singer has changed his idea about it. For years he was a preference utilitarian.

3:AM: Is an esoteric morality ok—and are we sometimes right to do in secret what would be wrong to advocate or do in public?

KLR: It seems that the idea of esoteric morality, that is a lack of total transparency, is a natural outcome of hedonistic act-utilitarianism. For example, on the whole it is good that we have a law forbidding torture, because we know that when torture is permitted, it is often used simply as a form of degrading others and demonstrating one's power over them. But imagine a situation in which you can really save many innocent lives by torturing a criminal, and there is no other way to save those lives. That might be the right thing to do, while still supporting the law that prohibits torture.

3:AM: The "repugnant conclusion" argument of Parfit regarding optimal population growth seems on the face of it a pretty decisive one for rejecting utilitarianism doesn't it? How do you handle this issue so we can remain utilitarians?

KLR: I don't see this as a ground for rejecting utilitarianism at all. Parfit's "repugnant conclusion" is an objection to one way of answering the simple question that Sidgwick was the first to raise: if by increasing the population, the average level of welfare decreases, but because everyone still has lives that are, on balance, happy, the total amount of happiness in the world increases, is that a good thing? What Parfit has shown is that all of the answers that seem plausible—not just those offered by Sidgwick or other utilitarians—lead to either inconsistency or counter-intuitive judgments. Therefore it isn't as if non-utilitarians do any better in answering the question than utilitarians.

3:AM: Is your view a non-reductive and non-naturalistic, non-metaphysical and non-ontological form of cognitive intuitionism of the sort that someone like Philip Kitcher would deplore—as he did with Parfit's *On What Matters*? Won't many think that we have evolved evaluative attitudes to help us survive and breed rather than because they are true—and isn't this fatal for Sidgwick's position? And isn't it strange that someone like Peter Singer would argue from a non-naturalistic point of view given his work in animal rights?

KLR: Yes, our view is the kind that Kitcher deplores, but, like Parfit and many other philosophers, we don't think naturalism in ethics is defensible.

Singer is a utilitarian and so does not base his arguments about animals on rights. But anyway, I don't see why you should think there is anything strange about rejecting naturalism in ethics, while defending the view that animals are sentient beings whose welfare should be considered alongside our own. I can't see what one has to do with the other. Perhaps there is some confusion going on here, because the term "nature" is used in so many different ways, but naturalism in ethics has nothing to do with whether one values "nature" in the sense of the world apart from human beings.

3:AM: Is the view of human reason you defend here with Sidgwick a ground for optimism or pessimism?

KLR: I never have thought of that in this way! First, as I have mentioned, our point about reason is a bit different from that of Sidgwick or Parfit. We try to argue that reason is always impartial, that what is on the side of egoism is not really rational. It can be pretty uncomfortable for us sometimes. But on the other hand, it leaves us with quite clear guidance about what we should do.

3:AM: And for the readers here at 3:AM who want to get further into your philosophical world are there five books you can recommend?

KLR: This is a cruel question indeed! How to choose 5 out of so many. Apart from Sidgwick's *Methods* I would recommend Scheffler's *Death and the Afterlife*—a book that will put your life into a perspective; how would you feel about the sense of your existence if you knew that life on our planet will end a few hours after your natural death as an old man? A lovely witty book on happiness is always good—if you have not read it yet, get Gilbert's *Stumbling on Happiness*. It seems to me that getting happy in your life can be a hard, rational work. If you want to be better to yourself read Kahnemans's *Thinking, Fast* *and Slow*. Maybe next time you will save yourself some troubles doing shopping! As for serious philosophy—Parfit's *On What Matters* is a must. Be quick though, as I have mentioned, the third volume is supposed to appear next year! If you are interested in ethics always and forever Singer's *Practical Ethics*.

Katarzyna de Lazari-Radek is the author of:

The Point of View of the Universe: Sigdwick and Contemporary Ethics (with Peter Singer) (Oxford University Press, 2014)

3 | Applied Ethics

17 | Rebecca Gordon: "Saying No to Jack Bauer"

Rebecca Gordon is a philosopher at the University of San Francisco. She is an applied ethicist, and here she discusses ways of forging a dialectical relationship to the rest of the world, current political realities, torture as a government-supported institution hidden in plain sight, torture and Alisdair MacIntyre's virtue ethics, torture as a practice, what Obama should do, "enhanced interrogation," why Jack Bauer is wrong, why Elizabeth Anscombe thinks certain thought experiments can erode ethical thinking, whether her own approach is universal, rival approaches, and whether there are reasons for optimism around this depressing reality.

3:AM: What made you become a philosopher?

REBECCA GORDON: It was an accident. I'd spent the previous 30-odd years as an activist in a variety of political movements, supporting myself as a bookkeeper and accountant. In 2000, it seemed that many of the movements I'd worked in (for women's liberation, for LGBT in solidarity with people in Central America, against apartheid in South Africa and for racial justice in the United States) had reached a kind of stasis. A long phase of my personal life was also drawing to a close; my partner and I had been caring for my mother for some years; now she was dying. It seemed like a good moment to do something new. Naturally, I thought, "I'll go back to school."

NEXT QUESTION: What to study? Mathematics? History? Small particle physics? I decided I might as well do something that encompasses the whole shebang and study theology. So I wandered over to the Graduate Theological Union, where I thought I'd spend a couple of years and emerge with an M.Div. from Starr King School for Religious Leadership. Once you're enrolled at GTU, you can take classes at any of the nine schools, and U.C. Berkeley. So I did. And, against all my expectations, I fell in love with scholarship.

The Graduate Theological Union in Berkeley, California gave me a full ride for the first two years of a doctoral program in Ethics and Social Theory. As I worked on the dissertation, I began teaching in the Philosophy department at the University of San Francisco. Now I had something entirely new to learn about: how to teach. For the last nine years I've had the privilege of talking with an economically, racially, and nationally diverse group of young people about their own deepest values—at the time in their lives when they are trying to figure out who they want to be in the world.

The work that became Mainstreaming Torture began as my dissertation at the GTU.

3:AM: You say that the world of philosophical ethics is divided into two very distinct segments—theoretical and applied ethics and that in the academy the theoretical is more esteemed. But you are an applied ethicist—so are you out to change the world—and do you think the academy should be too?

RG: I would never presume to seek to "change the world" as an individual actor. That is a project for many people thinking, deciding, and working together in organized ways. My goal for the students in my classes is that they emerge thinking of themselves as citizens—not necessarily, or only, of a single nation, but of the world. Do I think the academy should be out to change the world? I think that much of its work inevitably does change the world, and not always for the better. I think that those of us located in the academy have a responsibility to recognize that our institutions are embedded in a larger society, and that, as is true for any institution, we exist in dialectical relationship to the rest of the world.

3:AM: You've recently engaged with the highly topical issue of torture. Was the motivation political awareness of what's happening recently?

RG: Yes, and no. Yes in that I began thinking and writing about state torture within two months of the terrible attacks of 9/11. And no, in the sense that I had long known that my own government supported torture regimes in many places, including Greece, the Philippines, and large parts of Latin America.

In 1984 I spent six months in the war zones of Nicaragua. There I met survivors of torture at the hands of the counter-revolutionary force the Reagan administration was (at that time illegally) training, arming, and supporting, known as the contra. The contra had an intentional strategy of terrorizing civilians in rural areas, torturing them to death and leaving mutilated bodies to be discovered by others. I met at least one torturer as well.

A few years later, I served as interpreter for a U.S. delegation to El Salvador, just a few weeks before the murders of six Jesuits, their housekeeper, and her daughter at the Universidad Centroaméricana in San Salvador. At that time, the Salvadoran government enjoyed military and political support from United States. During our two weeks in El Salvador, one of our key contacts in the labor movement there was arrested. We were able to visit him in prison, where he described how he had been tortured. Not for information, but as a matter of course.

Within a few weeks of the 9/11 attacks, it became clear to anyone who wanted to know that one result was that people were going to be tortured. Of course this wasn't the first time the U.S. government has been involved with torture, but September 11 did mark a real change. Almost overnight, a question that many people believed had been resolved—whether or not torture is wrong—was reopened. In November of 2011, Jonathan Alter, a mainstream liberal columnist, wrote in Newsweek, "In this autumn of anger, even a liberal can find his thoughts turning to ... torture." He wondered whether it might be a good plan to deport the Muslims living in the United States whom the FBI had rounded up to "Saudi Arabia, land of beheadings." Americans who weren't thinking about new methods to "jump-start the stalled investigation of the greatest crime in American history" had failed to recognize that they lived in a transformed world. "Some people still argue," wrote Alter, "that we needn't rethink any of our old assumptions about law enforcement, but they're hopelessly "Sept. 10"—living in a country that no longer exists."

The people the FBI had rounded up turned out to have nothing to do with 9/11, but some of them were held for more than half a year in cells in Brooklyn, NY, where they were subjected to treatment that has since become very familiar: 23-hour-per-day isolation, short shackling, beatings, sexual humiliation, exposure to freezing temperatures, and in at least one case, anal rape with a police flashlight.

The more I think about institutionalized torture, the more I realize that it is hidden in plain sight all around us—in U.S. jails an prisons, and even in institutions for people with disabilities. So yes, it is topical. And it has been going on for a long time.

3:AM: Are you approaching this via virtue ethics, four cardinal virtues and Alisdair MacIntyre and what is the best way to understand what torture is?

RG: I'm going to reverse the order of these questions, because I think that once we understand what institutionalized state torture is, it becomes clearer why I think MacIntyre's contemporary virtue ethics provide a useful way of understanding torture's moral implications.

The torture that I am concerned with is institutionalized state torture—the kind of organized, intentional program carried on by governments. It's not

Jack Bauer saving Los Angeles on 24. It's not some brave person preventing a ticking time-bomb from going off by torturing the one person who can stop it. We must stop thinking of torture as a series of isolated actions taken by heroic individuals in moments of extremity, and begin instead to understand it as a socially embedded practice. A study of past and present torture regimes suggests that institutionalized state torture has its own histories, its own traditions, its own rituals of initiation. It encourages, both in its individual practitioners and in the society that harbors it, a particular set of moral habits, call them virtues or vices as you prefer.

Here's my definition of institutionalize state torture: It is the intentional infliction of severe mental or physical suffering by an official or agent of a political entity, which results in dismantling the victim's sensory, psychological, and social worlds, with the purpose of establishing or maintaining that entity's power. This definition can be expanded to reveal its legal, phenomenological, and political dimensions.

The language about "intentional infliction of severe mental or physical suffering by an agent of a political entity" mirrors the definition found in the UN Convention against Torture and Other Cruel, Inhumane, or Degrading Treatment, to which the U.S. is a signatory. A phenomenological definition describes the ways in which torture reduces and distorts its targets' orientation in time and space, its effects on language, and its destruction persons' social connections. The "political" portion deals with the purposes of torture, which when it is institutionalized by a state, has much less to do with "intelligence gathering" than it does with political and social control.

So what does this understanding of torture have to do with virtue ethics and Alasdair MacIntyre? I would argue that when we understand torture as an ongoing practice, we can begin to see how it affects moral habits. (I'll say more about how MacIntyre's approach in answer to a later question.) The "cardinal" virtues have been around in "western" philosophy since Plato and Aristotle (although the latter's catalogue of virtues was more varied and variable.) These virtues are courage, justice, temperance or moderation, and wisdom. In Mainstreaming, I describe ways that each of these is distorted by the practice of torture.'

Courage becomes not the ability to withstand fear and pain, but the ability to overcome instinctive squeamishness and inflict it.

Justice is tricky to define, but one thing is clear, which is that torture subverts the usual temporal order of legal justice. Ordinarily, trial precedes punishment. In torture, the order is reversed, and in many cases, no trial ever occurs.

Temperance can be thought of as a properly measured response to the joys and pleasures of life. In torture, what is prized is moderation in enjoyment of causing suffering. That is, interviews with torturers suggest that they have little respect for peers who torture because they like doing it. Thomas Aquinas includes the subsidiary virtue of humility within the category of temperance. Torture belies the humility that allows us to recognize that no human being can know the contents of another person's mind. We cannot identify with certainty the "really bad guys," who may in fact turn out to be unlucky men scooped up and sold on an Afghan battlefield.

The wisdom I am concerned with is practical wisdom, what Aristotle calls phronesis, and Thomas prudence, right reason about things to be done. It is the intellectual virtue, that allows us to think properly about moral questions. In Mainstreaming, I said,

"In commenting on the perpetrators of great evil, including torturers [Hannah Arendt] observed that the one thing they appeared to have in common was "something entirely negative; it was not stupidity but a curious, quite authentic inability to think." Elsewhere she writes, "Without taking into account the almost universal breakdown, not of personal responsibility, but of personal judgment in the early stages of the Nazi regime, it is impossible to understand what happened." The inability to think about what is happening around one, or to make a moral judgment about it, is a dangerous habit indeed.

The practice of institutionalized state torture requires precisely this "quite authentic inability to think" both in people directly involved, and in a public that learns not to think too hard about what is being done in our name for our supposed protection. I sometimes think it's useful to talk about "culpable ignorance," the failure to acknowledge something we could know if we chose to. Not that we haven't had help getting there. I've argued that in the case of the "war on terror" the government's "rhetoric of denial, the theater of fear with its manipulation of threat levels and [what William Cavanaugh calls] the "striptease of power," the apologias for torture by present and former government officials: All these serve to diminish ordinary citizens' capacity to think clearly about moral questions.

3:AM: There's always the danger that any definition will not cover all examples—so are you deliberately just focusing on the area where you think there's an urgent need for policy decisions given the post- 9/11 political landscape rather than trying to cover other areas?

RG: I actually think that the definition of institutionalized state torture also applies to practices carried out daily in U.S. jails and prisons. There are direct connections, in terms of personnel and techniques, between torture in the "war on terror" and in other sites of incarceration. For example, we are beginning to understand just how severe the mental suffering is of people held in solitary confinement. To take another example, the expectation that people held in jail or prison will be raped is so common that it has become a staple threat on television police procedurals: "How long do you think a pretty boy like you is going to last in Rikers?"

3:AM: How does MacIntyre's virtue ethics help your approach to condemning torture?

RG: It takes MacIntyre about 250 pages of After Virtue to unfold his virtue ethics schema. My attempt to summarize it here will doubtless be inadequate! There are four key concepts in MacIntyre's ethics: telos, practice, virtue, and tradition. For him, the human telos (goal, purpose of life) is essentially participation in the ongoing historic quest to understand and enact the good life for human beings. Much of this quest takes place within the context of practices, which he understands as complex, cooperative socially-embedded human activities. A practice involves the collective work of several or many people, although individuals participating in a practice, for example, landscape painting, may often work on their own. It has its own set of internal "goods"—things that can only be achieved through participation in that particular practice. It has rules and standards of excellence. Entering into, learning, and participating in a practice creates allows a person to form virtues: stable, transferrable habits of character, which are in turn necessary to weathering the dangers and difficulties found in the larger quest for telos. Finally, practices are embedded in traditions, which MacIntyre conceives of not as a set of hallowed ideas or beliefs, as an ongoing argument about aspects of the human telos.

It seems to me (with one caveat, which is addressed in your next question), that institutionalized state torture is a practice, in the sense that MacIntyre describes. It is complex and collaborative. It has its own rules and standards of excellence. There are specific internal goods achievable only through this practice, goods which I call the production of truth, the production of enemies, and the production and reproduction of torturers themselves. Torture also produces moral habits, I argue, both in the practitioners themselves, and to some extent in the members of the larger society that knowingly permits torture.

3:AM: Why is torture a "false practice"?

RG: This is an expression introduced by Christopher Stephen Lutz in Tradition in the Ethics of Alasdair MacIntyre, to describe a human activity that satisfies most of MacIntyre's definition of a practice, except that it is evil. In a false practice, the moral habits engendered inhibit rather than assisting a human being in her quest for the good life. In After Virtue, MacIntyre asks himself whether a human activity that is inherently evil can be called a practice. He answers in the negative, and cites torture precisely as the kind of complex, collaborative activity he would consider evil, and therefore not a practice.

3:AM: You suggest three responses to torture that Obama should heed. Can you tell us about them?

RG: I finished the manuscript for Mainstreaming Torture in June 2013. At that time I wrote that there were three things the U.S. government and specifically President Obama should do in the short term: Close the prison at Guantánamo Bay, Cuba, end the practice of extraordinary rendition (i.e., sending people to other countries for "interrogation'), and completely dismantle the torture apparatus of the tangle of intelligence and military agencies presently involved in torture.

I've also said that we still need a full accounting of the torture practices that evolved in the "war on terror." This would include, but certainly not be limited to, release of the Senate Intelligence Committee's 6,000-page report on the CIA's "enhanced interrogation" program. Of course, the CIA is not the only U.S. agency involved in torture. I've also argued that in addition to a full accounting, there must be real accountability for the U.S. torture programs. This means holding to account not just a few low-level soldiers like Lynndie England of Abu Ghraib fame, but the high public officials who directed these programs.

Unfortunately, a year later none of these steps have been taken. Guantánamo remains open, with a present detainee population of around 140. The U.S. government, and specifically the CIA, still explicitly expresses a right to "render" detainees to other countries, although with the proviso that they not be tortured. Since this proviso has always been in effect, if not effectual, skeptics might be forgiven for doubting the sincerity of that proviso. And finally, nothing has been done to address torture carried out by U.S. civilian and military entities other than the CIA. As Jeremy Scahill ably demonstrates in Dirty Wars, one of the most important of these is the Joint Special Operations Command, or JSOC, which ran its own "interrogation" program in Iraq. Just a few days ago, the UK Guardian reported that there is still at least one U.S.-run detention center near the Bagram Air Force base in Afghanistan. The United States has handed over all its Afghan detainees to the Afghan government, but it retains the right to hold non-Afghan prisoners indefinitely.

3:AM: What are we to make of the idea of "enhanced interrogation" and the CIA's claim that it worked to prevent future planned atrocities? If torturing one guy prevents a war where hundreds of thousands are affected isn't there a case? Is there never a justification?

RG: A couple of answers here. First, we are in no position to verify the CIA's (relatively vague) claims that torture worked to prevent future atrocities. We have only their word for it.

We know that torture worked to force Khalid Sheik Mohammed to admit to being the mastermind of the September 11 attacks. But that admission had nothing to do with preventing future attacks. Furthermore, neither U.S. law nor international law permits the use of torture for the purpose of producing a confession to a crime. The reasons for this are obvious: 1) If forced confessions were admissible in criminal courts, everyone who is arrested would be at risk of being tortured; and 2) Forced confessions are very likely to be false confessions.

We know that some people within the CIA have claimed that torture produced the missing piece of information about the identity of a courier to Osama bin Laden, which eventually allowed a U.S. team to find and kill him. Others have argued that in fact that information was already known, which is the public position of the Senate Intelligence Committee on the matter. But in either case, is torturing someone to find out the location of a criminal, even a very bad criminal, justified?

The scenario presented in your second question is a version of what's often called the "ticking time-bomb" problem. It usually involves a utilitarian argument that the unhappiness of the many outweighs that of the tortured individual. Other versions are consequentialist also, if not strictly utilitarian, positing for example, the imperative to torture one (guilty) criminal in order to find the location of one (innocent) kidnapped child. There are several difficulties with these hypothetical scenarios:

We wouldn't know how to do it right. It is not possible to torture someone "on the spur of the moment." Torture requires infrastructure and trained practitioners who keep their skills honed. Jack Bauer to the contrary, real life is not like 24. (And Bauer actually is pretty well-trained!)

The time-sensitive scenario is precisely the one in which someone who is concealing life-saving information is most likely to hold out; he knows exactly how long he has to resist.

We can't have what Fritz Alhoff calls "epistemic certainty" that we have captured the right guy, that he actually knows what we want to know, that he's right about what he thinks he knows, or that, as Henry Shue says, he won't just "vomit and die," instead of producing information.

These scenarios don't happen in the real world. There is no information "one guy" could produce that would prevent a war. Wars don't happen because one side or another doesn't know some key piece of information. Wars have their own logic and momentum, and their causes are often opaque, even to those who fight them. (Look at all the arguments a century later about the causes of WW I.)

I'm not picking on the torture-one-guy-to-prevent-a-war scenario in order to avoid the larger question, which is, isn't there some scenario in which time-senitive information that will save hundreds of thousands of lives can only be produced through torture? My answer is no, there isn't. This is not how institutional state torture works. G.E.M. Anscombe described the problem with this kind of hypothetical argumentation beautifully in a 1958 article:

"Finally, the point of considering hypothetical situations, perhaps very improbable ones, seems to be to elicit from yourself or someone else a hypothetical decision to do something of a bad kind. I don't doubt this has the effect of predisposing people–who will never get into the situations for which they have made hypothetical choices—to consent to similar bad actions, or to praise and flatter those who do them, so long as their crowd does so too, when the desperate circumstances imagined don't hold at all."

3:AM: Your discussion focuses on US policy but this isn't just a US issue is it? How effective are your arguments when placed outside of western style systems of politics and law? I guess this is a question about whether there are many presuppositions to your position that can't be universally granted or applied?

RG: This is a good question, and one that's not easily answered. Of course, the same question could be posed to an advocate of Kantian deontology, or utilitarianism, or any other ethical system arising out of the western philosophical traditions.

In a sense, this is a question that can best be answered empirically, by engaging in dialogue with specific traditions outside of "western" systems of politics and law. Here I think it very much matters which ethical system we're talking about. That is, my arguments might find many assumptions in common with some forms of buddhism (a way of life that privileges practice and virtue). It might be more difficult to find a shared starting place for a conversation with Korean animists. I don't honestly know.

I can think of a couple of relevant attempts to forge a universal approach to human rights not based specifically in western ethical traditions. The first is the process by which the Universal Declaration of Human Rights was written shortly after the United Nations was founded in 1945. The framers intentionally strove not to base the declaration's contents on any one ethical tradition, or in any one religious tradition. (Article 5, by the way, reads, "No one shall be subjected to torture or to cruel, inhuman or degrading treatment or punishment.") It is worth noting that in spite of the authors' efforts, the Declaration is not without its critics, who see it as a fundamentally western document.

The second is the efforts of Amartya Sen and Martha Nussbaum to transcend the problem of cultural relativism by developing the concept of "capabilities theory" as a means of making comparisons about justice across cultures and societies. In Women and Development, Nussbaum suggests that human animals in general are born with certain specific capabilities, including such things as life, bodily health, bodily integrity, senses, imagination, and thought, emotions, practical reason, affiliation, and play. A society is a just one, to the extent that it makes it possible for all its members to develop these capacities that are present in the human species as a whole. What that development looks like will vary tremendously across cultures, of course. Whether members of all societies would accept their assumptions about the capabilities of the human person remains an open question.

MacIntyre would argue that his own virtue ethics represents a sharp and intentional break with the Enlightenment framework that constrains most contemporary ethical systems. In that sense, you might say that his ethics are as much "Mediterranean" or "Aegean" as "western."

3:AM: There are of course rivals to the theories of virtue and ethics you put forward—why do you think your approach is superior to the rivals out there?

RG: I think that my approach to the ethical problem of institutionalized state torture is based on a more accurate representation of what torture is. If torture were simply a set of isolated actions, then consequentialist or deontological approaches might be adequate for judging each act. Torture is, in a sense, more than the sum of individual actions, each of which can be assessed de novo, weighed by an ethical calculus of costs and benefits, or through the mental testing of the effects of universalizing a maxim. Actions create habits. We become brave, as Aristotle says, by doing brave acts. And, in the case of allowing other people to be tortured as the price of an illusory guarantee of our own personal survival, we become cowards by doing cowardly ones.

I think that most of the time in real life, people act first and identify their reasons for acting later. If most of the time we act out of habit, shouldn't those habits be good ones?

3:AM: And is there any reason for optimism in this depressing area—are there developments that suggest that the use of torture will diminish in the near future?

RG: Actually, I think there is some. For one thing, I think hope is one of those virtues we need to cultivate in ourselves!

But more specifically, while some disturbing polling data suggests people in this country are more supportive of torture today than they were at the height of the 'war on terror," I see two hopeful trends. The first is a growing recognition in the United States that solitary confinement creates severe mental suffering and is in fact a form of torture. The second is the momentum building in opposition to capital punishment.

3:AM: And for those of us at 3:AM wanting to get further into your philosophical world are there five books you could recommend to us?

RG: Hmm . . . let's see . . .

Alasdair MacIntyre. *After Virtue and Rational, Dependent Animals.*
Elaine Scarry, *The Body in Pain: The Making and Unmaking of the World*

William Cavanaugh, *Torture and Eucharist: Theology, Politics and the Body of Christ*

Lawrence Wechsler, *A Miracle, a Universe: Settling Accounts with Torturers*

And if you want to have fun, try any of Terry Pratchett's Discworld novels.

Rebecca Gordon is the author of:

Mainstreaming Torture: Ethical Approaches in the Post-9/11 Period (Oxford University Press, 2014)

18 | Lori Gruen: "Philosophy of Captivity"

Lori Gruen is the William Griffin Professor of Philosophy and Professor
of Feminist, Gender, and Sexuality Studies, and Environmental Studies,
at Wesleyan University, where she also coordinates the Wesleyan Animal
Studies program. Here she discusses the ethics of captivity, and what we're
doing to nature. She thinks that human exceptionalism is a prejudice; thinks
that considering marginal cases is helpful and is skeptical about whether
intuitions about far-fetched cases bring about important ethical insights;
thinks that two big issues concerning ethics and animals are captivity
and industrial animal agriculture; thinks ecotourism is complicated; has
problems with holistic approaches to environmental ethics; thinks women
have it tough, that the ethics of captivity both are complex and have had little
philosophical treatment, that self-direction matters when considering how we
treat animals, that ideas of a wild free of human management are unrealistic,
and that some captivity is necessary.

3:AM: What made you become a philosopher?

LORI GRUEN: I went to college when I was quite young and I was pretty
idealistic. Philosophy sounded cool, but my first philosophy class kicked my
butt. I had absolutely no idea what was going on. Because I have a stubborn
streak, I decided to take another philosophy course and this time I got it. With
a couple of courses in the history of philosophy behind me, I was very excited
by my social and political philosophy courses. I found the work I was reading
liberating and still see philosophy as having the potential to change the world,
although there were periods when I was less sure.

I went to graduate school right out of college, so I was still young. And
while I was studying political philosophy I was increasingly interested in
practical ethical and political problems. And to that point I had not yet taken
any philosophy class, as an undergraduate or a graduate student, taught by a
woman. So I decided to leave graduate school to do activist work.

After several years working for various social justice causes, I began to miss doing philosophy. And I thought I might have more success trying to combat social woes by teaching students how to think more clearly and argue more rigorously. At the moment, I feel strongly that philosophy has the promise I thought it did in my youth. Teaching political philosophy in a maximum security men's prison has reinvigorated my excitement about the liberatory potential of philosophy. For example, philosophy not only gives the students tools for analyzing their incarceration but provides opportunities for them to imagine other possibilities.

3:AM: A recent book of yours looks at ethics and animals. You begin by looking at the position of human exceptionalism, something that goes back to at least Aristotle. What is the position, and is it a kind of default position for those who just don't think we should think about animals ethically?

LG: Human exceptionalism is a prejudice that not only sees humans as different from other animals but that also sees humans as better than other animals. Of course humans are unique in a variety of ways, although those differences are often articulated based on naïve views about other animals. In Ethics and Animals, I explore some of the claims that have been made to differentiate humans from other animals (that we are the only beings that use tools or that use language or that have a theory of mind) and show that they do not establish that humans are unique in the ways postulated. But I also discuss the ways that other animals are indeed different from us and different from each other. These differences are important for understanding them and for promoting, or at least not negatively impacting, their well being.

Human exceptionalism also underlies skepticism about including other animals in the sphere of moral concern. It is related to two other views that are discussed more often in the literature about moral considerability—speciesism and anthropocentrism. Speciesism is the view that I only owe moral consideration to members of my own species. Although this view is usually thought to be focused on humans, it seems consistent with the view that only Vulcans matter to members of that species, or only orangutans matter to that species. Anthopocentrism is the view that humans are at the center of everything and that everything is understood through our human interpretive lenses. Of course we humans experience everything as humans, so in some sense humans are necessarily the center of our own perceptions, but that doesn't mean we are unable to try to understand or care about non-humans. There is a sense in which we are inevitable anthropocentrists, but we needn't be human exceptionalists.

Human exceptionalism sees humans as the only beings worthy of moral concern. Normative exceptionalist arguments generally fail in one of two ways—they pick out a supposedly unique characteristic or property upon which moral worth is supposed to supervene but it turns out that either not all humans have that property or that humans aren't the only ones that have it.

3:AM: Are marginal cases relevant?

LG: And this is why marginal cases are relevant. If there are some humans who do not have the morally valuable traits that the human exceptionalist prize, but they are nonetheless included in the group of those who do have the traits, then this suggests that it isn't that trait that is morally important, but species membership. But membership in a species isn't morally interesting and assigning moral significance to membership in a species amounts to a prejudice in favor of those thought to be in one's group. I myself am uncomfortable with the "marginal" cases terminology, but it is a remnant of the human exceptionalist view that promotes the idea that all humans fit neatly into a category based on morally worthy properties that only humans share, when there are no such properties.

3:AM: Why is the ethical case about animals so important? If you want to stop people being nasty to animals then aren't there things other than morals you could or should appeal to? Couldn't taste do the job i.e. we ought squash bugs because it's disgusting? Or it's unfashionable now, so nineteenth century etc.?

LG: The magnitude of the harms done to animals is almost incomprehensible—60 billion suffer before they are slaughtered for food in global industrial agricultural production annually and that contributes more greenhouse gas emissions than any other sector, which in turn is wreaking havoc on animal habitats on land and in the sea. When we also consider the additional threats that other animals face from human activities, it becomes clearer that the problems are structural and remedies cannot solely rely on individual tastes. But there are some really hard philosophical questions about what, if anything, individuals can do to help curtail these harms.

Consider what sometimes gets called the "impotence problem." When one goes out to eat and orders bbq chicken rather than a veggie burger, the chicken isn't slaughtered-to-order, so buying the veggie burger doesn't save any particular chicken's life. It seems that whatever one orders, it doesn't really have an effect either way on whether chickens suffer and die in food production. But surely individual actions must have some impact since if everybody abstained from eating chickens that would make a very large difference to very large number of chickens. This is one sort of problem Derek Parfit discusses in Reasons and Persons and Shelley Kagan and others have taken up by considering the impacts of our choices on other animals. Though I won't rehearse some of the proposed solutions to the problem here, what I want to mention is that when we are exploring the bad consequences of complex systems, ethical and political analyses are crucial.

In saying that, I don't want to completely dismiss the role that taste and disgust can play in perhaps making people aware of an ethical problem and motivating and sustaining people to stop harming others. But to my mind, taste and disgust, which are themselves shaped by cultural and social norms as well as idiosyncratic personal histories, are not particularly reliable and in the face of mass harms and injustice, are not always helpful.

3:AM: How important is it for people arguing for animals to be treated ethically to know what is happening to them? Your book is really full of information about this—is there a sense that you feel people who resist the ethical stance are ignorant of current problems?

LG: I've always been puzzled by the way that some moral philosophers create extraordinarily far fetched examples and then ask us to see what sorts of intuitions we have about these cases. I am skeptical that any intuitions we might dig up contain important ethical insights. But I'm also puzzled by those who argue from abstract general principles, for example, about the unethical treatment of causing other animals to suffer or fail to flourish, without knowing many details about particular animals and what might constitute their well-being. Having specific details are crucial for making ethical judgments. So, I think we should try to engage in some version of the process Rawls' called reflective equilibrium in which we consider the details as we understand them (and we should also be reflective about what we see as details to start with), our intuitions, and our more general ethical and political commitments.

Having details about the general treatment of other animals combined with particular cases promotes the reflective process. But there is more needed than just knowing what is happening to them. I think an under theorized part of our ethical lives relationships—what relationships are we in, what is the nature and quality of those relationships, and what obligations those relationships generate? Once we see that we are in relationships with specific animal others and come to understand how our actions impact individuals and their conspecifics, we can view our responsibility or complicity differently. Nobody wants to be in a bad relationship, so part of what I do in my work is include descriptions of these relationships in ways that allow for re-consideration.

One of the central ideas that I have been developing is what I call "entangled empathy" which is a type of moral perception directed at attending to the well-being of others. Very briefly, the "entanglement" part of the idea is based on a recognition that we are in all sorts of inextricable relationships with one another. The "empathy" part is not the standard form of moral emotion often discussed in the literature, but rather it refers to a perceptive skill that involves affect and cognition. Entangled empathy is developed by having a fuller picture of what is happening to others, coming to discern what the interests of others may be, imagining how those interests are experienced, and figuring out how our actions directly and indirectly impact another's well-being.

3:AM: So what are some of the key contemporary issues that help mobilise ethical arguments towards animals?

LG: There are two current issues—captivity and industrial animal agriculture—that have generated a lot of attention to animals of late and that have lead to questions about our obligations to them, to ourselves, and to the rest of nature. The issue of keeping animals captive in zoos and aquaria has become a pressing topic again. The movie Blackfish that looks behind the scenes at Sea World, the plight of elephants and polar bears suffering in unnatural conditions in zoos, and the practice of publicly killing animals at zoos in Europe have lead to renewed discussion of questions about liberty, conservation, individual well-being vs. species protection, and reproductive freedom. (see my oup blog and Ethics of Captivity).

In addition, as concerns about climate change become more pressing, awareness of the destructive contribution from industrialized food production has lead many people to reevaluate what they eat. The United Nations conservatively estimates that roughly 18% of the total greenhouse gases emitted come from industrialized livestock production, more greenhouse gas emissions than all transportation—planes, trains, and cars—combined. Rajendra Pachauri, chair of the Intergovernmental Panel on Climate Change (IPCC), made an explicit call urging individuals to "Please eat less meat—meat is a very carbon intensive commodity. . . ."

More people are giving up animal products once they recognize that personal taste can't justify harms to other animals, the environment, and future generations. Of course, as human populations grow and wealth accumulates, more animals then ever before are being threatened and killed. Ethical arguments that convince individuals only go so far and there is a dire need for ethical engagement that can impact policy.

3:AM: You take a nuanced approach to ecotourism? Why not condemn it outright?

LG: Ecotourism is a complicated issue. On the one hand there are places where ecotourism has raised awareness of the complex ethical issues that arise in contexts in which animal well-being, environmental protection, and human flourishing come into direct conflict and ecotourism provides one mechanism for minimizing these conflicts. It also often motivates the "tourists" to work on behalf of protecting wild animals and their habitats. Coming face to face (so to speak) with an animal in her natural environment can deepen one's sense of responsibility. On the other hand, ecotourism has the potential to further instrumentalize other animals and perpetuate problematic arrogant attitudes about human relationships with the more than human world. I don't think a sound ethical judgment can be made about ecotourism unless the context is fully explored.

3:AM: You are unhappy with holistic approaches to environmental ethics. First of all, can you say what you mean by "holistic" in this context, and who are the main proponents?

LG: Holism in environmental ethics is the view that value lies in whole systems rather than individual parts of the system or particular members of the community. Aldo Leopold, a holist who developed "the land ethic," argued that an action is right when it preserves and protects "the integrity, stability, and beauty" of an ecological community because integrity, stability, and beauty are the locus of value. In Ethics and Animals, I explore the complicated issue of anthropogenic extinctions through the lens of holism in the hopes that it might provide an answer to the question of why species are valuable. Holists view extinctions as, what one prominent holist, Holmes Rolston III, calls superkillings. Holists find that the value of species is more than the sum of the welfare of individual members of the species. The holist view allows that the death of individual members of a species would be justified if those deaths led to the betterment of the species as a whole and, by extension, the preservation of the species.

3:AM: So what is the problem?

LG: There are a number of problems with holism of this sort. But my main worry is that they have a limited view of how to value nature. Holists tend to think we either value nature instrumentally, which for them amounts to not valuing nature at all, or intrinsically, where value attaches either to individuals or to collectives. But nature can be valued in a variety of ways; we can value both collectives and individuals; we can value things as means to ends (like money); we can value things as ultimate ends (much as we value our companions, partners, or children); and we can value things as neither ultimate ends nor mere means, but rather as constitutive of other things that we value (perhaps, freedom of choice and privacy are such things.). Some values lie between means values and ends values and, while it makes ethical analysis tricky, that may be the most sensible way to address tricky conflicts.

We could argue that species have value that doesn't reduce simply to the cumulative well being of each individual member of the species, but that value doesn't transcend the members either. There is value in the relations that the existence of the collective allows to be realized. For example, the well-being of most animals, particularly social animals, relies centrally on their ability to develop relations with others of their kind, to learn species-typical behaviors, to develop specific cultures, to communicate, to hunt, to play. Individual flourishing, in humans and other animals, crucially depends on a sustaining and sustainable context much larger than the individual, and thus valuing the individual necessitates valuing the whole within which the individual makes her life meaningful. Of course, that meaningful life is of value too.

3:AM: Things are particularly toxic for women across the globe at the moment. What are contemporary feminisms arguing to combat this situation?

LG: I don't think things are any worse now than they have always been, sadly, I just think with social media and 24/7 news we are hearing more about various manifestations of gender oppression and violence. Women and other marginal groups are being impacted in different ways now—for example, climate change and food scarcity will affect women and children first and harder than it will affect men initially. The arguments that feminists have long been making for equality and respect are rooted in an analysis of the indefensibility of exercises of unearned privilege, e.g. male privilege, white privilege, class privilege. Feminist philosophers and theorists continue to draw attention to the social construction of social categories that have been naturalized. We try to reveal the logic of domination that allows members of one group to create social structures that favor themselves while at the same time creating or perpetuating social structures that disadvantage "others." One of the strengths of contemporary feminist thinking about privilege and domination comes from increased attention to intersecting oppressions—the complex ways in which gender, gender non-conformity, sexuality, race, ethnicity, class, and I would suggest species as well, interact to generate very specific forms of injustice. Attention to intersecting oppressions complicates thinking about how we might achieve more just social arrangements and it has the potential to bring together groups that those with power have worked to keep apart and at odds.

3:AM: And in philosophy departments also there are big issues. There have been a few high profile cases recently. As a philosopher what is like from the inside, what do you think the reason is for academic philosophy being so poor in this respect and are there things that should be done?

LG: The high profile cases within philosophy departments are focused on sexual harassment and sexual predation. It is so important that women who are being harassed are speaking out. For too long that wasn't the case and I think part of the reason women are speaking out now is because there are many philosophers of all genders who are working to make changes in the profession so victims of sexual harassment feel they will be supported. I do worry a bit that the focus on sexual harassment in the profession has obscured the more day in and day out sexism that exists in philosophy.

I think the fact that the situation is so bad for women and minorities in the profession is, in some sense, over-determined. Old stereotypical views about women and scholars of color are still prevalent, if not as overt as they once were, and stereotype threat still operates. I have heard from more than a few students and colleagues that they have to spend energy battling the idea that they are "imposters" or "aren't smart enough." There is very little philosophical work by women or minority philosophers taught in most philosophy classes so for women students and students of color to pursue philosophy they have to have a deep passion as well as courage, we usually don't just "fall into" philosophy. One of the things I love about philosophy but I know drives non-philosophers a bit crazy is how we have a habit of trying to understand and explain things in great detail. Given this habit and that the majority of faculty are men in almost all philosophy departments, the phenomena popularly referred to as "mansplaining" is thus rather common and can subtly shape the climate.

There is a lot going on to try to remedy these problems. Changing what is taught in undergraduate courses; working to avoid conferences or edited volumes that only include men (see the gendered conference campaign); and talking more openly about what positive changes can be made to create more inclusive environments in individual departments and philosophy as a whole all are promising developments. But these changes will take time and require vigilance. As a profession, we have a long way to go.

3:AM: In your new book on captivity—which looks at both human and non-human captivity and the issues that arise—there are some examples that might strike some as strange, such as the inclusion of pets. Some might thinks that including pets in discussions about captivity takes us away from crucial examples, such as prisons and zoos? Do pets raise interesting issues at the margins that help bring into sharper focus what the issues are around captivity?

LG: The ethical issues around captivity are remarkably complex and it is surprising how little philosophical attention has been paid to them. You are right to think that prisons and zoos raise the most obvious issues –the individuals that are held captive in these environments are there against their wills, they endure a wide variety of restrictions on their liberty, and they are under the control of their captors. But when we describe captivity as a condition in which a competent adult is confined and controlled and is reliant on those in control to satisfy her basic needs, it becomes clearer that there are many captive environments beyond prisons and zoos, environments that are not ordinarily thought of in those terms.

When we start thinking about pets or "companion animals" as captives then we may start reflecting in new ways on how we treat them. Clare Palmer and Peter Sandoe wrote a provocative chapter in the book that questions the received wisdom that routinely confining cats indoors promotes their well-being. Cats may be happy with our affections and their lives may be longer if we keep them safe indoors, but there is a loss here, to their freedom to go where they want and interact with and shape their larger environment.

In captive contexts, the trade-offs, between safety and freedom, protection and choice, are often obscured. For example, in the US, over 2 million people are incarcerated and not only are they denied freedom but their families and communities are impoverished in the name of social "safety" which is often illusory. Within prisons too, as two of the chapters in the book vividly illustrate, autonomy and basic respect are sacrificed in the name of safety and security. Comparing various kinds of captive institutions provides an opportunity to analyze the language of "safety" and reveals its strategic use in obscuring the loss of other valuable things.

Seeing pets as captives, I think, does bring some of the complexities of captivity into sharper focus.

3:AM: At first it seems obvious that conditions of captivity are really important—but then again, even a well looked after slave is still a slave—and no one is going to use the conditions as a justification in that kind of case are they? So where do you stand on this—how far should we be interested in conditions of captivity?

LG: One justification for keeping individuals captive has been that captivity is better for them. In the context of companion animals and zoo animals, for example, one often hears that they will live longer lives and they won't have to worry about injury or predation or hunger. The sense is that they are better off having lost their freedom. The same sorts of justifications were also heard in the case of slaves. Captors wanted to believe that slaves were better off, became more civilized, more human, because of their captivity. Of course, this is odious in the case of human beings, and there are some who argue that this attitude is equally objectionable in the case of other animals.

Comparing captivity to a type of slavery, some animal advocates are opposed to all forms of captivity, even keeping pets. They take the label "abolitionist" as a way of linking their views to earlier abolitionist struggles to end slavery.

But I think our relationships with other animals (of course humans, but also nonhumans) are a central part of what makes lives meaningful. Rather than thinking we must end all captivity and thus all our relationships with other animals, we'd do better working to improve those relationships by being more perceptive of and more responsive to others' needs and interests and sensibilities. Since we are already, inevitably, in relationships, rather than ending them we might try to figure out how to make them better, more meaningful, and more mutually satisfying. Importantly, by recognizing that we are inevitably in relationships to other animals, replete with vulnerability, dependency, and even some instrumentalization, and working to understand and improve these relationships, I'm not condoning exploitation. Acknowledging that we are in relationships doesn't mean that all relationships are equally defensible or should stay as they are. Relationships of exploitation or complete instrumentalization are precisely the sorts of relationships that should change.

And this is where an exploration of conditions of captivity and the complexity of the individual captives' interests comes in. Some animals, like whales and elephants, cannot thrive in captive conditions. As much as we might want to have closer relationships with them, it isn't good for them. Others, like dogs and chimpanzees, can live meaningful lives in captivity but only if the conditions they are captive in are conducive to their flourishing and they are respected. Part of the problem with captivity is the relationship of domination that it tends to maintain. By re-evaluating captivity (and for many in our non-ideal situation, there is no real alternative) we can start to ask questions about whether and how captive conditions can, while denying certain freedoms, still promote the dignity of the captives.

3:AM: Putting a wasp in a jar seems less bad than putting a chimp in a cage. Does this intuition track anything ethical?

LG: The loss of freedom has different implications for different individuals within the same species and for members of other species. Usually, denying individuals their liberty negatively impacts the quality of their lives, but this can happen in two ways. Doing what one wants, being free to make choices and to act on them, and not being interfered with in the pursuit of one's desires are important because they contribute to making an individual's life go better. Individuals who are confined, restrained, or subordinated can't follow their desires. Putting the wasp in a jar and putting a chimpanzee in a cage denies them both freedom of movement and the freedom to get what they want.

But perhaps what underlies the intuition that it is worse to make a chimpanzee captive than to confine a wasp is the sophisticated cognitive capacities of the chimpanzee who values her freedom, not just instrumentally because of what it gets her, but because it is constitutive of her well-being. This may sound odd, but I think from what is now known about chimpanzee cognition, the boredom and frustration that accompanies captivity and the documented need for environmental, emotional, social, and intellectual enrichment suggests that chimpanzees do value their freedom. The process of satisfying one's own interests and correcting one's self when she changes her mind or makes bad choices are part of what makes a life a good life for beings who have these sorts of cognitive capacities. I believe chimpanzees can do these things, so it makes sense to think that they, like us, value their freedom more than just instrumentally.

And its not just chimpanzees. Many other animals are self-directed, adapt to changing circumstances, make choices and resist changes, and improve their environments, often through collective action. Other animals learn from con-specifics and modify what they learn to suit themselves and their needs. Not all animals in a social group do exactly the same things, eat exactly the same things, or spend time with the same individuals. They are making independent choices. There are species-typical behavioral repertoires that constrain an individual's absolute expression of this their autonomy, but none of us is ever completely free of constraints. So I think there are a lot of other animals for whom captivity is ethically problematic because it violates their autonomy, but probably not wasps.

But, maybe I just don't know enough about wasps.

3:AM: Some animals wouldn't exist if they weren't in captivity. How do we decide whether species death or life is morally justified?

LG: There is a long-standing debate about the conservationist justification for keeping animals captive rather than let them go extinct. Some have argued that we shouldn't sacrifice the interests of the one for the good of the many. But I confess, I'm vexed by the hard questions of extinction and also worry about whether "we" can make much useful difference.

In Ethics and Animals I recount the story of the dwindling existence of rhinoceros. I wrote about the death of one of the rarest large mammals on the planet, the Javan rhinoceros who was found shot dead in Vietnam's Cat Tien National Park. The rhino was shot by poachers so they could to take the horn. At the time, conservation authorities said there are only three to five Javan rhinos left in Vietnam. In 2013, they were declared extinct. Also last year, the Western Black rhino was declared extinct. Elephants, orangutans, tigers, and a host of other less "charismatic" animals will not be around (outside of zoos and preserves) for much longer.

If there were a way to hold some individuals in ideal captive conditions in the hopes of reintroducing them to the wild in order to avoid extinction that might justify captivity. But that is no longer realistic. In fact, the very idea that there is a "wild" free of human management is itself unrealistic. One of the new ways of thinking about what used to be considered a choice between individuals in captivity and wild populations free of human interference, is to recognize that all endangered or threatened animals are in some sense already in captivity—not in zoos, but rather in conditions in which they have their freedom managed and controlled.

3:AM: There are lots of reasons for captivity that aren't ethical—practical, aesthetic, taste, politics, emotive and so on—so do you think the ethical reason must always override these other possible reasons?

LG: This question bumps up against discussions about the scope and nature of ethical reasoning. I have sympathies with broadly consequentialist answers to this sort of question—the divisions between types of reasons can be helpful for a variety of purposes, but basically whatever divisions one makes, we can evaluate reasons in ethical terms. So if I have a taste for hamburgers, the production of which causes intense suffering, my aesthetic desire for burgers can be evaluated on ethical grounds. It may be politically expedient to disproportionately stop and frisk black youth, but the implications of acting on reasons of expedience can be evaluated ethically.

Captivity is the same way. In fact, in many instances, the only thing to do is keep some individuals captive. My own interest in the ethics of captivity arose in my working with captive chimpanzees almost a decade ago. I felt truly conflicted about the fact that these incredibly smart, sociable, often charming, always complicated, individuals had to spend their lives (some live to be 50–60) in captivity. Many of the chimpanzees I know are 5th or 6th generation captives. Chimpanzee habitats are being decimated and the fastest growing populations of captive chimpanzees are in Africa, in native range countries for chimpanzees, where they are orphaned due to bush meat hunting and forest destruction. So even if it was possible to teach individuals who have only known captivity to survive outside of captivity, there really isn't a safe place to release them. This raised a genuine moral dilemma—any thing we do, release them or hold them captive, can be considered wrong. So that lead me to thinking about whether and how we could minimize the ethical costs of captivity.

3:AM: And for the curious readers here at 3:AM are there five books (other than your own) you could recommend that would take us further into your philosophical world?

LG: I know many of those you interview have a hard time coming up with only five books and I'm having a hard time too. There are so many important books in practical ethics and social and political philosophy, but here are five books that have been important to my current thinking—*Feminist Theory: From Margin to Center* by bell hooks, *The New Jim Crow* by Michelle Alexander, *Resisting Reality* by Sally Haslanger, *Every Twelve Seconds* by Timothy Pachirat, edited by Cheshire Calhoun.

Lori Gruen is the author of:

Animal Liberation: A Graphic Guide (with Peter Singer) (Camden Press, 1987)
Sex, Morality and the Law (with George E. Panichas) (Routledge, 1997)

Ethics and Animals (Cambridge University Press, 2011)

Reflecting on Nature: Readings in Environmental Ethics and Philosophy (with Dale Jamieson and Christopher Schlottmann) (Oxford University Press, 2nd ed., 2012)

Entangled Empathy: An Alternative Ethic for Our Relationships with Animals (Lantern Books, 2014)

Ecofeminism: Feminist Intersections with Other Animals and the Earth (Bloomsbury 2014)

The Ethics of Captivity (Oxford University Press 2015)

19 | Japa Pallikkathayil: "Rethinking the Formula of Humanity"

Japa Pallikkathayil is an Assistant Professor in the Department of Philosophy at the University of Pittsburgh. Here she discusses the relationship between morality and politics, the problems facing women in philosophy, Kant, what an ideal government should be like, bodily rights, and coercion.

3:AM: Can you say how you became a philosopher. Were you always asking philosophical questions even when little or is it something that gradually happened in reaction to experience of the world?

JAPA PALLIKKATHAYIL: I have long been interested in philosophy but it took me a while to decide on philosophy as a career. As a high school debater, I read a lot of philosophy and enjoyed it. But back then I was more practically oriented and was very involved in local politics in my hometown (Kansas City, Missouri). In college, I was a double major in government and philosophy and I initially planned to go to law school and eventually pursue a career in government. I really wanted to make the world a better place. But eventually I realized that I didn't know what the world should look like and, in particular, what the role of the government in our lives should be. These kinds of questions gripped me and never let go. So, philosophy seemed the right fit for me.

3:AM: You have focused on ethical issues connected in particular with the use of coercion. My initial thought is that coercion is a bad thing. But you want to get clear just what makes me think that and so you pull apart the idea of coercion. So can you say what makes coercion bad?

JP: I actually think that it is sometimes okay to use coercion. The state, for example, threatens to put people in jail for committing crimes like robbery or assault. At least in a just state, maybe this use of coercion is not morally suspect. I think that coercion is objectionable when what the coercer threatens to do is wrong. This takes away options that the person being threatened is entitled to have. So, the mugger who says "Your money or your life," wrongfully takes away your option of keeping both your money and your life. That's the first problem with wrongful coercion. And I think this first problem leads to a second. If you don't have the options you are entitled to have, your choices don't have the same significance that they usually do. Normally, if you hand your money to someone, you are consenting to let that person have it. But that's not true in the interaction with the mugger. In that way, the mugger deprives you of a kind of authority over your money. So, I think that the second problem with wrongful coercion is that it deprives victims of what I call "normative authority."

3:AM: You make a distinction between what you call "physical coercion" on the one hand and "volitional coercion" on the other. This is a crucial distinction for you so could you tell us what they are?

JP: Physical coercion involves taking physical control of at least some part of another's body. So, for example, consider grabbing someone's arm and pulling her out of her chair. Volitional coercion operates on another's actions rather than her body. The mugger, for example, is trying to get you to act in a certain way without taking control of your body by, say, wrestling you to the ground and prying the wallet out of your pocket.

3:AM: You argue that we often mistakenly think about these two kinds of coercion as being pretty much the same and involving the same kind of thing. But you think that this is a mistake. Can you tell us about this?

JP: Someone who is physically coerced is not able to move as she chooses. There is a temptation to understand what volitional coercion involves in the same way, so that someone who is volitionally coerced is not able to act as she chooses. But if you think about it, this can't be quite right. The point of the mugger's threat is to get you to make a particular choice rather than preventing your choice from being effective.

3:AM: So the "volitional coercion" idea makes us worry that somehow we are choosing to do what a bully, for example, is asking us to do. So this is about analysing what is happening when the mugger says "Give me your money" or the rapist says "let me rape you" and I agree and give up my money or my body? This is the issue that you're interested in isn't it? Can you say something about the background to this issue and how philosophers have looked at it before you.

JP: One natural way of understanding what goes wrong in those kinds of interactions involves describing the victim's autonomy as somehow compromised. That idea, however, involves an ambiguity that I think people working on this issue have sometimes lost track of. The idea of autonomy and related ideas like freedom are often understood in terms of an agent's internal psychological states and how those are connected with her actions. But autonomy might also be thought to have some kind of interpersonal element so that in order to be autonomous one must stand in certain relationships to others. So, in locating the problem with wrongful coercion in its effect on the victim's autonomy, it's easy to slide between these two senses of autonomy. To avoid this problem, I try to set aside the talk of autonomy and just focus on whether wrongful coercion's problematic effect on a victim is best understood in terms of its effect on her internal states or on her relationships with others. And I think that the latter story is the right one.

3:AM: You discuss the contrasting ideas of "impaired action" and kind of reject it don't you? So could you say something about what's wrong with saying that my choosing to act (i.e. handing over my money to a mugger or allowing a rapist to rape me) is only my action in a broken or impaired way?

JP: This view locates the problematic effect of coercion in the internal states I was just mentioning. The idea is that the victim is in some sense not properly connected with her actions. I think it is important to recognize that victims of wrongful coercion are still acting in a meaningful sense because there is a way in which we still regard those people as responsible for their choices. So suppose a terrorist threatens to kill your family unless you help her plant her bombs. Here the terrorist is certainly wrongfully coercing you. But it is still true that you are responsible for the choice you make in response. Of course, if you give in, the circumstances might lead us to evaluate your conduct less harshly than if you were an eager participant. But we need to recognize you as really acting in order for your conduct to be evaluable in the first place.

3:AM: You also reject some ideas of contemporary Kantians such as Christine Korsgaard and Onora O'Neill about "impaired consent" but find something of value in this account. Is that right? Can you say something about this.

JP: Let's go back to the case of the mugger. As I mentioned, when you hand over your money, you can't consent to let the mugger keep it. And this is a kind of problematic effect on the victim's relationship with others. But the ability to consent isn't the only kind of normative authority that you lack if you are the victim of impermissible coercion. So, suppose someone tried to wrongfully coerce you into making a promise. That promise wouldn't bind you for the very same reason you can't give consent to the mugger, namely, you lack the options you are entitled to have when deciding about whether to make the promise. So, I think that focusing on the victim's impaired ability to consent is illuminating but not the whole story.

3:AM: One of the things you say about your approach is that we don't need to completely define coercion before we can come to a sensible and rational position about the ethics of coercion. Can you say something about why you think this rejection of the definitional project is very important? Is it an approach that you have found obstructive to other aspects of philosophical investigation?

JP: The definitional project has occupied most of the recent work on coercion. And the way that project has typically been pursued involves reflecting on cases and trying to assess intuitively whether they involve coercion and then developing a definition on the basis of this data. None of the accounts that have resulted from this strategy have quite been able to capture all of the cases in a way that seems satisfying. I think that this is good evidence that the way we use the term "coercion" involves some confusion or ambiguity.

So, instead of trying to settle on a definition from the outset, I focus on paradigmatic cases of coercion, like that of the mugger, and ask normative questions like why is what the mugger is doing wrong and how does this action affect the victim's responsibility for her response. And by answering these questions in paradigmatic cases, we arrive at the features that are relevant for answering these questions in other cases. We can thereby answer the normative questions without labeling an act coercive or not. And I think that the normative project can then shed light on where the confusions or ambiguities are in our use of the term "coercion." While the preoccupation with a definition has been particularly striking in the work on coercion, I think that many of the concepts that are familiar in moral discourse are also better explored using the more normatively focused strategy.

3:AM: Your work focuses not just on coercion, but also deception and exploitation. Sadly these are issues of immense traction and relevance. The link between morals and politics often raises issues about deception, exploitation and coercion. You have written about this in your essay Deriving Morality from Politics: Rethinking the Formula of Humanity. So can you say something about the formula: what was it and what should it be?

JP: Kant's formula of humanity requires that we treat people as ends in themselves rather than merely as a means. In one way, this is a very intuitive idea. We shouldn't use other people but should instead let them live their own lives. The trick is in articulating what this involves. To do this, most Kantians have focused on one-on-one interactions. I think that this focus misses the way in which our political relationships shape our interactions.

In order to recognize people as separate individuals with their own lives to live, we need to respect their rights. And I don't think that we can do this without just political institutions. Without such institutions, we face three problems. First, our rights are indeterminate. For example, how loudly can you play your music without violating your neighbor's rights? There isn't an obvious rule settling this and, as equals, none of us is uniquely entitled to decide what this rule should be. Just political institutions give us a way of impartially establishing these kinds of rules. Second, however detailed these rules are, there will still be cases in which there may be reasonable disagreement about how the rules apply. Once again we need an impartial procedure for settling this, and just political institutions provide this procedure. Finally, rights only give people the space to live their own lives if others don't violate those rights. Just political institutions give people the assurance that their rights will be observed. It turns out, then, that respecting others in the way that the formula of humanity indicates crucially involves being in just political relationships with them.

3:AM: Many of us look at politics and just see a miasma of immorality and corruption, greedy immoralists exploiting our hopes for private selfish gain. So how do we get morality from politics?

JP: Just political institutions create a space within which we can situate everyday one-on-one interactions. So, suppose you need a ride to the airport. Your friend might want to help you out, but it wouldn't be okay for her to steal someone's car to do that. In this way, people's rights place limits on the kinds of interactions we may have and so shape our moral duties. In this case, the content of our duty to help other people depends on the resources we have a right to control.

I think a lot of moral duties involve this kind of sensitivity to people's rights. And since our rights are indeterminate without political institutions, we need those institutions in order to be able to fulfill our moral duties. That's how politics gives content to morality. But of course here I am talking about just political institutions and, as your question brings out, most of the political institutions we are familiar with fail to realize that ideal to some extent. While no one doubts that injustice is a problem, my account suggests that it is an even deeper problem than we might have realized. By failing to properly establish our rights, unjust political institutions disrupt our ability to discharge even moral duties that do not initially seem to have much to do with politics.

3:AM: When we look out at vast areas of the globe there seems to be abuse at all levels. War, inequality, bullying, just a general swamp of nastyness.

Are you driven to these philosophical questions by recognition of the general screwed up world? Do you think philosophizing can help? What would you say to someone who cried out in despair: look, thinking isn't helping, we need action?

JP: Action is certainly important, but we should also not underestimate the role of ideas in producing change. Action without a vision is bound to be unfocused and runs the risk of being counterproductive. On the other hand, without real engagement with the world, ideas are bound to be empty. So, ideally, action and reflection go hand in hand.

While we are trying to address the serious problems in the world, we should not shy away from asking questions about the big picture. At the same time, we shouldn't get so caught up in abstract theories that we lose sight of the problems that motivate them. Of course philosophers are especially susceptible to making the latter mistake, but I think that there are many philosophers who are really making an effort to contribute to the public discourse about important issues. Change can sometimes be fostered simply by helping people understand their own commitments, and sometimes change requires an entirely fresh way of looking at things. Philosophers are particularly well positioned to help on both these fronts.

3:AM: Talking to some women philosophers and reading reports, academic philosophy seems to be pretty bad at recognizing women philosophers. You are of course an exception to this, being a top philosopher in the top department for philosophy. But is this an issue that concerns you and have you any thoughts about why this is so and what might be done?

JP: There are lots of layers to the problems facing women in philosophy. To start with, unfortunately, overt sexism still exists. I have been lucky enough not to have much first hand experience with the kind of horror stories reported on the blog "What is it like to be a woman in philosophy?" But the posts there are very revealing. It's really hard to know what to do about the situation when sexist attitudes are pervasive. But sometimes there are just one or two problematic professors who everyone knows are problematic but no one does anything about. In these cases, I think other faculty members need to be more proactive in addressing the situation. While this is not easy, not intervening fails to take seriously the very pernicious effect even a few people can have on the entire climate of a department.

There are also ways in which practices in the discipline are poorly suited to manage implicit biases. To take just one example, consider a problematic element of the hiring process. Many of the first round interviews of job candidates take place at the Eastern Division meeting of the American

Philosophical Association. In the evening, after the formal interviews, everyone gathers for a kind of cocktail hour during which candidates are supposed to seek out and chitchat with the people from the schools they interviewed with. This is a format that seems likely to exacerbate the influence of implicit biases and other irrelevant factors on the judgments of those involved in hiring. Given this, it is mysterious to me why this practice persists.

Another layer of the problem facing women just has to do with the numbers. As I understand it, fewer women major in philosophy, even fewer apply to graduate school, and so on. I don't know if there are ways of improving the experience of women in particular in their first exposure to the discipline, but I do think that there are ways in which the discipline might be healthier for all involved. We can choose to approach our interactions with others in the discipline in a way that is collaborative rather than competitive. The very same questions can be posed in ways that are constructive rather than combative. The latter approach shuts people out of the conversation and closes down lines of inquiry rather than opening them up. Individuals and departments differ in the extent to which this issue of approach is a problem for them. But I think that if we were all more mindful of how we are interacting and what we are conveying when we do so, we would all be better off.

3:AM: What do you make of the experimental philosophers who utilise findings in cognitive science and psychology to test out the moral intuitions of folk. Is this something that you find helpful or useful? Will you be burning any of your armchairs any time soon?

JP: For the topics that I have been working on recently, like coercion, I don't think that studying people's intuitions is likely to be very helpful because, as I mentioned, I think that people's intuitions on these subjects are muddled. So, I prefer the more normatively focused strategy to the study of intuitions about hard cases, regardless of whether those intuitions are from the armchair or from the laboratory.

3:AM: Finally, have there been books outside of philosophy that you have found enlightening for you as you brood on these essential moral issues?

JP: When I first started thinking about these issues, I enjoyed the classic dystopian novels 1984 and Brave New World. And I must confess a recent fondness for The Hunger Games trilogy.

3:AM: And finally finally, for the sassy crowd here at 3:AM, are there five books you could recommend that would get them thinking about these issues?

JP: The classic *Watership Down* by Richard Adams engages issues of authority and coercion in a very compelling way. *Ender's Game* by Orson Scott Card is also an enjoyable read. For a more recent novel, *Cloud Atlas* by David Mitchell is worth checking out. For some historical accounts involving these issues, try *Homage to Catalonia* by George Orwell and *Hiroshima* by John Hersey. I also want to throw in two movies that involve these themes and are worth checking out: The Sea Inside and The Greatest Happiness Space.

20 | Kimberlie Brownlee: "Conscience and Conviction"

Kimberlie Brownlee is an Associate Professor in Legal and Moral Philosophy at Warwick University. Here she talks about conscience and conviction, Rawls's narrow views, Raz's wider ones, her reversals of the standard liberal picture, her rejection of moral conviction as passion, the good reasons for a defense of civil disobedience, about the difference between conscientious objection and civil disobedience, the role of the state and its offices, punishment, the missing voice of offenders, and the ethics and law regarding social deprivation.

3:AM: What made you become a philosopher? Were you always asking tricky questions?

KIMBERLEY BROWNLEE: Although I've always been interested in who we are and how we should live, I didn't know what Philosophy was until my final years of high school in the International Baccalaureate (IB) programme. I had a special teacher for the compulsory Theory of Knowledge course, who was fond of asking: "How do you know?" at disconcerting moments. He was also entirely irreverent and spontaneous in his teaching methods. He held seminars on the roof of the classroom (until we were told by the administrators to get down), and he held seminars where we faced the outer walls instead of each other to see if this would hinder or enhance discussion. From him, I learned about some famous thought experiments in philosophy, such as Nozick's experience machine, the brain in a vat, and the trolley problem, and I was hooked for life.

3:AM: Your new book presents the case for civil disobedience in terms of conscience and conviction. Before saying what your approach is, could you first say something about traditional liberal approaches to this issue? Is Rawls the key figure in this?

KB: Henry David Thoreau coined the term "civil disobedience" in the late 1840's to describe his refusal to pay the state poll tax that was funding the Fugitive Slave Law and the US government's war in Mexico. Although Thoreau gave us the term, his own breach of law is not a paradigm case of civil disobedience as we understand it since his act was less aimed at changing the law than paradigm cases are. Some paradigm cases of civil disobedience from the Civil Rights era are Rosa Parks's refusal in 1955 to give up her bus seat, the Woolworth's lunch counter sit-ins in the early 1960s, and the 1963 Birmingham marches led by Martin Luther King Jr. The most influential account of civil disobedience in the liberal tradition is John Rawls's distinctively narrow account, outlined in *A Theory of Justice* (1971). Rawls defines "civil disobedience" very narrowly as a public, non-violent, conscientious breach of law taken with the aim of bringing about a change in law or policy while at the same time maintaining a broad fidelity to the legal system. On this definition, someone like Mahatma Gandhi did not engage in civil disobedience because he had revolutionary aims that lacked fidelity to British rule in India. And, on this definition, someone like Nelson Mandela did not engage in civil disobedience either because he advocated constrained forms of violence such as sabotage. Finally, on this definition, someone who sneaks into a research lab to release animals does not engage in civil disobedience even if she publicizes it afterward because her act lacks the distinctive publicity of forewarning authorities of her intended disobedience.

Rawls is equally narrow in his views on when civil disobedience is justified and when we have a moral right to use it. Rawls says that, in a just society, there is a right to civil disobedience only when our act satisfies three conditions for justifiability: 1) it responds to substantial injustice, 2) it is taken as a last resort, and 3) it is done in coordination with other minority groups. Rawls has been criticised, rightly, for not properly distinguishing his account of justified civil disobedience from the civil disobedience we have a right to take. And, he has been criticised for not explaining how to extrapolate his account from the ideal, just society to our messy, non-ideal, real societies. In the real world, it's a lot to ask of someone like Martin Luther King Jr that he coordinate with other minority groups when those groups ask him to wait for a "better season."

Joseph Raz defends a broader account of civil disobedience that does not restrict the acts that can be protected by a right. Instead, Raz rejects the idea that this right exists in all societies. He says that only in an illiberal society is there a right to civil disobedience and this right is reserved for those people whose rights to political participation are violated. They have a right to reclaim that portion of their political participation rights that are not recognised in law. So, in Martin Luther King Jr's America, black Americans had a right to civil disobedience, but white Americans did not even if they supported the same causes. In a liberal society, there is no right at all to civil disobedience, Raz says, because the law adequately protects our rights to political participation. What Raz's view ignores is that civil disobedients might not be criticising the law for outlawing their action, but instead doing the best they can to honour their conscientious moral convictions. Standard liberal theories say that civil disobedience is less conscientious and less defensible than private, non-communicative "conscientious" objection.

Conscientious objection is associated with pacifism (dating from the First World War), but is also practised in healthcare, education, retail work, and so on. Examples include the doctor who refuses to perform abortions and the religious grocery store clerk who refuses to process the sale of alcohol or to wear or not wear certain clothing in public. Unlike the civil disobedient, the private objector does not try to persuade others of her view or to change laws. She aims simply to act as she believes she ought to act. In standard liberal theory, private objection is seen as a modest, unassuming act of deep personal conviction, and civil disobedience is seen as a strategic, political act whose costs are only sometimes worth bearing. Standard liberal views say that, if there were a general moral right to engage in disobedience on grounds of conscientious conviction, then only private, non-communicative acts would be protected by it.

3:AM: So how does your approach differ?

KB: My account reverses the standard liberal picture and shows that civil disobedience is more conscientious and more defensible than private objection is. As such, civil disobedience has the better claim to the protections that liberal societies tend to give to conscientious breaches of law. True conscientiousness requires not just that we act as we think we ought to act, but also that we be willing to be seen to hold the views we have. We must be willing to communicate our views to others and to bear the costs for our dissent. This is what I call the communicative principle of conscientiousness. The person who disobeys the law privately or evasively raises a doubt about the sincerity of her convictions since she is unwilling to be seen and to engage others in deliberation about her cause. In addition, I argue that there is a general moral right to engage in civil disobedience and this right is not limited either to people who are justified in disobeying or to illiberal societies where people have political rights to reclaim. The moral right to civil disobedience is rooted in a humanistic respect for our dignity and agency as reasoning and feeling beings capable of cultivating deep commitments. Respecting dignity and agency requires respecting that genuine moral convictions have a non-evasive and communicative element, which can include constrained, communicative disobedience of law. Indeed, the moral right to engage in civil disobedience entails a moral right against punishment for civil disobedience.

3:AM: You have a pretty stringent approach to conscientious convictions. You don't allow hot-headed brutal ones. You stress rationality, but don't insist that they have to be correct or sound don't you? Wouldn't that mean that bad morals would be as effective as good ones in avoiding the law?

KB: I reject the idea that moral conviction is a type of passion that can be measured by how all-consuming it is. Such hot-headed, unthinking devotion is best described as an obsession, not a conviction. A genuine conscientious conviction does not have to be factually or morally correct, but it does have to pass some logical and evidential tests. Consider, for example, the religious parents who believe that they can heal their daughter who has curable diabetes through prayer alone even though the evidence is that she is dying, and even though they would have taken her to a doctor had she broken her leg. Their belief fails the tests of logical coherence and minimal evidential satisfactoriness. Hence, it is not a genuine conscientious conviction, and it cannot exempt them from ordinary expectations of decent childcare. It's true that, in my view, people with morally bad views could escape legal consequences for their civil disobedience if their views are genuinely conscientious. The reason rests on the principle of humanism noted above that society has a duty to honour our human dignity and autonomy by recognising that we're reasoning and feeling beings capable of forming deep moral convictions which are, by nature, non-evasive and communicative. It follows that society and the law place too much pressure on us when they coerce us always to put the law before our deep convictions. If our convictions are genuinely conscientious, and if we defend them through suitably constrained methods of civil disobedience, then the law should not impose punitive sanctions on us.

3:AM: How would you deal with convictions rooted in faith communities rather than rationality? And further to this, aren't you making too much of rationality. Don't sometimes we have to act out of desperation or fear or an unproven suspicion?

KB: Someone who believes something on the basis of divine revelation would have to show why we should accept a belief because it is acquired through a certain process rather than because it has a certain content. This would be difficult to show, but not impossible. My account puts only modest constraints on the kinds of beliefs that can be genuinely conscientious. Indeed, my account is more inclusive than standard liberal views are. I say that the staunch anti-abortion activist can be just as conscientious as the environmentalist or the animal rights activist because what matters is that they are sincere, serious, consistent, non-evasive, and communicative in ways that are respectful of their audience as people they seek to persuade of their views. This kind of respect requires that the anti-abortion activist use highly constrained breaches of law that try to engage others in reasoned deliberation about her cause and not to coerce them into accepting it through bombings, killings, threats, or other extreme tactics. It is true that the constraints on the methods of true civil disobedience demand a certain reasonableness from disobedients. They have to aim to communicate with others at the level of reason. But, this demand is not a constraint on the content of their beliefs. And, it's a demand that disobedients should want to meet since they should want to be able to show that their view is sufficiently credible that reasoned arguments can be given in its defence.

3:AM: How do you characterise conscience in this?

KB: A key aim in my book *Conscience and Conviction* is to distinguish the two concepts in its title. Although the terms "conscientious conviction" and "conscience" are similar, the concepts they pick out are quite different. Conscientious moral convictions are necessary for conscience because they show that we take morality seriously. But, they're not enough for conscience because our convictions can be mistaken. Conscience, by contrast, is genuine moral responsiveness and understanding. The more we have of it, the better we understand what really matters morally. People like Mahatma Gandhi and Aung San Suu Kyi exemplify true conscience. Gandhi was an extraordinary figure in 20th century history, whose non-violent, non-hating resistance of British rule in India achieved remarkable political change and gave us an enduring model of serene goodness. He was someone who could say truly "My life is my message." The same might be said of Aung San Suu Kyi, the leader of the National League for Democracy in Burma, who was inspired by Gandhi to adopt a stance of non-violent, non-hating resistance against the brutal dictatorship in Myanmar/Burma and who endured the better part of 20 years under house arrest between 1989 and 2010 in isolation from her family.

In the book, I situate conscience within a pluralistic moral framework, and show that, even though we cannot have unequivocally right answers to many moral questions, we can nonetheless cultivate both an inward moral knowledge of the workings of our own mind and heart and a rich practical set of moral skills to make morally justifiable decisions.

3:AM: So what are good reasons for legal defence in cases of civil disobedience?

KB: I argue for two legal defences for civil disobedience. The first is a legal excuse and is available, in principle, for any act of civil disobedience. This excuse is called the demands-of-conviction defence. It is rooted in the humanistic principle of respect for dignity and agency that I mentioned above. By recognising a demands-of-conviction defence, society would honour the links between autonomy, psychological integrity, and conscientiousness. It would do this by not forcing us either always to put the law first before our deep commitments or always to be surreptitious when we distance ourselves from laws we oppose. Since truly conscientious breaches of law are non-evasive and communicative, this legal excuse applies more readily to civil disobedience than to private objection. The second legal defence for civil disobedience is a legal justification. It is a necessity defence rooted in a needs-based notion of necessity and is available only for those acts of civil disobedience that are driven by true conscience.

This defence is not available to bigots, xenophobes, and misguided do-gooders. We can claim necessity when our civil disobedience is animated by a legitimate concern for people's non-contingent basic needs and rights. Those needs include brute survival needs as well as fundamental humanistic needs of political recognition, social inclusion, and respect. For example, we could plead necessity if we engage in civil disobedience to defend the basic rights of prisoners not to be subjected to degrading, cruel, and inhumane conditions.

3:AM: At a time when organised labour and the rights of the poor, for example, are diminishing, your views seem very important. How possible is it for public officials like soldiers or the police to take stands supporting civil disobedience when so much seemed stacked to wipe it out?

KB: In general, liberal societies could take a harsher stance than they tend to take toward evasive "conscientious" objectors. And, they should take a far less harsh stance than they sometimes take toward civil disobedients. To achieve this, individual officials could take a closer look at the underlying moral responsibilities that animate their own offices and consider whether civil disobedience is sometimes the only legitimate course of action for them when they're expected to act contrary to those moral responsibilities. In my book, I discuss the case of two UK community support police officers (CSOs) who tried to save a child who was drowning in a pond, not by attempting a rescue, but by radioing for a trained emergency crew to come to the scene as their professional code required. In the interim, the child died. While the officers were praised by their superior for following proper procedure, they were censured by their community and by former Home Secretary David Blunkett, who said that, "What was appropriate in this circumstance for a uniformed officer would be appropriate for CSOs as human beings, never mind the job."

In my view, the CSOs should also have considered their special moral responsibilities as CSOs. They should have considered not the rulebook, but their responsibilities to protect the members of their community. If police officers, soldiers, and other lower-level officials are willing to question the formal demands made of them, then they are in a better position to be responsive to the civil disobedience of others including that of ordinary citizens.

3:AM: Locke thought that we could go against the sovereign state if property rights were no longer protected. Hobbes thought we could fight the state if it no longer protected us. Isn't your moral argument just another way of undermining the sovereign state and supporting a neo-liberal agenda, which is clearly not what you would intend?

KB: In Conscience and Conviction, I argue that the state and its offices have an important role to play even though their norms and dictates do not have absolute priority. The formal, interlocking web of public offices that a reasonably good society sets up are normatively important because they identify broadly the limits of persons' spheres of responsibility when the system is working well. A reasonably good society is one that tries to set up offices to deal with major issues, such as crime and war, that do not place unduly heavy moral burdens on any would-be occupants of those offices. Unduly burdensome offices not only are unjust to their holders, but also make break downs in official function more likely. I call this the minimum moral burdens principle. For example, in US states such as California, the office that doctors were asked to play in overseeing executions by lethal injection fails the minimum moral burdens test because doctors were asked not just to reduce the condemned person's suffering, but also to intervene to facilitate death if the person wakes up. This task deeply conflicts with doctors' special responsibilities as healers and carers to promote people's wellbeing. And, it's no solution to this kind of problem to set up a special medical office of "execution overseer" because that office would be, by nature, unduly morally burdensome for any would-be occupant.

When fundamentally important moral roles are formalised into decent offices to address the biggest problems of our society, and when the holders of these offices honour their moral responsibilities largely as they should, then all occupants must respect the efforts of their colleagues and not seek to do each other's jobs. When, however, some people do not fulfil the moral responsibilities that are theirs in virtue of the roles that underpin their offices, this affects others' moral responsibilities. It widens the gap between formal expectations and genuine moral responsibilities, and can make conscientious refusal and civil disobedience the only morally acceptable courses of action.

3:AM: You've written about the offender's part in the dialogue of crime and punishment. Is this a voice that is missing?

KB: Yes, the offender's voice is missing in the theory and practice of punishment. One influential theory of state punishment is the communicative theory of punishment. The best-known version of it, defended by Antony Duff, says that, in a liberal society, punishment is the state's effort to engage an offender in a moral dialogue about his conduct. The justification for punishment here is backward-looking. As a society, we look at the wrong done and we see the appropriateness of publicly communicating condemnation of it. Punishment is essentially a secular form of penance that vividly confronts the offender with the nature and effects of his crime. My complaint is that, although this theory shows that punishment is communicative, it does not show that it is dialogic. The theory falls prey to what I call the Scripting Problem.

Punishment requires an offender to undergo the public ritual of apology and penance with its expected expressions of grief and remorse irrespective of his attitudes toward the judgement on him. This kind of forced response not only fails to respect the offender as a person and a citizen, but also fails to satisfy a plausible set of conditions for genuine moral dialogue. In a genuine dialogue, the state would be responsive to the offender's stance toward his punishment. This leads to another problem, which I call the Generic Script Problem. Some offenders—such as repentant offenders and civil disobedients—should not want to follow the formal script of apology because they differ relevantly from unrepentant offenders. The formal script assigned to offenders by the state signals growing awareness and remorsefulness for wrongdoing as well as apology and commitment to reparation. This script misrepresents those offenders who are repentant prior to punishment. It misrepresents them as being unrepentant offenders who need to go through the punishment ritual to come to appreciate the wrong they've done. And, it also misrepresent civil disobedients as being unrepentant or perversely defiant when in fact civil disobedients are trying to engage society in a dialogue different from that ostensibly pursued by punishing them.

A third problem is what I call the Status-Change Problem. When the state condemns someone, it engages in a performative act. It changes that person's legal and moral status in the same way that a minister changes two persons' legal and moral status when she says "I now pronounce you husband and wife." If the state is not responsive to the offender's communicative efforts about his punishment, then the performative act of condemning him alters his status in a way that undermines the conditions for genuine moral dialogue.

3:AM: What role should offenders have?

KB: Offenders should have opportunities to respond to the state's condemnation and to communicate to victims and society the attitude they take toward the apology ritual of punishment. If an offender is fully repentant prior to punishment, then she should not be misrepresented as needing to undergo the full process of punishment to be brought to repent. There may be other reasons for her to accept punishment, such as to show through deeds and not just speech that she is committed to repairing relations with her victim. But, she should have a forum to communicate her repentant attitude, and the state should be responsive to that by imposing a less harsh punishment on her since part of the aims of punishment have already been achieved in her case. Similarly, the civil disobedient should be given a forum in which to signal that she differs from ordinary offenders. She should not be misrepresented as being merely defiant when she actually seeks to engage society in a dialogue.

3:AM: Social deprivation is now an endemic and increasingly virulent blight in societies all over. Is social deprivation a key context for your thinking about legal matters?

KB: My interests in communication and sociability are leading me now to explore the ethics of sociability and, in particular, the merits of social human rights. Debates about human rights tend to neglect social rights. By "social rights," I do not mean economic rights, such as basic subsistence, health, and education, which have received considerable attention. Rather, I mean the rights that protect our fundamental interpersonal, associative, and community-membership needs regardless of our economic circumstances. My current book project, provisionally titled, No Entry: The Evils of Social Deprivation, tries to remedy the neglect of our fundamental social needs and rights. Within the category of social human rights, there is a fundamental, but unacknowledged right, which I call the human right against social deprivation. By "social deprivation," I do not mean poverty, but a persisting lack of minimally adequate opportunities for decent human contact. Social deprivation is a common experience for people subjected to long-term medical quarantine or solitary confinement in prison. It is also a common experience for people whose principal forms of social interaction are degrading and cruel.

Neurological studies by John T. Cacioppo and others indicate that chronic loneliness, understood as perceived social isolation, generates anxiety-inducing physiological threat responses known as the "fight or flight" response. Studies associate chronic loneliness with obesity, the progression of Alzheimer's disease, increased vascular resistance, elevated blood pressure, diminished immunity, reduction in independent living, alcoholism, depression, suicidal ideation and behaviour, and mortality in older adults. In the most extreme cases of isolation, such as coercive isolation in long-term solitary confinement where people are forcibly denied access to human contact, people tend to suffer hallucinations, self-mutilation, psychosis, and suicidal ideation and behaviour. Coercive social deprivation is the most extreme variant of a more general, pervasive phenomenon of social isolation that includes people, many of whom are elderly or disabled, who are chronically, acutely lonely and unable to remedy their situation. Such severe unwanted loneliness is an important concern, particularly in western societies, given aging populations and the individualistic bent of Western culture and policymaking that threatens social support structures.

3:AM: How should the law change in response to deprivation? Are there signs that the law has noticed this context, or is it business as usual?

KB: For a start, state institutions should not be allowed to use socially privative forms of detention. If the immigration, healthcare, and criminal justice systems use solitary confinement in their detention facilities, then they are guilty of social human rights violations. More broadly, the state should pay attention to the incidental and chronic loneliness of disadvantaged and vulnerable groups of people such as elderly people, people with disabilities, and immigrants.

3:AM: And finally, for the readers here at 3:AM, are there five books (other than your own) which you'd recommend we should read to get to grips with these issues?

KB: For discussions on civil disobedience, Hugo Bedau's collection *Civil Disobedience in Focus* is a useful compilation of seminal papers in the liberal tradition. For discussions on human rights, I turn again and again to James Nickel's *Making Sense of Human Rights*; Henry Shue's *Basic Rights*; and James Griffin's *On Human Rights*. For a rewarding discussion on punishment, I recommend Antony Duff's *Punishment, Communication, and Community* .

Kimberley Brownlee is the author of:

Conscience and Conviction: The Case for Civil Disobedience (Oxford University Press, 2012)

21 | Sibyl Schwarzenbach: "Civic Friendship"

Sibyl Schwarzenbach is Professor of Ethics, Political Philosophy, and Feminist Philosophy at Baruch College and the Graduate Center at the City University of New York. Here she discusses the philosophy of civic friendship, Rawls as an abstract individualist, the growing inequality in the United States and the world, Locke and feminism, the way metaphysics underdetermines a thinker's practical position in ethics and politics, Aristotle, paradigms of labor and activity, Marx's understanding of social labor and the emotions, how relations between nations might better be conceived, women's roles, why Kantian dignity is not enough, and sexism in academic philosophy.

3:AM: What made you become a philosopher? Has it been what you hoped it to be so far?

SIBYL A. Schwarzenbach: I often think I would not have become a philosopher had my older brother not been killed one night in a car accident when I was eleven. It turns out that many writers and thinkers have a death somewhere in their childhoods. Before that I had been passionate about sports, piano, and the great outdoors, but I quit all these and moved inwards, was forced to reevaluate things. Death certainly makes one stop and think. Of course, it was also the 1960s and not only my own family, but the entire world was convulsing around me. The U.S. was in the midst of the Vietnam War, the Civil Rights movement, women's liberation, drugs, sex, rock & roll. It was a heady time and I tried to participate as best I could, but when I later enrolled in my first philosophy course in college, I took to it like a fish to water. Here were others who doubted the existence of God and pondered suicide (the Existentialists), and there was this one guy (Descartes) who actually questioned whether the external world existed—just like me! I fell in love with one philosopher after another: Plato and the ancient Greeks, Marx, Kant, Wittgenstein.

With regard to my becoming a professional philosopher, it both has and has not turned out to be what I hoped. There were few women studying philosophy in the 1970s. I had no female philosophy professors during my entire undergraduate years and the only one I had in graduate school (Martha Nussbaum) was fired while I was there. Naturally, I was concerned whether I could make a living in such a male-dominated field. In some ways, this part turned out better than I expected. After a few rather unpleasant episodes, I managed to secure a tenured position in the middle of Manhattan with wonderful students and some great colleagues.

But academia can be frustrating, there is no doubt about it—and it is not just the deep sexism that pervades the field. There is also a certain pusillanimous character to the life of the academic mind –at least in recent decades and in the U.S. Perhaps it is because academic philosophizing today so often refers to and feeds upon itself instead of on the outside world. Far too much effort and thought is directed towards a small circle of initiatives who are meant to further one's career, and so forth. There is indeed much brilliance within the university but much is also wasted on self-promotion, pandering and trivial matters, while outside its walls all sorts of important projects lack intelligent guidance. This is particularly painful for a political philosopher nurtured in the fervent and socially aware 60s and 70s.

3:AM: You contextualise your work on Rawls and communitarianism by drawing attention to the influence of Hegel. You argued then that you were hoping to revive that Hegelian influence. Perhaps a way of seeing why what you are up to is important is to point up the contrast between readings of Rawls that see him as a Kantian. So what's the difference between the Hegelian Rawls and the Kantian one?

SAS: By now the Hegelian influence on Rawls's thought has pretty much been revived and even explicitly acknowledged by the later Rawls himself. But at the time of my 1991 article comparing Rawls and Hegel, communitarians such as MacIntrye, Sandel and C. Taylor were criticizing Rawls ad nauseum for being a Kantian "abstract individualist," and they interpreted his original position as articulating an ahistorical, absolute vantage point sub specie aeternitatis and so on. In the article I tried to show that this misreading was due to the fact that few bothered to understand or even to read Parts II & III of *A Theory of Justice*. The confusion may be compared to reading only Part I of Hegel's *Philosophy of Right* and concluding that the great communal thinker Hegel was really only an abstract individualist; it couldn't be further from the truth. If one considers the whole of *A Theory of Justice*, however, not only the book's tri-partite structure but Rawls's debt to the holist methodology of the German Idealists emerges (see the book's last pages), and one realizes that his construction of the original position is grounded in a specific set of modern social and historical institutions. This is all clarified in Rawls's later works, of course, but it is already present in *A Theory of Justice* if one reads it closely enough.

To answer the second part of your question: perhaps the most important insight Rawls takes from Hegel is the central role of the "basic structure" in his theory. With this term Rawls refers to the way a society's major social, economic, and political institutions hang together in one scheme, and it is to this set of background institutions that justice as fairness applies in the first instance. This emphasis, comparable to Hegel's Sittlichkeit and absent in in Kant's moral and political philosophy, is of critical importance, for it is only by reference to some set of background institutions and cultural ways of life—the basic rules of the game, as it were—that one can adequately understand and evaluate the significance of individual actions, say, or the nature of individual rights (not only how these rights are secured but how they are delineated and constituted in the first place). To use a well-known analogy, one can't understand what a "knight" is or "check mate" in the game of chess, if one hasn't a clue regarding the rules and goal of the game in the first place. Many don't realize the extent to which Rawls was also influenced by the thought of the later Wittgenstein . . .

3:AM: Why do you argue that this Hegelian perspective is more satisfactory?

SAS: I actually don't think it is more satisfactory, only that it is necessary. The degree to which we should focus upon and emphasize the basic structure of society (or Sittlichkeit) is an issue still up for grabs, but one must at least be aware of its critical role and importance. Libertarians, for instance, characteristically have no conception of the basic structure in their theories and it is why their analyses are so misleading and (in my view) superficial.

Still, the emphasis on background social, political and economic institutions (what I am calling the Hegelian insight) is developed to such an extent in Rawls's later work– particularly in his *The Law of Peoples*—that I think he goes too far. The late Rawls risks loosing the original insight with which his greatest work *A Theory of Justice* begins: the inviolability of the individual from the perspective of justice. As a committed feminist, I shudder whenever Rawls writes of a "decent consultation hierarchy" in non-western cultures, for we all know that such a hierarchy refers to a group of men ensconced in power. I don't believe for one minute that the appeal to the dignity of each individual is just some bourgeois, western imperialist notion being imposed upon the rest of the world. On the contrary, western nations such as the U.S. violate this dignity all too frequently when the "individual" happens to be of another race, gender, or religion.

I therefore find myself in growing sympathy once again with that great individualist Kant and at a time when the current mood (on the left) appears to have swung in the opposite—more communal and culturally relativist—direction. In the end, the only thing that bleeds is an individual.

3:AM: Rawls is probably the greatest political theorist of liberalism since Locke. But he's closer to a socialist worldview than a Lockean conception of liberalism isn't he? How would you place Rawls now? Is his brand of liberalism dead in the USA and more relevant in, say, Europe?

SAS: Oh dear, let's hope his brand of social democratic liberalism isn't dead in the United States, for then we are all in big trouble. Again, Rawls did us a great service in the 1970s by focusing our attention on the basic structure of our society. If one ignores this underlying set of background institutions and how they interact, one observes only the most superficial results of far deeper processes at work.

Consider, for instance, the growing inequality in the United States today (and in the world generally). This development can't possibly be explained by the fact that "some individuals are talented and work hard, while others lack capabilities and drive"—as libertarians and neo-liberals are wants to claim. On the contrary, it is important to see that our present set of U.S. institution is deeply flawed. The system permits a handful of persons to inherit billions at birth due to rather arbitrary property, tax, and inheritance laws, together with a crumbling public educational system, etc., while other individuals inherit a crack addiction in utero, are born into dire poverty and a racist culture. How could fairness ever emerge from such unequal—and thoroughly undeserved—starting points? A few individuals may indeed buck the odds of their birth circumstances and claw their way to the top, but statistically speaking these individuals are pretty insignificant. In fact, recent studies have revealed that social and economic mobility—and the chances of individual advancement due to his or her talent—is far greater today in "socialist" Europe than in the U.S.

3:AM: You have engaged with feminist readings of John Locke. Locke's not a feminist but he did have the idea of "no fault divorce," equal education for the sexes and thought women were as smart as men, had no problem with women in political power and so according to Shanley and Butler his thinking contained the "seeds of feminism." But there's stuff that works against that thesis as well. So was Locke a proto-feminist or not?

SAS: One can find "seeds of feminism" all over the map and in the most unlikely places; so, I don't put too much emphasis on the proto-feminist side of Locke. Plato claims in the Republic that unless women as a group are freed from the burdens of child care, they will never become philosopher-queens—a seed of feminism which is having difficulty sprouting even today—but then he goes on to depict any actual ruler as a man.

The situation is similar with Locke. Despite the various progressive elements you mention, there are other deeper tendencies that work against the collective liberation of women. Remember, Locke still explicitly claimed the "natural superiority" of men over women in his *Second Treatise*, and he was a member of the early modern medical establishment that was wrestling health care and reproductive control out of the hands of women and midwives and into those of men. (Sociologists have shown that the dominant class of persons burned as "witches" in the 16th and 17th centuries were lower-class midwives.) So too Locke is probably best known for his defense of the modern institution of private property, which has bewitched us all.

With regard to this last point, Locke famously proclaimed that man originally "owns" that with which he has "mixed his labor" and he argued further that the aim of private property is perhaps the greatest incentive to productive laboring activity. This powerful metaphor certainly seems to apply to free agricultural labor, to craftwork, and even still to private wage-labor in a factory. But where does this new grounding of property in individual labor leave the vast majority of women who, whatever else they did, were also "mixing their labor" with their children and family members, satisfying the needs of the household and larger community? Since persons could no longer be privately owned (for the most part) in the 17th century, Locke's labor theory gave a clever new grounding for the gendered status quo: women's traditional labor and activity quite naturally generates no property rights. Not only was this the case in Locke's time, but it still remains so for much of the world today. In my own view, for any genuine society-wide liberation of women to take place, we must dethrone Locke's powerful mixing metaphor—and the productive model of (market) labor—from the dominant place it still holds in our thinking and practice, and move on to an ethical reproductive model: to a model of ethical labor and praxis where reproducing our human (and animal) relationships in the best way possible—what I call friendship—becomes the goal. On this alternative model, one analyzes not just how to care for another properly or feed them well, but how to educate, further another's abilities, perceive and alleviate their pain, as well as how to maintain long term equal relations with them in the midst of change, as well as simply enjoy and appreciate them.

3:AM: You're well known for your work on the notion of civic friendship. Now this is really cool. To get a grip on what it is, it might be best to contrast it with well-known rivals. Masculine fraternity and Marxist solidarity are two chief rivals. Can you say something about these two and why they don't work?

SAS: I'm pleased that you think the notion of civic friendship is "cool." Our modern concept of friendship has become so privatized (as with many of our other public goods) that the idea of a public friendship between citizens strikes most, especially most Americans, as a contradiction in terms.

Let me contrast the idea of civic friendship first with some of its rivals. The political theorist Jane Mansbridge revealed years ago that when democratic theorists appeal to "fraternity" they primarily have relations between men in mind: a feeling of camaraderie, the recognition of equality among productive citizens, of shared economic interests or common male pursuits. So one problem with the notion of "fraternity" is (as you mention) that it is thoroughly masculine: women and their historical ethical reproductive activities become afterthoughts to a fundamentally male conception of citizenship. But so too, fraternity or the appeal to "the spirit of brotherhood" has frequently been used in the name of dubious and partial ends: in the ancient world, it referred primarily to relations between upper-class male citizens, and more recently to those among the Nazi elite or the KKK. Justice is hardly built into the notion.

A similar difficulty taints Marxist notions of solidarity—at least on my reading. The term originally meant "being solid," "a standing together," and in Roman Law it designated a "shared responsibility," but for what end is not yet specified. By the 19th century, solidarity takes on the meaning of working class unification against capitalist exploitation, and in the 20th it comes to connote the collective liberation of Third World peoples from European colonial rule. This is all good. But in all these cases, we should note that the model of "liberation" is still that of traditionally male forms of activity and labor even if women participate and try to adapt: marching off to war or meeting the enemy at the barricades (military activity), organizing trade unions and labor strikes in factories (confrontational economic production) or ideological battle (philosophy as activity between men). So too, as with the term fraternity, the appeal to solidarity historically has been exercised in the name of gross injustices, e.g. among Stalinist party members. This is not to say that recent solidarity theorists aren't trying to make good on this ethical lacuna within the notion, and elaborating new conceptions of moral or civic solidarity between groups and peoples.

But here, I believe, the concept of civic friendship has distinct advantages. For one, it has a good deal less male historical baggage than the other notions, if only because the idea is still rare when applied to contemporary circumstances. Far more importantly, however, the work of genuine friendship is furthered by activities of ethical reproductive praxis and labor, and not by either economic production or aggressive martial action, no matter how communal. On my reading, the aim of ethical praxis is the initiation and reproduction of flourishing human (and animal) relations for their own sake, whether personal or civic. So the idea of a civic friendship necessarily includes—and even focuses upon—the vast repertoire of ethical reproductive activity and praxis that women have traditionally performed, instead on any characteristically male behavior. Unlike fraternity, therefore, the work and relations between women are central to the modern notion of civic friendship, while in contrast to the notion of solidarity, the stress is on a different type of action and labor; the emphasis is neither on military nor productive activity, but on that which creates and maintains genuine friendships.

With the idea of a civic friendship, moreover, not only do women and their activities become central but the notion necessarily now applies to all citizens, and thus no longer to only a particular group, class or elite; the injustices historically perpetuated in the name of fraternity or solidarity by individuals or classes actually become impossible. Of course, as mentioned, solidarity theorists are beginning to speak of a "civic solidarity" as well. But my sense is that not only will it be difficult for the term solidarity to shake off its masculine heritage, but beyond entailing a negative freedom from (slavery, exploitation) it tells us little more. It does not tell us for which positive end we are "standing together." By contrast, the idea of civic friendship is far more explicit about the goal: the reproduction of political relations analogous to friendship among all citizens.

Allow me to clarify this last point a bit further, for I am frequently misunderstood here. In claiming that a just society must embody a significant degree of civic friendship (and an unjust one necessarily a lack), I do not mean that all citizens must be personal friends with one another (which is impossible). Nor do I mean that there must be some fuzzy warm feeling all citizens have for one another, or the like. Rather, my claim is that at least three essential traits of all friendship—a reciprocal awareness of equality, reciprocal good will and practical doing—must now be evidenced and operate publicly, at least to a certain degree, in a society's laws, its social and economic institutions, as well as expressed in the everyday habits and practices of citizens. Thus, for instance, a reciprocal civic awareness of citizen equality may be evidenced in what citizens know of and can expect from each other, in what rights they grant each other and are guaranteed by their constitution (both the content of the rights and whether they are upheld in practice). Here, of course, the state plays an indispensible role in mediating and regulating information and the press, or in mandating requirements for its schools.

Similarly, the trait of a practical doing may be revealed by the actual duties citizens are willing to perform for one another simply as such (these can range anywhere from not begrudging the paying of one's fair share of taxes, to helping fellow citizens in emergencies, to performing mandatory civil service, etc.). Finally, traits of friendship may be embodied in a society's economic institutions, whereby the extremes of rich and poor will not be tolerated, just as friends help each other out in this area. Civic friendship must always be kept distinct from personal friendship, however; in fact, the former requires that I often surmount the partiality I feel for personal friends or enemies when it comes to treating fellow citizens fairly. I may thus personally know and even dislike Peter, but I can still remain his civic friend: this means only that I will treat him in ways a citizen of this society ought to be treated. Another way of understanding the phenomenon of civic friendship is by realizing that the traits of all friendship—reciprocal awareness, reciprocal good will and practical doing—may apply to and become embodied in the basic structure of a society, to use the language of Rawls. Or a society can express their lack.

3:AM: So your idea of civic friendship is supposed to replace these ideas. You take the idea from Aristotle's notion of philia and find this egalitarian and reciprocal. You go with Aristotle in some detail, so you agree with his notion of the three-part soul don't you? Can you say some more about this and whether it's a straight lift from Aristotle—making him a feminist I guess—or whether it has been tweaked? And does the idea of philia survive if Aristotelian metaphysics doesn't?

SAS: You have asked me a good deal here. I'll begin with your last question. I am of the school that believes much "metaphysics" simply underdetermines a thinker's practical position in ethics or politics; the latter spheres are at the very least semi-autonomous. Hobbes was a metaphysical materialist, after all, and Hegel an idealist but both supported political monarchy in practice. Practical reason is not some mere "application" of our theoretical reason (the reigning view) but has its own subject matter—on this point I am a thorough Kantian. Per Kant, whereas theoretical reason deals with objects known, practical reason deals with how we produce objects or act in the world. Understanding our own ethical reasoning and human practice is practical reason's proper subject matter, and thus it has a different structure from theoretical reason (which can be about anything). I therefore have no difficulty in carving out a position, which respects a number of Aristotle's substantive ethical arguments and insights, while simultaneously jettisoning many (or even most) of his metaphysical claims. Strictly speaking, the former don't derive from the latter anyway.

That having been said, I begin with Aristotle for a number of reasons. First, he views the political state or polis as grounded in an entirely different set of activities (in ethical praxis and action) than do the vast majority of moderns. Today the primary justification for the state, especially in the U.S., tends to be viewed still in terms of providing security (military protection) and the regulation of property and the economy (production). Second, I develop what I take to be Aristotle's basic insight here: that civic friendship is a necessary condition for genuine justice in any state. Perhaps the easiest way to understand this claim is by way of considering its opposite. Without the expression of a minimal and reciprocal good will, recognition and practical doing between citizens—in a general atmosphere of hostility or ill-will, that is, or in one of widespread indifference—the rich and powerful in a society will characteristically pursue their own interests and bend the rules to their liking, while the poor and dispossessed will avoid, whenever and wherever possible, the laws being imposed on them. Without a minimal civic friendship embodied in society's basic structure of institutions, that is, only force and cunning will reign, and genuine justice becomes impossible.

Clearly Aristotle's notion of political friendship (politike philia) is being tweaked. Not merely because I zero in on, and include, the traditional activities of women, but also because my examination is now of our modern society's basic structure and not that of the ancient polis. In my view, any modern (post-Reformation) notion of political friendship must operate via a doctrine of universal individual rights and this I now label "civic" (in contrast to political) friendship. On this point, political liberalism strikes me as correct. In today's pluralistic societies, it is the height of dogmatism for the state to try to impose one comprehensive conception of the good life on all citizens. Nonetheless, the state may still reasonably require a minimal civic friendship between all citizens as a precondition of justice.

Aristotle's notion of philia is also clearly being tweaked. I wish to retain the original broad reference of the Greek term philia, whereby it refers to the best relations between parents and children, or between siblings, husbands and wives, lovers and even fellow citizens. In all these best-case scenarios, one finds the three essential traits of friendship mentioned above: a reciprocal awareness of the other as a moral equal, goodwill and practical doing over an extended period of time. Our contemporary English notion of "friendship" by contrast, has grown narrower and narrower over the centuries such that today all familial, sexual, and civic relations are held up in opposition to friendship relations strictly speaking—no matter the quality of these other relations. This I find perverse, and it is a trend I am trying to reverse, for the important reason that such conceptual narrowness obscures and even excludes from view, all those best-case, qualitative traits (or their lack), which these otherwise diverse relations (of family, siblings, lovers, citizens) may hold in common. Focusing on their commonalities gets us to focus on their quality. It is a different way of dividing up our social world.

Still, it was Aristotle's himself who began to narrow the notion of friendship down to what I call "the equal fraternal model." That is, beginning with an astute analysis of the broad notion of philia, Aristotle ends by proposing his more limited ideal of the best friendship relations: the reciprocal awareness, good will, and doing between two similar and similarly situated men of roughly equal age, class, endowment and virtue. In Aristotle's ideal of friendship the equality and similarity between the friends is presupposed from the start.

My own work, by contrast, tries to develop an alternative, but equally important, conception. In many cases of genuine friendship, for instance, equality (of age, class, gender, or race, etc.) need hardly be there from the start, but only the aim of a rough reciprocal equality over a complete life. Certainly many women's friendships have been far more flexible than Aristotle's ideal. Women have spent much of their lives with each other, raising their own and each other's children (of both sexes), have helped and educated and enjoyed time with them, supported in-laws and the old, even neighbors, etc. The best of these relationships surely produce genuine life-long friendships only now these relations stretch across generations, genders, difference in circumstances, and evolve in the midst of a diverse and developing (or declining sets) of individual abilities. In the best instances of such relations, no actual equality but only the aim of a rough equality between the two friends, need be maintained. Once a (good) child has reached independence, for instance, they often help the aged parent in turn. The same may be said of (good) pupils and teachers, or between peoples from different cultures and classes and so forth. Particularly today, there are many genuine ethical friendships but they develop in the midst of a far greater diversity in age, class, circumstance and ability. An alternative and largely still submerged model of "difference friendship" is at work.

Finally, in regard to Aristotle's analysis of "the reproductive soul" (at least someone is theorizing reproduction!), I begin from his analysis in the *De Anima* and ethical writings, but hardly end there. Aristotle never explicitly distinguishes a biological from an ethical reading of the reproductive soul (the threptikon): that part of all living creatures by which we nourish and reproduce ourselves. In his ethical writings, however, he clearly provides a normative account of nourishment. How we decide which type of food to eat, the right amounts, when, etc. is of critical concern to the human good life, and hitting the virtuous mean here entails not merely right habit and educated pathos, but right reason as well. Indeed, one could say that I attempt something similar in distinguishing ethical from biological reproduction. I am less interested in the reproduction of biological processes (in menstruation, how egg meets sperm, etc.) and more in developing an ethical account of how we—as creatures of reason, moral awareness and foresight—ought to reproduce ourselves, not simply individually each day or with a family, but as a civic society and even as a species: with whom should we live, ought we reproduce biologically, what should the nature of our civic society be, and how to conceive our duties to our fellow citizens and the next generation. As in the proper study of good nourishment, the way humans reproduce themselves and their civic relations is not a mere "natural" process (despite what many may think) but ought to be done consciously with reason, foresight and a universal concern for the whole, and even other, species. But it so rarely is!

3:AM: You say, "For the construction of a plausible modern conception of a civic friendship between citizens, the vast repertoire of particular moral convictions hitherto relegated to the "private," the "personal," and the pre-political "merely social" realm can no longer be excluded from the original data pool from which a political reflective equilibrium begins. On the contrary, it is precisely from this sphere of close personal and social relations—the traditional home of women—that one of the most powerful resources for a renewed conception of civic friendship is to be found.' You want to get theorists to start reflecting on what makes women's traditional activities work and see that this is a better notion of civic communitarianism that the alternatives. Is that right?

SAS: Yes, along with many other feminists, I would like philosophers to begin serious reflection upon a different paradigm of human labor and activity— one we share and which happens every day all around us. However, I have never advocated stopping there and accepting present practices of reproduction, whether individual or civic. On the contrary, not only have women been disproportionately burdened by such labor, but they have performed it under conditions akin to slavery and in ideological thrall to woman's "true nature." In the above quote, I ask only that we allow the diverse insights and moral intuitions of ethical reproductive praxis back into the balancing act of a political reflective equilibrium, at which point such insights will necessarily be refined, developed, and transformed. If we begin, by contrast, from the "tradition of moral philosophy" or from "our public political sphere"— Rawls's starting points—the slight of hand of the conjuring trick has already been committed—women have been excluded from these areas for thousands of year and largely still are. One can't help but then go on to develop a one-sided, partial, and distorted picture of the human community, including of the modern democratic state.

3:AM: You're interesting in your criticism of Marx. You think Marx's *Economic and Philosophical Manuscripts* of 1844 were a working of Aristotle's *De Anima* and that Marx was trying to revive both praxis and philia. But you say he lacked a sense of social labour and didn't understand the structure of emotions right. Is this right? Can you say more about why Marx was off?

SAS: Yes, that's pretty close. We know Marx was translating Aristotle's De Anima from the Greek into German (sections are still extant) while he was writing the 1844 *Manuscripts*. Much of the discussion regarding human capacities for nourishment, sensation/perception and universal intellect, uses the language of the *De Anima*. Marx also quotes directly from Aristotle's Politics but there is no evidence to my knowledge that he was influenced in any significant way by Aristotle's ethical writings (perhaps some Marx scholar can set me straight here). It is in these ethical works, however, that Aristotle gives his account of the emotions and their critical importance for the exercise of practical wisdom, for correctly apprehending the concrete particulars among which action always takes place, and for hitting the mean not only in individual action, but in just political rule. So it is not exactly the case that Marx didn't get the structure of our emotions right—Marx hardly discusses the emotions at all.

This being the case, both his theory of revolution and his account of the transition to socialism lack a few key elements. How, for instance, is the modern egoistic individual (including the wage-laborer), educated for and competing upon the capitalist market place, suddenly meant to rise up and collectively throw off, not merely the exploitative capitalists rulers, but his or her own egoistic tendencies? What are the conditions under which this still selfish individual will not merely cooperate and work with others to produce (indirect social labor) but actually work for others directly, seek the satisfaction of the other's needs and even (sometimes) enjoy it? The latter may be called directly social or other-directed labor, but there is no account of it in any of Marx's writings. The possibility of a genuine socialist revolution strikes me as far more plausible, however, if one begins from the immense amount of other-directed praxis that has been performed over the centuries primarily (but not exclusively) by women, even if much of this work remained un-free and in the private sphere.

3:AM: Part of what you seem to be arguing is that emotional illiteracy is what hampers civic friendship. Political theorists are too buttoned up and male. Is this right?

SAS: Not quite. Emotional illiteracy is part of the problem, but many of our theoretical self-understandings –the metaphors and models bequeathed to us and by which we recognize ourselves—also hamper and perpetuate the lacuna of civic friendship in our societies. If one is repeatedly told, and thus also ends up holding the self-conception, that human beings are in general egotistical, greedy, hell bent on domination and the accumulation of money and power, then the chances are pretty good that one is going to act in these ways as well. Much of what feminists (and others) are trying to do today is to whittle away at such narrow and dogmatic self-conceptions. They are dangerous because they help reproduce in reality what they at first proclaimed only in thought.

Think again of Locke's powerful "mixing" metaphor discussed earlier. This metaphor not only focuses our attention on so-called "productive labor" and the incentive of private property, but it simultaneously gets us to look away from and neglect other types of work and social incentives that motivate people in actual fact: when they are serving their communities or building common places of worship, when engaged in music or the theatre for its own sake, when beautifying towns, helping save animal species on the brink of extinction, fighting for another's rights or trying to end world poverty and suffering, not to mention all the activities entailed in maintaining good relations with their friends and families. On the reigning production model of labor aimed at private property (and consumption), it becomes difficult to imagine how people could ever act in these far more social and other-directed ways—and yet they do.

Finally, I believe our emotional illiteracy and our narrow self-understandings may both be traced back to dominant institutions and social practices: to the modern capitalist market where insecurity and egoism are nurtured and greed rewarded, where more money, consumption, and economic "growth" are considered leading individual and collective goals, and where a maze of illogical and historically haphazard property laws exist privileging the wealthy, etc. In the U.S. there has also been a striking lack of concern for educating the whole of the next generation (ethical civic reproduction) and this neglect goes back to our Constitution and even earlier. My point is thus not so much that males are emotionally dead or buttoned up—female corporate executives on Wall Street can be just as bad or worse—but that we must in addition to educating the emotions also consciously re-work reigning conceptions of ourselves that allow us to see only part of the story. This in turn would help alter our practice and our social institutions accordingly.

3:AM: You also worry that feminist theories of "care" haven't the scope to achieve full justice for all that your idea of civic friendship has. What's the problem with "care"?

SAS: Yes, some feminists are trying to develop entire theories based on the concept of care and some consider care ethics an entirely new approach to ethics. It just won't work in my opinion—much like Christian "love" didn't work—for the concept of care is neither structured nor differentiated enough, and one can't get blood from a turnip. By now, of course, there have been many good general criticisms of care ethics, among the most important being that the whole movement of the last thirty years remains far too closely tied to mothering (or parenting) practices and to specific and un-free bourgeois mothering practices at that; care theory remains parochial and partial. But to be a bit more specific, the concept of care strikes me as particularly unhelpful at best and profoundly misguided at worst, when it comes to modelling the normative relation between the ideal of democratic citizens. Here again, the concept of friendship has distinct advantages.

To begin with, not everyone wants to be nor should become "a parent," whereas nearly everyone, but for the odd hermit, seeks genuine friendships (no one wants merely apparent ones). Friendship is the more universal and comprehensive category, and it typically incorporates the concept of care but the reverse is not the case. Secondly, a one way or unequal caring relationship is not only possible, but appears to have been the historical norm: the feudal lord "cared" for his serfs, the slave-owner for his property, and the nurse for her dying patient. In all these instances of care, there is little reciprocity, no equality, and no real autonomy of the other.

By contrast, a one-way friendship is strictly speaking impossible; it is no friendship at all. Precisely when a friendship becomes one-sided or domineering, we consider it an unhealthy one and near its end. Friendship—unlike care—by definition requires reciprocity, the autonomy of the other and (as I argued above) at least the aim of a reciprocal equality. And for such reasons friendship emerges as the more appropriate ideal for modeling the future democratic citizen relation. This is not to say that how we, as a society, organize our child and sick and elderly care is not of crucial importance. It is only to say that for political purposes, to assert care as the central relation between citizens, or as the citizen's leading characteristic entails far too much paternalism, dependency, and even intimacy between citizens than appears healthy or appropriate.

Of course, I am also not denying that one may construct a concept of "genuine" care in which a minimal reciprocity, autonomy, and even equality between persons or citizens is simply stipulated. Historically, it can be argued, much care was one-sided and unequal, but we need not stick with this limited historical meaning. . . . In response to the care theorist here, I would argue; this is all fine and well, but by building equality and reciprocity into the very concept of care, what you are actually doing is moving further and further into the territory of the concept of friendship and leaving that of care behind. Finally, we mustn't forget that care ethics can be, and has been, utilized for reactionary purposes. Various U.S. court decisions, and even presidents of famous universities (c.f. the scandal over Lawrence Summers' remarks at Harvard) have argued that it is "not unfair" that women continue to be disproportionally under-represented in society's most prestigious jobs and fields (whether airline pilot or physics professor) and for the reason that women seem to prefer more caring jobs.

For all these reasons, the ideal of friendship and not care seems the superior normative model for the future democratic civic relation (I might mention, the deep connection between the idea of democracy and that of friendship was already noted by Aristotle). The desire for friendship is near universal, it includes everyone (men as well!) and by definition it entails a minimal reciprocal awareness and good will of the other's autonomy, as well as a practical doing and the aim of maintaining equality. Grounding a civic friendship in our alternative model of difference friendship, moreover, only mirrors the norms and requirements of the ever-growing pluralism of modern (in contrast to ancient) democratic societies. This alternative civic ideal now rejects Aristotle's equal fraternal model. It is an ideal of democratic citizens who are highly complex and diverse but who nonetheless recognize the autonomy of each (secured by modern doctrines of individual rights) in the midst of change, who willingly cooperate in educating the next generation to a civic good will, and who endeavor to aim at and maintain a rough equality of background material conditions and opportunities for all. Finally, these citizens will seek to resolve disagreements and conflicts—not through caring for or loving one another, but also not through guns, exploitation, deception or wile—but rather through expanding political procedures of dialogue and discussion, a more inclusive listening to one another other and, finally, by transforming such talk into a practical doing as a recognized civic duty—as if between friends.

3:AM: Rawls plays a key role in your theory doesn't he? How does he help get your civic friendship into place?

SAS: Yes, Rawls's thought has been critical for me. Rawls not only placed the emphasis (like Hegel) on society's basic structure once again, but he went further and called for the embodiment of the value of fraternity in that basic structure. Rawls considers his difference principle, remember, to be a political interpretation of fraternity. It states that any systematic inequalities allowed in society's basic structure must be tied to bettering the position of the worst off as well; no group is to be left behind. I would even claim that articulating this difference principle is the real substantive contribution that Rawls makes to the history of political liberalism, but it is a move that has been pretty much buried of late (not least of all by the later Rawls himself.) One could say, I am trying to reawaken Rawls's original concern with interpreting fraternity politically and seeing the value embodied in our economic institutions too. It is one of the great failures of Rawls's later work, in my view, that he never went on to elaborate, refine, and defend the fundamental substantive insight embodied in his second principle of justice: that individual parties may rightfully have and own more but only if they contribute to a fair structure that helps everyone—including the worst off. No exceptions.

3:AM: You see a role for this approach not just in changing internal political settlement but also as redefining relations between nations. How would that work?

SAS: Yes, again, our attitudes, emotional stance and our self-conceptions—how we conceive ourselves as individuals (whether as egotistical, competitive, going it alone or as cooperative, good willed, fun loving, etc.)—is crucial to how we end up acting in the world, always taking the possibility of various self-deceptions into account. Much the same is true with regard to our dominant collective self-understandings whether those of the state, peoples or nations. International Relations theory (IR)—the reigning theory of our day—continues to conceive of states as independent, self-sufficient and in constant competition with other states; any "friendships" we might hold with other states are either knee-jerk and unquestioning (e.g. US friendships with England or Israel) or else they are reduced to the instrumental use of other nations in the furtherance of our own national self-interest à la Carl Schmidt (here Saudi Arabia is a good example). In actual fact, however, states are hardly independent and self-sufficient any longer, if they ever were. Particularly since WWII, the doctrine and practice of universal human rights and the development of international law are restricting the political sovereignty of nation states, and their economic independence is being undermined daily due to increased global trade, climate change and so forth. Hence, the international realm too needs new and richer collective self-conceptions to replace old inadequate models and to help us better understand ourselves, whether as a nation or a global people in the future. We certainly need guidance on how we might all get along peaceably on a crowded planet with ever diminishing resources. . . .

3:AM: You argue that the values of philia are rooted originally in traditional women roles. Many women reject those roles. So is it your view that it's a model that is no longer feminist in a sense, that it's a historical accident that it has been found in women's traditional social realities but nevertheless this is something that has universal appeal? And if that's right, why isn't something like Kantian dignity just as good?

SAS: No, no, no. I think my long answer above should at least partly answer your questions here. Some version of philia (friendship taken broadly) I believe has universal appeal and is not found merely in women's roles or their social reality; it is crucial for men as well (cf. Aristotle's discussion) and found all over the world. But I do think analyzing traditional women's activities and their friendships in our societies today adds something important to the historical and cross-cultural debate, and allows us to dislodge the equal fraternal model.

In our advanced capitalist society (particularly in our American rugged-individualist one) our public economic, social, and political institutions are revealing ever fewer traits of a civic friendship: from the extreme material inequalities so blithely allowed, to the dearth of corporate social responsibility, to our crumbling public school systems, we are all to often abandoning the poor to their lot (including the global poor). Recent neo-liberal and libertarian thought appears to believe that we can do without any fellow-feeling, any other directed ethical praxis in our public political life, or in our economic institutions and even in our social theory and policy (witness the dismantling of many welfare and unemployment policies in recent decades). But neo-liberal policies have only proven once again that such privatization leaves vast swaths of the population behind and fortifies primarily those at the top. So one last concentrated (secular) place one still finds philia (and use value) today is, yes, in traditional women's activities of taking care of the household as well as in individual friendships, although again, I do not advocate maintaining this privatized care in the home, nor its glorification.

The reason the Kantian notion of dignity is not enough, I believe, is that genuine human (or even animal) dignity needs support. Just like that of a young child, the dignity of self and others needs to be acknowledged and cultivated; the absolute value of dignity cannot merely be proclaimed in the abstract (a weak point in Kant's theory) but must be nurtured, educated, and reinforced in individual, social, and institutional practice. But all this takes thought and work: a special kind of work. I don't believe one can recognize and reinforce the dignity of another human being, at the same time as one is trying to sell them coke-a-cola or some other worthless item.

3:AM: A question troubling philosophers in the academy is the place of women. Although better than it was the situation is still pretty dire. As a top philosopher what are your thoughts about the state of sexism in academic philosophy. Is civic friendship precisely what is needed? And you have written pretty harshly about certain "feminist" theories of psychoanalysis and philosophy that strike you as being misguided on many levels. Is this a symptom or a cause of some of the problems?

SAS: Ah, yes, the question of sexism in philosophy. Gaining any sort of recognition in this field is a constant and tiring struggle for women. If I had to sum up in a nutshell why sexism is particularly bad in philosophy (unlike in, say, the fields of literature or psychology or history), I would probably say because male philosophers can't stomach the thought of not being the torch bearers of "reason"– at least over and against women. This sense of self and entitlement runs deep. For at least two thousand years, one of the oldest pursuits—philosophy—pretty much by definition was an activity done by and between men only: like smoking cigars or going to war. And, as my generation in particular has discovered, things change slowly.

If by a greater civic friendship playing a role in ending sexism you mean merely a generalized sympathy and sentimental feeling towards women, such good will is clearly not enough. Many a colleague is well intentioned and sympathetic, but they come down hard the minute their male prerogatives are even slightly questioned. If, however, one takes civic friendship as the attempt to transform the basic structure of society such that developing mature, lasting relations between adult equals might become more important and fulfilling than gaining a larger piece of the pie, greater status, making loads of money or being "on top," then yes, greater incorporation of this value into the background rules of the game would help women as a group. I have no doubt.

3:AM: Have there been any books, films, music that have inspired you outside of philosophy?

SAS: Oh, many. As I grow older and the practical problems of finding a good job, publishing, obtaining tenure, etc. all recede into the distance, I find myself turning ever more frequently to areas outside philosophy for inspiration, insight, and simple delight. I have always loved literature and poetry— from *Charlotte's Web* (earth shattering at age 10) to the Greek tragedies, to Hölderlin, Thomas Mann, Emily Dickenson and Arundhati Roy. At the moment I am translating from the German some of the literary and journalistic essays of a Swiss cousin who wrote on and photographed the U.S. during the Great Depression (Annemarie Schwarzenbach, 1908-1942). I love being immersed in poetic language again, and photography has always been a special love of mine. But there were many other books and films that were crucial to me earlier, a number of which I don't know if anyone reads anymore: for instance, R.D. Laing's *The Divided Self* comes to mind or Wilhelm Reich's *The Mass Psychology of Fascism* which altered my development in the 1970s, and films such as Children of Paradise, Cocteau's Blood of a Poet, Bertollucci's The Conformist or those by Fellini and Bergman (the latter, of course, still well known). I'm also a big opera fan—especially Verdi and Wagner– and the Ring Cycle is something I go to hear and see over and again. There are many things in heaven and on earth about which philosophy has little to add.

3:AM: And for the civic friendship buffs here at 3am, are there five books (other than your own which of course we'll be reading straight after this) that you'd recommend so we get a better handle of what philia is all about?

SAS: I can't even think of five books on the topic of civic friendship or philia at the moment. There is Aristotle's *Nicomachean Ethics*, of course, and all the secondary literature on it. I was influenced in particular by John Cooper's and Martha Nussbaum's readings of Aristotle. Oh, I suppose I should mention that a number of us have started a new international journal (on-line, for the moment) called Amity: The Journal of Friendship Studies (eds. Preston King and Heather Devere) that anyone interested in the subject might enjoy (the first volume is ready and should be out soon). But at least as important as reading anything more on the topic is for people honestly to assess the role friendship has played in their lives and to consider not only which traits genuine friendship exhibits, but which might be important to develop politically.

Finally, working to deepen and strengthen our good relations, not just personally but with our fellow citizens and other nations, entails consciously foregoing enticements of power and the ideology of production: of being "the best," winning ever more prizes (I always think of Plato's cave), seeking higher status and more things, but also aiming to produce ever more books, articles or children—for none of these activities will help stop the earth from overrun or future catastrophes, whether with respect to war, starvation or dangerous climate change. To enjoy the actual relations we have, both human and animal, to conceive and build better ones, and to learn to live in the world modestly with all the other diverse peoples and animal species as if they were our friends—that is the great political task of the future, in my view, and one that it would serve us well to learn quickly.

Sibyl Schwarzenbach is the author of:

Women and the United States Constitution: History, Interpretation and Practice (ed. and contributing author) (Columbia University Press, 2004)
On Civic Friendship: Including Women in the State (Columbia University Press, 2009)

22 | Christopher Lebron: "The Color of Our Shame"

Christopher Lebron is Assistant Professor of African American Studies and Philosophy at Yale University. Here he discusses theories of justice appropriate for race. He discusses bridging the gap between abstraction and lived experiences, American democracy and racial inequality, marginalization and oppression, the idea of character and how it helps explain racial inequality, the problem of social value, why Rawls isn't enough, "white power," despair and blame, perfectionism and egalitarianism, soulcraft politics, three principles of racial justice, and the lamentable number of black philosophers currently working in the academy.

3:AM: What made you become a philosopher?

CHRIS LEBRON: I consider myself to be a person who has, even from a young age, harbored a certain kind of discontent with what I personally refer to as the tragedy of humankind. By this I mean to refer to the fact that people are possessed of extraordinary powers of imagination, reasoning, industry, magnanimity, but also of malice, destruction, and meanness. So far as I can tell we seem as a species tightly bound to this tragedy. But we each, personally, have a particular relationship to it and though I can often be deeply cynical, I can admit to cultivating an enduring hope that we individually have the potential to better comprehend our relationship to this tragedy so that we can do our small part to remain on the right side of the ledger. To my mind, this is the struggle of humanity vs. humankind. But how to do so, how might we do so, how ought we to do so?—this is a very great question. This question has been a part of my own complicated vacillation between love for humanity and resentment towards it.

I became a philosopher and theorist initially because I wanted to answer the question on how we get and stay on the right side of the ledger. As I mature in my career, though, I am coming to learn that I do philosophy because I want to know how I might get and stay on the right side of the ledge and in my personal struggle with the question I hope to invite others to take up my reflections and when they are pointed in the right direction, follow thusly, and when they are not, to help me and others find that direction, if it is there to be found.

3:AM: Your starting point for working out a theory of justice is to presuppose that if you're black then you're not part of society as democracy supposes isn't it? Is this what you mean when you discuss "lonely citizens" and shame?

CL: A theory of justice appropriate for race has one central obligation and that is to bridge the gap between abstract notions of the good, the right, fairness, etc. and the lived experience of race, the way history and power converge on the being and the fabric of reality of blacks in America. There are many kinds of injustices in the world and racial injustice certainly isn't the only one to be marked by asymmetries of power. However, it has a singular place in American history—racial domination made America what we know it to be today. What is the nature of this thing we refer to as America? Well, it has at least a few discernible and significant attributes. One is that it is a liberal democracy—that is, it is regulated by a form of governance that takes the freedom and liberty of its citizens to widely participate in politics to be fundamental; this feature is itself underwritten by a deeper normatively inflected commitment which is to treat persons in a certain way—as possessing autonomy and having the station of equal standing among peers in the social and political scheme. Another is that it is a liberal democracy founded in the course of practicing racial domination. My position here is not unique in the history of (black) thought—to found a nation's constitution and develop its institutions in this manner settles early lessons about which persons are supposed to be the legitimate beneficiaries of the constitution and institutions. A beautiful thing about a democratic government is that it can be made to change, but the nature of change required to address racial inequality have historically left not only scars but present-day battlegrounds of difference rooted in resentment on both sides of the racial divide, whites' sense of being threatened by change, and insecurity of a many kinds for all involved. A democracy's struggles largely constitute not only its history but its culture which itself teaches a variety of lessons to those constantly learning how to be citizens and how to assess other citizens. The bases for both these lessons and our apparatus for judgment is thus fraught with serious problems that affect the content of those lessons and our practices of judgment.

Finally, America is a liberal democracy that, despite that description and despite the passage of the Civil Rights Act of 1964, continues to be a functioning and quite vibrant site not only of common indicators of racial inequality (income, wealth, resources, employment) but of racial marginalization (segregation, the reproduction of disparaging racial stereotypes in our popular media) as well as racial oppression (disproportionate jailing and the devaluation of black life by the institutions of criminal justice whether it be by disproportionate application of the death penalty or unpunished acts of violence against blacks by police). So we have to ask ourselves: just what kind of "liberal democracy" is marked by a strain of deep and disrespectful injustice that is contrary to the very idea of liberal democracy? My answer is: One that doesn't merely marginalize but one that explicitly and implicitly rejects the humanity of black Americans. So it is more than not being part of American society. It is deeper. It is not being seen fully as the kind of thing that can vie for membership in American society—a human being. So here, the question of loneliness is not itself as central as the diminished value of black humanity.

I noted the slippage between the standards and principles entailed by the form of governance we describe as liberal democracy on the one hand, while on the other, the consistent demeaning and unjust treatment of black Americans. The very notion of slippage between the principles to which we subscribe and the reasoning, attitudes, and actions we take up provides the grounds for shame. That we might or ought to feel shame in any instance is not in itself in the ordinary course of things always a reason to raise questions of justice. When as a parent we affirm the virtue of generosity towards our children but act meanly on an occasion, this seems appropriately remedied by a genuine apology and show of affection. So the question here is, what, for me, raises the question of justice in the case under consideration—racial inequality? This is the role I set for character.

3:AM: Can you explain what you mean when you say that you think the USA suffers from bad character? How does it help explain systematic racial inequality?

CL: The idea of character has not typically been deployed in contemporary theories of justice and this has been so for a fairly straightforward reason. Theories of justice have mostly been concerned with distributive justice (the division of goods that are the product of a scheme of ongoing cooperation) and the role of institutional design in achieving distributive justice. Apart from the general and prior commitments of ideal theory, this focus tilts us away from certain ideas central to our ethical traditions, among them virtue and character. This has a bit to do with what some would claim is a category mistake in applying these ideas to institutions in addition to or instead of persons—philosophers do not tend to think of virtues like kindness or bravery applying to institutions, and in some instances that hesitation is justified. But this also has to do with what one has to go in for in mobilizing these ideas. If you seek to work out an approach to institutional design that is a fit for a certain conception of distributive justice then what you will really be attentive to will be matters of fairness, procedure, and properly structured deliberation. If you turn towards ideas like character, then you have to extend the theory, if it can be so extended, into an analysis of history and political development and an interpretation of our social landscape. But this will not be interesting if you think you can theorize fairness prior to politics and history, or if you are concerned that these particulars are sufficiently myriad to systematically organize for the purposes of prescriptive arguments.

And this is how the idea of character helps explain racial inequality. I might identify at least two approaches to that idea. One says that character has to do with the complex of habits and principles we possess and affirm and the way we develop, fail to develop, apply, fail to apply those principles and habits appropriately given the relationship we are addressing at a given point. Another, (attributable to Joan Didion) equates character with moral nerve— standing by our convictions and denying opportunities to regret our actions because doing so is on a par with rejecting our earlier selves—the self that made the decision we wish we might not have made. Now, I don't agree with this idea of regret in its particulars since I don't think regret amounts to rejecting our earlier selves, but there really is something to the idea of moral nerve that is to the point here: a failure to abide by the principle undergirding the form of government we endorse and ostensibly practice is not itself a failure or moral nerve—that can just be moral error. However, when that error—to put it mildly—persists for a few centuries without thorough and (consistently) sincere address, that is a failure or moral nerve. To overcome that failure, we also need to keep in view the first approach to character having to do with habits, virtues, and moral learning. When we observe the persistence, range, and depth of racial injustice, we are not talking merely about blacks not getting one good or another, we are talking about a polity unable to bring into right relationship the duties of democratic citizenship with the moral obligation to respect other persons as persons. This, I have argued, is fundamental to justice because without that relationship coming to bear, nothing else can effectively be done.

3:AM: Can you explain what you are arguing when you say that the problem of racial inequality is the problem of social value—does this mean you're arguing out of a tradition of social theorists led by W.E.B. Du Bois and Frederick Douglas?

CL: The problem of social value stipulates that blacks are not accorded the appropriate care and concern that motivates the proper distribution of goods in the first place. So it is an idea that attempts to bridge the gap between norms, history, sociology, and moral motivation—it is an analytic heuristic to support the argument for shame and character in a theory of racial justice as I above briefly reviewed. However, while I have coined this term and given it analytic shape, two things must be said about it. First, within the realm of intellectual inquiry, the substance of "social value" is not new in my work at all. Indeed, the problem of social value is a kind of concern expressed by Douglass, Du Bois, Baldwin, and many others in the history of black thought.

Second, that said and acknowledged, it was not my intention to argue out of that tradition, as you have put it. I formulated the idea out of frustration with my existence as a person of color and my observation of the kinds of things that have, do, and will continue for the foreseeable future to frustrate brown Americans. What's interesting here, though, is that I suppose it puts me right back in that tradition precisely because for Douglass, et al these concerns were not motivated by the intrigue of conceptual puzzles but by the urgency that is a result of facing marginalization as fact of everyday life.

3:AM: Why is a philosophical project like John Rawls's theory of justice not capable of gaining the necessary traction with racism in the USA? Is it because it can't grip hold of the question: "why don"t/won't can't you accept us as your equals?' and without being able to engage with that its going to evade the issue? And is this a theory specifically about racial inequality in the USA or are we to suppose it can be generalised?

CL: I have an imagining I like to share with my students regarding John Rawls—one that I don't in fact know whether it is true, but I imagine it to be perfectly possible. Here it is: It is 1963 and Rawls, like many Americans is watching on television the use of fire hoses and dogs to violently suppress peaceful black protesters in Birmingham, Alabama. And he is thinking, my God—how on earth do you get people as opposed in their positions to come to an agreement concerning how to move forward in a democratic society? With this question he becomes increasingly certain that his device, the original position behind the veil of ignorance is the only way to secure reasonable deliberation regarding principles of social justice precisely because each of the parties to this shameful event and the history that gives rise to it, has a great deal to lose or gain, thus won't be able to think the way (Rawls thinks we need to think) in order to derive rational principles of justice.

When I share this narrative, I myself can see how someone at the time could see a device like the original position as not only reasonable, but necessary. But now, the passage of an additional fifty years since the Civil Rights Act suggests a quite insidious form of racial inequality—one that can reproduce many of the effects from the days of Jim Crow under the watch of full formal equality. This should give the normative political theorist pause. My understanding of the issue has evolved into the position that it's not even really a matter of whether Rawls's framework can get a grip on the question, "why don't /won't/ can't you treat me like an equal?" It is that it is not really interested in asking that question at all. To ask that question requires that one take stock of what has been going wrong in our democratic dealings, but that can't be in view when on a theorist's own description strict compliance is being assumed.

I'd like to be more clear in ways that I have not been before that sometimes my discontent is directed right at Rawls's work, but other times my criticisms of Rawls is really meant to call to account his followers. I suspect Rawls himself would not argue that his work can be stretched to answer questions having to do with racial or gender inequality. But many of his followers, who occupy various positions of power and influence in the field have insisted that the work can do that, and by doing so, have as a consequence relegated direct questions of racial ethics to a kind of low-level status.

So, yes, without asking that very specific question—why don't/won't/can't you treat me as an equal?—being addressed, we do evade the issue because we pass over the very essential questions having to do with the intersection of moral motivation and social power. That said, I didn't devise my theory to be generalizable. When I was a graduate student, a theory that can "travel" was often portrayed as a sign of not only intellectual elegance but of analytic utility. I won't quarrel with that in general, but the attribute of generalizability is often portrayed not merely as an attractive virtue but a necessary one—one that shows the work really is rigorous. I do disagree with this latter stance. When I developed the arguments that would ultimately shape *The Color of Our Shame* in my dissertation, I intentionally sought to devise a theory good for one thing: to say something new (to political philosophers/theorists) about racial inequality in America. It would please me very much if a person considering race in the United Kingdom, for example, found something helpful in my work—I think there are some ideas in there that would travel, like social value, but I also think that that idea would have its most potent meaning only if modulated by that theorist as called for by the specific conditions of the United Kingdom. If it turned out that the idea didn't need modulating that would be interesting but that kind of outcome was and isn't my goal.

3:AM: You don't reject everything in Rawls though do you?

CL: I tend to think it's a bad idea to reject everything found in any writer's work because even when confused, work that makes it to the public is really trying to say something to us and it is an offense to reason to close one's ears to it, or refuse it an audience a second time because we didn't agree the first time. And when you have a work like *A Theory of Justice*, it is really silly to put the whole book to the side; it has shaped an entire field, for better and worse.

I don't reject everything in Rawls because there is a sincerity and elegance in the work that results in ideas that are worth thinking about: what is it about a scheme of ongoing cooperation that makes attending to moral equality distinctly important? Why should we allow undeserved attributes and resources shape the potential for a person to achieve a good life of her own choosing?

These and many others are really important questions that enliven our conceptual apparatus to features of normative political inquiry that should always remain front and center. My issue isn't that Rawls doesn't ask and skillfully attempt to answer worthwhile questions, it is that there are many other questions to be asked and also that our answers need to really embody imaginative reach when put to the test of our experiences, and here I sometimes find the work wanting.

3:AM: Why are you doubtful that the term "white power" can grip the complexity of racial subordination?

CL: When we think of the term "white power" we often conjure up something like the specter of angry white men in hoods taking the liberty to publicly terrorize blacks in the name of racial supremacy, shouting "White power! White power!" The possibility of that image depends on many features of American society that do not hold today. Before I move on, I do not want to be mistaken as saying there are no white racists today; some of them even subscribe to the doctrine of white power. But we need to be clear-eyed about our contemporary condition and realize that the real issue is the relationship between consistency and dissonance and not only consistency. What do I mean by this?

Nothing could be more obvious, I hope, than that in many ways, the facts and features of black inequality have remained startlingly steady for over a century since the Emancipation Proclamation. This is consistency. However, it is also clear that the nature of the expression of racial ire has modulated on account of the prominence of implicit bias as contrasted with explicit racism. It is also a fact that we have a black president, something beyond the realm of possibility even twenty years ago, I think. But this is the thing—we have these very significant shifts which ostensibly indicate progress overlaid on the persistence of the many forms of racial inequality already listed earlier. That is dissonance. If we were talking only consistency we would also be talking about the presence of similar mechanisms and conduits of oppression and terror. But we are talking about dissonance here—the confusing co-habitation of formal equality and wide-spread marginalization and often terror by different means, such as when a white cop abuses or takes the life of a black man often with impunity. When we are trying to make sense of that kind of a thing, it seems to me that the notion of white power is going to limit rather than expand our analytic capacities to get a grip on the nature of racial inequality today. Insisting on deploying the term white power is certainly provocative, and sometimes helpfully so, but I also think that mostly it commits the same offense I above charged Rawls/Rawlsians with—it leads not only to confusion about how to answer certain important questions, but also is not interested in or does not permit asking those questions.

3:AM: A key idea you argue for is that we need to engage with the characters of the people inside institutions rather than ignoring this element. Your approach is subtle. You say character is influenced by an interplay of the environments and structures we find ourselves in. Can you unpack what you mean when you say the best way to understand this interplay is "to understand whites as under the influence of moral disadvantage and blacks as under the influence of ethical disadvantage"?

CL: Analysis of racial inequality at the level of persons is burdened by important issues. On the one hand, the fact of the matter is, the number of explicit/ intentional racists among the white population in America is comparatively small, certainly smaller than it was in the middle of the 20th century, for example. On the other, implicating blacks in their own inequality is not only often wrong (which is not to say it is never justified or necessary or right) but fraught with the baggage left behind by commentary, such as that found in the Moynihan Report, in the late 1960's and 1970's that sought, in the wake of the passage of the Civil Rights Act, to quickly offload responsibility for blacks' woes onto blacks themselves. Here, two things come into view. The error of (entirely) blaming blacks for blight, as an empirical matter. But, also, substantively, there is the basic issue of blaming the victim which is understandably deeply taboo for blacks—consider the kinds of reactions Bill Cosby generates, for example, when he says not entirely unreasonable things like that young black men should not be eager to dress in stereotypically provocative ways (e.g. sagging jeans). This is seen as a kind of treason by many, and the reaction is understandable if sometimes unfortunate.

Thus, we are left with a really important issue. We need a way to bring into view the persons who populate institutions and we need to hold them to some account for not only past actions but also for prospective ones in helping to realize justice and we need to not act as if all whites are racists and as if blacks have merely been the force of their own undoing. This is how I conceive the relevance of moral and ethical disadvantage. As we've already reviewed, my theory is one that takes as central questions of character, and one idea that is important in speaking about character is habits or moral learning. We can learn our moral and ethical lessons in better or worse ways and when we think about the socializing effects of fields of power, in this case racial, we are all bound to learn some lessons badly and develop unfortunate, even offensive and harmful habits.

The divide I wanted to draw had to do with how one group treats another, and how the other group treats itself. But I wanted to ask this question from the perspective of gauging readiness to participate in realizing social justice. Taking the idea of implicit bias both seriously and as more widely representing the essential failing in white Americans, I wanted to argue that these are people with (generally) the right basic conceptions of democratic morality but whose grasp or understanding of these conceptions warp once blacks come into view. Here, we want to think about folks who, for example, are forgiving of whites on welfare, but then when blacks are on welfare denigrate blacks as free-riders and the welfare system as enabling deviant behavior. In this kind of instance, the basic virtue of generosity comes undone for little reason other than those receiving the benefit are the wrong color. We want to try and establish consistency in the relationship of generosity and compassion to public policy across all cases. The inability to do so (and to fail in similar kinds of instances of reasoning) is a moral disadvantage—a habit of moral reasoning that is the result of badly learned lessons or improper lessons altogether. What is important here is that the agent is not himself the source of a kind of explicit evil but is definitely a vehicle for an instance of it that is in conversation with history and we should be concerned to sever that relationship.

On the other hand, precisely because of fairly severe systems of exclusion, deprivation, and disrespect, it is the case that some in the black community have less than desirable conceptions of some normative ideas. Let's take honor, for instance. I find it personally despairing to recall the way friends (and sometimes, I) back in my early years would gladly and confidently look down on other kids who took book learning very seriously. To do so was to "sell out"—to lack integrity thus not act honorably. But surely that can't be right. That claim supposes that there is something intrinsically valuable, intrinsically black about ignorance—I can't imagine that any culture could seriously affirm that position, Western or otherwise, yet, it is not an uncommon one in the black community. There are of course clear and understandable reasons why these kinds of attitudes take hold. When your life and circumstances are deprived of power and authority, you naturally seek to assert it organically in ways that are available to you, so when you tell a young man, from the position of institutional authority he perceives as complicit in his deprivation, that he needs to see things like you do and go to class, how can we not expect him to snub his nose at us? But this is absolutely not a pathology as has been asserted by conservatives—this is a bad ethical lesson, it is a disadvantage, and just as with whites, we should hope to correct it.

3:AM: If schemes of power cripple white's attempts to avow anti-racism, and the power structures sustain these schemes, isn't this a recipe for despair rather than shame? And what role has blame got in this analysis? And is this where your idea of the contrast between "the disadvantaged agent" and the "determined agent" finds its force?

CL: I need to begin answering this question by disclosing that exactly something like a sense of despair often took hold of me in working out my theory. Some days it still does. But no matter how cynical one is, normative theory is necessarily optimistic (since it is trying to figure out how to develop a world better than the one we have got) and the source of my optimism resides in a distinction I must draw given the way the question has been put. I'm not convinced whites' capacity for appropriate care and concern are "crippled"—that word usually indicates a permanent/irreparable injury to a particular capacity. There is a position one can trace in the tradition of black thought, especially (for me) in James Baldwin—but maybe it really is just a hope—that whites are not beyond redemption, that there is no way for them to come into right relationship with their democratic commitments on the one hand (even the minimal ones) and racial equality on the other (even when thinly conceived). We do have some reason for despair—I have been pressing the case that the kinds of inequality we see reproduced fifty years after the Civil Rights Act is deeply alarming.

On the other hand, no one can deny that there has been some progress. To take something very basic, 3am wouldn't have interviewed me fifty years ago, first because I most likely would not have had a position at an institution (thus acquiring the attendant goods, such as a university press book), and second, even if I did, I would likely have been discriminated against by its editors—that's just the way it was. But here I am today and that is something. I want to say, then, that we should take the changes we can't deny as providing evidence of the existence of resources for further changes we often seem to resist. So, yes, this is where the contrast between disadvantaged and determined agents matters in my work, for if whites and blacks are both determined in their shortcomings, then not only are Rawls and (some) critical race theorists asking the wrong questions, so am I.

I think here is where blame has some role but we have to be careful with how loose we are with that word. Blame is easy, and resentment of it is even easier. What I mean by blame, in at least one sense, amounts to something like moral notification—you have done or are doing something that requires your ethical attention for us to be able to move forward together. Maybe somebody will remark that I am not really talking about blame precisely, but I see little harm in speaking of it in this way for our purposes. The point is, it is almost always useful to make that kind of claim; what is less useful is when its only expression comes in the form that indicates there is a score to be settled. But here I want to be careful because I don't want to foreclose radical politics—it just is the case sometimes that a score does need to be settled. But the point at which that stance is taken, we're not talking blame anymore but the synthesis of accusation and judgment, and then, we are often past the point of dialogue. If anything causes me despair it is that I sense, I feel that if racial inequality is not resolved sooner than later, (more) blacks will decisively move past being interested in blaming toward accusation/judgment.

3:AM: You advocate a type of perfectionism don't you? Can you unpack it and say what it is and what it isn't?

CL: I consider myself an egalitarian. Briefly, by this I mean someone who believes that all people are equal in a deeply moral sense of that word and should be treated as such; that thick moral duties can be derived from the fact of shared humanity. But what few people know about me is that one of the biggest influences on my thought is the strand of perfectionism that runs through John Stuart Mills's *On Liberty* as well as Friedrich Nietzsche's *The Geneaology of Morals* (though not only there in his work). This strand of perfectionism, as I interpret it goes something like this: there is no offense in saying that there are people who not only do some things better than others but that some people are better than others more generally; the real offense to my mind is when we are complacent about that fact or possibility, thus the person who can be better qua human potential, refuses to tax his or her own capacities, or—and this is actually important for my own brand of egalitarianism—those who are more advantageously positioned in this way withhold the resources (capaciously conceived) for others to more fully develop their skills. (I admit, little support for this last condition can be found in Nietzsche, but can be found in Mill.) I think some will find my position odd because on the one hand it affirms a position that most find inherently aristocratic but then tries to retrofit an egalitarian ideal over it. How does that work? I suppose it depends on an empirical hypothesis that could prove to be confused but in the absence of such proof I am supposing that each of us possesses a certain kind of genius to be better than merely competent moral agents.

Here I tend to think of the idea of moral literacy as put forward by Barbara Herman. Her analogy is that our capacity for reading is merely latent when we begin to learn to read, but through practice and instruction we get better and better at it to a point that not only do others not need to read to us, but we become more and more responsible for increasingly sophisticated interpretations of what we read. Her view is that our moral capacities work something like this and this is how we become more moral and are also susceptible to being held responsible for what we do, for lapses in judgment. Thus, the kind of perfectionism I advocate is, analogously, a very rigorous literacy program—one wherein Americans better learn to not only rationally understand but affectively sympathize with the racial harms they are complicit in bringing to bear. This does require a more sophisticated moral apparatus; I will reserve my despair if ever I become convinced that we are not all equally possessed of the requisite apparatus.

3:AM: Why can this be the central normative ideal?

CL: I'm not sure I can answer why it can be the central normative ideal. I can say, though, why I think it must be—the preponderance of evidence that our moral habits are lax and dislocated is too great to ask those responsible for injustice to try and address it from within their extant capacities and dispositions. To my mind it is simple: we must be better to do better; otherwise, in thirty years you and I will be having this conversation again and I will be asked, "What do you think has prevented us from achieving racial justice over the three decades since we last spoke? . . ."

3:AM: And what political vehicle do you suggest is needed to drive this ideal forward?

CL: Half of the answer to this question was given in *The Color of Our Shame* in the form of three principles of justice meant to assist in the project of soul-craft politics—policies to get the previously discussed brand of perfectionism off the ground. Political philosophers tend to be quite bad at thinking in terms of concrete policies, even non-ideal theorists and I'm no better in this regard. That said, my aim was to suggest guidelines for conceiving of policies that accorded appropriately with both widely held liberal norms and more rigorously argued perfectionist standards.

The real difficulty for me in answering this question, however, has to do with the fact that *The Color of Our Shame* forms only half of my philosophical/theoretical program. I am currently at work on my new book, *From A Human Point of View: (Re)Imagining Racial Egalitarianism* and this book is being conceived as part of a system, if I can put it that way, that once in place offers a more full approach or response to racial injustice. The new book is something of a significant departure not in terms of conceptual groundings since I am still very much concerned with matters of character and the like. Rather, the book is being written as a work having to do with personal ethics. The central claim of the book builds on a pairing between Baldwin and Bernard Williams to argue for a human point of view of equality—a perspective on equality wherein the salient aspects of our humanity count for a great deal in ordering our political affairs. The attendant claim is that an act of imagination that prompts us to explore what it is like to be the person making a claim of equality is needed or at least helpful. In the course of the project I enlist a selection of black novels to serve as a form of testimony on the experience of racial inequality and all of this leads to be me revisiting some central ideas in moral and liberal theory—the reactive attitudes, consensus, and blame—under the light of this approach to equality. I say all of this because I'm not sure I have in view a political vehicle to convey, as it were, my preferred brand of perfectionism. Rather, I have an intellectual agenda the next step of which is to try and write this book as the kind of book I would want all citizens to read and react to.

3:AM: Can you say something about the three principles of racial justice you discuss and perhaps indicate how had these been in play we'd have handled recent notorious cases of racial injustice such as the Trayvon Martin case and the Ferguson murder?

CL: Of the three principles I articulate in *The Color of Our Shame*, one is epistemic, another is propagandistic, and the final is participatory. The American Re-Education Act principle calls for wide spread programs of full and honest disclosure of America's racist past and racially fraught present. The example I use in the book is how the Civil Rights Act is typically taught—Martin Luther King, Jr. is often presented as the guiding light and representative of the struggle. There is no offense there, save that more difficult questions of Malcolm X's or the Black Panther's roles much less the conditions that gave rise to each are put to the side. When this happens, schools do not prepare students for effective citizenship that is sensitive to marginality and the effect of oppression. Rather, a package of neatly ordered ideas and facts is handed over conveying the senses that America has been more fair than it in fact has and black people never have had nor do not now have cause for rage. The Just Trojan Horse principle endorses the use of state power to present messages meant to condition our attitudes towards blacks and about ourselves. As I am now sitting here and writing my responses I've just watched a news report containing police car footage of a white office in South Carolina who stopped a black man supposedly for a seat belt violation as he was pulling into a gas station—he exits his car, gun drawn and asks the man for his license and registration; the black man makes a move towards his car to retrieve what the officer has asked him to produce and the officer, instead of advising the man to move slowly fires three rounds.

My principle would allow the following: a state sponsored Public Service Announcement during prime television that shows this video (or the increasingly countless number of others depicting this kind of abuse) and says the following at the end: "If you are white, and middle class and live in the suburbs, this would probably never happen to you or your child." Because it's true—it most probably wouldn't. The final principle is the Boondocks principle. I'll defer on explaining the reason for the name. The substance of the principle calls for extensive institutional reform that allows for widespread establishment of citizen councils to provide local oversight over various administrative procedures—law enforcement, economic development, districting, etc.—and further, to subsidize participation of those not sufficiently wealthy to participate in the event of lost income from participating rather than working, and finally, to implement stringent labor laws to prevent workers from being fired from their jobs for being civically engaged rather than economically productive. Together, the principles are really meant to indicate a muscular strategy for soulcraft politics, for the moral improvement of the polity on matters of race and racial sympathy.

Now, you ask what difference my proposals might have made in cases like the shooting of Trayvon Martin or Michael Brown (or Oscar Grant, or the choking of Eric Garner or....and on) and I have to say that it depends on when we are imagining these changes would have been implemented. If we are imagining just a few years ago, probably little difference. Habits and norms are slow to change, which I can accept as a fact of social psychology. If the Civil Rights Act had eventuated in something like this and we imagine it is done successfully these men might still be alive today. There are two phenomena that are the cause of black ire today, and we are seeing this in the Michael Brown/Ferguson case. On the one hand blacks perceive a degree of hypocrisy in the enforcement of the law because no black can imagine a black officer shooting and killing a white youth in the way Michael Brown was shot and killed and not being immediately vilified widely in the American public and arrested immediately. On the other, there is something more sinister that black folks sense and that is quite distinct from vagaries in public sentiment and institutional procedure after the fact; there is something preceding these tragedies—these men were all seen as legitimate objects of violence in the first place, as persons who by virtue of their skin color were deemed dangerous thus as warranting a shoot first ask later attitude. But how awful is that? The principles I offer are meant to deeply reshape how we value black humanity and to trigger shame when we realize we prize it far less than we do whites' for no other reason than that whites are white and that blacks are black.

3:AM: Congratulations for being awarded the American Political Science Foundations of Political Theory Best First Book prize for *The Color of Our Shame*. But there are hardly any black philosophers; it's a situation even worse than the lamentable number of women. Why do you think philosophy is worse than other departments in this respect and what can be done?

CL: Thank you for your congratulations. The prize was a great honor to me personally, but it was also a significant gesture of respect towards the field of race and philosophy/theory as one attending to a real and urgent moral problem. The fact that philosophers of race are generally attending to an urgent moral problem helps highlight the unfortunate if not perverse observation that we are not better represented in a field where normative inquiry is central.

According to a research note recently published in Critical Philosophy of Race by Tina Fernandes Botts, Liam Kofi Bright, Myisha Cherry, Guntur Mallarangeng, and Quayshawn Spencer, there are currently 156 black philosophers across the career spectrum—doctoral students, non-tenure track, tenure track, tenured; fifty percent are tenured faculty—seventy-three tenured black philosophers. To put that number in perspective consider that the membership of the American Philosophical Association is estimated at about 11,000 members. That means black philosophers (and let's just assume that all 156 are dues paying members) represent just 1.4 percent of the field. Surely some of the 11,000 dues paying members are not American academics, but that wouldn't change just how unsettling the percentage is.

So the question naturally arises: why does the field have this problem? I can't pretend to know the answer. I doubt the question has one answer. To my mind, there are two kinds of sociological problems—one that has not that much to do with the discipline per se and one that does. Philosophy by its nature benefits from a certain amount of leisure—a hefty library of books and lots of time to reflect. But in America time is money and money is not something that a significant proportion of blacks have had much to dispose of. Additionally, my own experience of the discipline and observations of its practitioners is that having access to it at a sufficiently high level prior to grad school or even prior to undergraduate studies is a privilege. American education has increasingly prized math and science preparedness, and even when the humanities are favored, literature and history tend to be the winners in public schools. That means that by the time that students make it to college, they have already begun to learn the tools of math and science and a select group of the humanities—a kind of preparation that helps even if bypassing technical fields and pursuing more "practical" fields of interest like public relations, accounting, etc. By contrast, the barrier to entry in philosophy is pretty high. Generally one greatly benefits from having (one might be tempted to say, is required to have) read or being familiar with (at least) some of the ancients as well as a significant number of the modern German thinkers. The point being, these are texts that are not commonly taught and do not present themselves as accessible—one can only imagine the difficult experience of making sense of The Critique of Pure Reason or The *Phenomenology of Spirit* on one's own with neither guidance nor prior preparation. Here, we see a pipeline problem in a very deep sense that extends beyond grad school admissions to the very nature of what it means to be prepared for study in the field.

The other sociology problem concerns the sociology of knowledge. In *We Who Are Dark*, Tommie Shelby rightly notes that philosophy of race is often grouped with applied philosophy and is thus seen as less worthy and rigorous than "pure" philosophy. I need to be fair in noting that many fields are home to methodology fights—right now, for example, political science seems to be at a crossroads where it seems those smitten with econometrics are increasingly trying to edge out scholars who think the study of politics is comprised of more than running elaborate models with large-N data sets. But what is ironic here is that while that approach is not especially friendly to scholars who study race, there are many who have been able to find a place at the table in journal publications, high profile faculty appointments, landed books with the preferred academic presses, and so on. Not even this, though, can be said for philosophy. Part of the issue is methodological—ideal theory makes it very difficult to reflect on race in its particulars. Once one sufficiently abstracts from facts of the case, the distinctive moral gravity of the problem begins to slip away. Then when one realizes that the most prized journals remain under the influence of the tradition of analytic liberal theory, then one also begins to understand why so little work on race makes it into these journals. The effect snowballs and becomes self-reinforcing. If you are a working normative theorists who cannot place in Ethics, or Philosophy & Public Affairs and similar journals then it is presumed that the work just really isn't that good, and if that is the case, then you may not be good enough to be at X top ranked department, and if you're not at X top ranked department then you must not be good enough to be brought out for talks at Y top-ranked department … One can easily see just how black philosophers quickly become invisible and by way of that invisibility presumed less skilled.

Apart from the methodological aspect of the problem there are also worries about how the substance is perceived and how we are treated on account of that perception. I once sat down with a senior colleague as I prepared a response for an R&R. The paper began with a strong claim about the absence of race in our most prized theories of justice. Two things happened at this meeting. First, I was told "I don't see what's especially interesting about racial inequality.' Second, I was presented a rather long lesson on the importance of humility—apparently, I appear and act too self-possessed—it was hard to not hear the word "uppity" in the speech I was given by this "liberal." And I know I am not alone in this kind of experience where the very basic issue of whether the questions black philosophers often want to ask are sufficiently "interesting." When a field faces these two rather broad problems concerning social practices, habits, and norms, the almost complete statistical absence of blacks from philosophy becomes much less mysterious.

As to what can be done to rectify the situation, the discipline has more direct control over the second sociological problem—that of knowledge—and here it is a difficult thing because we're talking about people being made to undo various causes of behavior: in some cases it is merely habit, in other cases it is stubbornness and ignorance, and in other cases, it is straightaway bias. My observation is that a significant contingent of younger white philosophers are actually on the right side of this, and they are often getting jobs in "influential" departments, the departments many blacks are not. My position is that they have a duty to act from their convictions and help police behavior: a colloquium invite list is comprised of one hundred percent white speakers, somebody needs to say something; a specialized conference on normative political theory is organized and race is not part of the conversation, somebody needs to say something; a high profile journal has not accepted a piece on race in the course of a year or two, somebody needs to ask why—is this really a matter that no submission passed muster? Maybe that is the case as I'm sure it sometimes is, but as of now there is not enough serious inquiry as to why certain journals' issues look the way they do sociologically; it is simply presumed that the peer review process more or less works and that's just how it goes. There's been a good deal of turmoil lately in the field where men accused of behaving badly in a number of shameful ways have been called out publicly and brought to account—these are the kinds of incidents that used to be somewhat beyond the reach of reproach and action. Those days are over, or, if they are not fully over, we need to keep doing what we can to make sure the field is brought into accordance with fully reasonable norms of acceptance and inclusion.

3:AM: And what five books can you recommend for us here at 3:AM to go further into this philosophical world of yours?

CL: *The Street* by Ann Petry; *The Genealogy of Morals* by Friedrich Nietzsch; Anything and everything by James Baldwin (sorry—I had to cheat here); *The White Boy Shuffle* by Paul Beatty and *Medicine for Melancholy* (a film by Barry Jenkins)

Chris Lebron is the author of:

The Color of Our Shame: Race and Justice in Our Time (Oxford University Press, 2013)

23 | Virginia Held: "The Ethics of Care"

Virginia Held is a philosopher at the Graduate Center of the City University of New York. She discusses the philosophy of care ethics, which she thinks is a feminist ethics that preserves the persuasive aspects of Kantian, utilitarian, and virtue ethics, but is better. She thinks the strength of her ethical position is that it is based on experience, that it should be equally considered from the point of view of the recipient as well as the provider, and that it implies a lot of liberal values. She thinks all the time about the nature of care relations, meeting the needs of others, and how paying attention to these things has radical transformational implications. She thinks it is hard to know which are the right questions to be asking, but easy to see that neoconservatives have been wrong on all foreign policy since Vietnam and that the United States is more deluded than bewildered these days.

3:AM: What made you become a philosopher? Has it lived up to expectations so far?

VIRGINIA HELD: I had intended to be an architect, but in my first course in philosophy in college, I fell in love with philosophy. By the time I graduated, however, I had travelled in Europe and become directly aware of the horrors of war, and I became disillusioned with philosophy. It was not addressing the problems that really mattered, and it seemed to me to be an intellectual luxury. After a year of graduate work in Europe, I left philosophy for a decade and worked for a political magazine in NYC. Another reason was that my husband was a graduate student and one of us needed to earn some money. But then I had a serious falling out with the editor of the magazine over US foreign policy, and the intellectual independence of academic life looked extremely attractive, so I went back to philosophy. At that time, jobs for women were very rare, but I was lucky. And yes, it has lived up to expectations in the sense that the field has changed and it is now possible to deal with what seem to me the most important questions, and I consider myself extremely fortunate to have been able to earn an adequate income doing something I am really interested in doing.

3:AM: You've developed an ethical theory around "care." You see this as an alternative to the dominant ethical theories of the last couple of centuries. It's important to you that it isn't an ethics to be added on to Kantianism or utilitarianism or virtue ethics. Can you say something about why it is so important that a care ethics is not an adjunct but is a fresh start? The Kantian Christine Korsgaard has placed reciprocity and human relations at the heart of Kantianism. Onora O'Neill has argued that justice and care are not opposed. In the light of these views, would you still defend the break, or would you be happier to see it as a continuation?

VH: I don't find it satisfactory merely to add some considerations of care to the traditional moral theories for reasons similar to why it is not enough to simply insert women into the traditional structures of society and politics built on gender domination. Feminists should understand that the structures themselves have to change. The history of ethics shows it to be a very biased enterprise. Very roughly, what men have done in public life has been deemed important and relevant to moral theory, and what women have done in the household has been considered irrelevant. I think it plausible to see Kantian ethics and utilitarianism as expansions to the whole of morality of what can be thought appropriate for law and for public policy.

I have come to see, in contrast, caring relations as the wider network, and the ethics of care as the comprehensive morality, within which we should develop legal and political institutions. Caring relations should be guided by the ethics of care, which we can best understand and which is most applicable in contexts of families and friendship. But we can and should also have weaker forms of caring relations with all persons, and within these, the more limited institutions of law should be guided, roughly, by Kantian norms, and the more limited political institutions by utilitarian ones. Yes I see the legal and political as importantly different, and both as significantly different from the contexts of family and friendship. This is a very oversimplified statement of a complex position but I try to clarify and delineate these matters in my written work.

3:AM: So "care" is at the heart of this new ethic but it isn't to replace justice. So how do you get from care to justice in your system? Do we end up losing the common use of "care" for a more term of art, technical use, as is the wont with philosophers? And isn't that a cheat?

VH: Yes, various Kantians are trying to acknowledge the concerns of care, and various philosophers interested in the ethics of care are trying to combine it with Kantian ethics. I think the ethics of care has the resources to be an alternative moral theory that can include persuasive aspects of Kantian ethics and also of utilitarianism and virtue theory. It's nevertheless a feminist ethics that includes the goal of overcoming gender domination, in our thinking as well as our institutions. And I see it as the more comprehensive view. Korsgaard and O'Neill are still Kantians, though more persuasive ones than some traditional Kantians. I think ethics should start with a vast amount of experience (the experience of caring and being cared for) overlooked by traditional moral theories, and see how the many important and valid concerns of other moral theories can be brought into care ethics. I think it is a strength of care ethics that it is based on experience. It is experience which everyone has had: no one would have survived without enormous amounts of care, in childhood at least. Most women, and increasingly men, have also had a great deal of experience providing care, especially for children.

3:AM: So "care" is at the heart of this new ethic but it isn't to replace justice. So how do you get from care to justice in your system? Do we end up losing the common use of "care" for a more term of art, technical use, as is the wont with philosophers? And isn't that a cheat?

VH: The values incorporated into this care can be reflected on. Existing practices of care can be evaluated, and reformed as appropriate, for instance so that parenting is shared and not primarily the responsibility of women. Care should always be considered as much from the point of view of the recipient as of the provider, and care that is domineering or demeaning should be reformed. Rationalistic moral theory purports to be universal but is less so than it imagines. Another advantage of the ethics of care is that it has no need to appeal to religion, which can be divisive, whereas the experience of care really is universal. Of course care ethics builds on previous moral theory. The sentimentalist tradition and Hume are important for the ethics of care. I'm very sympathetic to aspects of Kantian ethics, for instance that actions should be judged by the intentions with which we act. But the ethics of care can include this, as it evaluates what our actions express as well as being concerned with the effectiveness and results of our caring labours. The centrality of respect for persons in Kantian ethics is appealing, but can too easily be combined with notions of negative freedom such that we respect people by just leaving them alone. Kant's imperfect duties seem to me weak motivation for actually meeting people's needs. The concerns of care are much more compelling.

I think caring relations should form the wider network within which we should develop various more limited ties that give priority to justice. But care is more fundamental. We need to care enough about distant others to care that their rights are respected. Justice should be the primary value for interactions that are primarily legal ones, but many relations should not be interpreted as primarily legal. Our relations with our children, for instance, are primarily caring ones and only legal in a minimal sense. Justice, or fairness, should not be absent in these relations, but it doesn't have priority here.

3:AM: You place your ethics in a traditional liberal setting. Why do you argue that it is a better approach than its rivals, not just in personal morality but also on wider political and cultural issues? You even see it as playing a decisive role in global politics, so that for example the current crisis in the Eurozone would benefit from a dose of care. Is that right?

VH: Rather than saying that care should be developed in a liberal setting, I think I would say that care implies a lot of liberal values. Good care requires respect for others, including for their individuality and often developing freedom. Yes, the ethics of care is better than other moral theories at handling many global problems, such as the vast migrations of care workers that are occurring. And as I have recently argued in an article in "Ethics and Global Politics," I think it is a better foundation for international law than are the traditional moral and political theories with their Hobbesian assumptions about states. The ethics of care has fundamental implications for economic activity—that it ought to be structured and engaged in to promote the well-being of all, not primarily the economic interests of those with economic power. And it implies that markets and market values should be appropriately limited, and that market values should not be increasingly the dominant values, as in the U.S., in areas where other values should have priority, such as in childcare, healthcare, education, and the production of culture.

3:AM: You note that virtue ethics seems at times to have some things in common with care but nevertheless think care is a superior approach? Can you say something about this and how that particular contrast works?

VH: Virtue ethics seems to me focused on individuals and their dispositions, their virtuous characters etc. Care ethics focuses instead on caring relations, and evaluates relations, such as whether they are trusting, characterised by mutuality, etc. The activity of care involves meeting the needs of another, with sensitivity and responsiveness. This is not altruism because the situation is not a zero-sum contest between individuals but the building of a relation good for both or all persons involved. When parents care for children, they benefit together. When members of a community care for one another, all can gain.

3:AM: Now this ethics of care could well be seen as a "feminist ethic" and you're well known for writing about that. But I started asking questions like

I did just to see if gender doesn't actually need to be a starting point for understanding the theory. So I guess I'm wondering whether we need feminism to get the theory, or is the point that in enacting the theory of care we're implicitly engaged in feminism? How important is it that this is positioned as an explicitly feminism position?

VH: Historically, it was through paying attention, often for the first time, to caring activities, especially mothering, that the ethics of care was developed. This was experience of which women had a great deal and most men rather little. As men assume more responsibility for caring for children and engage more equally in other caring activities, I think they are quite capable of appreciating the values of care. But I think it would be a mistake to forget the feminist origins of these ways of thinking, or to overlook the feminist goals embedded in them. The implications of the ethics of care for transformations of society are very dramatic. Imagine, as a thought experiment, a society that really did make childcare of central importance, and economic or military power of more marginal interest, or that paid kindergarten teachers more than bank executives.

3:AM: You approach feminism to remind us about the pernicious omissions and commissions that make traditional liberal theories of ethics fatally flawed. You want to get us to see how a sexist gaze holds our institutions in their thrall. You wrote Feminist Morality: Transforming Culture, Society, and Politics back in 1993. Have things changed in the intervening time to an extent that you'd reject some of the things you set out there, or add stuff?

VH: In Feminist Morality I was just beginning to work out what I thought about the ethics of care. In *The Ethics of Care*, and in quite a few subsequent papers, I've come to have what I think is a much better picture of it as an alternative moral approach.

3:AM: I guess what might seem strange to some is that you continue to work in the liberal tradition even though liberal individialism seems anathema to you. Why not go Marxist or anarchist?

VH: I've been very influenced by Marxism in the past. I've always found anarchism too unrealistic about human beings. I don't think I see liberal individualism as anathema. I think it's often appropriate for limited domains of human activity and interactions, like legal ones. What I object to is the prevalent way it is seen as applicable everywhere and to everything, or as the way to think about all sorts of domains where it doesn't belong, or only belongs in very limited ways.

3:AM: We're in a continuous state of war and terrorism is the justification for lots of it. You've written extensively on political violence and I'm struck that you say it's not just the answers that are hard but knowing which are the right questions to ask about this subject. Why do you think it is so hard, and what questions are beginning to feel like the ones we should be asking? I'm interested in your idea of wide and narrow definitions of "terrorism" guiding our thinking. You prefer a wide definition don't you? Why is this a superior approach?

VH: It's often hard to know if we are asking the right questions in a lot of domains, but perhaps especially so with violence and terrorism because so much of the discussion has been distorted by strongly identifying with those on "our side." Frequently, in violent conflicts, both sides think that violence is being used against them and that they themselves are using violence to defend themselves. They use the weapons available. The definitions are often chosen so that the conclusion can be reached that what "we" do is to justifiably defend ourselves, and what "they" do is engage in terrorism.

3:AM: I guess the ethics of care guides much of your thinking here: what kinds of answers have you to these questions? How different would the political landscape of terrorism look if your ideas were taken into the policy arena do you think?

VH: Care encourages us to try to understand the feelings and thinking of our opponents as well as of our friends, of those our actions harm as well as those they protect. Violence is most obviously antithetical to care. As I have put it: violence destroys what care takes pains to create. With an outlook guided by care we will be steadily reminded that our goal must be to reduce the use of violence. Care does not, in my view, imply pacifism. It can recognise that some violence will be with us for the foreseeable future, and it can see some genuinely defensive uses of violence as justified, but it will work tirelessly and effectively to greatly reduce the uses of violence in multiple areas of life. It will point out that using violence to maintain a status quo needs moral justification as much as does using violence to change it.

3:AM: You worried in your early book *Rights and Goods: Justifying Social Action* about clever casuists constructing ethical arguments to defend whatever they liked. But you defended the idea of an applied ethics. I'd have thought these days it's been difficult to get ethics into any policy discourse. Economics since the Reaganite/Thatcherite eighties has been part of a neo-liberalism of performativity and managerialism marketisation that has successfully ousted moral talk about fairness and justice, hasn't it? So how do you see the place of ethics in policy discourses at the moment?

VH: I think it is actually easier now than it used to be to raise moral questions, to frame an issue as a moral one: what ought we to do about climate change, health care, education, and so on. Moral positions are not so often thought to be nothing but mere personal preferences. I agree that in the wider culture, "the market" has taken on mythical proportions as it is imagined to be capable of achieving best outcomes without requiring that we bring in moral considerations. But I think, or at least hope, that this very ideological and distorted way of thinking has about reached its limits and more plausible ways of understanding the issues will prevail. Certainly among thinking persons there is a willingness to ask about the morality of for-profit schools and hospitals and the buying and selling of human organs. And, for good reason, the satisfactoriness of a moral theory has seldom been judged by its immediate influence on policy.

3:AM: In her recent "Tanner Lectures" the economist Diane Coyle argued that we need to bring back ethical discourse into economic theory and that economists were at fault for mistaking market mechanisms for distributing ideas and materials and describing the processes of making stuff with markets as arbiters of value. And also of associating markets with a business lobby. This seems to be close to what you are arguing for. What sort of approach does your care ethics take in economics?

VH: I agree that we need to bring ethical discourse into economic theory, in the sense that economic processes ought to be evaluated morally. Many questions in economics are straightforwardly empirical rather than normative or moral, but we ought to ask routinely about the moral justifiability of economic arrangements and activities. I have argued in *The Ethics of Care* that education, healthcare, childcare, and the production of culture, ought not to be in the market, where economic gain has the highest priority. Yes they should value efficiency, and competition can often be helpful, but other values than profit should be given priority.

3:AM: An alternative to your care ethics position is the "civic friendship" ethic proposed by Sibyl Schwarzenbach. Why is your approach preferable?

VH: I think care is a more fundamental and a wider concept than friendship. No one can exist without having been cared for. So I would see civic friendship as a more limited kind of caring relation, relevant especially to political life. It's closer to the social contract model of agreements between equals voluntarily entered into, a model that plays such a central and often misleading role in political theory and then is expanded, often wrongly in my view, to the whole of moral theory. Care is more of a contrast and I think there are good reasons to make this contrast for understanding human relations and the moral questions involved. Caring relations are often unchosen and between those of very unequal power, and lots of other human relations than family ones are more like this than like voluntary contracts between equals, so it's illuminating to explore this contrast even if we want to conclude by supporting social contract models for legal matters.

3:AM: Although a top philosopher yourself, the position of women in academic philosophy is pretty bad, although improving by all accounts. So what's your thinking about this? Why is philosophy so much worse than other humanities subjects which you'd think shared a profile? What can be done?

VH: As you say, the position of women in academic philosophy is improving. Some parts of philosophy are more like mathematics and science than like other humanities, so perhaps these are relevant comparisons. Progress has been slow, but to someone my age it has been significant.

3:AM: In 1962 you wrote a report on the ethical attitudes in the USA. 40 years on, is the US still bewildered? And are you optimistic or pessimistic about the way things are going?

VH: More deluded than bewildered, perhaps. People are less hesitant to take moral positions or positions that might be considered based on ideology, but I think the positions taken are often wrong. I have been appalled by the success of the imperialism of the market, with market takeovers of all sorts of activities where market values are not the right ones to be dominant. And I find the corporate control of culture very depressing. And the neoconservative influence on foreign policy has been almost entirely a bad influence.

The neoconservatives have been wrong about just about every foreign policy issue from Vietnam to Iraq, and yet they continue to have a thoroughly outsize influence. So my optimism and pessimism vary. When I read that as many people in the U.S. believe in creationism as in evolution, and that the figures are the same for college students, or when I hear about how many people in this country have been misled into doubting that climate change is a problem, it's very depressing. But then I watch Stephen Colbert puncturing such delusions, and that he can appear on television night after night, with his extraordinary cleverness and effective wit, and actually be a commercial success doing so, restores my sense that there's hope. And if I reflect on the progress that women, and gays, have made in my lifetime, I am sometimes cautiously optimistic as the diplomats may say.

3:AM: And finally, for all us feminists here at 3:AM Magazine, which five books (other than your own which we'll all be dashing away to read straight after this) would you recommend to give us deeper insights?

VH: I spend more time reading the New York Times than I wish I did, but I find it so hard not to! All my life I have been especially attracted to art museums, so I like going to exhibitions at the Met and elsewhere. I'd like to read more novels but I rarely do. If I'm not working on care I'm apt to be trying to read up on international law or global theories of justice or some other topic I plan to write some essays on.

Five books I'd recommend to understand how the ethics of care developed and where it may be going are:

Sara Ruddick, *Maternal Thinking: Toward a Politics of Peace*
Joan C. Tronto, *Moral Boundaries: A Political Argument for an Ethic of Care*
Nel Noddings, *Caring: A Feminine Approach to Ethics and Moral Education*
Engster, *The Heart of Justice: A Political Theory of Caring*
Fiona Robinson, *The Ethics of Care: A Feminist Approach to Human Security.*

Virginia Held is the author of:

The Public Interest and Individual Interests (Basic Books, 1972)
Philosophy, Morality, and International Affairs (coed.) (Oxford University Press, 1974)
Property, Profits, and Economic Justice (ed.) (Wadsworth, 1980)
Rights and Goods: Justifying Social Action (Free Press/Macmillan, 1984)
Feminist Morality: Transforming Culture, Society and Politics (University of Chicago, 1993)
Justice and Care: Essential Readings in Feminist Ethics (ed.) (Westview, 1995)
The Ethics of Care: Personal, Political, and Global (Oxford University Press, 2006)
How Terrorism Is Wrong: Morality and Political Violence (Oxford University Press, 2008)

24 | Clare Chambers: "Sex, Culture, Justice"

Clare Chambers is University Senior Lecturer in Philosophy and Fellow of
Jesus College, University of Cambridge. Here she discusses some of the core
philosophical issues of sex, culture, and justice for liberal feminists; practices
of physical modification; social construction's role in negotiating claims
of universalism and tolerance; Foucault and the Panopticon; Bourdieu and
habitus; Mackinnon's critique of liberal feminism; taking violence against
women seriously; Benhabib's discourse ethics; how not to be a relativist; what
kind of universality is worth defending; and the state of academic philosophy
and feminism.

3:AM: What made you become a philosopher?

CLARE CHAMBERS: I came to philosophy via politics, and discovered my love of political philosophy very early on. I took Government and Politics A Level largely because I loved political debate, and chose the political theory option within that. I soon realized, with the help of an inspiring teacher, that the ideas behind political debate motivated me more than the outcome: I wasn't interested so much in whether or how a political party wins but in whether the winning party is right. I went on to study Politics, Philosophy and Economics at Oxford, strengthening my love of philosophical argument in general but particularly the situated urgency of political philosophy. A year as a civil servant in the Cabinet Office convinced me that my calling is in the meaningful, concise precision of philosophical thought, something that is really only possible in any sustained way within academia.

3:AM: In *Sex, Culture, and Justice* one of the big issues you're confronting is how liberal feminists can negotiate the commitment to universal values on the one hand and sensitivity to different cultures on the other. Your book is full of vivid examples of the issues your philosophical work engages with. So perhaps it's a good idea to start with you telling us about some of the examples that motivate your thinking in this area.

CC: Feminism has always seemed obviously right to me as a political movement. And it provides such rich pickings for philosophical analysis, for so much of our gendered behaviour is difficult to understand without such analysis. I'm particularly interested in practices of physical modification: the ways in which we feel that our natural bodies are somehow wrong, and the ways in which we can be motivated to modify or alter (in many cases I would say damage or injure) those bodies despite the physical, mental and financial costs of doing so. It's familiar for Western liberals to critically assess the body modification practices of "other" cultures: practices like Female Genital Mutilation (FGM) are fairly widely dismissed as abhorrent by most contemporary liberals, even those sympathetic to multiculturalism. I offer an assessment of this practice in *Sex, Culture, and Justice*. But I'm also interested in practices of body modification in Western cultures, practices which Western liberals don't tend to submit to scrutiny. So I trace the genealogy of routine secular male circumcision, and argue that while the practice is less physically extreme than FGM it has shared many of the same justifications over its recent history and can usefully be understood in the same light. Another example that recurs throughout the book is that of female appearance or "beauty" norms, something that feminists have long analysed and criticized. But in recent years cosmetic surgery has become a huge growth industry, one in which the vast majority of patients are women. I want to offer a philosophical explanation of how it is that women and men can choose to submit to practices that are harmful to them, without relying on concepts such as irrationality or false consciousness.

3:AM: A key idea that you draw on and develop to negotiate claims of universalism and tolerance of difference is the idea of social construction. Can you say a little about you mean by this before discussing how it helps the liberal feminist?

CC: The idea of social construction helps us to understand why people choose to harm themselves without relying on claims about irrationality or false consciousness. Social construction is the process by which social norms and social influence shapes our behaviour. I understand social consciousness as occurring in two main ways. First, social norms shape our options. The structure and norms of the particular society in which an individual lives affect both which options are available to her (you can't be an opera singer in a society that doesn't have opera) and which options are appropriate for her (in the UK the vast majority of childcare workers are female and the vast majority of plumbers are male). Second, social norms shape our preferences. Most people want to conform to the everyday norms that apply in their societies. In most Western cultures, for example, there is a strong social norm that men should wear trousers and not skirts or dresses. While some men experience this norm as the constraint that it truly is, most do not. Most men do not even consider wearing a dress in the morning, and if you asked them "would you like to wear a dress today?" most will answer, truthfully, "no." But of course this preference to wear trousers and not dresses is not innate, or rational in some objective meaning of the word, just as women's willingness to wear dresses is neither innate nor irrational. The gendered preference makes sense only in the context of a society that emphasizes, even insists on, it.

This idea of social construction helps the liberal feminist because it enables her to maintain a critical, feminist line on the inequalities of gendered behaviour without dismissing women and men who follow gendered norms as irrational. That is to say, it enables us to see why women's and men's choices may not be in their interests, and why the fact that an individual has chosen to follow some practice does not in itself mean that the practice is just. After all, if our choices are strongly shaped by our social context, we cannot use the fact of choice to legitimate that social context or its parts.

3:AM: Foucault is one of the key players for you isn't he in developing this notion? What is important about Foucault's approach?

CC: Foucault is one of the key theorists of social construction. In particular his idea of society as being like a Panopticon has been extremely useful to feminist analysis. The Panopticon is a prison, designed by Jeremy Bentham, which is designed in such as way that the prisoners can never be sure when they are being watched by the prison guards. The result is that the prisoners become self-policing. They become habitual rule-followers: at first out of active fear of being watched, but after a while merely as a result of habit and unconscious compliance. Foucault argues that society is like the Panopticon, in that we comply with social norms for the most part without those norms having to be actively or coercively enforced. Foucault doesn't apply his analysis to gender in any great detail but many feminists have, particular Sandra Lee Bartky, who memorably writes: "a panoptical male connoisseur resides within the consciousness of most women: they stand perpetually before his gaze and under his judgment. Woman lives her body as seen by another, by an anonymous patriarchal Other."

3:AM: Pierre Bourdieu is another key figure in your analysis. What does he bring to the party?

CC: Much of Bourdieu's analysis echoes Foucault, in that it also emphasizes the significance of social construction and the way that social norms imprint themselves on the body. Bourdieu uses the concept of the habitus to explain how it is that our very physical existence is conditioned by habitual adherence to the rules and expectations of our social context. Unlike Foucault, though, Bourdieu offers a sustained analysis of gender, in an account that owes a lot to radical feminist Catharine MacKinnon, and he uses terms like "symbolic violence" that invite normative critique of the process of social construction. Bourdieu also explicitly theorises the possibility of change, predominantly through the disjunction between habitus and social context ("field," in his terms) that can occur as the result of social mobility. Nonetheless, there are crucial elements missing from his account, such as the recognition of the transformative potential of consciousness-raising and a deep engagement with normative analysis.

3:AM: Catharine MacKinnon calls out liberalism on its inability to notice the humanity of women in the first place. You're sympathetic to this challenge aren't you—how do you see this problem? Why has liberal theory been so slow on this issue? I think you see the liberal's fundamental relationship with "choice" as being at the heart of the problem don't you?

CC: An uncontroversial way to define liberalism is as a commitment to the twin values of equality and liberty. As such most liberals will happily endorse gender equality and decry all forms of discrimination against women. From that perspective, feminism does not challenge liberalism conceptually, it merely highlights important areas in which the liberal commitment to equality has not yet been realized in practice. MacKinnon is skeptical. As she puts it, we should ask "why liberalism as a whole, long ruling ideology, needed feminism to notice the humanity of women in the first place, and why it has yet to face either the facts or the implications of women's material inequality as a group, has not controlled male violence societywide, and has not equalized the status of women relative to men. If liberalism "inherently" can meet feminism's challenges, having had the chance for some time, why hasn't it?"

What MacKinnon highlights here is that liberalism has happily coexisted with women's oppression for centuries. When the liberal Founding Fathers wrote in the Declaration of Independence that "all men are created equal" they really did mean all men and not women (or, for that matter, black people of either sex). While contemporary liberal societies are formally committed to gender equality they contain significant gendered inequalities in wealth, job prospects, political influence, and susceptibility to violence. A recurring theme of MacKinnon's work is that it is extremely difficult to get violence against women taken seriously. MacKinnon's fundamental claim is that the violence and abuse routinely inflicted on women by men is not treated with the same seriousness accorded to a human rights violation, or torture, or terrorism, or a war crime, or a crime against humanity, or an atrocity. So she asks, for example, why atrocities against women "do not count as war crimes unless a war among men is going on at the same time" and why, when approximately 3,000 women are killed by men in the United States each year, we refer to that state of affairs as "peacetime."

Liberalism's enduring complacency on these issues is hard to account for, and many factors must play a part in any explanation. But one part of the picture is a deep-seated conviction among liberals that formal, legal equality and freedom are the proper focus of liberal justice. Once this formal framework is in place, liberals want to protect individuals' freedom to choose, even if they end up choosing things that harm them or render them inferior. That is to say, they ignore the power of social construction that we've been discussing so far.

Now this focus on choice doesn't explain liberal unwillingness to engage deeply in the enduring nature of sex inequality, because of course women don't choose to be the victims of violence and low pay. But I think liberals see these matters as mere imperfections of the real world, without recognising that the continuing oppression of women demonstrates a profound inability of traditional liberal analysis to theorise or rectify injustice. Feminists have been much more successful at this, in part because feminists understand that how women fare in the world is intimately connected to how women and men are portrayed, represented and constructed in that world. Legal freedoms and formal equality, though important, are just not enough.

3:AM: You are sympathetic to Benhabib's principles of strong universalism combined with sensitivity to cultural difference but criticize her discourse ethics as a way of achieving this. Can you explain the argument here, and how do you propose we move forward?

CC: Benhabib's discourse ethics are part of a general movement towards deliberative democracy as a means of protecting freedom and equality while at the same time respecting cultural differences. The idea is that a suitable process of deliberation or discourse can result in an outcome that is acceptable to all but that goes beyond mere prejudice, self-interest, or unexamined opinion. By engaging in discourse individuals come to understand each other's views more closely, and also develop and modify their own views. The problem with discourse ethics and other versions of deliberative democracy is that, if it really is to transcend direct or representative democracy and become more than mere preference aggregation, the deliberation must take place within normative constraints. These typically include fairly substantive equality requirements, requirements which may go beyond the conception of equality held by those participating in the deliberation. And so my argument is that those equality requirements must constrain the outcome as well as the process of deliberation, which is to say that we can do a great deal of theorizing from that substantive commitment to equality just on its own.

3:AM: There are problems in reconciling liberal values with social constructivism that run through any position advocating universalism and social constructivism aren't there? For one, if all social forms constrain people, how can the liberal desire to liberate everyone from such constraints be deemed appropriate or even desirable? Is autonomy ruled out?

CC: Liberals and anyone else are fighting a losing battle if they hope to liberate people from the constraints of social construction. That's partly why I use the term "social construction" rather than "social constraint." As Foucault reminds us, power is creative and not merely repressive, and there is no autonomous subject if by that is meant "a person immune from social influence." Autonomy is not ruled out on this analysis, but it is reconceptualised. We are autonomous insofar as we exist in a social context that affirms our equality and that provides us with significant choices from a baseline of equality.

Where liberalism comes into its own is in its insistence that we can and must normatively evaluate different societies, states and policies: that we can distinguish between justice and injustice. This liberal commitment to normativity demonstrates that the task is not (can never be) to liberate people from social construction; instead, the task is to distinguish just and unjust norms and work to promote the former and eliminate the latter.

3:AM: And the obvious one is the one that ends with a relativist position: if normative values are socially constructed, how can we criticize values? Isn't universalism as dreamed up by the liberal feminist just a dead duck in the spit-roast of relativism?

CC: My response to this question includes the idea that, while liberalism may be particular in origin, it is universal in application. That's to say, while it is true that a commitment to liberalism is a culturally and historically situated commitment, liberal values themselves do not make sense if they are not applied universally. Non-universal equality is inequality. Non-universal freedom is constraint. Whether one holds liberal values may be culturally contingent. But it doesn't follow that, once one holds those values, one ought to view their application as also culturally contingent. Quite the opposite.

3:AM: And how on earth do we deal with the desirability of difference from a liberal perspective? By insisting on universality aren't we in danger of throwing out something that is just as valuable as universality?

CC: It depends what it is we are committed to by insisting on universality. Of course a commitment to cultural homogeneity will be inhospitable to difference. But that's not the sort of universality I defend. I defend a universality of fundamental equality and autonomy. It's actually pretty hard to argue against that from the point of view of difference in a coherent way, because any such arguments usually invoke the rights of those who are non-liberals to live in an illiberal way. But what reason could we have to respect other people's lives other than a commitment to their equal worth and autonomy? If equality and autonomy were not important what would be wrong with a liberal state forcibly quashing other cultures? On the other hand, if difference should be respected out of a commitment to the equality and autonomy of non-liberals, it follows that those non-liberals must themselves respect their own members' equality and autonomy.

3:AM: Will Kymlicka has the idea that a cultural framework is the required context for personal autonomy . You don't fully endorse this idea do you? What do you think he gets wrong?

CC: Kymlicka's work is valuable in that it combines a commitment to liberal autonomy with a recognition of the value and impact of community—a version of social construction. One problem with his work is that the distinction he wishes to draw between internal restrictions—restrictions that a culture might impose on its members and which Kymlicka argues are impermissible—and external protections—legal measures and exemptions that a culture needs for its own survival—is not clear-cut. Another problem is that Kymlicka's account is somewhat ambiguous about the level of liberalization required of a culture if it is to be worthy of the multicultural protections he endorses.

3:AM: Perhaps a good test case for you to show how your theory might be applied is academic philosophy departments in universities. How do you analyse the problem and how might you speak to a solution?

CC: There's been a lot of attention focused recently on the status of women in philosophy, with sites like "What is it like to be a woman in Philosophy?" and "Feminist Philosophers" drawing attention to the sexism that is endemic in many academic departments. Jennifer Saul in particular has worked on the importance of implicit bias and stereotype threat. Both are often unconsciously experienced and perpetuated. Implicit biases are those prejudices that even committed egalitarians hold, often unwittingly, against minority or oppressed groups. Stereotype threat is what happens when members of stigmatized groups perform worse than they otherwise would because they are "unconsciously preoccupied by fears of confirming the stereotypes about their group." Implicit bias and stereotype threat are specific examples of social construction. Implicit bias is a form of the social construction of options, and stereotype threat is a form of social construction of preferences and behaviour. Together they show that much of the activities of academic departments, whether it be hiring decisions, teaching practices, research culture or staff attitudes, must be scrutinized with a view to eliminating unjust inequality.

3:AM: Some recent feminist thought has been critical of a "white feminist" discourse and argues that minorities feminism would need to take a different stand. Is there merit in this position?

CC: Absolutely. There's always merit with engaging with alternative perspectives and considering whether (or perhaps that should be how) dominant discourse conceals assumptions and prejudice that only make sense from, and serve to reify, a majority standpoint.

3:AM: And why stick with liberal feminism? Why not abandon liberalism and go for a Marxist or Pragmatist position, for example, where the antagonism between universalism and celebration of difference is not so pressing?

CC: My aim in *Sex, Culture, and Justice* is primarily to talk to liberals. Liberalism is the dominant approach within contemporary Anglo-American analytical political philosophy. I want to show liberals that they need to pay attention to social construction, and that there is more to being a feminist liberal than simply paying lip-service to gender equality. Real conceptual change is required.

3:AM: And for those of us wanting to follow you into this philosophical world, can you recommend five books we should be reading?

CC: The obvious answer is my book and the works discussed there! Apart from that, I would start with anything by Andrea Dworkin and anything by Catharine MacKinnon, two profoundly important philosophers who are rarely read with the seriousness and attention to detail they deserve. If I had to pick just one introductory book by each it would be Dworkin's *Letters from a War Zone* and MacKinnon's *Feminism Unmodified*. Martha Nussbaum's *Sex and Social Justice* is a book of two halves: while some chapters defend the sort of liberalism that I critique, others powerfully describe the problem of social construction, so it offers a perfect example of the problems with liberalism as well as some of the solutions. Joan Williams' *Unbending Gender: Why Family and Work Conflict and What To Do About* It is an excellent piece of applied normative political philosophy that embodies just the sort of awareness we need. And Cordelia Fine's *Delusions of Gender* banishes any suspicion that nature might be the explanation for gender difference.

Clare Chambers is the author of:

Sex, Culture, and Justice: The Limits of Choice (Pennsylvania State University Press, 2008)

Teach Yourself Political Philosophy: A Complete Introduction (Hodder, 2012)

25 | Luciano Floridi: "Philosophy of the Zettabyte"

Luciano Floridi is Professor of Philosophy and Ethics of Information at the University of Oxford, where he is also Director of Research and Senior Research Fellow of the Oxford Internet Institute and Governing Body Fellow of St Cross College. He is a member of the Google Advisory Council on the Right to be Forgotten. Here he discusses the history of philosophy as a sine wave, why the philosophy of Information and Communication Technology is ultimately a species of the philosophy of ethics, what information is, a postanalytic continental divide, hyperhistory, the infosphere, the ethics and politics of information, responsibility, privacy, Google's the Right to be Forgotten, the quality of information, and why artificial intelligence is interesting because of what it tells us about ourselves.

3:AM: What made you become a philosopher? Are those reasons still sustaining you or are there new reasons why you continue as a philosopher?

LUCIANO FLORIDI: I was exposed to philosophy very early. My parents are passionate about it and my father introduced me to Russell, and in Italy philosophy is taught for three years in high school. By the time I was seventeen, I had three answers to the proverbial question "when I grow up I want to be. . . ." An economist, to understand the human world. A mathematician, to understand the world. Or a philosopher, to understand. Since I wanted a license to study any subject in abstract terms, the choice was easy, intellectually. I followed Terence's advice: "Homo sum, humani nihil a me alienum puto" ("I am a human being, nothing human is alien to me"). In practice, it was much harder. At some point in the nineties I was close to giving up, for what I wanted to do, namely to develop a philosophy of information, did not seem to interest any philosophy department, anywhere. Today things are very different. But my motivation has not changed. I still want to understand. I am still searching, like a teenager, for the ultimate meaning of life (there, I said it). I still wish to be a student of everything. I agree with Shakespeare that "All the world's a stage," but I disagree that "all the men and women merely players." Some of us have the privilege of being in the audience and study the play. However, whatever understanding I have gained so far has come at a price. I have lost two fundamental beliefs. I have become agnostic (mind, not atheist, for I do not believe in the non existence of God either), and I have now realised, with the certainty of the heart, that I will die not knowing. I miss God deeply. And my irrecoverable uncertainty (questions without answers) hurts badly.

3:AM: You argue that there's an information revolution going on, that it's very important and to ignore it is not an option just as it wasn't with the first three—the Copernican, the Darwinian and the Freudian. What is it about the zettabyte era that is causing the revolution?

LF: The history of philosophy looks a bit like a sine wave (or a roller coaster, if you prefer). It goes up and then down, up again, and then down. The ups, the crests of the wave, are the innovative periods, when we deal with philosophical problems. These are the times when philosophy is engaged with open and fundamental problems in relation to its own time. Once successful, philosophy fells in love with its own image, which is admittedly beautiful and attractive to any speculative mind. And like Narcissus it drowns, unable to leave the beauty of its reflection. The downs, the troughts of the wave, are the scholastic periods, when we deal with philosophers' problems. I believe that the information revolution is a great opportunity to renovate philosophy and climb up again on a new crest. Academic philosophy is definitely too narcissistic today. It would be very healthy to make it look at the world, instead of itself. And the world itself is in great need of philosophical understanding and design of new ideas. We need philosophy on board while we are creating the information society and re-thinking what I like to call the human project.

But what kind of philosophy? It seems to me that it should be a philosophy engaged with the profound transformations caused by information and communication technologies (ICTs). No aspect of human life is being left untouched by ICTs: education, work, conflicts, social interactions, entertainment, politics, art, literature, cinema, law, health, business, science ... it is hard to think of anything that is not being transformed or redefined by the information revolution. This means that old philosophical problems are being upgraded, think of issues about personal identity, memory, the nature of knowledge, the foundations of science, ethics, and so forth. And new philosophical problems acquire prominence: what is the nature of information? What happens to power in an information society? Can we reconcile human freedom and its predictability by smart machines? These are just a few examples among many.

Unfortunately, if you talk to philosophers, most of them are dismissive of technology. They tend to reduce it to a matter of tools and practical skills. I disagree. I guess I am not Platonic enough. The philosophy of information is not a matter of developing a philosophy of the next gadget. It is about engaging with the deep transformations caused by ICTs in how we understand the world, hence in our epistemology and metaphysics; in how we make sense of it, hence in our semantics; in how we conceptualise ourselves, and what we think we can be or become, hence in our theories of education, identity, and our philosophical anthropology; in how we interact with each other, how we manage and shape collaborative and conflicting relations, and how we may construct the society we want, hence in our socio-economic and political thinking. ICTs and the infosphere they are creating are providing the new environments in which we live and think. To use a word I introduced some time ago, they are re-ontologising our realities. Surely this is what philosophy should try to understand and help to shape properly. So, ultimately, it is a question of ethics, or, as I prrefer to put it, of e-nvironmental ethics. It is time to go back on top of the crest of the sine wave.

3:AM: You have argued that the mind doesn't want to get information for its own sake, nor to just represent reality but rather wants it to build a model of it so it makes sense so it can defend itself from it and survive. Is this where you begin defining what you mean when you talk about the philosophy of information?

LF: It is one way of approaching it. Imagine reality in itself as a sender of messages. Reality, understood as the Big Radio, broadcasts a very wide spectrum of signals. We, humans, are able to receive some of them directly, some others indirectly. For example, the visible spectrum is the portion of the electromagnetic spectrum that is detectable by the human eye; we perceive invisible radiant energy (infrared, electromagnetic radiation with longer wavelengths than those of visible light) through technological mediations. Out of all those signals, we make sense of the sender itself. It would be utterly naïve to think that the signals are a description of the sender, yet this does not mean that they are any less real. We only have to admit that the Big Radio is not sending selfies. With two other, different analogies, we cook with some ingredients (data from the world) but the dish we obtain (information) is not a copy of the ingredients. Or, we build with some materials (data in the world), but the house we obtain (information) is not a copy of the bricks we used. Human knowledge works in this constructionist (not constructivist, mind) way, it is not mimetic, it is poietic.

The mind reacts to the non-mental (call it the noumenon, if you prefer a Kantian vocabulary, although, to be utterly honest, the dialectics I am referring to is more Fichtean) by producing a meaningful interpretation of it. Some parts of this interpretation are heavily constrained by the signals we receive. In the long run, we ask more questions to get more data, as Francis Bacon already suggested. We manipulate the data to see what further data we obtain, and all this leads to scientific theories, which are our best ways of making sense of the constraining affordances (my preferred definition of data) provided by the realities we are studying. Some other parts of this interpretation are more flexible and malleable, the constraining affordances provide much more latitude, and well-informed, rational disagreement is more difficult to resolve, think of economic policies during a financial crisis.

The mind emerges from reality by detaching and differentiating itself from it through informational layers that end up in the creation of a language and a culture, a vision of the world and a scientific explanation of it, all things that the mind calls home. It is this meaningful environment that is essential for the mind to flourish, and the mind will do anything in order to generate it, including telling stories about mythological creatures, magic energies, or anonymous market forces. There is nothing relativistic, or anti-realist (to use some common jargon) in this, in the same sense in which there is nothing relativistic or anti-realist in the dish we cooked or the house we built. Humanity has taken advantage of the signals sent by the Big Radio progressively well, this is why our knowledge works so successfully. But we do not need to embrace any naïve realism, or representational theory of knowledge, or a correspondentist theory of truth. We should think about our knowledge of the world not in terms of painting it but in terms of engineering a model of it.

3:AM: You say that you're coming from a post-analytic-continental divide perspective. Why is this important to understanding your approach to the philosophy of information? Are you suggesting that the philosophy of information should be considered a new kind of first philosophy?

LF: It is important because I would like to see a better balance between control and power. Allow me to explain this with two caricatures.

On the one hand, analytic philosophy excels at controlling the philosophical discourse. An exact vocabulary, logic, formal distinctions, scientific information, empirical or thought experiments, mathematical formulations, statistical data, cogent and coherent arguments, a piecemeal and inferential way of discussing problems ... these are all ways in which analytic philosophy can exercise a high degree of control over a philosophical topic. The "but" is represented by the risk that so much technical control may be exercised over nothing, minutiae and irrelevancies, what I called above philosophers' problems. As John Locke once remarked, logicians keep sharpening their pens, but never write. It may get worse, if the degree of what can be controlled ends up determining the scope of what is worth investigating philosophically.

On the other hand, continental philosophy excels at enriching the philosophical discourse with powerful thoughts. An evocative vocabulary, rhetoric, scholarly references, literature, art, poetry, socio-political analyses, historical facts and interpretations, a more narrative style, existential and religious approaches to problems . . . these are all ways in which continental philosophy can add profound, powerful contents to a philosophical topic. The other "but" is represented by the risk that so much rich and powerful content may spill all over the place and be vague, confusing, incoherent, and sometimes downright mistaken. As a famous slogan of Pirelli (the tyre company) reminds us "power is nothing without control." In this case too, it may get worse, if the power of the content ends up promoting irrationality and an irritated impatience towards logic, or anti-scientific views, relativism, obscurantism, and an oracular philosophy.

The best philosophy (the one you find on the crests of the sine wave) has always combined a high degree of control with very powerful ideas. And this is what I hope a post-analytic-continental divide perspective may regain. It is certainly what we need today.

As for the philosophy of information, I can only hope that it will mature into a first philosophy. Anything less and it will have failed in its task of providing us with the powerful and controlled ideas that we need to shape and make sense of the human project in the twenty-first century.

3:AM: Should we approach this philosophy metaphysically or analytically, or both?

LF: Actually, I would say neither. We need to approach it from a design perspective, which I guess cuts transversally across the analytical-metaphysical divide. Philosophy deals with open problems, that is, problems that are constrained by facts and figures but ultimately solved by neither. These are problems such that you and I could be informed, rational, and not stubborn about them and still disagree about their acceptable solutions. We move forward when we can design (not invent, not discover) ways in which they can be solved satisfactorily. Yet opting for a metaphysical approach means having the illusion that we can talk about reality in itself, without accepting any level of abstraction, that is, any level at which questions may become sensibly solvable. With an analogy, it would be as if you and I disagreed on the value of a second-hand automobile without even being willing to accept that such value must be given within a framework of considerations (financial value, historical value, emotional value, running-cost effectiveness value and so forth).

However, I suspect that opting for an analytical approach would mean denying that the same philosophical problem, precisely because it is philosophical, is open to disagreement, and hence subject to more than one solution. Even in mathematics we are used to equations that have more than one solution, infinitely many solutions, no solutions at all, or solutions that can only be approximated. Philosophical problems are not different. If we wish to find their solutions, a reasonable approach is to clarify what the purpose is that determines the level of abstraction at which the question that is being asked is actually answerable, in case agree on further constraints, and ultimately accept that there may be many solutions, some preferable to others depending on the purpose for which a level of abstraction has been privileged. Plenty of philosophers' problems fail to be clear about all this, and become sources of endless diatribes, turning into cottage industries and scholastic monopolies.

3:AM: You use the term "hyperhistory" to mark the end of old history and the start of this new era. Is this the sort of shift that fashionable ideas of "singularity," "posthumanism," cyberculture', for example, are supposed to mark? Why do you find them unconvincing and that "the hole is way deeper"? Why do you think philosophy can help in this? Why not leave it to the scientists and IT boffins?

LF: I use "hyperhistory" to mean "more historical than before," in the following sense. Prehistory is any stage of human social life characterised by the absence of ways to record the present for future consumption. This normally means writing, and more generally ICTs. Then we talk about history whenever individual well-being and social welfare start being related to the development of ICTs. Once individual well-being and social welfare start depending on ICTs increasingly heavily, then we can speak of hyperhistory. As a test, you know you live in a hyperhistorical society if this can be the target of a cyber attack. To put it more dramatically: in hyperhistorical societies those who live by the digit (may) die by the digit. Now, the appearance of hyperhistorical societies is related to a major shift in our philosophy and the appearance of a philosophy of information, not unlike historical events and philosophical ideas were coupled in the Enlightenment, for example. This macroscopic shift has generated attempts to explain what is happening under our eyes. We sense a deep and widespread transformation. So, fashionable ideas, such as "singularity," "posthumanism," "cyberculture," are at worst philosophical snake oil, at best evidence of growing pains: we are confused, in search of new certainties, in need of meaningful frameworks, and so we resort to the ageless practice of telling stories, some reassuring, some scary, all fanciful. What we need to do is to develop a robust, controlled and rich philosophy. This should not be left to bizarre speculations. But it cannot be delegated to "scientists and IT boffins" either. This because they usually do not deal with open problems and with the design of the ideas necessary to answer them, with the ultimate goal of making sense and shaping the world. When they do, they are simply stepping into a philosophical debate, often rather naively. You need experts in "multisolvability."

3:AM: What do you mean by the "infosphere" and why does it mean we need to rethink our philosophy of nature? Do you think the infosphere changes the way naturalism (tricky term) needs to be thought about?

LF: Infosphere may mean many things. It can be used as a better synonym with cyberspace. "Better" because it is more inclusive as it does not presuppose an online/offline divide, something that social media have made anachronistic in the last decade (I prefer to speak of "onlife"). Philosophically and more technically, I have also used it as synonymous with reality. But not with reality in itself, for I remain rather Kantian about this point. Rather, it is the way in which we make sense of reality today. Whatever the world is itself, today, for our culture, it is becoming an infosphere. By this I mean that we have moved from a view of the world that was Newtonian and mechanistic, made of things and then properties of things and then processes in which things and their properties are involved, to an informational view of the world, in which entities are nodes arising from networks of relations, properties are special kinds of relations (for example, being tall is a unary relation, as it takes only Alice to be satisfied, whereas being taller is a binary relations as it requires both Mary and Bob to be satisfied), and processes are transitions in which networks move from one state to another. I have been guilty in the past of simplifying this view by saying that what is real is informational and vice versa, but this has to be interpreted from a constructionist perspective, according to which real has an epistemological not an ontological meaning. The sort of informational realism I defend is not metaphysical but epistemological, to be a bit more precise. Using a Kantian terminology this means that what is real phenomenologically (not noumenally) is informational and vice versa.

3:AM: You argue that politics needs to change too, don't you, so that multi-agent systems can be set up to deal with global issues? Can you sketch out the issues here?

LF: Yes I do. Let me simplify as much as I can. Big problems require big agents to be solved. The big agents we have inherited from modernity are the Nations/States. In many cases, these have already evolved into multi-agent systems, think for example, of the separation of executive, legislative and judiciary powers in many democracies, the significant movement towards devolution within countries like the United Kingdom, or the federal organisation of countries like the United States. Unfortunately, Nations/States are not big enough. They are necessary but insufficient to deal with huge challenges—such as the financial crisis, global warming, health risks, terrorism, conflicts, inequality—that require more powerful agents. This is why I am moderately in favour of more robust approaches to the role of the EU, of the UN, or other similar international organisations, and of international treaties that can give humanity a better chance to rise to the global challenges it is facing today. The UN and the EU were the outcome of the Second World War. I very much hope that we will not need another tragic lesson and so much terrible suffering before we move forward in favour of the creation of some powerful multi-agent systems that may save us from our own mistakes. I am concerned that, currently, we are leaving this multi-agent systems policy in the hand of multinationals. They are the closest we have to global multi-agent systems. Nothing wrong with them, but politics should be done in terms of social agreements, rather than economic interests.

3:AM: And ethical concerns also get shifted. One of the things that you discuss is extending the scope of the ethical environment so that artificial, digital and synthetic environments are covered. Can you set out what this means for things such as the ethics of vandalism, bioengineering and/or death?

LF: I believe we can refine our sensitivity towards what deserves, initially and in an overriding sense, some degree of respect. This is not just Nature, but Reality more inclusively. The idea is not new. Precedents of it can be found in Plotin and Spinoza, for example and, according to colleagues more knowledgeable than me, in Buddhism. I think Martin Luther King Jr. put it very insightfully when he wrote, in Rediscovering Lost Values, that "If we are to go forward, we must go back and rediscover these precious values—that all reality hinges on moral foundations and that all reality has spiritual control." I completely agree. If one considers that nothing deserves to be proactively disrespected to begin with, then forms of vandalism, for example, become reprehensible even when they target inanimate things or artefacts that are not necessarily valuable to anyone. Vandalism—the most violent form of which is murder—impoverishes the world ontologically, decreasing its rich variety. In this sense, we can lament death as a loss of a special structure. And we can be open-minded about bioengineering as a way of adding new pages to Galileo's book of nature. The major difficulty in all this is to counterbalance an exclusively agent-oriented position with an equally important patient-oriented one. This means structuring the ethical discourse around the question of what is good for the receiver of the action, rather than for its source. Most applied ethics in recent times belongs to this patient-oriented tradition, from environmental ethic to medical ethics, from bioethics to feminist ethics.

3:AM: Does this new situation change the link between agency and ethics and law? We've seen law beginning to shift to extend legal responsibility to institutions such as banks, for example, rather than individuals working in the banks. Is this the kind of thing you're thinking we need to get a philosophical grip on?

LF: The ethics of responsibility could make a significant step forward by engaging with at least three problems that are becoming pressing. One is distributed responsibility, the case in which the interactions between many agents and technologies, through time and different circumstances, bring about good or evil effects. Another is the distinction between moral responsibility and accountability. There are many moral actions that can be traced back to non-individual and non-human sources, from a company to a software program. And finally, but perhaps most importantly, we should free ourselves from a logic of afterlife judgement, punishment and reward, which is typical of the Christian way of thinking of good and evil actions.

3:AM: You're advising Google at the moment aren't you? The big issue there is privacy isn't it? Can you say something about how your method of abstraction might be applied in this?

LF: I am a member of Google's Advisory Council to the Right to Be Forgotten. And yes, privacy is a major issue. Here is an elementary example of the importance of using a clear method of abstraction when discussing it. Privacy and freedom of speech are fundamental principles of any liberal and democratic society. However, if people are confused about the level of abstraction—if they use only a single agent model, for example, and apply "being fundamental" as the only criterion to evaluate the two principles—then they conclude that they must be compatible. Alice has a fundamental right to her privacy and a fundamental right to her freedom of speech and there is nothing that indicates a potential conflict. However, once we include the possibility that different agents may appeal to each principle with respect to the same contents, then Alice's privacy can easily conflict with Bob's freedom of speech. This is what happens with the so-called right to be forgotten, which needs to be modelled in terms of different agents' conflicting interests in implementing two fundamental principles.

3:AM: Have you recommendations about the way forward around this issue? And is there a later impact on this—one that changes views of who we are and how we relate to others?

LF: The ruling of the European Court of Justice was a wrong step in the right direction, which is that individuals must be able to exercise more control over information that concerns them. However, I doubt that putting Google in the driving seat may be a solution (it is currently Google that decides which information is or is not de-linked, people can then appeal; and it is Google that decides who counts as a public figure to whom the ruling of the Court does not apply). It should be a legal institution that decides. Google, or any other search engine, should merely comply with the decision. Yet the decision should not be about mere accessibility, that is, about the possible removal of links from a search engine result. It should be about availability, that is, about the possibility of blocking at the source a specific bit of information. This would solve the territoriality problem, for if you block a piece of information, it does not matter which search engine tries to index it. The trouble is that this measure is a form of censorship and therefore, being a serious move, it requires taking equally seriously the harmful nature of the information in question. Unpleasantness would not count. Unfortunately, I am not sure any of the parties involved wants to get this serious. This is a pity because who we are online is now fluidly mixing with who we are off line. I mentioned already that we have begun to live onlife. The consequence is that our social selves affect who we are and who other people think we are, and this affects who we may be or become, and how we may be treated. The construction of our personal identifies onlife will be increasingly important. We better take care of the modalities though which this happens.

3:AM: A related issue is about the quality of information in our new situation. Good quality information will help us thrive it is supposed—so what do we mean by information quality? Is there a settled view and if there isn't does this matter? What's your position on this?

LF: The most common definition of information quality is "fit for purpose." This helps but only partially. For it means that one needs to know the purpose and hence the level of abstraction at which the quality of the information in question is being evaluated. Ultimately, there are some parameters that can be used: accurate, complete, consistent, relevant, timely, updated, and so forth. However, the final evaluation requires an interpretation of the nature of the question which the information is supposed to answer. Asking whether some information is of good quality in itself is a bit like asking whether some food (grass? plankton? mice?) is of good quality in itself independently of the organisms that is going to eat it.

3:AM: AI was perhaps a key point for the kind of philosophical landscape you discuss, which raises the issue of the notion of whether there's still an element of hype in all this that might not be earned. I'm thinking of the way that the hard problem of consciousness hasn't been sorted despite films like "Ex Machina" suggesting that if you build a big enough and fast enough computerized thing then it will be. Searle and Chalmers' warnings loom over that project it seems to me and so it may be that some of the claims about the revolutionary changes aren't as clearly present as you claim. Is this a fair pushback and does it suggest that the change is maybe not as deep as it might appear?

LF: In broad terms, I agree with Searle and Chalmers, and I have very little philosophical interest in AI, if by this we mean the real thing, that is, the non-biological reproduction of human intelligence by engineering means. This is science fiction, which I enjoy enormously, but as entertainment. However, I do find smart technologies philosophically significant. They are replacing us in an increasing number of tasks, and they can predict our choices in an increasing number of cases. They are not important in themselves. What matters is what they say about us. We are the only intelligent and free agents in the universe that I know of (although the universe is a big place, and who knows what's happening in some of its distant corners). The special mix of consciousness and intelligence that characterises us may be a natural and yet unique phenomenon. We may be, to use a Greek word, a hapax legomenon in Galileo's Book of Nature. This is a word that occurs only once in a text, like "Honorificabilitudinitatibus" ("the state of being able to achieve honours"), which Shakespeare uses only once, in Love's Labour's Lost. There is nothing supernatural in a hapax legomenon, it just does not occur again. If so, we better come to terms with our solitude in the universe. There are neither gods nor machines that can be blamed for our mistakes, or to which we can delegate our responsibilities. There is only us, all the way down to the end of time.

3:AM: And which five books, other than your own which we'll all be rushing out to read, can you recommend for readers here at 3:AM to take them further into your philosophical world?

LF: If I restrain myself to five philosophical books, and I force myself to avoid the most obvious classics that readers are likely to know already, then I would recommend:

1. Gilles Deleuze and Felix Guattari, *What is Philosophy?*
2. Jean-Francois Lyotard, *The Postmodern Condition: A Report on Knowledge*
3. Herbert Simon, *The Sciences of the Artificial*, 3rd ed.
4. Alfred North Whitehead, *Process and Reality*, corrected ed.
5. Norbert Wiener, *The Human Use of Human Beings: Cybernetics and Society*, 2nd ed.

And if I may add six recommendations about reading, they would be:

Read only classics. There is no time to confront any lesser foes.

Choose your classics. Do not enter into other people's fights, it is your life, you are at least entitled to choose your foes.

Never read a classic defenceless. A classic will deeply and irreversibly conquer your mind, so entrench yourself carefully, by digging deeply into your own thoughts, and make these strong enough to withstand the assault that will be almost irresistible.

Never study a classic, interpret it. After resisting its assault, counterattack as violently as you can: misinterpret a classic, steal from it, use it for your own purposes, be unfair, force it to confesses what you need to know, reduce it to something else, never show any hermeneutical mercy.

Never underestimate your reading list. Choose your foes judiciously. The order in which you will engage with classics will forever determine who you are. Two minds will be very different, depending on whether they wrestled with *The Tempest* before or after *Faust*, with *Anna Karenina* before or after *Madame Bovary*, with *Life A User's Manual* before or after *Zen and the Art of Motorcycle Maintenance: An Inquiry into Values*, with *Waiting for the Barbarians* before or after *Waiting for Godot*.

Reread the classics. *The Leopard* is not the same classic at fifteen, thirty-five, or sixty-five. The more you read your classics the more you can make peace with them. What were once foes become loyal allies, who will join you in your new battles against other unknown classics.

Luciano Floridi is the author of:

l'estensione dell'intelligenza: Guida all'informatica per filosofi (Armando, 1996)
Scepticism and the Foundation of Epistemology: A Study in the Metalogical Fallacies (Brill, 1996)
Internet: Un manuale per capire; Un saggio per riflettere (Il Saggiatore, 1997)
Philosophy and Computing: An Introduction (Routledge, 1999)
Sextus Empiricus: The Recovery and Transmission of Pyrrhonism (Oxford University Press, 2002)
Infosfera: Etica e filosofia nell'età dell'informazione (Giappichelli, 2009)
Information: A Very Short Introduction (Oxford University Press, 2010)
The Philosophy of Information (Oxford University Press, 2011)
La rivoluzione dell'informazione (Codice, 2012)
The Ethics of Information (Oxford University Press, 2013)
The Fourth Revolution: How the Infosphere Is Reshaping Human Reality (Oxford University Press, 2014)

26 | Kathinka Evers: "Neuroethics"

Kathinka Evers is a Professor of Philosophy at the University of Uppsala and a codirector of the EU Flagship Human Brain Project. Here she thinks about what neuroethics is and what its questions are, about the distinction between fundamental and applied neuroethics, about the relationship between brain science and sociology, about how her approach avoids both dualism and naive reductionism, about mind-reading, about the ethical issues arising from disorders in consciousness, about brain simulation and its relation to philosophy, about whether tendencies in the brain lead to social or individualistic interpretation, about epigenesis, about human enhancement, about cognitive prosthetics, and about the singularity.

3:AM: What made you become a philosopher?

KATHINKA EVERS: I was raised in a home where philosophy was a frequent topic for dinner conversations. Both my parents are academics, my father a philosopher, and he inspired an enthusiasm for philosophy in me at a very early age. Also for logic, which he taught me simultaneously with my learning to read and write. Abstract thought appealed to me immensely ever since early childhood, and mathematics became the favourite topic at school from the first year and onwards. Later in life, in my early youth, I travelled extensively, and came into contact with profoundly different cultures, schools of though, and values. This human diversity intrigued me in numerous ways, also from a philosophical perspective, and I started studying philosophy at the university. I began with logic and philosophy of science, took my doctoral degree in this domain (on the concept of indeterminacy in logic, philosophy and physics), but was also interested in moral and political philosophy. The latter was largely due to my upbringing that taught me how the social responsibility of an individual increases in proportion to her/his education, rather like a social debt: one must contribute to benefit society through one's education (it is not just a private play-ground created for one's own amusement). Philosophy of

mind interested me deeply, but I was frustrated by the lack of empirical perspectives in the philosophical faculties when I was a student, where the road to
hell was paved with empirical propositions! Yet it never seemed possible to me
to understand the mind purely through a priori reasoning, ignoring the organ
that does the job. On the other hand, brain science took scant interest in conceptual, philosophical analyses at the time, which seemed equally lopsided.
Today the situation is fortunately different: philosophy and the neurosciences
collaborate in a very fruitful manner. And that is why I now have turned my
philosophical focus to studies of consciousness and neuroethics.

3:AM: You're working in the field of neuroethics. Can you sketch for the
uninitiated what this is—this isn't just about translating ethics into brain
science is it?

KE: It is partly that, but not only. Neuroethics is indeed concerned with the possible benefits and dangers of modern research on the brain. But neuroethics also
deals with more fundamental issues, such as our consciousness and sense of
self, and the values that this self develops: it is an interface between the empirical brain sciences, philosophy of mind, moral philosophy, ethics and the social
sciences. It is the study of the questions that arise when scientific findings about
the brain are carried into philosophical analyses, medical practice, legal interpretations, health and social policy, and can, by virtue of its interdisciplinary
character, be seen as a subdiscipline of, notably, neuroscience, philosophy or
bioethics, depending on which perspective one wishes to emphasise. Such questions are not new, they were raised already during the French Enlightenment,
notably by Diderot who stated in his *Eléments de Physiologie*: "C'est qu'il est
bien difficilie de faire de la bonne métaphysique et de la bonne morale sans
être anatomiste, naturaliste, physiologiste et médecin...." Moreover, ethical
problems arising from advances in neuroscience have long been dealt with by
ethical committees throughout the world, though not necessarily under the neuroethics label. Still, as an academic discipline labelled "neuroethics," it is a
very young discipline. The first "mapping conference" on neuroethics was held
in 2002, and references to neuroethics in the literature were made little more
than a decade earlier. These early articles described, for example, the role of the
neurologist as a neuroethicist faced with patient care and end-of-life decisions,
and philosophical perspectives on the brain and the self. Today, the pioneers of
modern neuroethics have developed an entire body of literature and scholarship
in the field of neuroethics that is rapidly expanding.

3:AM: In your view there are two types of neuroethics: fundamental and
applied neuroethics and that the "fundamental" aspect has been unrepresented
in the field. Is your thought here that if the fundamental aspect isn't worked out
the applied aspect won't be able to fully work?

KE: Yes. So far, researchers in neuroethics have focused mainly on the ethics of neuroscience, or applied neuroethics, such as ethical issues involved in neuroimaging techniques, cognitive enhancement, or neuropharmacology. Another important, though as yet less prevalent, scientific approach that I refer to as fundamental neuroethics questions how knowledge of the brain's functional architecture and its evolution can deepen our understanding of personal identity, consciousness and intentionality, including the development of moral thought and judgment. Fundamental neuroethics should provide adequate theoretical foundations required in order properly to address problems of applications.

The initial question for fundamental neuroethics to answer is: how can natural science deepen our understanding of moral thought? Indeed, is the former at all relevant for the latter? One can see this as a sub-question of the question whether human consciousness can be understood in biological terms, moral thought being a subset of thought in general. That is certainly not a new query, but a version of the classical mind-body problem that has been discussed for millennia and in quite modern terms from the French Enlightenment and onwards. What is comparatively new is the realisation of the extent to which ancient philosophical problems emerge in the rapidly advancing neurosciences, such as whether or not the human species as such possesses a free will, what it means to have personal responsibility, to be a self, the relations between emotions and cognition, or between emotions and memory.

Observe that neuroscience does not merely suggest areas for interesting applications of ethical reasoning, or call for assistance in solving problems arising from scientific discoveries, as scientists of diverse disciplines have long done, and been welcome to do. Neuroscience also purports to offer scientific explanations of important aspects of moral thought and judgment, which is more controversial in some quarters. However, whilst the understanding of ethics as a social phenomenon is primarily a matter of understanding cultural and social mechanisms, it is becoming increasingly apparent that knowledge of the brain is also relevant in the context. Progress in neuroscience; notably, on the dynamic functions of neural networks, can deepen our understanding of decision-making, choice, acquisition of character and temperament, and the development of moral dispositions.

3:AM: Some people in the social sciences express anxiety that brain science of this kind threatens the work of the social sciences. But you think it's a two way street, that the social sciences enrich neuroethics in certain areas. Is that right? Can you say something about this? Why shouldn't philosophers and social scientists be afraid of neuroscience?

KE: There are different possible reasons for this scepticism, which I can well understand, even though I regret very much when it leads to a rejection of collaboration across the fields. For, as you correctly point out, I consider the contribution of the social sciences and humanities deeply important, not only to neuroethics, but also to the natural sciences, notably neuroscience. Some of the reasons I see are the following four.

(1) Natural sciences have different degrees of explanatory power with respect to moral thought and judgment. The explanatory gap between our minds and our genetic structure is, I would say, larger than the explanatory gap between our minds and the architecture of our brains because the relationship between the latter two is closer than between the former in a manner that is explanatorily relevant. Simply phrased, neuroscience can explain more about why we think and feel the way we do than genetics does or can do. Even though an individual's genetic structure importantly determines who and what s/he becomes both physiologically and in terms of personality, genes only decide limited aspects of the individual's nature, and, at least so far as the mind is concerned, less than his or her brain structures do. In contrast, the brain is the organ of individuality: of intelligence, personality, behaviour, and conscience; characteristics that brain science increasingly is able to examine and explain in significant ways. Everything we do, think and feel is a function of the architecture of our brains; however, that fact is not yet quite integrated into our general world-views or self-conceptions.

The rapid neuroscientific advances may come to include profound changes in fundamental notions, such as human identity, self, integrity, personal responsibility, and freedom, but also, importantly, in neuroscience's models of the human brain and consciousness that has already moved away from modelling the brain as an artificial network, an input-output machine, to picturing it as awoken and dynamic matter. Through its strong explanatory power, neuroscience could be regarded as no less, and possibly even more controversial than genetics as a theoretical basis for ethical reasoning. Science can be, and has repeatedly been, ideologically hijacked, and the more dangerously so the stronger the science in question is. If, say, humans learn to design their own brain more potently than we already do by selecting what we believe to be brain-nourishing food and pursuing neuronally healthy life-styles, we could use that knowledge well—there is certainly room for improvements. On the other hand, the dream of the perfect human being has a sordid past providing ample cause for concern over such projects. Historic awareness is of utmost importance for neuroethics to assess suggested applications in a responsible and realistic manner.

(2) We know how genetics has lent itself to political prejudices of various kinds: conservative versus progressive, right-wing versus left-wing, male versus female, etc. Conservative ideologies trying to preserve the privileges of some specific class, race or gender sought support in genetic theories such as Mendelism, the theory of heredity emphasising the innate characteristics of the human being (some individuals could thus be said to be "born to poverty

and servitude" and social reforms would make less sense). Progressive ideologies were inspired more by Jean-Baptiste de Lamarck's doctrine allowing for the inheritance of acquired characteristics and, by extension, of social flexibility. Attempts in the 1970s to establish socio-biology spurred intense controversies, and were attacked for joining the long line of biological determinists. The reason for the survival of these recurrent determinist theories, argued critics, is that they consistently tend to provide a genetic justification of the status quo and of existing privileges for certain groups according to class, race or sex. That discussion became polarized in the extreme, where sociologists and biologists would sometimes reject all attempts to explain human identity and social life in any terms other than their own. Today, in contrast, biological and sociological explanations of human nature develop in parallel relations of complementarity rather than in stark opposition. Whilst some cases necessitate choices between the two perspectives (for example, if a specific disorder should primarily be medically or sociologically explained and treated), they are not seen as mutually conflicting generally. In some instances, of course, that peace may be frail. The ideological (and sometimes financial) interests in finding facts that suit a certain set of values are no less strong than they used to be, and their power to influence the scientific communities, through conditioned funding, political regulations, or by other methods has not diminished. Nevertheless, the all-out war of the trenches between biology and sociology appears to ebb away.

In contemporary neuroscience, the biological and socio-cultural perspectives dynamically interact in a symbiosis, which should reduce the tension further. This is particularly true of dynamic models of the brain arguing that whilst the genetic control over the brain's architecture is important, it is far from absolute; it develops in continuous interaction with the immediate physical and socio-cultural environments. The traditional opposition between sociology and biology is accordingly substituted by complementarity. An important task will be to unify different levels and types of knowledge combining technical and methodological approaches from distinct disciplines rather than to select one at the expense of another. Social sciences are extremely important for us to achieve an integrated and multi-level understanding of the brain. Note that homo sapiens is a species that spends large parts of its life developing the brain in response to learning and experience: culture leaves physical imprints on human brain architecture. And this symbiosis cannot be understood from a purely biological perspective.

(3) Another possible reason for scepticism has more to do with emotions or values. A central fear amongst those who reject the entry of natural science into moral philosophy and ethics is that the search for biological explanations of morality would somehow rob it of its moral, emotional, or human dimension, as people once feared the biochemical explanations of life. An equally central hope of those who see the development in a positive light is that the

realisation that morality is a product of brains functioning in social, cultural environments, will empower, and enrich, the field of ethics. Surely, knowledge need not erode human dignity: if anything, the reverse ought to be the case. Even so, I can in view of recent history also well understand if the new socio-cultural-biological research of neuroethics sets ideological alarm clocks ringing. The solution, clearly, is to beware of any ideological misuse of theories developed and to maintain a high level of vigilance in this regard. Mistakes have been made in the past that should admittedly not be repeated. However, these mistakes have not only been of a political nature.

(4) Yet another obvious motivation for scepticism against neurobiological explanations of social phenomena, such as moral thought and judgment, is the harsh destiny that awaited the concept of the conscious mind when science secularised that area of research and placed the human mind firmly in nature. Schools of thought emerged that did indeed rob the conscious mind of both meaning and content, scientifically speaking. In its eagerness to escape dualism, science in the 20th century became to no small extent psychophobic and that is important to bear in mind when we discuss the relevance and value of neurobiological explanations of thought and judgment.

The sciences of mind suffered from severe psychophobia until late in the 20th century, and it is perfectly legitimate not to want neuroethics to cross the same desert. The doctrines of behaviourism invaded psychology and were followed by naïve eliminativism and naïve cognitivism. One eliminated the mind; the other emotions and the brain from their pursuits, and the result was, of course, seriously lop-sided. I consider an interesting study of psychology the question why any thinking being would want to reduce its own mind to a behaviouristic slot-machine, or indeed to any machine, organic or otherwise. And, as Joseph LeDoux asks: Why would anyone want to conceive of minds without emotions?

The scientific situation today has evolved considerably from what it was a century, half a century or even a decade ago. Mind science is far less psychophobic (if at all), and radical eliminativism with respect to consciousness has lost most of the ground it once possessed. Modern neuroscience is in important ways and measures non-eliminativist both ontologically and epistemologically: it neither denies the existence of mind (conscious or non-conscious), nor does it deny that the mind is an important and relevant object of scientific study, nor does it necessarily presume to explain subjective experience without the use of self-reflection. The image of the brain that some contemporary neuroscientists offer if as far from behaviourism or the mind-machine model in which the brain's activity is depicted in an input-output manner as it is from the religious notions of an immaterial soul. Psychophil science has taken the ground.

Scientific theories about human nature and mind in the 19th and 20th centuries were occasionally caught in two major traps: ideological hijacking, and psychophobia in the form of naïve eliminativism and naïve cognitivism. In order to avoid repeating these mistakes, neuroethics needs to build on the sound scientific and philosophical foundations of informed materialism. This is a concept originally coined in chemistry (by Gaston Bachelard) that has been extended to neuroscience (by Jean-Pierre Changeux) and to philosophy (by KE) in a model of the brain/mind that opposes both dualism and naïve reductionism. This model is based on the notion that all the elementary cellular processes of brain networks are grounded on physico-chemical mechanisms and adopts an evolutionary view of consciousness as a biological function of neuronal activities, but describes the brain as an autonomously active, projective and variable system in which emotions and values are incorporated as necessary constraints. Due to the way in which our capacity-limited brains acquire knowledge of the world and ourselves, informed materialism acknowledges that adequate understanding of our subjective experience must take both self-reflective information and data gathered from physiological observations and physical measurement into account. Informed materialism depicts the brain as a plastic, projective and narrative organ evolved in socio-biological symbiosis, and posits cerebral emotion as the evolutionary hallmark of consciousness. Emotions made matter awaken and enabled it to develop a dynamic, flexible and open mind. The capacity for emotionally motivated evaluative selections are what distinguish the conscious organism from the automatically functioning machine. And herein lies the seed of morality.

3:AM: How do you see the relationship between the empirical research and the philosophical analysis of concepts of concepts such as "consciousness"? Presumably the analysis impacts on the research? I guess this is really a question about what role you think philosophy has in neuro science?

KE: If I may begin by paraphrasing Immanuel Kant: Conceptual analysis of mind without empirical content is empty; empirical analysis of mind without conceptual analyses is blind. The basic role of philosophy (as I see it) is to clarify concepts, theories and arguments; reveal underlying assumptions of suggested theories and data, as well as their implications both theoretically (e.g., epistemologically) and practically (e.g., ethically and socially). It is a help to interpret correctly the results of empirical experiments, such as what fMRI scans actually "reveal" in the brain, or what it means to say that we can "communicate" neurotechnologically with patients in vegetative states, or when we "read minds" without overt behaviour or speech. Philosophy is in quest of meaning, bringing understanding of concepts to a higher level, developing theories that are more refined, clearer, and more coherent. Without philosophy, neuroscience stands a much greater risk of misinterpretations and other errors.

3:AM: Philosophers like Goldman and Carruthers think about mind reading: from the perspective of neurophilosophy what do you think are the possibilities and limits of this?

KE: The possibilities of neurotechnological mind-reading that we have today allow access to mental states without 1st person overt external behaviour or speech. With the advancement of decoders of cerebral activity it is very likely that in the near future we will see a rapid progression in the capacity to observe—without mediation of language—contents of the others' mind. We are seemingly able to efficiently use a subject's cerebral cortex for rapid object recognition, even when the subject is not aware of having seen the recognized object. This may be extended as a great promise to the domain of dreams, to observe in real time the content of a visual narrative during sleep. We might be able to infer a myriad of simultaneous intentions whose deliberation process to reach explicit agency is not tangible even to the same subject. We might be able to use this technology in medical situations (most notably in patients with consciousness disorders) where this might be the only available tool to infer another person's will. Certainly, applications in commercial setups to control objects (games, cars, airplanes) that are currently under massive development will become more frequent and effective.

There is a logical limit to these pursuits, in that an individual cannot wholly share another's experience without merging with it. Their distinction necessarily introduces a filter, an interpretation that individuates their respective points of view. In other words, by virtue of our distinction we have a private room that cannot logically be violated. The presence of this logical limit says nothing about the extension of our privacy, except that it isn't null. It does not exclude that our unalienable privacy may be extremely small. Moreover, it does not entail that we need have privileged access to our on experiences: the fact that there is an essential incompleteness in any other person's knowledge or experience of you does not mean that there is no, or less, incompleteness in your own self-understanding. To the contrary, it is possible that a brain decoder may access more information about, say, the intention of a subject than that which may be simply accessed by introspection.

The specific benefits of neurotechnological mind reading include the following:

- For a person who suffers from behavioural incapacity for communication, the prospect of neurotechnological mind reading opens up promising vistas of developing alternative methods of communication.
- The development of these techniques holds promises of important medical breakthroughs, notably improvements in the care and therapeutic interventions of patients with disorders of consciousness.

- For those—parents, paediatrics, and others—interested in understanding the infant pre-verbal mind, the research opens promising vistas.
- For radiology or satellite reconnaissance, notably, optimizing image throughput by coupling human vision with computer speed is a promising area of research.
- For philosophy of mind and all sciences of mind, whether they are clinically orientated or not, the research into neurotechnological mind reading is exciting and appears theoretically promising.

The development of mind reading can also be perilous, however, increasingly so if or when the techniques advance. There is, notably, a risk for misuse as a consequence of hypes, exaggerations, or misinterpretations, and a potential threat to privacy unknown in history. At present, the possibilities of neurotechnological mind reading are so rudimentary that the techniques pose threats to privacy mainly in the form of misuse, but this threat might expand and increase if the techniques are refined. In that context, the question arises: who is best placed to know what goes on in a person's mind? Who is authorized to say? Does the 1stperson have privileged access, or the one to perform/interpret the cerebral measurements? Already, a person's unconscious recognition of an image can be detected. How far can that be taken? Today, at the present level of science and technology: not far. Yet in the future, if better models and measurements of brain functions and mental contents are developed, the day could come when another, with the use of neurotechnology, enters your mind further than you can yourself. Is that a threat, or a promise? How we evaluate the integrity of our mind depends in part on our trust in others and our views on society: in which society we live; and which society we want to see develop in the future.

3:AM: You've examined the ethics of treating people who have disorders in consciousness. Can you describe some of the conditions you are discussing and say what ethical issues arise from these situations?

KE: Three of the main diagnoses of disorders of consciousness (DOCs) are Minimally Conscious State (MCS), Vegetative State (VS), and Coma. Their distinction is often described in terms of two dimensions: wakefulness (referring to arousal and the level of consciousness) and awareness (referring to the content of consciousness and subjective first-person experience). Patients who are in MCS can, as the name suggests, show some signs of awareness: some MCS patients may retain widely distributed cortical systems with potential for cognitive and sensory function despite their inability to follow simple instructions or communicate reliably. In contrast, the diagnostic criteria of coma exclude the presence of awareness and responsiveness as well as wakefulness. Coma is defined as a state of unarousable unconsciousness due to dysfunction of the brain's ascending reticular activating system (ARAS), which is responsible for arousal and the maintenance of wakefulness.

The diagnostic criteria of VS likewise exclude the presence of awareness; however, these patients can move, open their eyes, or change facial expressions. By virtue of these bodily states and movements, VS is considered to be one of the most ethically troublesome conditions in modern medicine, since bodily states can be taken to be indexes of mental states, something that may cause psychological problems for the next of kin, and diagnostic doubts in the caregiver. Recent studies of DOC patients prompt a question that has ethical implications: is it accurate to describe patients with VS or coma as totally unaware of themselves and their environment? Or do some of those patients possess preserved mental abilities undetected by standard clinical methods that exclusively rely on behavioural indexes?

Numerous ethical issues arise in this clinical context, notably: the problem of misdiagnosis, assessment of detected residual consciousness in DOC patients and (if applicable) the interpretation of their 1st person experiences, developing communication with these patients (if possible), decisions on adequate treatment, adapting the living conditions of these patients taking their possibilities of enjoyment or suffering into account and providing support for those who are close to the patient, and the question whether life-sustaining care should be discontinued in case the patient suffers.

3:AM: Do the ethical and legal concerns overlap in these patients?

KE: In some cases, yes, for example the concern whether to discontinue life-sustaining care if a patient is believed to suffer. But all ethical concerns are not legally regulated. And all legal regulations are not as such ethical.

3:AM: A technological fix is an obvious thing to want if you're an engineer or scientist. So brain simulation seems equally an obvious thing to try if we're trying to fix problems of consciousness. But simulation raises interesting philosophical questions in you doesn't it. So first could you sketch out what simulation in this context looks like?

KE: To my knowledge, simulation is not yet used in the studies of consciousness disorders, but this could be an interesting future development. I am not an expert on simulation. I only began studying it a couple of years ago when I became involved in the Human Brain Project. What I say below are ideas published and co-authored with a colleague in neuroscience, Yadin Dudai. I will begin by discussing the goals of simulation. In experimental science, simulation is one of the four meta-methods that subserve systematic experimental research. These are: observation, the most fundamental of all the experimental methods, clearly preceding modern science; intervention, currently the most popular method in reductive research programs, with the aim of inferring function from the dysfunction or hyperfunction of the system; correlation of sets of observations or variables extracted from the observations, or of the effect of interventions, in order to identify links between explicit or implicit phenomena and processes; and simulation, to verify assumptions, test heuristic models, predict missing data, properties and performance, and generate new hypotheses and models in which these experimental meta-methods are commonly enwrapped (the order in which the meta-methods are listed above does not of course imply that they are used in that order in realistic research programs). Simulation is hence used here to provide a proof of concept in the course of research and to promote and achieve understanding of the system.

When scientists use simulation in this manner, they either explicitly or implicitly assume that in order genuinely to understand a system, one should be able to reconstruct it in detail from its components. This assumption resonates with a maxim of scholastic philosophy, resurging in Vico (1710): only the one who makes something can fully understand it. "Understanding" as a cognitive accomplishment is intuitively understood but its meaning(s) in science is debated. For many scientists, understanding refers to the ability to generate a specific mental model (or a more encompassing theory) that permits predictions based on scientific reasoning concerning the behavior of the system under different conditions at the specified or additional level(s) of description. One particular point that is highly pertinent to a philosophical discussion of simulation is the level of epistemic transparency assumed to be required to reach understanding of the system. In other words, what is the magnitude of the epistemic lacunae or "gaps in understanding" that one is willing to tolerate in a simulated model while still claiming that the simulation increases scientific understanding at the pertinent level of description. This point is particularly relevant to the understanding of complex, nonlinear systems such as the brain, i.e., systems with emergent properties in which the behavior of the system is unaccountable for by the linear contributions of the components.

In the brain sciences, understanding is currently realistic with respect to only a limited number of basic neural operations and brain functions. Some types of simulations, however, have a long history of being a productive tool in testing and advancing partial understanding of the mechanism of action of neural systems. They are also considered in attempts to impact the development of artificial computational systems and brain inspired technologies.

For instance, since the outset of the powerful reductionist approach to the neurobiology of plasticity and memory, perceptual input and motor output of neural systems have been simulated by substitution with direct electrical stimulation of nerve fibers and of identified sensory or motor nerve cells, respectively. In this type of approach, the artificial agent that simulates or functionally substitutes the natural component is further used to manipulate the system in order to demonstrate that the modeled state or process are indeed functioning as expected. Hence the input of the conditioned stimulus (CS) in Pavlovian or instrumental conditioning is replaced with artificial stimulation of the natural input to prove that identified parts of the neural circuit in vivo fulfill or at least take part in the role assigned to them in a model of the functional nervous system.

Another philosophically important question concerns the nature of the object: what is the "brain" that brain simulation targets? In real life, brains do not live in isolation. In other words, brains are complex adaptive systems nested in larger complex adaptive systems. They reside in bodies. The interaction between the brain and the other bodily systems is, in reality, impossible to disentangle. Our brain gets and sends information to all other bodily systems, and its state at any given point in time is determined to a substantial degree by this interaction. That the brain is a brain-in-a-body cannot be ignored in considering the goal to simulate the realistic brain. But the brain-in-a-body at any given point in time is in fact the outcome of the individual experience accumulated over the period preceding this specific point in time. In simulating the brain, one has therefore to consider the experienced-brain-in-a-body. Neglecting experience sets a severe limit on the outcome of brain simulation. On the other hand, taking experience into account necessitates simulating real-life contexts, a daunting task per se, specifically given that part of the real-life experience is the interaction over time with the functioning body. In specifically discussing a hypothetical human brain simulation, it seems logical to limit the goal to the individual, yet without ignoring the relevance of the natural, social and cultural interactions and contexts over time. Therefore, the question how this limitation may affect the adequacy of large-scale simulation attempts in due time and their results must be borne in mind. Some key considerations are the following:

Scarcity of knowledge: Collection of data for realistic large-scale brain simulation is not trivial. Even a highly productive large experimental laboratory investigating the mammalian brain can produce only limited amounts of data. Federating data from different labs has to take into account that even small differences in methodology and conditions can mean a lot in terms of neuronal state and activity, and different labs seldom if ever use exactly the same conditions and protocols. The invariants identified under these conditions may mask important features. This complicates the ability to merge data from different sources without losing important information. Heterogeneous data formats also present an obstacle in sharing. As far as data required for human brain simulation are concerned, it is sufficient to note that cellular physiology data are scarce and obtainable from patients only. Functional neuroimaging using fMRI has limited spatiotemporal resolution which currently constraints its applicability to high-resolution brain simulation, though is useful in obtaining important information on the role of identified brain areas and their functional connectivity in perceptual and cognitive processes. One possibility to bridge the gap from the cellular to the cognitive is to use data from the primate brain, but these data are also yet insufficient for the purpose of large-scale brain simulation.

Epistemic opacity: Is the aforementioned Vico maxim, that posits that one can only understand what one is able to build, i.e. that truth is realized through creation, applicable to computer simulation of complex systems? Having fed the information and let the machine run the computations involving strings of equations and come up with emergent properties, do we really understand the system better as long as part of the process is epistemically opaque? And what is it that creates the opaqueness, given that we in fact wrote the equations—the numerical iterations, high dimensionality, nonlinearity, emergence, all combined? This brings us back to the meaning of "understanding." Some will note that even in daily life, we claim to understand natural phenomena without really mentally grasping their inner working. For example, we predict that if we release a ball from a tower, the ball will fall because of gravity. But is the attraction of physical bodies transparent to us epistemically, or is our sense of understanding due to habituation with the phenomenon or the physical law? As noted above, the acceptable magnitude of epistemic opacity in a computer simulation that can predict the outcome of the behavior of the system, is for the individual scientist to decide, and will probably vary with the professional training and the level of description and analysis.

Computing power: The computing power required for large-scale simulation of a mammalian brain is yet unavailable. Exascale-level machines are required, that, if pursued by current technology, will demand daunting amounts of energy. However, given the fast pace of advances in computer technology, this issue will probably resolve prior to the resolution of the scarcity of knowledge problem mentioned above.

The toll of data sampling: Attempts at large-scale brain simulation differ with regard to their reliance on realistic and detailed brain data, but all currently rely on limited sampling and statistical typification. It is one thing to sample phenomena in experiments in search for mechanisms and to classify the data to facilitate understanding, another to rely on the sampling to faithfully build the system anew. The possibility cannot be excluded, hence, that important properties of real-life neurons in vivo are concealed or minimized in the process. It is noteworthy that relying on extracted invariants may result not only in missing data but also in going beyond the data, because of potentially erroneous generalizations. It is also of note that such methods may reduce the ability to rely on the simulation to perform new fine-grained experiments in silico "higher order simulation"), which is contemplated as one of the contributions of brain simulation (i.e. replace in vivo or in vitro experiments that are complex, time consuming and cause animal suffering). Further, it may result in a situation in which the outcome of an in silico experiment will have to be verified in vivo after all.

Reality checks: Large-scale simulations are expected to involve iterations in which the performance of the simulated systems is evaluated by benchmarks. However, scarcity of knowledge may raise doubts concerning the suitability of such benchmarks, as we do not yet know in most cases whether the correlation sought by us of the activity of an identified circuit with specific physiological or behavioral performance indeed reflects the native function of the circuit. For example, are place cells primarily sensitive to spatial coordinates, or amygdala circuits to fearful stimuli? Lack of knowledge on the native computational goal may result in optimizing simulations to misguided or secondary performance. On the other hand, one may consider using the fit of simulations to selected benchmarks to explore computational goals of the native circuit.

Representational parsimony: Much of our scientific progress, understanding and intellectual joy stems from our cognitive ability to extract and generalize laws of nature. Describing the universe in a minimal number of equations is often equated not only with ultimate understanding but also with beauty. If we aim to reproduce details in simulations, do we still advance in "understanding" in that respect, or just imitate nature? Proponents of large-scale simulations will claim that the reproductions of the details is practiced in order to extract new laws that may emerge from the simulation. Besides raising again the issue of epistemic opacity, a more practical question comes up: Should we expect a small set of laws to describe a complex adaptive system like the brain? Some will say that this depends on the level of description. The brain can be considered as a community of organs with different functions and phylogenetic history, which renders the hope to understand in detail the operation of each by the same task-relevant computations doubtful. It still leaves open the possibility that some basic principles of brain operation are explainable by a unified theory. But this depends on the level of description. One may claim that we already understand some fundamental principles of brain operation, for example, that spikes encode and transmitters convey information, but this level of description is obviously not what brain scientists have in mind in trying to "understand" the brain. It is of note that high parsimony in realistic models has the potential to ameliorate epistemic opacity.

3:AM: How do you think simulations and philosophy should be integrated in this approach? What should we be trying to achieve?

KE: For example: Science and society should aim to benefit from contemplating the future and prepare for it, even if this future is not necessarily around the corner. Suppose, for the sake of argument, that the brain and computer sciences combined will indeed be able one of these days to come up with a simulated human brain. What questions will we face?

Similarity of the simulation to the original: If the simulation is in silico, there is the obvious dissimilarity that the simulation versus the original are two different substrates. The relevance of this dissimilarity can be expected to vary with theoretical frameworks and contexts. If, for example, one takes the hypothetical position that consciousness can only arise in a biological organism (see below), the relevance of the difference in substrate will be very high, since it will entail the further dissimilarity of being capable versus incapable of possessing mental states.

The issue of similarity can also be raised, however, within an in silico universe. Suppose, for the sake of argument, that we succeed in some imaginary future to generate a faithful simulation of the native human brain that is embodied in neuromorphic devices, embedded, for example, in humanoid robots. Will we be able to create legions of identical brains? The question of similarity of such artificial copies of the human brain can be dissected in terms of internal structure, or spatiotemporal location. The question can be broken up into two levels: type similarity, i.e. will the process generate a type of machine that is similar to a generic brain, and token similarity, i.e. will the process generate specific copies of an individual brain. In that case, in theory, type similarity is a possibility. Yet token similarity is a different question. That issue can benefit from the classic discourse in analytic philosophy, related to Leibniz's principle (or "Law") of The Identity of Indiscernibles. This principle states that if, for every property F, object x has F if and only if object y has F, then x is identical to y. In other words, no two distinct things exactly resemble each other, because if they share all intrinsic and all relational qualities (e.g. spatiotemporal coordinates) they would then be not two but one. They can, however, share all intrinsic qualities and yet be relationally, e.g. spatially or temporally, distinct. Formally we do not expect, therefore, even a future perfect brain simulation project to produce token identity.

3:AM: Will consciousness emerge? When mental states of the human brain are considered, consciousness commonly comes up in the discussion. Can consciousness be simulated?

KE: A dominant conceptual framework posits that mental states are brain states. Will (or must) intrinsically identical brains have identical mental states? Will distinct simulated brains with identical mental states be considered distinct "individuals"? Will they be able to read each other's "mind"? (Presumably, yes, if they know their intrinsic identity and the answer to the first question is affirmative.) Will they significantly differentiate even if they share identical experiences? Many brain scientists will posit that they will diverge over time because they consider the possibility that at least some systems in the brain will be of the type that is sensitive to minuscule deviations in the initial states (this also reflects on the improbability of token identity, see above).

Further, mental states may not correspond on a one-to-one basis to brain states; or mental states are functions of the brain with some other relation to brain states, for example, they are only supervenient or consequential to brain states, come along with them, but are not necessarily entailed by them in a one-to-one relation, in a way that brain research can not yet account for. But could the computer be conscious at all? At present, available evidence justifies only a rather tame hypothetical stance: If consciousness is necessarily an outcome of a certain type of organization or function of biological matter, then brain simulation will never gain consciousness; whereas if consciousness is a matter of organisation alone, e.g. extensive functional interconnectivity in a complex system, then it might arise in simulations in silicon.

3:AM: How would we recognise whether a future brain simulation is conscious or not?

KE: Two main types of approaches can be raised. The first, a Turing-type test for a conscious entity. Yet by itself this is insufficient, because we can easily imagine a computer being able to mimic the expected responses of a conscious entity without experiencing consciousness. The second, provided we assume faithful imitation of the relevant native brain activity, identify activity signatures that reflect conscious awareness in the human brain. This is in principle similar to the way one attempts to identify sleep and dreams objectively, by looking for characteristic brain activity signatures. But on the one hand, we do not yet know such signatures; on the other, even if they are identified, they may not exhaust signatures of conscious awareness in a simulated system. A pragmatic heuristic approach could be combination of two elements, still short of a sufficient condition. One, a Turing-type test; the second, activity signature in the simulated entity that fits the one expected in the original biological brain, and is time locked to the responses taken to reflect conscious behaviour.

3:AM: Is realistic human brain simulation possible in the absence of consciousness?

KE: It is possible to consider brain simulation without the question of consciousness arising. However, when processes in the brain are simulated that are conscious in the human being (for example, declarative emotion), the question arises: if consciousness is not simulated, how adequate can that simulation be?

To illustrate, one of the proposed goals of human brain simulation is to increase our understanding of mental illnesses, and to ultimately simulate them in theory and possibly in silico, the aim being to understand them better and to develop improved therapies, in due course. But how adequate, or informative, can a simulation of, say, depression or anxiety be, if there is no conscious experience in the simulation? The role of consciousness and the effects of this role on the outcome of simulation of human brain faculties will be important to assess in this context.

3:AM: So: what can we gain from discussing brain simulation?

KE: Although the road to simulation of human brain, or even only part of its cognitive functions, is long and uncertain, on this road much will be learned about the mammalian brain in general and about the feasibility of transformation of some efforts in the brain sciences into big science. New methodologies and techniques are expected as well that will benefit neuroscience at large and probably other scientific disciplines as well.

But given the expected remoteness of the ultimate goal, why should we engage in discussing some of its conceptual and philosophical underpinnings now? Big science brain projects provide an opportunity to assess and preempt problems that may one day become acute. In other words, we can use the current attempt to simulate the mammalian brain as an opportunity to simulate what will happen if the human brain is ever simulated.

It is rather straightforward to imagine the types of problems a simulated human brain will incite, should it ever become reality in future generations. They will range from the personal (e.g. implications concerning alterations of the sense of personhood, human identity, or anxiety and fear in response to the too-similar other); social (e.g. how shall the new things be treated in terms of social status and involvement, the law, or medical care); and ethical (e.g. if we terminate the simulated brain, do we "kill" it, in a potentially morally relevant manner?). These problems also require foresight of safety measures to ensure that in due time, the outcome of ambitious brain projects do not harm individuals and societies. But most of all, by discussing the potential implications of such projects now, we contribute to the sense that scientists as individuals and science as a culture should take responsibility for the potential long-term implications of their daring projects.

3:AM: You think there are tendencies in the brain that place us in a predicament of whether we go social or whether we go individualistic. Could you first sketch out for us what it is about the brain causes the predicament and why this is significant?

KE: I think we are fundamentally social as well as individualistic. The problem, simply phrased, is that we may be biologically unable to apply certain values that we intellectually endorse, because we are imprisoned in a smaller context. Let me try to explain this more fully.

Self-awareness can only develop through social interaction. The human brain is fundamentally social, and develops in natural and social contexts that strongly influence its own architecture. In social creatures, self-interest is a source of interest in others, primarily those to whom the self can relate and with whom it identifies, such as the next of kin, the clan, the community, etc. In intelligent social species such as the human, the "I" is extended to endorse the group, "we," and distinctions drawn between "us" and "them." Sympathy and aid is typically extended to others in proportion to their closeness to us in terms of biology (e.g., face recognition, or racial outgroup versus ingroup distinctions), culture, ideology, etc.

Evolution seems to have predisposed social animals to develop norms and rules for their behaviour, for example assistance within the group, where failure to follow social rules or conventions can have serious consequences. However, even in favourable conditions, we are not necessarily biologically capable of following all social rules. Ample evidence shows how brain dysfunctions or damages can underlie a multitude of cognitive, emotional and behavioural disabilities, including self-indifference and social or moral incapacity, and how the structure of the supposedly healthy brain may also render some norms more or less inapplicable in practice.

Our capacity for understanding others or for sympathising with them is dependent on brain functions. Compassion, for example, requires an intellectual capacity to understand the other, as well as an emotional capacity to care about the other. Both of these functions in the brain can be disordered or damaged, and even in brains that are supposedly neither, these functions are pronouncedly selective.

The neurobiology of empathy, here understood as the ability to apprehend the mental states of other people, is today subject to extensive research suggesting that this ability is a complex higher cognitive function with large individual and contextual variations that depend on both biological and sociocultural factors. In some individuals, the capacity for empathy is seriously reduced. Those who suffer from Asperger's Disorder, for example, are largely unable to understand other people's minds, to envisage how they think or feel. Still, to the extent that they succeed, they are able to sympathise.

Individuals with a psychopathy disorder find themselves in the reverse situation: the structure of their brains makes them less able to experience certain emotions, such as sympathy, guilt, shame, or other morally relevant emotions, but they can nevertheless be well able to envisage what other people feel.

There is, accordingly, a biological distinction between moral and social understanding (knowing what is considered "right," "wrong," "good," "bad," etc.) and moral or social emotion, such as sympathy, embarrassment, shame, guilt, pride, etc.

Pjotr Kropotkin, whose idealistic interpretation of history made him see voluntary mutual helpfulness and sympathy in his studies of nature, emphasised in sharp contrast to Thomas Huxley the positive aspects of nature: the tendency to altruism and mutual aid that stems from our natural capacity for sympathy with others. However, Kropotkin's and Huxley's images can be wedded; for when sympathy and mutual aid is extended within a group, they are also (de facto) withheld from those that do not belong to this group. In other words, interest in others is ordinarily expressed positively or negatively through either sympathy or antipathy directed to specific groups—but very rarely, if ever, are attitudes extended to universal coverage, for example as attitudes towards the entire human species, let alone towards all sentient beings.

Our standards for normality versus mental illness or disorder reflect this feature.

Emotional inabilities can be diagnosed as signs of a psychiatric disorder, but there is no corresponding diagnosis of a person who is indisposed to feeling shame or sympathy in relation larger groups, e.g. humanity, so long as that person remains capable of relating "normally" to individuals. This is a rule rather than an exception, if we look at the standard works defining mental disorder, such as the DSM IV. In other words, our diagnostic criteria for mental disorders reflect relationships between individuals rather than between an individual and a large group. This may be realistic, but also reflects a serious human predicament.

Even in human beings that are not diagnosable as suffering from a brain disorder or mental illness, understanding does not entail compassion but is frequently combined with emotional dissociation from "the other." We can easily understand, say, that a child in a distant country probably reacts to hunger or pain in a way that is similar to that in which our own country's children react to it, but that does not mean that we care about the children in equal or even comparable measures. Indeed, if understanding had entailed sympathy, the world would be a far more pleasant dwelling place for many of its inhabitants.

Humans are biologically natural sympathisers with the groups to which they belong, and can understand groups to which they do not belong, but they are not equally disposed to sympathise with them. To the contrary, we behave towards the greater part of the world in a manner that may have suggested a psychopathic disorder had it been directed towards individuals.

We are natural empathetic xenophobes: empathetic by virtue of our intelligence and capacity to apprehend the mental life of a relatively wide range of creatures, but far more narrowly and selectively sympathetic to the closer group into which are born or choose to join, whereas we tend to remain indifferent or antipathetic to everyone else; neutral or hostile to most aliens.

Judging by present statistics on world poverty, distribution of health care, and the predominantly tense or bellicose relations between individuals, nations, cultures, ethnic groups, social classes, races, genders, religions, political ideologies, etc., the vast majority of human beings appear reluctant or unable to identify with, sympathise or show compassion towards those who are beyond (and sometimes even towards those who are within) "their" sphere. Whilst some societies or individuals may be more prone than others to develop strong ethnic identity, violence, racism, sexism, social hierarchies or exclusion, all exhibit some form and measure of xenophobia.

Thus, in spite of our natural capacity for selective sympathy and mutual assistance that Kropotkin emphasised, the human being also comes very close to Hobbes' description: a self-interested, control-oriented, fearful, violent, dissociative, conceited, megalomaniac, empathetic xenophobe. In view of their historic prevalence, it is not unlikely that these features have evolved to become a part of our innate neurobiological identity and that any attempt to construe social structures (rules, conventions, contracts, etc.) opposing this identity must, in order to have any degree of realism in application, take this formidable biological challenge into account in addition to the historically well known political, social and cultural challenges. The question can be raised, for example: can—understood as a biological "can"—we develop "global" attitudes (such as the famous first § in the UN Declaration on Human Rights, asserting the equal worth and dignity of all individuals), or are universal declarations doomed to remain mere abstractions because we are neurobiologically conditioned to remain emotionally, and therefore morally, selective and group-oriented? Can sympathy biologically be extended?

The natural egocentricity or individualism of the brain appears quite pronounced: the brain is in constant autonomous activity, projecting autonomously produced images onto its environment that it proceeds to test, and in this activity it refers all experiences to itself, to its own individual perspective. This perspective is naturally narrow, with physical as well as epistemic limitations. We can conceive the narrowness of the individual perspective in terms of space (and the finite perspective's epistemic limitations) and personal identity (with a typical preference for the self, the familiar, and that with which the individual can identify, to which he or she can relate). Another important aspect of the individual perspective's narrowness is temporal: it is extremely difficult, sometimes even impossible, for a human being to be emotionally concerned with, or clearly to envisage, actual or possible states or events that are temporally distant (for example, imagined to lie one or several generations ahead in the future) compared to how we are involved with the present. In other words, our cerebral egocentricity is psychological, somatic and spatio-temporal, which means that we, each of us, live in a minute and egocentric world: this-here-now (understanding the "now" as denoting a fairly wide personal time-perspective, since it is notoriously difficult for human beings to live in the "now" understood as the actual present). By nature, we are predisposed to do so: without this massive dissociation we could presumably not survive, at least not with our present cerebral architecture.

A major practical problem is that the effects of our actions are not equally limited. The difficulty of wide-range involvement (be that spatial, temporal or personal) is matched by a facility to cause large-scale destruction on a global scale. This factual tendency to mental myopia that seems to characterise us both culturally and biologically poses serious problems whenever long-term solutions are needed; say, to improve the global environment or reduce global poverty. Our societies are importantly construed around egocentric and short-term perspectives: politically, economically, environmentally, etc., making it extremely difficult to put global or long-term thought and foresight into practice, and this is of course only to be expected if that is the way our brains function.

In this light, it is, we suggest, an important task of neuroscience to diagnose the human predicament in neurobiological terms. What types of social creatures are we, from a neurobiological point of view? Such knowledge can, in addition to its theoretical relevance, be socially very useful and of methodological relevance, e.g., in the development of adequate educational structures and methods, or in the assessment of alternative methods to remedy social problems. In order to remedy an ill, we first need a proper diagnosis of this "ill"; its nature, underlying causes and theoretically possible remedies. In the absence of such diagnosis we risk opting for methods that may provide a superficial, cosmetic improvement at best, improve appearances perhaps, but without affecting the real situation in any enduring or profound manner.

Importantly, such diagnoses must include both biological and socio-cultural dimensions, as well as a clear understanding of how these perspectives are related. Culture and nature stand in a relationship of symbiosis and mutual causal influence: the architecture of our brains determines who we are and what types of societies we develop, but our social structures also have a strong impact on the brain's architecture; notably, through the cultural imprints epigenetically stored in our brains. The door to being epigenetically proactive is, accordingly, opened.

3:AM: And that leads me naturally onto my next two questions. Epigenesis is a key area for your thinking. It's about the way steering the way we evolve by influencing cultural imprints in our brains. Have I got that right? If so, why isn't this about "human enhancement" and cognitive prosthetics?

KE: The fundamental idea of epigenetic proaction is trying to understand and influence the genesis of human norms in the light of what we today know about the brain. Being epigenetically proactive also means adapting and creating social structures, in both the short and the long term, to constructively interact with the ever-developing neuronal architecture of our brains. It can be described as an educated form of ethical innovation. The scientific challenges involved are accompanied by important social and ethical challenges, some of which we describe below. It seems clear, at least so far as mammals are concerned, that Darwinian evolution has lead to the global expansion on the earth of the human species that spends a considerable part of its life developing its brain experiencing and appropriating its physical, social & cultural environment. This is noteworthy: the environmental influence on the brain's functional architecture yields an evolutionary strength to Homo sapiens, compared to other animals whose cerebral developmental period is comparatively much shorter, and less environmentally determined. That gives an increased importance to "epigenetic mechanisms" driven by interaction with the environment in the course of the long postnatal period of human brain maturation, during which reciprocal relationships grow between the brain and its physical, social, and cultural environments.

Thus our cerebral identity incorporates social interactions. Our brain progressively builds up its connectivity through a constant dialogue between the genetic endowment of the child brain and her/his experiences of the external world. Moreover, trans-generational transfer of information from adult to child takes place through the incorporation of the social and cultural environments in the developing infant brain. From a sociological perspective, these neuroscientific theories and data are important through the scientific support they lend to the idea of adapting social conditions for the benefit of brain functions and their balanced development.

Through epigenetic proaction, new ethical rules can be internally produced and stored in our cerebral architecture. The neuronal features that develop from socio-cultural impact (the results of learning and experience) can be stabilized and passed on through generations, i.e., be epigenetically transmitted. Accordingly, culture can help us in the construction of our brain and conversely, through creative and rational thinking, our brains may as well lead to the production of novel social structures that persist across generations and might be stored in extra-cerebral memories as inscriptions, codes or laws.

In view of this neuro-cultural symbiosis, we can describe this process both as a "neuralization" of the normative process itself, and as a "culturalization" of the brain through the selective stabilization of cultural circuits. Our cultural and social structures—including our normative reasoning—are importantly products of the neuronal structures of our brains, but these neuronal structures are also importantly products of our cultures and societies. Hence the possibility arises to influence our brains with the use of culture, and be epigenetically proactive, in other words: to invent, learn and transmit new ethical norms, forming some kind of new ethical languages. One of the motivating forces behind our suggestion of epigenetic proaction is a concern about the present state of the world, and the difficulties in dealing with the situation adequately. A similar concern also comes to expression in the current debates on "moral enhancement."

In these debates, it is often argued that human nature is inapt to handle the problems that humankind presently faces in part as a result of our own actions (environmental destruction, poverty, etc.), and that moral education has not been able to forestall the present global situation described as serious. Another similarity between these two discourses lies in the belief that human nature might be improved, much to the benefit of our societies. The main differences between these approaches lie in the solutions that are suggested.

In the "moral enhancement" debate, the focus is largely on the individual, and the methods suggested are often a kind of "quick-fix" of the brain (such as drugs or brain stimulation) ignoring their short and long term consequences on human brain functions that are under-evaluated and potentially dangerous. In contrast, epigenetic proaction (as I understand it) importantly focuses on the genesis and transmission of novel educational/management programs with long-term influences across generations, and makes no reference at all to direct and blind interventions on the brain. Epigenetic proaction can have important effects on the individual person, and on the individual generation, but it is not conceived as an individual short-cut contrasted to moral education.

3:AM: You discuss this by examining the epigenesis of selective stabilization of synapses. Could you explain what this is and what conclusions you draw?

KE: This part of my work has been inspired by the works of Jean-Pierre Changeux, and my ideas about epigenetic proaction owe much to our long-standing and very fruitful collaboration. During embryonic and postnatal development, the million billion (10^{15}) synapses that form the human brain network do not assemble like the parts of a computer according to a plan that defines precisely the disposition of all individual components. If this were the case, the slightest error in the instructions for carrying out this program could have catastrophic consequences. On the contrary, the mechanism appears to rely on the progressive setting of robust interneuronal connections through trial-and-error mechanisms that formally resemble an evolutionary process by variation selection. At sensitive periods of brain development, the phenotypic variability of nerve cell distribution and position, as well as the exuberant spreading and the multiple figures of the transiently formed connections originating from the erratic wandering of growth cone behaviour, introduce a maximal diversity of synaptic connections. This variability is then reduced by the selective stabilization of some of the labile contacts and the elimination (or retraction) of the others. The crucial hypothesis of the model is that the evolution of the connective state of each synaptic contact is governed globally, and within a given time window, by the overall message of signals experienced by the cell on which it terminates.

One consequence of this is that particular electrical and chemical spatiotemporal patterns of activity in developing neuronal networks are liable to be inscribed under the form of defined and stable topologies of connections within the frame of the genetic envelope. In humans, about half of all adult connections are formed after birth at a very fast rate (approximately 2 million synapses every minute in the baby's brain). The nesting of these multiple traces would directly contribute to forming and shaping the micro- and macroscopic architecture of the wiring network of the adult human brain, thus bringing an additional explanation to the above mentioned non-linearity paradox.

Another consequence of the synapse selection model is that the selection of networks with different connective topologies can lead to the same input-output behavioural relationship. This accounts for an important feature of the human brain: the constancy or invariance of defined states of behaviour despite the epigenetic variability between individual brains connectivity.

Finally, both the spontaneous and the evoked activity may contribute to the synapse selection. In this framework, the suggestion was made that reward signals received from the environment may control the developmental evolution of connectivity. In other words, reinforcement learning would modulate the epigenesis of the network. This process of synaptic selection by reward signals may concern the evolution of brain connectivity in single individuals but also exchange of information and shared emotions or rewards between individuals in the social group. It may thus play a critical role in social and cultural evolution.

3:AM: As research moves forward aren't we moving towards the notion of the singularity, the version where we are able to understand the brain to the extent that we can alter it, make it more powerful so we can understand issues that once seemed impossible? And once that happens then what we are doing now and what we are now will seem ultra stupid, in the same way we look at apes. Philosophers and scientists talk about naturalistic responsibility being born out of science's strong social relevance but that's never done much to stop the develop heinous stuff. Aren't there good reasons to fear the advancement of neuroscience—how many sci-fi scenarios do we need to think there could be a problem brewing when superbrains appear?

KE: I think we seem ultra stupid already now, in view of the mess we are making of the world we inhabit. I also think we have good reasons to fear ourselves: our capacities, strengths, and weaknesses. Arthur Koestler compared evolution to a labyrinth of blind alleys and suggested that there is nothing very strange or improbable in the assumption that the human native equipment, though superior to that of any other living species, nevertheless contains some built-in error or deficiency, which predisposes us to self-destruction.

Neuroscience can give us further tools for this destruction as well as help in finding, say, new cures for mental disorders, or better educational methods. But the notion of rapid brain improvement in the form of direct manipulation seems so unrealistic to me that I cannot see any reason to fear it. In spite of the impressive increase of data in neuroscience, our understanding of the brain remains quite modest, and the knowledge we have is not integrated in a manner that would allow us to manipulate it in the way suggested in some

SF-movies. That said, I enjoy SF-literature very much, and some of it is scientifically and technologically quite sophisticated.

As for whether or not we should as you query "fear the advancement of neuroscience," I would reformulate that: it is not the science itself that we should fear but some of the uses that human beings might make of it.

3:AM: And for the readers here at 3:AM, are there five books you could recommend that will take us further into your philosophical world?

KE: There are so many fantastic works to choose between ... but selecting a variety from different domains and historical eras, the following five have been rich sources of inspiration to my philosophical thinking in different ways:

> Epictetus (c. AD 55-135), the *Enchiridion,* or *Handbook.* Practical wisdom of stoicism.
>
> Benedictus Spinoza, *Ethica* (1677), or Ethics. The most beautiful geometric world-view ever to have been conceived. A forerunner of much modern thought, including monistic views of mind, the concept of libido, and the idea that energy constitutes matter.
>
> Immanuel Kant, *Kritik der reinen Vernunft* (1781/87), or *Critique of Pure Reason.* A fundamentally logical Weltanschauung that remains relevant to contemporary philosophy.
>
> Arthur Koestler, *The Ghost in the Machine* (Hutchinson, 1967). A thought-provoking philosophical-psychological treaty on human nature and human tendencies towards self-destruction.
>
> Jean-Pierre Changeux, *L'Homme de vérité* (Odile Jacob, 2002), or *Physiology of Truth* (Harvard University Press, 2004). A neuroscientific work of great philosophical importance about how the brain seeks knowledge.

Kathinka Evers is the author of:

Why Tolerance? Study into the Nature and Functions of Tolerance (Excalibur Press, 1997)
Neuroéthique: Quand la matière s'éveille (Éditions Odile Jacob, 2009). Also published as
  Neuroética: Cuando la materia se despierta (Katz, 2010)

INDEX